The Psychology of Imagination

History, Theory, and New Research Horizons

A Volume in
Niels Bohr Professorship Lectures in Cultural Psychology

Series Editors:
Brady Wagoner, *Aalborg University*
Nandita Chaudhary, *University of Delhi*
Pernille Hviid, *University of Copenhagen*

Niels Bohr Professorship Lectures in Cultural Psychology

Brady Wagoner, Nandita Chaudhary, and Pernille Hviid, Series Editors

The Psychology of Imagination: History, Theory, and New Research Horizons (2017)
Edited by Brady Wagoner, Ignacio Brescó de Luna, and Sarah H. Awad

Integrating Experiences: Body and Mind Moving Between Contexts (2015)
Edited by Brady Wagoner, Nandita Chaudhary, and Pernille Hviid

Cultural Psychology and Its Future: Complementarity in a New Key (2014)
Edited by Brady Wagoner, Nandita Chaudhary, and Pernille Hviid

The Psychology of Imagination

History, Theory, and New Research Horizons

Edited by

Brady Wagoner, Ignacio Bresó de Luna, and Sarah H. Awad

Aalborg University

Information Age Publishing, Inc.
Charlotte, North Carolina • www.infoagepub.com

Library of Congress Cataloging-in-Publication Data

CIP data for this book can be found on the Library of Congress website:
http://www.loc.gov/index.html

Paperback: 978-1-68123-709-1
Hardcover: 978-1-68123-710-7
E-Book: 978-1-68123-711-4

CONTENTS

PART VI:
CONCLUDING RESPONSE

INTRODUCTION

Imagination as a Psychological and Sociocultural Process

Brady Wagoner, Ignacio Brescó, and Sarah H. Awad

Denmark, the location of the Niels Bohr Lectures, has a rich history of fantasy and imagination. One immediately thinks of H. C. Andersen's fairytales, Kierkegaard's method of indirect communication, Niels Bohr's scientific imagination, Tivoli amusement park, and more recently the internationally renowned Nordic Noir, Danish architecture, and Nordic cuisine. By what social, cultural, and psychological processes are these products constructed, and how do they feed into the popular imagination and the everyday life of people? Although these are fundamental questions, they are difficult to answer from standard psychological theories. Psychology has generally tended to view the imagination as an intellectual process of representing and operating on unreal objects in front of the mind's eye. This has unfortunately led to a neglect of the aesthetic, emotional, social, cultural, and contextual dimensions of imagination that were essential to the 19th century concept of "fantasy," which "imagination" replaced.

Cultural psychology offers an alternative perspective, which brings these undeniable dimensions back to the fore. Fantasy and imagination are understood as the human capacity to distance oneself from the here-and-now situation in order to return to it with new possibilities (Vygotsky,

The Psychology of Imagination: History, Theory, and New Research Horizons
pp. ix–xii

1931; Zittoun & Gillespie, 2016). To do this, we use social-cultural means (e.g., language, stories, art, images, etc.) to conceive of imaginary scenarios, some of which may become real. Imagination is involved in every situation of our lives, though to different degrees. Sometimes this process can lead to concrete products (e.g., artistic works) that can be picked up and used by others for the purposes of their imagining. It is important to note that imagination is not here approached as an isolated cognitive faculty but as the means by which people anticipate and constructively move toward an indeterminate future. It is in this process of "living forward" (to use Kierkegaard's phrase) with the help of imagination that novelty appears and social change becomes possible.

This book has been developed from a workshop titled From Fantasy to Imagination, held at the Centre for Cultural Psychology at Aalborg University, Denmark. The intention of the workshop was to develop a cultural psychological approach to imagination. The keynote address was given by Carlos Cornejo, who provided us with an extensive cultural history of the concept that connected it to its romantic roots in Goethe and others. Drawing from this historical review, his lecture accounted for why we have been left with an impoverished notion of imagination, thus pointing to the necessity of reconstructing the earlier notion for (cultural) psychology today. This set the ground for the presentations to follow, which were given by social and cultural psychologists from all over the world. They were asked to reflect on the theme of imagination in general, and Cornejo's lecture in particular, from their own research backgrounds.

At the end of the event, selected participants were invited to prepare a chapter that develops a cultural psychological approach to imagination based on the discussions at the workshop. A number of other leading psychologists who had worked on the topic were also invited to write chapters for the book, where we saw gaps in the table of contents. We aimed to provide broad coverage of four main areas. Those make up the parts of the book coming after Cornejo's (this volume) leading chapter:

Part II: Conceptual and Historical Analyses to sketch out the key debates that have surrounded the concept of imagination through its history and what we might learn from them in a developing contemporary approach to the topic. In his chapter, Tateo complements Cornejo's chapter with a look at the concept from Ancient Greece through the 18th century, drawing out important issues, such as its relation to rationality, intersubjectivity, and the construction of reality. Klempe and Lehmann's conceptual history then focuses on theorizing the aesthetic dimension of human experience through a consideration of Baumgarten's work, which was a key source for Immanuel Kant. Christensen and Brock further proceed to elaborate context of Kant's theory, especially the imaginative link between sensuality and concepts, and how contemporary philosophers, such as

John McDowell and Rom Harré, have developed it in a culturally informed direction.

Part III: Theoretical Approaches and Developments makes connections with a variety of theoretical perspectives, such as materiality studies, phenomenology, psychoanalysis, cultural anthropology, and creativity. Beckstead looks at the topic of imagining the past using materiality studies and Simmel's theory, which owes much to Goethe's ideas. Zittoun explores one area in which fantasy kept its initial richness, namely psychoanalysis, followed by an outline of an attempt to theorize imagination within cultural psychology using a "loops" out and into the here-and-now situation. Winther-Lindqvist draws on existential-phenomenology to address hope as a reaction to parental somatic illness. With an empirical basis of 35 comprehensive interviews, Winther-Lindqvist provides a phenomenological description of hope as an imaginative activity, spurred as a reaction to parental illness in teenagers. Glaveanu takes up Cornejo's historical analysis on fantasy and imagination in order to contextualize the present-day debates about creativity studies, thus pointing out the need to recover the social and cultural dimensions of this emerging field.

Part IV: The Scientific Imagination in Psychology gathers different ways of approaching the role of imagination in knowledge construction. Shotter opens up this section by bringing Wittgenstein's question "What does one include in thinking?" to the field of imagination studies: What does one include in the word imagination? What have we learned to use this word for? From a more anthropological perspective, Guimarães focuses on imagination in Amerindian psychology. In contrast to the epistemologies resulting from modern sciences, this author advocates for alternative, and traditionally sidelined, ways of knowledge construction coming from the Amerindian in Brazilian tradition, such as empathy, physiognomic sensibilities, intuition, fantasy, and imagination. Following this epistemological approach, Mazur highlights the role of imagination in science, especially in situations of ambiguity leading to doubt, curiosity, and hope in the pursuit of knowledge. Finally, Watzlawik wraps up this section by taking up Goethe's stance on the fundamental role of personal experience in relation to knowledge construction. Starting with a personal experience that triggered a research project on sexual identity, this author shows that the attempt to capture a certain phenomenon scientifically often implies taking it apart, thus creating gaps that later need to be acknowledged and "worked with."

Part V: New Research Horizons provides a number of illustrative examples of how a sociocultural approach to imagination can be useful in research practice. These examples come from a wide range of different research settings. Awad looks at imagination as a coping mechanism in disempowering situations, expressed in poems and letters written by political prisoners from the Egyptian post-2011 revolution. Eckerdal explores imagination through ways in which humans relate to nature, drawing on empirical work about the meaning of picking flowers in Japan and Denmark. Hampl and Mihalits investigate the cultural imagination condensed into particular images, using a comparative picture interpretation with the Documentary Method to look specifically at the public representation of St. George and the dragon in the coat of arms of the Russian Federation.

In the final section of the book, Cornejo responds to the above chapters and renews his argument for the need to reenchant psychology. He concludes by clarifying some key ideas developed through the book, while highlighting some consequences of the historiographical analysis he offered.

REFERENCES

Vygotsky, L. S. (1931). *Imagination and creativity of the adolescent.* Retrieved from https://www.marxists.org/archive/vygotsky/works/1931/adolescent/ch12.htm

Zittoun, T., & Gillespie, A. (2016). *Imagination in human and cultural development.* London, England: Routledge.

PART I

NIELS BOHR LECTURE

CHAPTER 1

FROM FANTASY
TO IMAGINATION

A Cultural History
and a Moral for Psychology

Carlos Cornejo

Wenn ihr's nicht fühlt, ihr werdet's nicht erjagen
[If you don't feel it, you won't catch it].

—J. W. Goethe, *Faust I*

As any long-standing discipline, psychology has its own dictionary of forgotten words. Major technical terms of the 18th and 19th centuries, such
as *apperception*, *will*, *soul*, *sympathy*, or *genius*, scarcely appear in current
technical psychology language. Some of them disappeared by the end of
19th century, their meanings being thus hardly comprehensible at present. Other terms gradually were relocated in other intellectual domains so
that we have certain notion of them because of our familiarity with other
disciplines. We have furthermore the case where some antique words survive in modern jargon, but with a present use diverging from the prece-
dent in important ways. This is the case of *fantasy*. Whereas during the
18th century and until the first half of the 19th century, fantasy played a

The Psychology of Imagination: History, Theory, and New Research Horizons
pp. 3–44

central role in the then-current psychologies, its importance steadily decayed after the irruption of the "new psychology"—the successful research program developed by Wilhelm Wundt and others to recover by means of natural sciences methodology the pre-Kantian questions on mind. Our inquiry will mainly focus on the use of fantasy by prominent authors before 1870; that is, immediately before the institutionalization of modern scientific psychology. By contrasting those views with post-Wundtian psychology, we will be able to visualize what aspects of fantasy continued being considered part of psychology's object of knowledge and what aspects were left behind, so to say, in the prehistory of the discipline.

Words acquire their meanings only in a specific sentence—sentences in texts. In their turn, texts can only adequately be interpreted in the sociocultural context in which they are produced. A specific scientific term makes sense only within the entire language used by a discipline to approach its knowledge domain. Consequently, by following the historical course of a technical term such as fantasy, we obtain not mere anecdotal facts but valuable information on the implicit cosmological and anthropological models extant through the European societies where it was used. The changing role that fantasy satisfies in different theories of 19th century psychology offers us an entrance into the mutating anthropological models of that time. Knowingly, the 19th was the century when the objectifying view of Nature, long ago consolidated in the natural sciences, protracted to comprise human affairs. Not only Nature came to be considered as a complex machinery of causally related objects and things, but also personhood itself was deemed part of the mechanistic world. From social issues to mental functions, human life during the 19th century was progressively modeled after the same causal laws that proved predictive of the natural world. Because of its historical connections with creativity, aesthetics, and poetry, modifications of fantasy throughout time throw light on the model of person that made feasible and even obvious the project of a natural science of mind.

Today psychology is widely regarded as a discipline born at some point of the second half of the 19th century, when the first experimental laboratories to study psychophysiological processes were founded. Academics originally instructed in philosophy and natural sciences spearheaded this intellectual movement, whose aim was to create a natural science of mind. Conveniently Wilhelm Wundt named this new enterprise as "new psychology" establishing a liaison with, and a distinction from, Christian Wolff's old rational psychology of the 18th century (Wundt, 1907). In this view of history, pre-Wundtian psychological theories are regarded at best as precursory, not properly psychological approaches. Psychologies from before 1850 remain massively unknown, so much so, in fact, that we nowadays have only a faint idea of the forms that the discipline had, preserved mainly in important psychology textbooks from the first part of 19th century; for example, *Handbuch der Psychologie* (1804) by D. Tiedemann, *Psychologie zur Erklärung der Seelenerscheinungen* (1824) by E. Stiedenroth, or *Vorlesungen über Psychologie* by C. G. Carus (1831).

It is indeed true that the institutionalization of modern scientific psychology required the "huge influence ... of an increasingly prevalent positivistic small enterprise" (Wundt, 1907, p. 15). Yet it would be mistaken to underestimate the relevance and development of the psychological studies before the consolidation of the new psychology. Such "prescientific" psychology was quite extended by the end of 18th century, and it was the arena where models of man[1] were proposed and discussed. Moreover, certain beliefs established by old psychologies were incorporated in experimental psychology and persist even today. Thus, from a wider point of view, modern psychology looks more like another chapter of the large book of the human studies—neither the first one, nor the last.

Our exploration of the concept of fantasy will begin about two generations before the emergence of the positivistic-oriented scientific psychology—"Wundt's creature" as Sigmund Koch (1969) once named it. To situate the right place of modern psychology in the history of human studies, we need to visualize the evolution of the ideas of person and mind. We will begin this exploration with the philosophical and scientific ideas of one of the most important intellectual figures of Germany at the turn of the 18th century, Johann Wolfgang Goethe, whose importance as poet transcended his time but whose scientific contributions were, and still today are, greatly ignored. We would like to show him as heir of the long tradition of holism, and by this way, one of the forgotten precursors of cultural psychology. His theoretical position on fantasy offers remarkable dissimilarities with the other big name in the German culture of his time, Immanuel Kant. The muffled collision between the models of man defended by Germany's two main sages in the aftermath of the 18th century can be observed in their contrasting modes of approaching fantasy. This cultural dispute laid the foundations on which the new psychology was planned and successfully implemented.

Goethe's Science

Although Johann W. Goethe gained international renown very early in his life because of his works as poet and prose writer, his contributions to philosophy and natural sciences never received an even remotely similar acknowledgment. Goethe was intensively concerned with natural scientific issues, as expressed in his *The Metamorphosis of Plants* (1790) and *Theory of Colors* (1810), as well as in diverse brief commentaries and reflections. Despite the limited impact of his scientific works, Goethe's interest in science was not a secondary one. His close friend Johann Peter Eckermann reported the following valuation made by Goethe:

> As for what I have done as a poet ... I take no pride in it whatever ... Excellent poets have lived at the same time with myself, poets more excellent have lived before me, and others will come after me ... But that in my century I am the only person who knows the truth in the difficult science of colours—of that, I say, I am not a little proud, and here I have a consciousness of a superiority to many. (Eckermann, 1850b, p. 145)

To have a notion of the relevance that Goethe assigned to fantasy, it is important to keep in mind three main features of his approach to science, and to life in general, as we will soon see: developmental perspective, holism, and personal experience as the source of knowledge. The first feature delineates his whole scientific effort as genetic. Goethe developed by means of many examples the primordial idea that the true knowledge about an object of inquiry can only be adequately obtained by capturing its development instead of fixed states of it:

> If I look at the created object, inquire into its creation, and follow this process back as far as I can, I will find a series of steps. Since these are not actually seen together before me, I must visualize them in my memory so that they form a certain ideal whole ... At first I will tend to think in terms of steps, but nature leaves no gaps, and thus, in the end, I will have to see this progression of uninterrupted activity as a whole. I can do so by dissolving the particular without destroying the impression itself. (Goethe, 1785/1998a, p. 75)

Goethe's description of Nature as a living process, in permanent development, grows up from his observation that even though one plant species may vary across latitudes and times, still we are capable of identifying it as one. This is the seed of Goethe's genetic method, which from a historical perspective played a catalyzing role in promoting a new worldview, in which not only the botanic world, but every form of life is seen as an evolving process (Miller, 2009). Knowingly, the 19th century has been described as the century when the idea of evolution was discovered as pervading the whole universe (Jespersen, 1922). The developmental approaches emerge at the verge of the 19th century in different strands: from Buffon's geological descriptions of soil strata as signals of a prolonged evolution of earth, through the conception of languages as evolving from a common root (which makes possible the concept of "language family"), to Hegel's notion of history as evolving trough cultures and epochs, until Darwin's depiction of biological species as permanently adapting and changing across times (Cornejo & Olivares, 2015). Goethe is not merely part of this developmental spirit: He represents one of the most influential voices of his time, bringing the genetic thinking forth. It is not difficult to reconstruct his influence on the Humboldt brothers and, indirectly, through Alexander's epochal voyage, on Darwin's evolution theory. Furthermore, it is clear that he had also a remarkable impact on Kantian philosophers such as Hegel, Fichte, and Schelling. He is therefore a key author to understand *Naturphilosophie* [natural philosophy] and, by this means, *Lebensphilosophie* [philosophy of life]. Unfortunately, his philosophical-scientific contributions to advancing the idea of development in the 19th century intellectual landscape have been overshadowed by his prominence as a poet. Nonetheless, he was one of the fundamental precursors of the major change that took place from a worldview of static things united by mechanical connections to a developmental one.

A tight related feature of Goethe's conception of science is the primacy of wholeness over atoms and parts. He writes,

> All things in nature, especially the commoner forces and elements, work incessantly upon one another; we can say that each phenomenon is connected with countless others just as we can say that a point of light floating in space sends its rays in all directions. (1792/1998b, p. 15f)

Nature, that is, the very object of knowledge of the natural sciences, is, for Goethe, a living organism, whose proper apprehension requires looking for connections, because she "hides amid a thousand names and terms, and is always the same" (Goethe, 1783/1998c, p. 5). Good science is that which grants priority to the perception of the wholeness, that which demands the scientist's capacity to see connections that initially may appear distant and dissimilar. Modern natural sciences, argues Goethe, err by focusing solely on analysis, neglecting the need for synthesis. The plain accumulation of separate elements does not guarantee we will gain a better understanding of a subject matter. On the contrary, the more analyses the sciences run, the finer the grain, but also the farther the comprehensive vision: in such a case, the observations turn out to be obstructions to the vision. To see the wholeness of which Sanskrit and English are part, our attention should be detached from specific parts of them; only then we can see the wholeness that unites a multiplicity of languages. Scientific analysis works only when it is oriented by a theoretical synthesis: "the sciences come to life only when the two exist side by side like exhaling and inhaling" (Goethe, 1829/1998d, p. 49).

The methodological question of how scientists can advance their analysis without losing sight of the synthetic wholeness leads us to the third feature of Goethe's scientific approach. The capacity to see that the unity in diversity requires restoring "to the human spirit its ancient right *to come face to face with nature*" (Goethe, 1829/1998d, p. 48; emphasis in the original). For Goethe, the right way to do science involves a personal commitment to directly see, touch, and feel by oneself the phenomenon at stake. Goethe himself incarnated this prescription. *The Metamorphosis of Plants* (1790/2009) is ripe with examples and remarks from his significant first journey to Italy (1787–1788). His *Theory of Colors* (1810), where he defends a holistic approach to colors opposed to Newton's analytical view, began also with a personal experience, which he discloses at the conclusion of the historical part of the *Theory of Colors*. When asked to return the prisms Mr. Büttner had lent him, Goethe reports,

> I had taken the crate in order to give it to the messenger, when it occurred to me that I quickly wanted to see through a prism, something I hadn't done since my early youth … I was in a totally white room. As I held the prism before my eyes, I expected keeping Newtonian theory in mind, that the entire white wall would be gradated into different colors … But I was quite amazed that the white wall showing through the prism remained as white as before. Only where there was something dark did a more or less distinct color show. The cross frames of the window appeared most actively colored, while the light-gray outside did not have the slightest trace of color. It required little thought to recognize that an edge was necessary to bring about colors. I immediately spoke out loud to myself, through instinct, that Newtonian theory was erroneous. (1810/1971, p. 199)

This passage reveals a central aspect of Goethe's theory of knowledge: Knowledge [*Wissen*] is ultimately a form of experience [*Erlebnis*]. Accordingly, concepts should be grounded in lived experiences rather than in logical or formal connections. For Goethe, every rational construction should start from the personal experience of being in contact with the phenomenon of interest. Our scientific theories are not separable from the life experiences that have fed our curiosity for that aspect of the world which the theory is about. Moreover, the aim of any scientific inquiry is precisely to rationally expand an intuitive perception[2] [*Anschauung*], which we not infrequently have even before any of our experimentally controlled observations: "In general, events we become aware of through experience are simply those we can categorize empirically after some observation" (Goethe, 1810/1998e, p. 194). Clarity of thought comes to our minds not after a painstaking ascending logical process but from our intuitive perception of the phenomenon. The abstract principles and laws governing certain aspects of the natural world are not revealed "to our reason through words and hypothesis, but to our intuitive perception through phenomena" (Goethe, 1810/1998e, p. 194f). Goethe calls these intuitively captured phenomena "*archetypal phenomena*, because nothing higher manifests itself in the world" (1810/1998e, p. 195; emphasis in the original). Thus, scientific formalizations emerge from an intuitive perception, not the reverse.

The statement that such intuitive perception is humanly possible situates Goethe in clear contrast with Kant, who assigns this possibility only to a divinity and thus limits human judgment to discursive reason, which needs concepts and logical structures. Goethe asks, "Why should it not also hold true in the intellectual area that through an intuitive perception of eternally creative nature we may become worthy of participating spiritually in its creative processes?" (1817/1998f, p. 31). Significantly, he counterargues Kant from his own life experiences: "Impelled from the start by an *inner need*, I had striven unconsciously and incessantly toward primal image and prototype, and had even succeeded in building up a method of representing it which conformed to nature" (Goethe, 1817/ 1998f, p. 31f; emphasis added). The existence of an intuitive perception is thus in Goethe a conviction rooted in his personal experience; it is something felt, not the result of a logical conclusion. The priority of the intuitive perception over logical soundness corresponds to the conceptual manifestation of the mentioned third feature of his whole scientific work: personal commitment. From this insight, he develops his criticism to modern natural science. He repeatedly complains that Newtonians "put some distance between themselves and life" (Goethe, 1998g, p. 306) and that the only way to be faithful to a formal discipline is not to lose the wholeness of life: "And this exactitude [of mathematics]—does it not flow from an inner feeling for the truth?... A mathematician is perfect only to the degree that he is a perfect human being, to the degree that he can experience the beauty in what is true" (Goethe, 1998g, p. 310f).

One corollary of personal commitment is Goethe's dismissal of the use of scientific instruments that would potentially obstruct the guiding intuitive perception. Insofar as he privileges the sensual [*sinnlich*] access, not every scientific device seems suitable to see the phenomenon:

> Man himself is the best and most exact scientific instrument possible ... The greatest misfortune of modern physics is that its experiments have been set apart from man, as it were; physics refuses to recognize nature in anything not shown by artificial instruments, and even uses this as a measure of its accomplishments. (Goethe, 1998g, p. 311)

In a conversation with Frederic J. Soret, he reflects,

> I have never affected anything in my poetry ... I have never uttered anything which I have not experienced, and which has not urged me to production ... I have only composed love-songs when I have loved ... How could I write songs of hatred without hating! (Eckermann, 1850b, p. 259)

Similarly, in *Conversations to Eckermann*, he confessed,

> I have ... attempted natural science in nearly every department; but, never-
> theless, my tendencies have always been confined to such objects as lay ter-
> restrially around me, and could be immediately perceived by the senses. On
> this account, I have never occupied myself with astronomy, because here the
> senses are not sufficient, and one must have recourse to instruments, calcu-
> lations, and mechanics, which require a whole life, and were not in my line.
> (Eckermann, 1850a, p. 360f)

To better understand why the use of technical instruments impedes
feeling and palpating the phenomenon of interest, we have to explore
Goethe's model of man and its position in nature. This vision allows us to
clarify why instruments, calculations, and mechanics are not in his line.

Goethe's *Theory of Colors*

In *Theory of Colors*, published in 1810 after 10 years of preparation,
Goethe argues vehemently against the Newtonian view that light is the
additive product of the colors. Instead, he states, "Colors are the deeds of
light" (Goethe, 1810/1998e, p. 158), and although colors and light are
intimately related to each other, "we must consider both as belonging to
all nature" (Goethe, 1810/1998e, p. 158). Light should be considered not
as a secondary compound but a primary phenomenon; and the same
holds for the eye: Nature as a whole reveals itself to the eye through color:

> Though it may sound a bit strange, we will now assert that the eye does not
> see shape as such, since brightness, darkness, and color operate together as
> the sole means for the eye to distinguish among objects or parts of objects.
> (Goethe, 1810/1998e, p. 163f)

Light is not the summation of colors; this only appears when light suffers
alterations from shadowing. To see colors we need the interplay of light
and dark.

While light shows itself and objects in a "generally characterless way"
(Goethe, 1810/1998e, p. 267), each color is expressive from its very creation: "Color ... always appears as specific, full of character and meaning"
(Goethe, 1810/1998e, p. 267). This insight requires a mind disposition
that already in Goethe's times was almost forgotten in natural science: to
pay careful attention to the senses before promoting these observations to
abstractions via reflection: "Two needs arise in us when we observe nature;
to gain complete knowledge of the phenomena themselves, and then the
to make them our own by reflection upon them" (Goethe, 1998h, p. 155).

The fact that colors are imbued with meaning from the start receives confirmation not from abstraction but from the careful attention to our sensitive reaction in the whole organism whenever we are immersed in a colored landscape:

> Thus nature also speaks to other senses which lie even deeper, to known, misunderstood, and unknown senses. Thus it converses with itself and with us through a thousand phenomena. No one who is observant will ever find nature dead or silent. It has even provided a confidant for the rigid body of the earth, a metal the least fragment of which tells us about what is taking place in the entire mass. (Goethe, 1810/1998e, p. 158)

Colors, accordingly, do have effects on man's inner nature, those being sensorial, moral, and aesthetic. However, each color brings about a specific impression to the mind so that these connections are not arbitrary and not interchangeable. To capture such effects, we have to be completely surrounded by a determined color, for example, in a room of a single hue or by looking through a colored glass. In such cases "we will then identify ourselves with the color; our eye and spirit will be brought into unison with it" (Goethe, 1810/1998e, p. 279). Through the concept of *polarity*[3] Goethe opposes the primary colors yellow and blue. Both represent, respectively, the active and passive sides of light. Considered as a whole (that is, becoming aware of their sensory, moral, and aesthetic effects), such a polarity may be extended in this way (see Table 1.1).

The diversity of colors comes basically from this original polarity by means of intensification.[4] Intensified colors bring unexpectedly new colors. When blue and yellow intensify, they become violet and orange,

Table 1.1. Yellow-Blue Polarity and Their Corresponding Sensorial-Moral Effects

Plus	Minus
Yellow	Blue
Causation	Deprivation
Light	Shadow
Brightness	Darkness
Power	Weakness
Warmth	Cold
Nearness	Distance
Repulsion	Attraction
Affinity to acids	Affinity to alkalis

Goethe (1810/1998e, p. 267f).

respectively. The reddish impression in violet and orange will increase at the highest degree of intensification. Such color turns out to be purple or pure red. This is the "most exalted of color phenomena" (Goethe, 1810/1998e, p. 282), whose effect is

> as unique as its character ... It may take a serious and dignified impression, or one of grace and charm; the first effect arises when it is dark and condensed, the second when light and dilute ... Thus the dignity of age and the charm of youth may be clad in a single color. (Goethe, 1810/1998e, p. 282)

In the case that the opposites yellow and blue join without being intensified, the color green appears. In the green, yellow and blue are evenly balanced, producing in the eye and the soul the impression of simplicity and rest: "We cannot and will not go beyond it" (Goethe, 1810/1998e, p. 283).

The diverse colors originated by intensification and the new oppositions they form can be adequately expressed through the color wheel [*Farbenkreis*]. Goethe presents his own version of it in part VI of his *Theory of Colors*. Figure 1.1 shows Goethe's own watercolor drawing from 1809. Several aspects are worth mentioning from this diagram. First, colors opposed within the circles are not strictly opposite but rather complementary, in the sense that whenever the eye sees a color, "by nature it unconsciously and necessarily produces another color on the spot, and the two colors together will contain the whole circle of colors" (Goethe, 1810/1998e, p. 283). The eye, in brief, is constantly looking for the complementary colors to recover the totality and find satisfaction. Thus, the contemplation of yellow demands violet, purple (pure red) demands green, blue demands orange, and vice versa. Second, Goethe's color wheel includes the symbolic effects that each color produces in human souls at sensorial, moral, and aesthetic levels.[5] Thus, purple produces in us the sentiment of the beautiful [*schön*]; orange is noble [*edel*]; yellow represents the good [*gut*]; green stand for useful [*nützlich*]; blue evokes the sentiment of mean or common [*gemein*]; while violet corresponds to unnecessary [*unnöthig*].

Third and most important for our discussion, Goethe establishes in his color wheel the association between specific colors and their symbolic effects to four powers of soul: fantasy [*Phantasie*]; reason [*Vernunft*]; intellect [*Verstand*]; sensuality [*Sinnlichkeit*]. Fantasy occupies the red-blue (violet) space of the color wheel, possibly producing effects of that which is unnecessary, but beautiful. Reason is placed in the orange space, being associated with nobleness and beauty. In its turn, human intellect stays in the yellow-green part of the wheel, becoming associated with sentiments of goodness and usefulness. Finally, sensuality corresponds to the green-blue part of the circle, connecting the soul with the common and the useful.

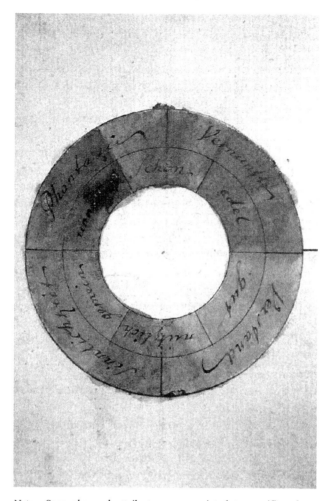

Note: Sensual-moral attributes are associated to specific colors. Original in the Freies Deutsches Hochstift-Frankfurter Goethe-Museum.

Figure 1.1.   Goethe's color wheel, with associated symbolic qualities, after his own drawing (1809).

Fantasy in Goethe

A golden goal for philosophy is, according to Goethe, to bring together again what nature originally created unified. This also applies to human soul faculties. Under such orientation, the anthropology proposed by Goethe defines the integration of capacities associated to the active colors on the wheel (reason and intellect) with the passive powers (fantasy and sensuality). This meant recovering human faculties that were at that time already disappearing little by little in the scientific communities in favor of the more and more central "active" capacities of intellect and rationality.

Goethe is writing at the dawn of the 19th century, when the theory of knowledge that supported the growth of the natural sciences was a broadly extended philosophy, beyond the scientific domain. In fact, European society as a whole was at that time rapidly changing because of the scientific revolution and its practical consequence, the industrial revolution. The astounding success of the natural sciences not only modified the physiognomy of cities, social composition and economy structure, but importantly expanded the modern-rational worldview, which progressively relegated human activities and faculties that were unrelated to the logical analysis. During the 19th century the same vocabulary used to describe physical processes began to be applied to human processes, from the social institutions to mental life. Words such as *system, causal relations, mechanisms, effects, associations, reflexes, atoms* became usual forms for describing and explaining aspects of human reality. If science could formalize the celestial region, making it possible to explain and predict the stellar movements, was it not reasonable to expect the good day in which social behavior and human affairs would also be modeled and predicted? During the 19th century, it gently became self-evident to understand the human body, social institutions, and the very inner life of humans as mechanically constituted. The belief that Kantian transcendental categories of space and time pervade and structure not only natural phenomena but also the social world and the individual mind was mere common sense in industrial societies.

This expansion of the mechanical-objectifying cosmology toward society and human dimensions is concomitant with the rise of intellect and reason as the central powers of the human soul. This is the growing movement against which Goethe is trying to oppose. He vigorously argues for the need to integrate the common sensuality and the beautiful but unproductive fantasy to the rational powers of the human soul. Modern science conceives a rationally ordered universe whose unveiling requires the methodic exercise of reason and intellect. Such unilateral emphasis leads only to the impoverishment of science, since analyses need syntheses in the same way as breathing is both inhalation and exhalation. Soul powers conform a totality, whose division may originate quarrels and biases that distort the original harmony among the parts of the whole:

We are well enough aware that some skill, some ability, usually predominates in the character of each human being. This leads necessarily to one-sided thinking since man knows the world only through himself, and thus has the naïve arrogance to believe that the world is constructed by him and for his sake. It follows that he puts his special skills in the foreground, while seeking to reject those he lacks, to banish them from his own totality. As a correction, he needs to develop all the manifestations of human character— sensuality [*Sinnlichkeit*] and reason [*Vernunft*], imagination [*Phantasie*] and common sense [*Verstand*]—into a coherent whole, no matter which quality predominates in him. If he fails to do so, he will labor on under his painful limitations without ever understanding why he has so many stubborn enemies, why he sometimes meets even himself as an enemy. (Goethe, 1824/1998i, p 45f)

Goethe's aim was to balance the rationally biased model of man by integrating sensorial and imaginative powers. Consequently, it is the scientist's task to develop "all manifestations of human character" (Goeth, 1824/1998i, p. 45) into a coherent whole. Even more, as the color wheel suggests, the primordial tension between sensuality and intellect gives birth via intensification to beauty, a mixture between fantasy and reason, represented by pure red—the perfect color. A rational model of reality phenomena does not come from the mere intensification of the coldness and calm of the intellectual apprehension; it also requires similar intensification of the senses in order to obtain "an exact sensuous fantasy" [*eine exakte sinnliche Phantasie*] (Goethe, 1824/1998i, p. 45f). No rationality is possible without feeling. "If you don't feel it, you won't catch it," admonishes Faust to Wagner. Fantasy, for Goethe, is not opposed to reason and does not consist in a poetic faculty to put ourselves outside the mechanically ordered world; it is not a human capacity to rest in a parallel world where logic does not rule. Instead, fantasy represents the faculty to fully feel this world, that is, to see nature's inner relationships and not merely the superficial ones. Hence, fantasy is a precondition to achieve an ideal science, one that respects nature by depicting it faithfully. As a consequence, fantasy is not a faculty reserved for poetry and art only. In a conversation dated January 27, 1830, Eckermann reports the following reflection by Goethe:

In fact ... a great natural philosopher without this high gift [fantasy/imagination] is impossible. I do not mean an imagination which goes into the vague and imagines things which do not exist; but I mean one which does not abandon the actual soil of the earth, and which steps to supposed and conjectured things by the standard of the real and the known. Then it may prove whether this or that supposition be possible, and whether it is not in contradiction with known laws. Such an imagination presupposes an enlarged tranquil mind, which has at its command a wide survey of the living world and its laws. (1850b, p. 220)

Fantasy is a necessary faculty to unveil the hidden relationships of nature. The capacity to see these connections depends on an exact sensorial fantasy: "Although arguments may deal with utterly separate matters, wit and imagination can group them around a single point to create a surprising semblance of right and wrong, true and false" (Goethe, 1792/1998b, p. 16). Thus, the final goal of knowledge, namely, to have an intuitive perception [*Anschaaung*] of the wholeness in which the phenomenon of interest is partaking, does depend on our capacity to feel within ourselves the inner connections of nature. Out of such an intuition the human mind is capable of constructing rational models and theories of the phenomenon. If abstract reason rests on "the actual soil of earth," scientific formalizations are meaningful and full-fledged; if, on the contrary, a sensorial basis is not provided, scientific formalizations risk being hollow abstractions: these are pitfalls of abstraction. Fantasy nourishes rationality, making concepts and abstractions intuitive and vivid. Scientific theories lacking in fantasy are exercises of empty abstraction.

The vividness and concreteness given by the sensorial-bounded fantasy close the gap between nature and mind. The more formally science proceeds, the greater the risk of constructing hollow models. For nature is not a book written in the language of mathematics; nature "has neither language nor speech, but she makes tongues and hearts with which to feel and speak" (Goethe, 1783/1998c, p. 4). The ability to feel in our inner self the movements of nature is thus a requisite to create a trustworthy science. "It is yourself you should scrutinize to see/whether you're center or periphery [of nature]," as he writes in the poem *Spontaneous Outburst* (Goethe, 1820/1998j, p. 37). He also reflects, "The human being knows himself only insofar as he knows the world; he perceives the world only in himself, and himself only in the world ... Every new object, *clearly seen*, opens up a new organ of perception in us" (Goethe, 1820/1998j, p. 38; emphasis added). To see clearly means here to develop a sensorial-imaginative approach to reality. Modern science only does justice to nature when its models are tightly tied to the soil of earth. The sensorial-imaginative mode of perceiving is a requisite to the intuitive perception [*Anschauung*], the golden goal of science and poetry. This special kind of knowing implies seeing clearly natural phenomena, not just having a precise set of concepts about them. Concepts and models are certainly necessary for doing science, but if they lack in visual, sensorial, palpable imagery, they will not lead us to the sought intuitive perception.

To be sure, sensuousness and vividness provided by sensuality and fantasy cannot be exhaustively translated into words and abstract language. An epistemological corollary of this is Goethe's skepticism concerning the capacity of science to offer a complete formalization of nature: "Neither things nor ourselves find full expression in our words" (Goethe, 1805/ 1998k, p. 26).

Even though intellectual rationality offers logical precision, such clearness will be empty without the content provided by the sensorial-based fantasy. Since sensuality and fantasy are rooted in the vital organization of human beings, science needs a direct, personal involvement in scientific inquiry: "My intention is to collect all the empirical evidence in this area, *do every experiment myself*" (Goethe, 1792/1998b, p. 17; emphasis added). Thus the rational constructions are meaningful insofar as they have a sensorial-imaginative grounding, which however cannot be exhaustively described through abstractions. Fantasy and sensorial vividness refuse to be tied to discrete concepts. Nature and life offer the ground to intellectual and rational constructions, not the reverse. The priority of life over intellect and the consequent skepticism over scientific knowledge will be a central tenet for the *Philosophy of Nature* of the following generation and, at the end of the 19th century, for the *Philosophy of Life*. Nevertheless it would be misleading to circumscribe its beginning to Goethe's way of science. Goethe's position doubtlessly represents a remarkable moment of the critical spirit against the potential dangers of a hegemonic mechanical worldview, but it incorporates insights gained centuries ago.

Mystical-Theological Background

The primacy of intuition over intellectual understanding can be traced back at least to the early Renaissance. The role of faith in human understanding and its relation with intellectual knowledge became an important question ever since the first Latin translation of Aristotle's *De Anima* (Hicks, 1907) and its Arabian commentaries became available. During the second half of the 13th century, most prominent theologians devoted themselves to discerning how the Aristotelian concept of mind, including his distinction between vegetative, animal, and rational souls, could be coherently assimilated to the vernacular patristic tradition. Besides many critical issues for Christian theology, including the immortality of soul, free will, and divine determinism, or the role of the intellect and love in revelation, an important question extensively discussed at the verge of the Middle Ages and modernity is the nature of faith. Is it a kind of knowledge? If so, what exactly do I know when I believe in God? And what is the difference between knowing God and knowing the workings of earthly reality? Several late-medieval thinkers developed anthropological perspectives to bring together the emerging scientific approach, conspicuously represented by Aristotle, and the scholastic theological tradition. In the context of the present chapter, my aim is to sketch the main features of these anthropologies, emphasizing the proposed relationship of faith and knowledge and the role that fantasy plays in it. Having this in mind, I will focus on only one of these transitional authors, Nicholas of Cusa. We have two main reasons to explore his work. First, during the 19th century he was identified as the first modern philosopher (e.g., Cassirer, 1906; Falckenberg, 1880; Windelband, 1911). Second, as we will soon see, he developed a sophisticated anthropology whose echoes can be heard until the 19th century.

Nicholas of Cusa (1401–1464; original: Nicolai de Cusa), born in Cues (Germany), cardinal and bishop of Brixen (Italy) was an important theologian and philosopher, who at the same time intensively handled diplomatic functions on behalf of the Pope. In one of these diplomatic missions, Nicholas of Cusa was sent to Constantinople to arrange the visit of representatives of the Eastern Church to the Council of Ferrara-Florence of 1438. Nicholas himself wrote that during his return from Constantinople he received as a divine gift the insight that beyond the rational knowledge, where the Aristotelian principle of noncontradiction applies, there is a deeper and more robust knowledge: the *docta ignorantia* or learned ignorance. Since divine infiniteness and absoluteness exceeds human intellectual capacities, the only way human beings can obtain a faint idea of God's absolute presence is by means of a sort of knowing not-knowing, where although we understand, we are incapable of giving grounds for such understanding. This level of knowledge is governed by the *coincidentia oppositorum* principle, through which opposites may coincide. The learned ignorance allows for seeing the unity where the ratio discovers differences. The square and the circle become one and the same when we add progressively n-angles to the square. Apparent dualities dissolve when approached from the cultivated ignorance: God and Christ; Earth and Heaven; maximum and minimum; sense and ratio.

> Therefore, if the foregoing points are true, then since the desire in us is not in vain, assuredly we desire to know that we do not know. If we can fully attain unto this [knowledge of our ignorance], we will attain unto learned ignorance. For a man—even one very well versed in learning—will attain unto nothing more perfect than to be found to be most learned in the ignorance which is distinctively his. The more he knows that he is unknowing, the more learned he will be. (Nicholas of Cusa, 1440/1990, p. 6)

Like in Goethe's intuitive perception, the certainty and vividness of the knowledge reached through *docta ignorantia* contrasts with its ineffability: "Someone who desires to grasp the meaning must elevate his intellect above the import of the words rather than insisting upon the proper significations of words which cannot be properly adapted to such great intellectual mysteries" (Nicholas of Cusa, 1440/1990, p. 7). The *docta ignorantia* "will suitably lead you ... unto wondrous delight ... (provided you rise from the sign upward to the truth, by understanding [the meaning of] words symbolically)"[6] (Nicholas of Cusa, 1440/1990, p. 18). The latin expression *verba transsumptive intelligendo* [understanding beyond the words] denotes the requirement to surpass language in order to see what by pure intellectual means is incomprehensible.

The relinquishment of words and intellect as condition for deeper understanding seems to be a heritage from the mystical movement from the middle of the 13th century, about 150 years before Nicholas of Cusa (Windelband, 1911). Meister Eckhart, for example, defended the primacy of the unspeakable intuition [*unaussprechliches Anschauen*] within the human soul as the fundament of faith over the intellectual knowledge of scholars (Windelband, 1911). Human thought, although important, is secondary to faith felt inwardly, since "essence and knowledge are one ... Knowledge is ... the unity of essences between the knower and the known" (Windelband, 1911, p. 28, translation mine). This connection illustrates the historical gravity of the German verb *anschauen* [literally to see or to contemplate], usually translated into the Latin form *intuitio* and their variants in modern European languages.[7]

It is not difficult to perceive the commonalities between Goethe's intuitive perception and Nicholas of Cusa's *docta ignorantia*. In both cases, a special attitude toward reality is necessary to obtain an understanding of a higher level. Such an attitude implies overcoming the pure intellective mode of approaching the world so that we can assume a contemplative approach to see the reality rather than impose on it a conceptual framework implicit in our linguistic distinctions. This is a call for grounding the higher forms of knowledge in a simple, direct, visible intuition (a *visio sine comprehensione*) rather than in formal arguments or rational procedures. The *docta ignorantia* expresses such certainty that cannot be thoroughly translated by language. In the same way Goethe's intuitive perception does not "find full expression in our words" (Goethe, 1998k, p. 26).

Moreover, Goethe's model of four powers of the soul seems to be a modern version of the model offered by Nicholas of Cusa in *Idiota: De Mente* [*The Layman on Mind*] (1450/1983). In this text, Nicholas of Cusa integrates in one common frame the kind of knowing that his *docta ignorantia* guarantees with the inherited three Aristotelian souls. He establishes four levels of knowledge, from the lower to the higher: senses; imagination; reason; intellect/intuition. At all levels, the human mind [*mens humana*] characterizes itself as being an "assimilative power," that is, it tries, by perceiving and conceiving, to assimilate [*assimilatio*] itself or to adopt the configurations [*configuratio*] of the form [*forma*] of the perceived object or thought:

> Mind is so assimilative that in the sense of sight it assimilates itself to things visible, in the sense of hearing it assimilates itself to things audible, in the sense of taste to things tasteable, in the sense of smell to things that can be smelled, in the sense of touch to things touchable. In the senses [mind assimilates itself] to things perceptible, in the imagination to things imaginable, and in reason to things accessible by reasoning. (Nicholas of Cusa, 1450/1996, para. 100)

While the sensorial organs are the first way to assimilate to objects, there is still another "arterial spirit" (i.e., corporeal, material spirit), which is "configurable, though in a gross and nondiscrete manner, to all perceptual forms" (Nicholas of Cusa, 1450/1996, para. 101), namely, imagination [*imaginatio*]. This power of soul differs from the senses only in the fact that it apprehends (though confusedly) objects when these are absent. In addition to this, the human mind is capable of assimilating objects in a more clear and subtle way by means of the identification of concepts from the perceptible objects. This function requires the third power of the soul: reason [*ratio*], which allows the soul to distinguish among mental states. Importantly, even through reason, "the soul does not grasp the true nature of things, since it apprehends forms united to matter ... But the matter distorts the form, so that the form's true nature cannot be grasped" (Nicholas of Cusa, 1450/1996, para. 115). Sense, imagination, and reason are assimilations for perceptible objects because they all are assimilations of "corporeal spirits" (Nicholas of Cusa, 1450/1996, para. 102). Mind perceives, imagines, and discerns concepts insofar as "mind acts as a soul, enlivening the body" (Nicholas of Cusa, 1450/1996, para. 102). Hence, these three powers of soul are in fact three different ways in which "the soul uses the bodily instrument" (Nicholas of Cusa, 1450/1996, para. 115). As reason apprehends "forms united to matter" and "the matter distorts the form," rational knowledge is necessarily conjectural: "So, then, I maintain that concepts which are attained by means of assimilations made by reason are subject to uncertainty, because they are [made] in accordance with images of the [true] formal natures rather than in accordance with the true formal natures themselves" (Nicholas of Cusa, 1450/1996, para. 102). Reason is conjectural since it is tied to the body, and therefore not free from matter.

There is still an intellectual power of the soul by which the mind conceives the immutable essence of things "using itself as its own instrument, apart from any instrumental [corporeal] spirit" (Nicholas of Cusa, 1450/1996, para. 103). This is possible because our mind does not only act operatively in a body, but it is also in itself, that is, it is "free from matter" (Nicholas of Cusa, 1450/1996, para. 104). When mind per se, not tied to matter, looks on its own immutability, it "makes assimilations of forms not as they are embedded in matter but as they are in and of themselves"

(Nicholas of Cusa, 1450/1996, para. 103). When this happen, mind assimilates itself not to things, but to abstract forms, that is, incorporeal forms. This is the origin of mathematical branches. This procedure leads to discovering truth, but still in a partial way. That is, the mind discovers a certain necessity in a specific domain of reality, or in another. In this condition, "mind is still unsatisfied, because it does not behold the precise truth of all things" (Nicholas of Cusa, 1450/1996, para. 105). To reach the truth in its own infinite precision, mind should advance from intellect to intuition:

> Mind, looking unto its own simplicity ... uses this simplicity as an instrument, in order to assimilate itself to all things—assimilate itself not only abstractly, apart from matter, but also in terms of a simplicity that is incommunicable to matter. And in this way mind beholds, in its own simplicity, all things ... And within its own simplicity mind beholds all things as without any composition of parts—beholds them not as one thing is this and another is that but as (1) all things are something one and (2) something one is all things. And this is the intuiting of absolute truth [*Et haec est intuitio veritatis absolutae*]. (Nicholas of Cusa, 1450/1996, para. 105f)

At this point we can make explicit similarities between Goethe's intuitive perception and Nicholas of Cusa's intuition or *docta ignorantia*. First, in both cases intuition is simple and direct. Intuition does not emerge from strengthened efforts for rationality or the construction of models of increasing abstraction, but rather from the attention to the more simple and direct aspects of our own experience. The totality intuitively experienced is lived with full certainty or self-evidence. Second, intuition is something that can be seen. While reason "assimilates concepts by conceiving," intuition produces "intellectual viewings" (Nicholas of Cusa, 1450/1996, para. 99). Even though intuition is holistically lived and felt, the visual dimension of this experience receives an outstanding place in the descriptions of both authors.[8] Third, intuition cannot be translatable exhaustively. As described above, for Goethe, intuitive perception will never find full expression in words, while Nicholas of Cusa declares that on intuition "enough could never be said" (Nicholas of Cusa, 1450/1996, para. 106). Finally, in both cases, knowledge obtained by intuition is always accompanied with a remarkable positive affectivity, described as tranquility, delight, beauty, and pleasure by Nicholas of Cusa and as sublimity and beauty by Goethe.

Nonetheless, two important differences between Goethe and Nicholas of Cusa on intuition should be addressed. First, intuition in Nicholas of Cusa is the right way for understanding God and his creation. It also fulfills theological aims. For Goethe, intuitive perception is oriented mainly toward aesthetical goals. A just apprehension of reality, even the objective, scientific one, involves a ubiquitous aesthetic dimension that emerges from a contemplative attitude rather than from an analytic one. It is true that for both authors theological speculations and aesthetic feelings are not contradictory, as a cosmic order pervades the whole nature, a divine order experienced as beauty. But it is also true that they were writing in radically different historical and cultural contexts so that their aims differentiate undoubtedly.

The second difference between Goethe and Nicholas of Cusa's theories of knowledge concerns the role of fantasy or imagination. Nicholas of Cusa understands imagination as a "chamber" [*cellula*] in the mind, where the images originally produced by sensorial stimulation are again brought to life. Its productivity is accordingly rather limited to having images in the absence of the corresponding objects—it can generate only what once was perceived and now is absent. Imagination provides images to the ulterior intellectual abstraction of forms from material perceptions. For Nicholas of Cusa, imagination is disconnected from the power of intuiting, because it is still attached to the material world; intellect, on the contrary, unites the human soul with the immaterial world. Thus, the "intellectual viewing" [*visio intellectualis*] produced by the intuition remains closely related to the revelation of Christian tradition. This is a personal illumination as a consequence of God's gift to those who faithfully contemplate the world. Since this kind of intuition involves the immaterial soul, it implies a detachment from the material body. In Nicholas of Cusa's case, there can be intuition only when immaterial soul understands "free from material world," whereas imagination corresponds to an "arterial spirit," since the soul uses the body as instrument to re-create images.

In spite of Nicholas of Cusa's separating imagination from intuition, his descriptions of the latter reveal features that Goethe attributes to fantasy. Goethe describes it as an instrument to penetrate into the living world—an indispensable faculty to obtain the intuitive perception. On theorizing about intuition, Nicholas of Cusa connects it with God's agentivity:

> For our mind differs from the Divine Mind as seeing differs from doing. The Divine Mind creates by conceiving; our mind assimilates by conceiving—i.e., by making concepts, or intellectual viewings. The Divine Mind is a reifying power; our mind is an assimilative power. (Nicholas of Cusa, 1450/1996, para. 99)

Human intuition reflects imperfectly God's creative power. God creates and human intellectively apprehends the creation. Their knowledge powers define human being as second creator [*secundum creator*] (see Westhof, 2013). Whenever human beings strive for knowing the world, they "assimilate" it, that is, they become the world themselves. These second creators apply the intellective powers to re-create within themselves the order of the cosmos. In this sense, the human being is described by Nicholas of Cusa as a living image of God: "And God, who is all things, shines forth in mind when mind, as a *living image of God* [*viva imago dei*], turns to its own Exemplar and assimilates itself thereto with all its effort" (Nicholas of Cusa, 1450/1996, para. 106; emphasis added).

From the fact that the human being is a second creator, Nicholas of Cusa draws the epistemological insight that humans know the world insofar as they reflect the world as a living mirror:

> Similarly, God, through the movement of the heavens and from a suitable material, brought forth a proportion [viz., a body] in which animality would shine forth in a very perfect manner. To this proportion He then added mind as a *living mirror* [*vivum speculum*]. (Nicholas of Cusa, 1450/1996, para. 87; emphasis added)

The capacity of knowing by feeling into oneself is the main source of knowledge for both Nicholas of Cusa and Goethe. For the former, this capacity allows an immaterial access to God's creation; for Goethe this is precisely fantasy. In both cases, this capacity obviously implies that human beings have an active role in knowing the world. Insofar as the active role of the human being in the act of knowing becomes more prominent, fantasy/imagination comes nearer to intuitive perception. For Nicholas of Cusa, imagination does not take the part of intuition; for Goethe, fantasy is a *conditio sine qua non* for having intuitive perceptions. The critical difference seems to reside in the role played by the human being in the act of knowing. For Nicholas of Cusa, the intuition lays still near to the divine revelation, which is a gift, not a personal achievement. For Goethe, intuitive perception requires the intentioned cultivation of the skill to anchor abstractions with the actual soil of earth. Having intuitions demands active efforts to give vitality and sensuality to the intellective constructions. The contrasts between Nicholas of Cusa and Goethe profile the change from a passive to an active mode of knowing. A transitional author that shows the increasing importance of fantasy in the act of knowing the world is Giambattista Vico.

Fantasy in Vico's Thought

Giambattista Vico (1670–1744) developed one of the first criticisms to the Cartesian method. The formal method, argued Vico, turns out to be inapplicable to the field of human issues. This claim is the corollary of his tenet *verum et factum convertuntur*, with which Vico abruptly begins his *De antiquissima italorum sapientia* (1710): "For the latins, *verum* (the true) and *factum* (what is made) are interchangeable, or to use the customary language of the Schools, they are convertible" (1710/1988, p. 45). True knowledge can be obtained only about something that was created by us, since only in such a case do we know the reasons for every detail of this object. Since God is Nature's creator, He is the only true knower of the natural world. Natural sciences are therefore merely conjectural and cannot provide the certainty and clearness that Cartesians allegedly sustain.

There is another corollary of the *verum et factum convertuntur* principle: there are reality domains from which we can indeed have true knowledge, namely, those that are created by ourselves. Such domains include foremost what Vico calls the "civil world," that is, human social life. Hence, Vico inverts the Cartesian hierarchy of epistemic supremacy, putting the natural sciences below the human sciences, since the latter but not the former may have access to true knowledge. The method to understand human social life, particularly that of ancient nations, is the fantasy ("imagination" in the English translation), described by Vico as an imaginative effort performed by the scientist on the object of knowledge. By analyzing ancient times in European culture, he states, "For when we wish to give utterance to our understanding of spiritual things, *we must seek aid from our imagination to explain them* and, like painters, form human images of them" (Vico, 1725/1948, para. 402; emphasis added).

Fantasy becomes for Vico the more genuine and exact way to discover true knowledge in human affairs. The imaginative capacities of the scientist become the method for a new science. The discovery of the principles of the civil society demands that the scientists look "within the modifications of our own human mind" (Vico, 1725/1948, para. 331). Thus, the method of fantasy

> seeks its proofs not in the external world but *within the modifications of the mind of him who meditates it.* For, as we have said above, since this world of nations has certainly been made by men, it is within these modifications that its principles should have been sought. (Vico, 1725/1948, para. 374; emphasis added)

The fantasy, argues Vico, implies the task of abandoning momentarily one's own culture to enter into an alien culture, perhaps already disappeared. This procedure may not be as easy as one could think, since we have to overcome the difficulties of imagining symbolic worlds far distant from our own. For example, when understanding past cultures we have "to descend from these human and refined natures of ours to those quite wild and savage natures, which we cannot at all imagine and can apprehend only with *great effort*" (Vico, 1725/1948, para. 338; emphasis added).

In the same spirit of Nicholas of Cusa's *assimilatio*, for Vico the modifications of our mind implied in the method of the fantasy correspond to a transformation by which the scientist becomes the inquired object:

> So that as rational metaphysics teaches that man becomes all things by understanding them (*homo intelligendo fit omnia*), this imaginative metaphysics shows that man becomes all things by not understanding them (*homo non intelligendo fit omnia*) and perhaps *the latter proposition is truer than the former*, for when man understands he extends his mind and takes in the things, but when he does not understand he makes the things out of himself and becomes them by transforming himself into them. (Vico, 1725/1948, para. 405, emphasis added)

Many aspects of the method proposed by Vico are quite similar to the Nicholas of Cusa description of the maximal intellectual power (the *intuitio*). The big difference is that for Vico such intuition is dependent on corporeal imagination. Vico is therefore strongly arguing for granting fantasy an epistemic role. As we saw above, for Nicholas of Cusa, imagination does not participate in knowledge of higher levels, intellect and intuition, because of its corporeal determination; rather, it is the intellect, the immaterial part of the microcosm of man, the faculty responsible for intuition. Intellect and imagination run separately in Nicholas of Cusa's theory, precisely as form and matter or as divinity and humanity do. Vico, on the contrary, affirms that there is no real intellectual access to human reality without integrating imagination as the key instrument to understanding. The form of this claim is expressive of an anti-intellectualist position: man becomes all things not by understanding them but rather by not understanding them. A real comprehension of social life requires incorporating in us the modes of thinking of others; not applying our own concepts and distinctions to an unknown culture. This act of knowledge is not intellectual; it is imaginative.

Concerning Vico's tacit anthropology, he explicitly opposed imagination to intellect; for example, "Imagination is more robust in proportion as reasoning power is weak" (Vico, 1725/1948, para. 185). In his analysis of the development of civilization, rationality and abstraction are considered recent achievements of humankind when compared to the "poetic wisdom" of the primordial times of Greek culture. The "power of ratiocination" (Vico, 1725/1948, para. 375), that is, rationality and abstraction capacities, are developed later than "sense and vigorous imagination" (Vico, 1725/1948, para. 375). Vico uses the known four capacities of the soul in a sociocultural developmental sequence that follows the late medieval hierarchy. More interesting is, nonetheless, the epistemological claim that the human scientist should combine abstraction and rationality with an epistemic attitude of imaginative contemplation. Without imagination (in Vico's words, *fantasia*) we will never experience the "divine pleasure" of contemplate the principles extended along the "world of nations in all the extent of its places, times and varieties" (Vico, 1725/1948, para. 345).

Fantasy in Kant

Let us return to Goethe. Considering the historical background, it becomes clearer how significant was Goethe's aim of bringing together again what Nature created as unity. In his anthropology, this maxim takes the form of the integration of fantasy and reason. The union of imagination and rationality, of synthesis and analysis, turns out to be a condition to intuitive perception—the apodictic vision of a global truth. The importance that Goethe assigns to fantasy represents a significant development for what was a rather limited contribution in Nicholas of Cusa's thought. It plays an even more central role than that of an indispensable methodological instrument, as in Vico's work. Fantasy seems to advance from a supplier of images for intellectual tasks to come, to the a force that modifies our own intellectual constructions so that we may understand the social and natural realities. It provides flexibility and adaptability to rational concepts. Thus, fantasy seems to encrypt the ancient idea of an active movement from the spirit, or *pneuma*, that leads to deep truths by a simple but certain in-tuition (i.e., in-sight). It tacitly represents hence the connection between the modern rational science with the mystical and Christian revelation.

The fate of Goethe's attempt to raise an integrative anthropology and its impact in the emerging psychology may be better understood when we take into account that he was coetaneous with Immanuel Kant, for many the greatest philosopher of modern times, whose influence on 19th century psychology was immense (Valsiner, 2012). Knowingly, in his *Critique of Pure Reason* (1781/1998), Kant analyzes the question of how the mind should be constituted in order to reach accurate knowledge. His analysis leads to what he called his own Copernican Revolution: the constitution of the sensible objects depends on the structure of our own faculty of reason and not the reverse, as was assumed by empiricism and rationalism. Kant inquires accordingly into the conditions of possibility of our reason; not what is beyond our rational understanding, but what makes it possible at all. This is his "trascendental method," which does not concern transcendent knowledge, that is, knowledge on substances outside of this world, but the *a priori* conditions that make knowledge possible, where *a priori* means before we have any sensible experience. Kant will dismiss the questions concerning the domain beyond sensible experience as metaphysical. Thus, Kant is interested in the conditions that make possible our sensible experience (*sinnliche Erfahrung*), rejecting the suprasensible domain whereof we cannot have experiences. Any attempt to theorize on the suprasensible leads unavoidably to aporias or antinomies.

Important for the coming psychology are Kant's statements on mind. He postulates three faculties of the mind: sensibility [*Sinnlichkeit*], understanding [*Verstand*], and reason [*Vernunft*]. Sensibility corresponds to the capacity to have sensible experience, which does not function like a passive reception instance, because all what we perceive is spatiotemporally structured. Since neither time nor space is externally given, Kant assumes those are *a priori* forms given to the sensible data. We cannot perceive the things in themselves, but only structured in time and space; we perceive phenomena not noumena. In line with Locke, Kant advances that self-knowledge pertains also to the category of perceptions; when we observe our own internal states, we have an internal experience [*inner Sinn*], which is also matter structured by space and time. According to Kant, we perceive the world and ourselves from the start within a spatiotemporal structure. We are constituted for perceiving the world (and ourselves) in a mathematical way. Any attempt to get rid of this framework is misleading. Such a belief will be fundamental for ulterior experimental psychology. The second mental capacity, understanding, allows clarifying the sensible experiences by bringing a multiplicity of partial impressions in unified perceptions. This process takes place insofar as the mind applies logic—formal functions to the (already spatiotemporally structured) perceptions, giving them unity. These functions are the transcendental categories (e.g., causality, unity, persistence, etc.), as they are *a priori* and determine our understanding of reality. Thus, for Kant, knowledge is the blend of sensible experience with concepts. Finally, reason represents the highest knowledge capacity. It gives unity to the rules of understanding and therefore produces increasing levels of integration through abstraction.

Interestingly, Kant assigns a main role in his framework to fantasy [*Einbildungskraft*]. Imagination explains the function of synthesis, that is, the fact that from a multiplicity of impressions, one object is experienced; or that from a multiplicity of experiences, one picture is obtained: "Synthesis in general is ... the mere effect of the imagination, of a blind though indispensable function of the soul, without which we should have no cognition [*Erkenntnis*] at all, but of which we are seldom even conscious" (Kant, 1781/1998, p. 211). Kant distinguished two kinds of imagination: reproductive and productive. The reproductive imagination produces synthesis following the empirical laws of association and explains the psychological fact that representations are connected one after another. The productive imagination produces a transcendental synthesis that relates sensibility, in the form of certain sensorial impressions, with understanding—transcendental categories. The productive imagination grants the structure of forms to that which is given by the senses, as well as it gives the unity of thought to a mass of perceptions:

> No psychologist has yet thought that the imagination is a necessary ingredient of perception itself. This is so partly because this faculty has been limited to reproduction, and partly because it has been believed that the senses do not merely afford us impressions but also put them together, and produce images of objects, for which without doubt something more than the receptivity of impressions is required, namely a function of the synthesis of them (Kant, 1781/1998, p. 239, fn.)

Unlike Goethe's notion of fantasy, Kant's definition of imagination lacks any relation with feelings and organismic processes. For Kant, imagination has an intermediary role between sensibility and understanding; it is a force that produces synthesis in the form of sensible experiences, concepts, and ideas. It satisfies therefore a function strictly intellectual, and its possible grounding in feelings is plainly ignored or conspicuously minimized. Kant's anthropology represents fully the model of man for the Illuminism, as it conceives the human being as cognizing subject rather than as person. Human actions, from the ordinary to the moral, are governed by rational principles, that is, logicoformal rules. Even sensible experiences are regarded as rationally structured, since they become experiences proper when the raw sensorial data become structured by means of *a priori* forms. Through such descriptions, Kant does not aim to do psychology but to establish what he calls "the conditions of the possibility" of knowledge. To study the human nature does demand an empirical inquiry; but to search for its conditions of possibility has a transcendental character. He is not interested in understanding the developmental origins of cognition, but in its fundaments. Kant delimitates his focus on the epistemological subject, an abstract instance endowed with sensibility and reason whose activity makes the existence of knowledge possible. It is important to note that the epistemological subject does not correspond to a person, since a person is an empirical instance. In fact, activities that people do and that are not related with knowledge gaining are simply not considered in Kant's analysis.

The cleavage between epistemological subject and person runs in parallel with Kant's conception of imagination. He separated the empirical reproductive imagination—the capacity to have representations of an absent object—from the transcendental productive imagination, which articulates sensations and experiences by means of *a priori* forms and categories. Reproductive imagination becomes part of psychology; productive imagination, part of the theory of knowledge. In Kant's version, imagination is devoid of the sensuous and organismic aspects implied in Goethe's understanding of the term *Sinnlichkeit*.[9] Its role is making reason possible; there is no equivalence to Goethe's exact sensuous imagination that leads to an intuitive perception. In fact, the very term *intuition* [*Anschauung*] undergoes a fundamental transformation to denote sensible experiences, that is, spatiotemporally structured sensorial impressions, while the primordial idea of an intuitive perception, a *docta ignorantia*, is discarded by Kant since our understanding can only be discursive, that is, category based:

> And further, it is not at all necessary here to prove that such an *intellectus archetypus* is possible, but only that in the contrast of it with our discursive, image-dependent understanding (*intellectus ectypus*) and the contingency of such a constitution we are led to that idea (of an *intellectus archetypus*), and that this does not contain any contradiction. (Kant, 1790/2000, p. 277)

Kant's empirical assumptions are that there cannot be human understanding of a nondiscursive nature and that human scientific language satisfies by definition his logicoformal conception of transcendental categories. Take notice that such tenets are psychological, that is, empirical. As such, they fall outside the field circumscribed by Kant as transcendental. Thus, they are accepted with no further arguments than that they have to exist to make rational science possible. Kant's aim is not to describe how the human mind really is, a task assigned to psychology, instead it is to describe how the mind should be in order to make objective knowledge possible. This description depicts an abstract subject, not a real person. Thus, this epistemological subject is fully rational and her feelings (if she has them) do not interfere with the knowledge act. Accordingly, her imagination, far from being a critical force connecting sensuousness with reason, as in Goethe's model, either provides images in a reproductive fashion (reproductive imagination) or imprints transcendental categories on sensorial data. In both cases, imagination for Kant satisfies only intellective functions and is disconnected from feelings and organismic processes.

Goethe and Kant were the greatest exponents of two different approaches to humanity and nature extant at the beginning of the 19th century, and their influence would endure the whole century. Goethe represents the humanist attempting to correct the crooked growth of natural sciences by remembering the old truths of harmony and beauty. Kant embodies the illuminist thinker, who designs a complex metaphysical skeleton to sustain the vision of man as a rational knower.

Fantasy at the Dawn of the New Psychology

Psychology textbooks of the first half of the 19th century evidence the incorporation of Goethe's fantasy as well as Kant's distinction between a reproductive imagination and productive one. While the intellectual function to reproduce images in absence of the objects tends to be indentified with reproductive imagination, Kant's productive imagination is progressively devoid of its original transcendental sense, becoming equivalent to Goethe's notion of fantasy. A nice example of this transformation can be read in Carl Gustav Carus' *Vorlesungen über Psychologie* [*Lectures on Psychology*] (1831). In this text, he distinguishes a reproductive imagination [*reproduktive Einbildungskraft*] from a capacity autonomous and productive that he calls fantasy [*Phantasie*]: "The fantasy is a creating imagination, a call for representations to dress up in some way emerging ideas from the soul, where those representations ... suffer essential modifications" (Carus, 1831/1958, p. 423f.; our translation). Fantasy, argues Carus, is the result of the union of productivity with imagination. On the other side, like Kant, Carus understands that the reproductive imagination deploys representations [*Vorstellungen*] according to the laws of association (simultaneity, similarity, opposition), and that its activity is limited to calling back earlier states and sensorial impressions.

Carus' real intellectual interest was fantasy rather than imagination. Following the long tradition that connects psychology with the Renaissance philosophy, he recurred to the notion of "man as microcosm" (see Cornejo, 2015), to assert that fantasy becomes the "germ of all visual arts," when it grabs and imitates "the organs and skills of natural life." By means of the imitation capacities awakened by fantasy, human beings learn to protect themselves and to adapt to their environments. Fantasy is also responsible for "the first art of making through imitation" (Carus, 1831/1958, p. 423f.; our translation). The centrality of fantasy in Carus' psychology becomes more evident in his *opus magmun* of 1846, *Psyche*, where he advances a theory of the developmental phases of the human soul from its first expressions in animals toward adult human beings. He proposes basically three ontogenetic phases: understanding [*Verstand*], fantasy [*Phantasie*], and reason [*Vernunft*]. In understanding, the mind learns to recognize and order its own representations [*Vorstellungen*]. Then

> At a higher level, the mind begins to produce autonomously with the already comprehended representations, to combine them properly to generate from them new ones that never were externally perceived. This happens during the driving youth period of the mind ... that we call the development of puberty in the real organism. Insofar as the mind manages to create something new, we call this level *Fantasy*. But at last the mind arrives at perceiving ... the mystery of unity in multiplicity; in its capacity of creation the mind becomes aware of its own divine nature and of the divinity that underlies any form of being. In brief, the mind arrives at perceiving the idea, i.e., at *reason*. (Carus, 1831/1958, p. 129f.; our translation, emphasis in original)

Far from merely reproducing images to feed ulterior rational processes, fantasy is for Carus the core of artistic and scientific creativity. That "an exact sensorial fantasy" was a necessary component of scientific activity was precisely the point raised by Goethe. The same insight is visible in the *Lehrbuch zur Psychologie* [Handbook of Psychology] (1816) by Johann Friedrich Herbart: "To do poetry, in the broadest sense, is the essence of any invention ... There is as much fantasy in scientific thinking as in poetic production; and it is very doubtful whether Newton or Shakespeare possessed the more fantasy" (Herbart, 1816/1834, p. 74; our translation). Herbart assumed the fourfold model of mind, separating sensibility and imagination as "lower capacities" from "higher capacities", namely, understanding and reason. Despite the hierarchy, Herbart maintained that imagination/fantasy takes part of the production of rational conclusions:

> To the extent that we ascribe to reason [Vernunft] the capacity to draw conclusions, an inadmissible demarcation becomes visible between the faculties of the soul. To extract inferences and to prove and verify them are two very different affairs, which in fact are in the majority of cases quite separated. The first may be attributed to fantasy [Einbildungskraft], whereas the second to reason. (Herbart, 1816/1834, p. 69; our translation)

Similarly, Ernst Stiedenroth,[10] in his *Psychologie zur Erklärung der Seelenerscheinungen* (1824) [Psychology for the Explanation of the Phenomena of Soul], expresses that fantasy and intellect [*Verstand*] permanently blend, so that it would be more appropriate to talk of one activity rather than two separated faculties:

> Furthermore, it is known from poetry that imagining [Phantasieren] and thinking [Verstand] mix constantly. It would be wishful that one could experience whether fantasy first brings up images, for which the reason prepare concepts, or whether fantasy fosters imagery to preexisting thoughts. Nothing about such strange split operations will be found in the soul. Rather it is obvious that both—concept and image—are constantly mixing, and that they represent only *one activity*, so that if anyone wants to split it, nothing will remain a secure property neither of the one nor of the other. (Stiedenroth, 1824, p. 15; our translation, emphasis in original)

Coherently with his criticism of the more or less arbitrary segmentation of the soul in different faculties or capacities, Stiedenroth (1824) writes about "the thinking" [*das Denken*] and "the fantasizing" [*das Phantasieren*] as actions of the soul rather than static properties, whose nature is doubtful. Moreover, according to Stiedenroth's holistic description, the fantasizing can play an important role in the scientific inquiry. For Stiedenroth, fantasy can "complete a representation [Vorstellung] or a sequence of representations" even when this representation is a concept. However, the "thinking in the narrow sense [i.e., *reason*] wishes to be objective ... [but] the fantasizing does not want to be objective thinking" (Stiedenroth, 1824, p. 173). Therefore, the fantasizing cannot complete a concept in itself, but only "outside itself, i.e., by sensualization [Versinnlichung], by depiction [Darstellung]" (Stiedenroth, 1824, p. 173). When fantasy takes part of the thinking, the result is thus an intuition [*Anschauung*]. At this point, Stiedenroth connects again, as Goethe, as Vico, as Nicholas of Cusa, fantasy with intuitive perception: "Therefore, fantasy is everywhere related with intuition and its products will be intuitable or will give an intuitive perception" (Stiedenroth, 1824, p. 173). Fantasy completes intellectual concepts by giving them vividness and physiognomy that should be examined in later operations by reason:

> In this way, fantasy is therefore able to intervene in the thinking in the narrow sense [*reason*]; it prefigures or imitates vivid [*anschaulich*] relationships, which the thinking in the narrow sense has to objectify, i.e., it has to examine and prove their concordance with valid concepts and thoughts. (Stiedenroth, 1824, p. 173; our translation)

Like Carus, Stiedenroth maintains the inseparability of fantasy from thinking, between sensorial-imaginative aspects of human experience and the intellectual functions. Furthermore, both authors agree that the specific contribution of fantasy to reason is to "prefigure or imitate vivid relationships." Carus calls this process imitation [*Nachahmung*], referring to the human capacity to assimilate and to become the inquired object.

Scientific Psychology and an Irony of History

In 1911, looking retrospectively at the history of psychology, Max Dessoir called it "an irony of history," that despite Kant's skepticism toward the possibility of a scientific psychology, this discipline had followed in a rather disciplined way his metaphysical scientific worldview and his anthropology. As a general framework, Kantian philosophy contributed decisively to the view of inner experiences as a succession of spatiotemporal events. By the middle of the 19th century, this worldview was so commonsensical that it was natural to measure human subjective processes as extended in time and space the same way that electric stream was measured upon physiological tissues.

Concerning the term *fantasy*, the second half of the 19th century shows the tendency to keep the psychological interpretation of the Kantian distinction between a reproductive and a productive imagination, reserving, in German language, the label *fantasy* to the second kind. For example,

Oswald Külpe in his *Grundriss der Psychologie* (1893) [*Outlines of Psychology*] argues that "the activity of memory is reproductive: that of fancy or imagination [*Phantasie*] seems in contrast to it to be productive, creative" (Külpe, 1893/1895, p. 170). As seen above, the "psychological" character of fantasy obeys the fact that it was not understood as the *a priori* condition that unites sensorial data and transcendental categories, but rather as a psychological, that is, empirical process of synthesis. Thus, in his own *Grundriss der Psychologie* (1896) Wundt pointed out that the basic "psychic elements" (sensations [*Empfindungenen*] and sentiments [*Gefühle*]) form more complex images [*Gebilde*], which in turn become related by means of either associative or apperceptive connections. Wundt described two "composite apperception functions," namely, analysis and synthesis, that is, the apperceptive activities of comparing and connecting representations. For Wundt, fantasy is the activity involved in the synthetic function of building a total representation from elemental images, particularly when this composite corresponds to an "arbitrary synthesis" (Wundt, 1897, p. 306). Clearly the synthesis to which Wundt is referring here differs radically from the metaphysical function originally presented by Kant. Wundt's synthesis takes place in a real person, not in an abstract subject.

A second tendency is assuming Kant's belief that sensibility is passive, while understanding and reason are active capacities of the soul. This assumption, together with the introduction of methods from physiology, influenced the increasing bias toward the "passive part" of the human mind in the scientifically oriented research of the "new psychology." The initial studies by Ernst H. Weber, Gustav Fechner, and H. von Helmholtz were precisely conducted on sensorial perception (Dessoir, 1911; Klemm, 1911). Wundt's later expansion of the methodological innovation in the broader context of a new "science of immediate experience" does not promote applying experimentation to higher, more active functions of the human mind.[11] The consequence of this for the study of fantasy is that its scientific validity came to be in question in the same way that every psychological process that could not be experimentally or psychometrically measured. This progressively produced a sentiment of dissatisfaction with the productive fantasy, which may explain its gradually disappearing from scientific psychological research. It is true that fantasy still occupies an important role in introductory books to the discipline (Erdmann, 1873; Külpe, 1895; Wundt, 1874, 1897). But it is also true that its description is lacking in experimental grounding, which characterizes the more basic processes, such as sensation, perception, and even memory. On the whole, it was only the doctrine of the elements, and the experimental methods for their study, that outlasted Wundt's approach; not his voluntarism, which included the apperceptive modes to combine representations and fantasy activity; nor less his *Völkerpsychologie*.

A third trend concerning fantasy is its progressive displacement from psychology toward other knowledge domains. Insofar as psychology focused in the mental processes more susceptible to mechanical modeling, and subsequently dismissed the creative capacities of the human being, fantasy, that is, productive imagination, became of interest in other disciplines, in which the model of person has creativity and activity as central features. An example of this movement is Theodor Lipps' *Grundlegung der Ästhetik* (1903) [*Fundaments of Aesthetics*]. In this work, Lipps develops a psychological approach to the aesthetic perception by using the concept of *empathy* [*Einfühlung*]. By doing descriptive phenomenology, that is, by describing in the first person the own experiencing in front of natural scenes of reality, Lipps rediscovers the old insight that we permanently perceive the world not as a set of things and states emotionally neutral, but rather expressively. Lipps argues that objects are directly expressive, even the unanimated ones, so that they impress immediately on us as beautiful, ugly, brilliant, hopeful, fearful, and such. The reason is that persons directly and unavoidably empathize, that is, they feel in themselves what they perceive. In the encounter with the world, people act internally, moving themselves according to the expressive features perceived. But not only when we perceive do we have expressive impressions but also when we imagine. Lipps argues that the external action is not the only kind of "real acting." There are in fact three kinds of action:

> One is the *acting in the sphere of fantasy*, by which the will directs itself toward mere objects of the imagination; this is the plain "mental" working ... Next there is the *intellectual acting* or the acting by reasoning, by reflecting, by thinking, by judging, by deduction, etc. And there is finally the acting that only gets satisfied in the *real existence*, i.e., in the perception and in the awareness that something is real. (Lipps, 1903/1923, p. 129; emphasis added; our translation)

In fantasy there is a sort of "inner acting," by which we experience in a vivid manner the imagined object. This is the modern version of Nicholas of Cusa's living mirror, Vico's "modifications of the own mind," as well as Carus and Stiedenroth's imitation. An important point in Lipps' proposal is the observation that the fantasizing entails aesthetic feelings: In the Gestalts formed by fantasy "lies beauty" (Lipps, 1903/1923, p. 166). Fantasy re-creates life, and its products are in the same way aesthetically experienced.

In a similar vein, Wilhelm Dilthey (1910/1922) defines poetic imagination [*dichterische Phantasie*] as the capacity present in especially talented persons to produce vivid images whose content is intuitable but at the same time leads to novel ways to understand reality. In contrast to the intellectual discernment, the poetic imagination would connect with the vital forces of life, since "life already contains the forces operative in the imagination" (Dilthey, 1910/1985, p. 238). The poetic imagination makes contact not with the objects denoted by the literary work, but with their "life-value": "The life I find in my own self, my situations, and the people and things around me constitutes their life-value ... It is this life-value that the literary work shows first of all" (Dilthey, 1910/1985, p. 237). In this way, the poetic imagination reveals new aspects of reality. Even though a poem can refer to specific states of affairs, it is "wholly saturated by the universal" (Dilthey, 1910/1985, p. 243) because of the connection with deep aspects of our existence. Imagination opens up new ways to understand life and its multiple aspects: "For by representing some part of reality, every genuine poetic work accentuates some characteristic of life which has not been seen in this way before ... The event is thus raised into something significant" (Dilthey, 1910/1985, p. 251). The modifications that imagination actively performs in memories and representations lead to new intuitive forms, which in turn influence our "representational images" of the denoted objects or events. Thus,

> A thinking in images emerges, and in it the imagination attains a new freedom.... The forces which produce this series of formative processes originate in the depths of the psyche as it is moved by life in various ways toward pleasure, pain, mood, passion, and striving. (Dilthey, 1910/1985, p. 241; emphasis added)

Dilthey invites us to go beyond language to "attain a new freedom" (Dilthey, 1910/1985, p. 241) by creating intuitive images capable of connecting our mood with the vital forces of nature. Of course, Dilthey is also escaping from the scientific language, entirely colonized by the early 1900s by logical-positivism. The connection to the depth of life transforms poetic images into escape windows to obtain new freedom. The poetic image fosters a wholly new approach to a certain aspect of reality through visible and sensuous means, liberating our imagination from Kantian "discursive understanding" (Kant, 1790/2000, p. 277). For sure, Dilthey separates the poetic imagination that he praises from the "regulated imagination" of the scientist, "whose steady self-control hangs on the imagining processes to the standard of reality" (Dilthey, 1910/1922, p. 184; our translation). Dilthey relinquishes Goethe's aim to integrate imagination with reason to create a new science; instead he formalizes the division of labor between natural sciences and sciences of spirit. By doing this, scientific psychology is left with reproductive imagination, while the creative part of imagination, the "poetic imagination," is left outside its reach. In fact, the concept of *poetic image* has proven to be very useful and productive in literary fields, as the following observation by Northrop Frye eloquently expresses:

> The simple point is that literature belongs to the world man constructs, not to the world he sees; to his home, not his environment. Literature's world is a concrete human world of immediate experience. The poet uses images and objects and sensations much more than he uses abstract ideas; the novelist is concerned with telling stories, not with working out arguments. (Frye, 1964, p. 27f)

A further consequence of psychology's adoption of Kant's anthropology ought finally to be mentioned. Kant's epistemological interest is bounded necessarily to the knowledge capacities of the knower. Therefore the Kantian model of reason excludes the realm of feelings, emotions, and moods of human beings. Nonetheless there are many descriptions converging on the fact that without the dimension of feeling, no fantasy is possible. Vico spoke of the "divine pleasure" (Vico, 1725/1948, para. 345) of understanding remote cultures via fantasy, while Lipps (1903/1923) made explicit also the connection by arguing that fantasy always entails aesthetical impressions. Dilthey maintained that "feeling is the vital source of all poetry" (Dilthey, 1910/1985, p. 243). Also Felix Krüger, some years later, pointed out that "the 'momentum' of fantasy as well as its capacity of anticipating, of completing, of creating images are supported and conducted primarily by *feelings*" (Krüger, 1953, p. 293; emphasis in the original; our translation). In general, the new psychology's absorption of the golden goal of epistemology—to study abstractly the conditions of possibility of knowledge—altered its primordial interest in people to their intellective faculties. Consequently, those dimensions of human existence that were considered peripheral to the action of rational knowing, like feelings and fantasy, were minimized or plainly disregarded.

CONCLUSION

At the dawn of the 19th century, the modern natural sciences had completed about 250 years of successful growth. The expansion of their rationale and methods had been continuous from then onward. By the end of the 18th century, the French revolution and the industrial revolution seemed to converge in the suggestion that a more promising civilizatory order was beginning. In the new worldview, rational planning according to scientific theories occupied a central role. The conception that a mechanical order susceptible to mathematical modeling governed the whole cosmos became commonsensical for the European intellectual world. Hence, the implementation of modern rationality on the human and moral sciences of that time advanced progressively throughout the 18th century. This was the context where the anti-intellectual revolt by the Romantic Movement took place. Even though the entire cosmos may be mechanically constituted, for Romanticists the human soul could not be part of any formally explainable machinery, no matter how complex. They vehemently defended passion instead of reason, nature instead of civilization and spontaneity instead of planning. Human scientists of the early 1800s stood at the cultural crossroads of either, rationally, conceiving human soul as part of the mechanized natural world or, romantically, abandoning the very idea to do science.

Kant and Goethe represent two different ways to dissolve the "either science or art" dichotomy to which anyone interested in humanities was confronted during the 19th century. Kant designed a metaphysical architecture that, on the one hand, guarantees the modern sciences privileged access to phenomena. This is so because our perceived world is unavoidably structured through *a priori* transcendental categories. On the other hand, Kant grants philosophy a special supervision role over sciences, since philosophy is the discipline in charge of rationally delimitating the conditions of possibility of knowledge. Thus, the same architecture reserves for philosophy the transcendental role of judging the legitimacy of scientific procedures (see Rorty, 1979). This solution reaches a compromise between natural sciences and philosophy; the first rules on synthetic fields, the second on analytic ones. Kant generates for philosophy a legitimated and honorific new place in an intellectual world dominated from now on by natural science. This approach forces human sciences to choose between translating the human soul into the "discursive" knowledge used for any other natural phenomenon or analyzing it transcendentally in the frame of a rational metaphysics. The human soul should be either materialistically or idealistically redefined. This is one of the origins of the dispute between materialism and idealism.

Goethe offered a different solution. He strove for integrating science and art by starting from anthropological assumptions other than Kant's. He recovered the Renaissance model of soul, as advanced by Nicholas of Cusa, to propose that true knowledge can only be reached by combining intellectual efforts with "an exact sensuous fantasy," that grants vividness and simplicity to the intellectual statement. The knowledge aimed at is clear though ineffable: It is an intuitive perception, a kind of knowledge rooted into the mystical-religious intuition or *docta ignorantia*. Goethe prescribes accordingly aesthetical education for scientists to enhance their diminished powers of fantasy and sensuousness. Fantasy has not the function to put scientists outside of this world, in a parallel reality beautiful but unreal. Instead, fantasy gives flesh to abstract ideas; it makes them concrete and palpable. It prevents the vices of idealism, confounding nature with the abstractions developed to model it. But it also prevents us from the failures of materialism, since nature is an organic wholeness, neither machinery nor system. The human soul should also be neither materialistically nor idealistically studied. Such a polarity is based on a wrong anthropological assumption, namely, that people are epistemological subjects. For human sciences, Goethe's way of science allows talking about the human soul while rejecting its mechanization and recovering its nonrational capacities. Fantasy and organismic sensibilities also play a crucial role in science, as they express the connectedness between human organisms with the wholeness of nature. Ideas are not only thought, but also felt, seen, and sensual-morally experienced. As Faust advises Wagner, "If you don't feel it, you won't understand."

Goethe drew a middle way between materialism and idealism by proposing a "poetic science" (Kaufmann, 1980/1998, p. 49). His scientific contribution was decisive for the ulterior philosophy of nature, later on for the philosophy of life, and for the holistic schools of 20th century psychology. He is certainly a precursor of holistic thinking and should too be recognized as a precursor of cultural psychology, or at least part of it. However, from the advantageous point of view of the present, it is rather clear that Goethe's production as scientist and as philosopher of science received scarce attention both during and after his lifetime. Psychology as a whole respected Kant's general framework and attempted to revert his dictum on the impossibility of having a scientific psychology. Psychology set about translating the human soul and its capacities into a mechanical worldview and refrained from including terms incompatible with such a cosmology. In 1895, W. Heinrich retrospectively described this process with these words: "It is not difficult to find which was the moment that decisively interfered with the posterior progression of the philosophical and psychological research ... This is the boom of the natural sciences" (Heinrich, 1895, p. 31; our translation). By the middle of the 19th century, a "new psychology" was born: "From a 'psychology with soul' has emerged a 'psychology without soul'" (Heinrich, 1895, p. 32; our translation).

The fate of fantasy in psychology reflects precisely the emergence of a psychology without soul. Already in the work of Giambattista Vico, imagination [*fantasy* is Vico's word] gains epistemological status. For Vico, the "modifications of mind" produced during an effort of fantasy is the better instrument to know the human world. Even though psychology formally incorporates fantasy in its epistemological function, it does so by distinguishing a merely reproductive imagination that unites images according to the laws of association and fantasy proper, or productive imagination, which creates novelty from existing images. The two kinds of imagination followed different paths in the second half of 19th century, when the program for a "psychology without soul" became more explicit. On the one side, reproductive imagination was conveniently adapted to a mechanical view of mind. On the other, fantasy, that is, productive imagination, was slowly displaced from scientific psychology to nonscientific disciplines, such as aesthetics and literature.

Reproductive imagination was transmuted into a preintellective instance of a mechanical mind. It foreshadows what will be massively understood as imagination in 20th century psychology: an intellective operation, whose aim is to recover information in the form of mental pictures previously registered for ulterior intellectual processing (e.g., Kosslyn, 1992; Pylyshyn, 1992). At about the same time, the power of fantasy becomes poetic imagination and a quality of talented persons. Its function as grounds for scientific knowledge faded. Fantasy was disconnected from the fabric of scientific knowledge and accordingly was progressively abandoned by scientific psychology, much more interested in repetitive processes rather than in creative ones.

Fantasy constitutes a prime example of what happens with nonrational processes in a psychology without soul. Since early times, fantasy has been described as a felt experience, in which feelings and organismic sensibilities have a central importance. The ultimate claim of fantasy is to become the contemplated object: Mind modifies itself in order to reflect the features of the object, as a living mirror, pointed out Nicholas of Cusa. Fantasy is purely experiential and therefore fully nourished by feelings and sensualities. The insight obtained is pictorial—visual, nonlinguistic, and sensitively charged. Given this nondiscursive character, images produced by fantasy were considered as belonging to the zone of irrational forces and expelled from the illuminated zone of rational powers. This is one of the reasons why the term *fantasy* still survives in psychoanalysis.

Psychology embraced the Kantian model of man, which paradoxically enough was never a description of a human being, but rather a prescription of "*what mind had to be like* to make the certainty of Euclidean geometry and Newtonian science possible" (Kaufmann, 1980/1998, p. 94; emphasis in the original). By adopting Kant's model of the human being, psychology introduced epistemology at the core of its scientific program. By the middle of the 19th century, psychology was accordingly prone to studying perceptions and intellectual functions; the former experimentally, the latter analytically. Human dimensions that pre-Kantian psychology summarized in feeling and desire capacities were banished from the rational mind. Thus, psychology began its scientific path by making an ontological redefinition of its subject matter: the discipline is not about all that people experience, but instead about the rational aspects of such experiences. From then on, psychology pursues epistemological rather than anthropological aims.

This history has a moral for cultural psychology. Even though its sources are manifold, the interest in cultural psychology grew particularly as a reaction to the reductionisms of the new scientific psychology. As such, it inherits the dichotomy between idealism and materialism. Many founding authors of cultural psychology argued strongly against the axiom of *first cogito* as the starting point for human psychology. The very adjective *cultural* underlines that the starting point should be found instead in supraindividual instances. But remember that the noun is psychology. The moral is also this: We have to overcome Kant. Goethe's poetic science can be helpful to this goal. The constructive task of cultural psychology will not be completed until a psychology that includes all the aspects of human experience is recomposed. Let us imagine again a psychology with soul.

ACKNOWLEDGMENTS

I am deeply grateful to Roberto Musa for his corrections and commentaries to the first version of this manuscript. I thank also Himmbler Olivares and Cristián Hernández for constructive insights incorporated in this text.

NOTES

1. I use the expression *models of man* following the 19th century style. No sexism is meant by this usage. The notion of man encompasses both sexes throughout this manuscript.
2. I follow here the translation for the term *Anschauung*, suggested by Douglas Miller, editor and careful translator of Goethe's *Scientific Studies* (see translator's note on p. 315 in Goethe, 1998).
3. Goethe understands *polarity* in the most general sense of one of the "two great driving forces in all nature" (Goethe, 1998, p. 6); the other one being *intensification*, as we explain in what follows. Polarity corresponds to "a state of constant attraction and repulsion" (Goethe, 1998, p. 6) and can be observed in a myriad of dualities: "We and the objects/Light and dark/ Body and soul/Two souls/Spirit and matter/God and the world/Thought and extension/Ideal and real/*Sensuality and reason/Fantasy and practical thought*/Being and yearning/Two halves of the body/Right and left/ Breathing" (Goethe, 1799/1998h, p. 155; emphasis added).
4. *Intensification* is, besides *polarity*, Goethe's second great driving force of nature. It "is a state of ever striving ascent" (Goethe, 1998, p. 6). This upward force pervades the whole nature: the development from seed into plant; the crystallization of minerals; as well as the major keys in music (Miller, 1998). Goethe applies it also to color formation.

5. Goethe identifies three kinds of sensorial, moral, and aesthetic effects: symbolic, allegorical, and mystical. Symbolic effects are those consistent with nature (e.g., purple as majesty); allegorical effects, which are more conventional and therefore they may be learned (e.g., green as hope); mystical effects, i.e., archetypical relationships, which are "as much a part of human intuitive perception as they are of nature" (Goethe, 1998, p. 296). These last effects imply having an intuitive perception of a certain "spiritual meaning": "When we see them [yellow and blue] bring forth green below and red above, it will be hard to resist the thought that green is connected with the earthly creation of the Elohim, and the red with the heavenly creation" (Goethe, 1998, p. 296).

6. Here I use Jasper Hopkins' translation from German. The original latin text says: "*si ex signo ad veritatem te elevaveris verba transsumptive intelligendo, in stupendam suavitatem adducent*" (Nicolai de Cusa, 1440/1983, para. 29), that may also be translated as: "if you rise from the sign to the truth, by understanding beyond the words, toward a delightful softness" [translation by the author].

7. The connection with the Christian philosophy helps incidentally to explain the Faustian expression *If you don't feel it, you won't catch it*. This can be reconstructed as the Goethian version of St. Augustine *If you don't believe, you'll not understand*, which in its turn seems to be St. Augustine's version of *If you do not stand firm in your faith, you will not stand at all* from Isaiah 7:9. Thus, "Dost thou whish to understand? Believe. For God has said by the prophet: "Except ye believe, ye shall not understand" For understanding is the reward of faith. Therefore do not seek to understand in order to believe, but believe that thou mayest understand; since "except ye believe, ye shall not understand" (St. Augustine, c. 414/1874, p. 405).

8. As a matter of fact, the Latin word *intuitio* comes from the verb *intueri* "to look at"; etymologically: *in-* (in, on) and *tueri* (to see). German *Anschauung* [intuitive perception] corresponds hence to a precise translation of the Latin *intuitio*.

9. Goethe and Kant use the same word: *Sinnlichkeit*. Although strictly its more precise translation would be *sensuality* or *sensuousness*, in the specific case of Kant, *sensibility* is an arguably better translation (see Kaufmann, 1980/ 1998). This is also the preferred option in the Paul Guyer and Allen W. Wood English translation of *Critique of Pure Reason* (Kant, 1781/1998).

10. Ernst Stiedenroth's *Psychologie zur Erklärung der Seelenerscheinungen* (1824) [*A Psychology in Clarification of Phenomena From the Soul*] represents a surprising case of oblivion in the history of psychology. To my better knowledge it is the only *psychology* book reviewed (and highly praised) by Goethe (1998/ 1824): "I always considered myself fortunate if an important book came into my hands at a moment when it coincided with my own work, strengthening and furthering my activity ... In the above book I again met with this pleasant experience" (Goethe, 1998/1824, p. 45).

11. Wundt will raise severe criticisms of the expansion of experimental methods to higher mental functions (memory, thinking, will), qualifying, for example, the experiments on thinking by the Würzburg School as "pseudo

experiments" and "a youth sin of experimental psychology" (Wundt as cited in Lenk, 1996, p. 76).

REFERENCES

Carus, C. G. (1831/1958). *Vorlesungen über psychologie*. Darmstadt, Germany: Wissenschaftliche Buchgesellschaft.

Carus, C. G. (1846). *Psyche: Zur entwicklungsgeschichte der Seele*. Pforzheim, Germany: Flammer und Hoffmann.

Cassirer, E. (1906). *Das Erkenntnisproblem in der Philosophie und Wissenschaft der neueren Zeit, Vol. 1*. Berlin, Germany: Cassirer.

Cornejo, C. (2015). Searching for the microcosm: A glimpse into the roots of Vygotsky's holism. *History of the Human Sciences, 28*(2), 72–92.

Cornejo, C., Olivares, H. (2015). Living and observing: Two modes of understanding time. In L. M. Simao, D. S. Guimaraes, & J. Valsiner (Eds.), *Temporality: Culture in the flow of human experience* (pp. 95–114). Charlotte, NC: Information Age.

Dessoir, M. (1911). *Abriss einer Geschichte der Psychologie*. Heidelberg, Germany: Carl Winter's Universitätsbuchhandlung.

Dilthey, W. (1910/1922). *Das Erlebnis und die Dichtung: Lessing, Goethe, Novalis, Hölderlin, 8th Edition*. Leipzig, Germany: Teubner.

Dilthey, W. (1910/1985). Goethe and the poetic imagination. In R. A. Makreel & F. Rodi (Eds.), *Wilhelm Dilthey: Selected works, Vol. V Poetry and experience* (pp. 235–302). Princeton, NJ: Princeton University Press.

Eckermann, J. P. (1850a). *Conversations of Goethe with Eckermann and Soret, Vol. I*. London, England: Smith, Elder.

Eckermann, J. P. (1850b). *Conversations of Goethe with Eckermann and Soret, Vol. II*. London, England: Smith, Elder.

Erdmann, J. E. (1873). *Grundriss der Psychologie für Vorlesungen*. Leipzig, Germany: Vogel.

Falckenberg, R. (1880). *Die Philosophie des Nicolaus Cusanus mit besonderer Berücksichtigung der Lehre vom Erkennen*. Breslau, Germany: Koebner.

Frye, N. (1964). *The educated imagination*. Bloomington: Indiana University Press.

Goethe, J. W. (1810/1971). *Theory of colors*. New York, NY: Reinhold.

Goethe, J. W. (1785/1998a). Excerpt from "Studies for a physiology of plants." In D. Miller (Ed.), *Goethe: The collected works, Vol. 12, Scientific studies* (pp. 73–75). New York, NY: Suhrkamp.

Goethe, J. W. (1792/1998b). The experiment as a mediator between object and subject. In D. Miller (Ed.), *Goethe: The collected works, Vol. 12, Scientific studies* (pp. 11–1). New York, NY: Suhrkamp.

Goethe, J. W. (1783/1998c). Nature. In D. Miller (Ed.), *Goethe: The collected works, Vol. 12, Scientific studies* (pp. 3–5). New York, NY: Suhrkamp.

Goethe, J. W. (1829/1998d). Analysis and synthesis. In D. Miller (Ed.), *Goethe: The collected works, Vol. 12, Scientific studies* (pp. 48–50). New York, NY: Suhrkamp.

Goethe, J. W. (1810/1998e). Theory of colors. In D. Miller (Ed.), *Goethe: The collected works, Vol. 12, Scientific studies* (pp. 157–298). New York, NY: Suhrkamp.

Goethe, J. W. (1817/1998f). Judgment through intuitive perception. In D. Miller (Ed.), *Goethe: The collected works, Vol. 12, Scientific studies* (pp. 31–32). New York, NY: Suhrkamp.

Goethe, J. W. (1998g). Selections from *Maxims and reflections*. In D. Miller (Ed.), *Goethe: The collected works, Vol. 12, Scientific studies* (pp. 303–312). New York, NY: Suhrkamp.

Goethe, J. W. (1799/1998h). Polarity. In D. Miller (Ed.), *Goethe: The collected works, Vol. 12, Scientific studies* (pp. 155–156). New York, NY: Suhrkamp.

Goethe, J. W. (1824/1998i). Ernst Stiedenroth: A psychology in clarification of phenomena from the soul (Part one, Berlin: 1824). In D. Miller (Ed.), *Goethe: The collected works, Vol. 12, Scientific studies* (pp. 45–46). New York, NY: Suhrkamp.

Goethe, J. W. (1820/1998j). A friendly greeting. In D. Miller (Ed.), *Goethe: The collected works, Vol. 12, Scientific studies* (pp. 37–38). New York, NY: Suhrkamp.

Goethe, J. W. (1805/1998k). Symbolism. In D. Miller (Ed.), *Goethe: The collected works, Vol. 12, Scientific studies* (pp. 26–27). New York, NY: Suhrkamp.

Goethe, J. W. (1790/2009). *The metamorphosis of plants.* Cambridge, MA: MIT Press.

Heinrich, W. (1895). *Die moderne physiologische Psychologie in Deutschland: eine historisch-kritische Untersuchung mit besonderer Berücksichtigung des Problems der Aufmerksamkeit.* Zürich, Switzerland: Speidel.

Herbart, J. F. (1816/1834). *Lehrbuch zur Psychologie [Handbook of Psychology]* (2nd ed.). Königsberg, Germany: Unzer.

Hicks, R. D. (1907). Aristotle De Anima, with translation, introduction and notes. Cambridge, England: Cambridge University Press.

Jespersen, O. (1922). *Language: Its nature, development, and origin.* London, England: Allen & Unwin.

Kant, I. (1781/1998). *Critique of pure reason.* Cambridge, MA: Cambridge University Press.

Kant, I. (1790/2000). *Critique of the power of judgment.* Cambridge, MA: Cambridge University Press.

Kaufmann, W. (1980/1998). *Goethe, Kant and Hegel: Discovering the mind, Vol. 1.* New Brunswick, NJ: Transaction.

Klemm, O. (1911). *Geschichte der Psychologie.* Leipzig, Germany: Teubner.

Koch, S. (1969/1992). Wundt's creature at age zero—and as centenarian: Some aspects of the institutionalization of the "new psychology." In S. Koch & D. E. Leary (Eds.), *A century of psychology as science* (pp. 7–35). Washington, DC: American Psychological Association.

Kosslyn, S. (1992). Demand characteristics? The second phase of the debate. In B. Beakley & P. Ludlow (Eds.), *The philosophy of mind: Classical problems, contemporary issues* (pp. 241–242). Cambridge, MA: MIT Press.

Krüger, F. (1953). *Zur Philosophie und Psychologie der Ganzheit: Schriften aus den Jahren 1918–1940.* Berlin, Germany: Springer.

Külpe, O. (1895). *Outlines of psychology: Based upon the results of experimental investigation.* London, England: Swan, Sonneschein.

Lipps, T. (1923). *Grundlegung der Ästertik* (3rd ed.). Leipzig, Germany: Leopold Voss. (Original work published 1903)

Lenk, H. E. (1996). *Geschichte der Psychologie* (2nd ed.). Stuttgart, Germany: Kohlhammer.

Miller, G. L. (2009). Appendix: The genetic method. In J. W. Goethe (Ed.), *The metamorphosis of plants* (pp. 104–117). Cambridge, MA: MIT Press.

Nicholas of Cusa (1450/1983). *Opera omnia, Vol. V Idiota: De sapientia, de mente, de staticis experimentis.* Hamburg, Germany: Meiner.

Nicholas of Cusa (1440/1990). *On learned ignorance.* Minneapolis, MN: Arthur J. Banning Press.

Nicholas of Cusa (1450/1996). *On wisdom and knowledge.* Minneapolis, MN: Arthur J. Banning Press.

Pylyshyn, Z. W. (1992). Tacit knowledge and "mental scanning." In B. Beakley & P. Ludlow (Eds.), *The philosophy of mind: Classical problems, contemporary issues* (pp. 229–239). Cambridge, MA: MIT Press.

Rorty, R. (1979). *Philosophy and the mirror of nature.* Princeton, NJ: Princeton University Press.

St. Augustine of Hippo (c.415/1873). *The works of Aurelius Augustine, bishop of Hippo. Vol. X Lectures or Tractates on the gospel according to St. John, Vol. 1.* Edinburgh, Scotland: Clark.

Stiedenroth, E. (1824). *Psychologie zur Erklärung der Seelenerscheinungen, Vol. I [Psychology for the Explanation of the Phenomena of Soul].* Berlin, Germany: Dümmler.

Tiedemann, D. (1804). *Handbuch der Psychologie.* Leipzig, Germany: Sarth.

Valsiner, J. (2012). *A guided science: History of psychology in the mirror of its making.* New Brunswick, NJ: Transaction.

Vico, G. (1710/1988). *On the most ancient wisdom of the Italians.* Ithaca, NY: Cornell University Press.

Vico, G. (1725/1948). *The new science.* Ithaca, NY: Cornell University Press.

Westhof, N. (2013). Goethe und Cusanus. Ein Vergleich ihrer Anthropologie in kulturgeschichtlicher Absicht. *Cusanus Jahrbuch, 5,* 49–60.

Windelband, W. (1911). *Geschichte der neueren Philosophie in ihrem Zusammenhange mit der allgemeinen Kultur und den besonderen Wissenschaften, Vol. 1.* Leipzig, Germany: Breitkopf & Härtel.

Wundt, W. (1874). *Grundzüge der physiologischen Psychologie.* Leipzig, Germany. Engelmann.

Wundt, W. (1897). *Grundriss der Psychologie* (2nd ed.). Leipzig, Germany. Engelmann.

Wundt, W. (1907). Psychologie. In W. Windelband (ed.), *Die Philosophie im Beginn des zwanzigsten Jahrhunderts: Festschrift für Kuno Fischer* (pp. 1–57). Heidelberg, Germany: Carl Winter's Universitätsbuchhandlung.

PART II

CONCEPTUAL AND HISTORICAL ANALYSES

CHAPTER 2

USE YOUR IMAGINATION

The History of a Higher Mental Function

Luca Tateo

WHAT DO WE MEAN BY IMAGINATION?

Imagination is one of those words which has been heavily invested with commonsense meanings before entering psychological jargon. I would therefore like to start by exploring commonsense knowledge in order to grasp the system of everyday meanings that is necessarily part of the object of study. Then I will try to complement Carlos Cornejo's (this volume) historical reconstruction of the concept of imagination by discussing it from ancient Greek history until the 18th century. Finally, I will propose possible directions to achieve a better understanding of imaginative processes in the context of cultural psychology.

Let us start from a simple suggestion that probably everybody received at least once in their lifetime: "Use your imagination." Personally, when I have received such an invitation it was related to situations in which I was somehow lacking the resources to find a solution. It could have been at school, when I had to do my homework or with my friends or when I had to play. My teacher could have been telling me "Use your imagination" when I was stuck on a blank page during a writing exercise. Or else at

The Psychology of Imagination: History, Theory, and New Research Horizons
pp. 47–66
Copyright © 2017 by Information Age Publishing

home while I was bored on a rainy winter afternoon, my parents could have invited me to switch off the television and invent a game to play with my younger sister. Later on, when I was a goofy adolescent, a winking girl could have told me "Use your imagination" with a come-on look. Or in adulthood, during a work meeting, when everybody got bogged down on a research problem apparently without solution and a creative outburst was required. I am sure that if anyone looks back, they can come out with several similar examples. We are prompted to use our imagination when we must behave in a creative way.

Therefore, we are invited to use our imagination when there is no ordinary, ready-made solution to make sense of a situation. On the other hand, I would emphasize another part of this utterance: "Use *your* imagination." We are never told to use our or their imagination or the like. It means that in common sense, imagination is something personal, something that you can have or miss to a certain degree. As in the case of intelligence, it seems like an individual property that can never be totally absent but can be possessed by the person with individual differences in magnitude. In fact, there are some projects, especially in the United States, that are trying to develop a measure of imagination on the model of IQ.[1]

Nevertheless, taking a closer look, we can find many examples of situations in which imagination, or something very similar, is involved. The ubiquitous nature of imaginative processes in everyday activities shows how often imagination is at stake—from the child's animistic world to the joys of sex in *Fifty Shades of Grey* (James, 2011); or the visionary Steve Jobs, who from a garage became an apostle of technology; from the mystic of hermits' visions to works of art; from the mythological hybrid creatures to the theorization in physics.

Let us now look at the opposite kind of experience, when we have been told by someone: "Don't use your imagination." It could have happened at school, during a math test, when you were lost in trying to solve a difficult equation. Then your teacher warned you, "Don't use your imagination, make calculations and find the right answer." Or when you realized that the very same girl didn't actually give you a come-on look so when you tried to talk to her, she answered, "Don't even imagine it!" Thus, imagination is banned when one is prompted by everyday life situations to face real life, with its disillusions, harshness, practical sense, and mostly, when a scientific approach is required. In other words, don't use your imagination when you are supposed to behave in a rational way. Actually, long tradition of thought has opposed rationality and imagination, the latter having been incorporated into common sense, underestimating what is "a mere product of our imagination." Such an opposition has been promoted even in the case of those thinkers who appreciated the role of imaginative processes in psychological life.

Nevertheless, we know from direct experience and from the history of mankind that imaginative processes are somehow involved in even the most mundane activities. Imagination is at work in experiencing both past and future, bringing to life something that is no longer or not yet here and now. I anticipate a bit here my argument that imagination is as much a way to embody signs as to produce signs. Imagination is a higher psychological function that enables us to manipulate complex meanings of both linguistic and iconic forms in the process of experiencing, "consisting of lived-by action and counter-action, that is contextual inter-action with the world in the form of an experiencing subject and other-ness" (Tateo, 2015, p. 188). As I will argue in the last section, imagination is a fundamental symbolic process creating signs, linguistic and iconic at the same time, that represents experience, detaching it from the immediate presence. It is used to self-regulate behavior in different conditions and can be communicated to other people in different situations. But I've already gone too far. As I promised, I will first try to go with you along the origins of the received views and counterviews about imagination by looking back at the history of ideas.

History of Imagination: The Origins

Imagination is one of those concepts that crossed the history of Western culture as "a category of mental activity whose definition and interpretation has varied very greatly from age to age and from author to author" (Cocking, 2005, p. xiii). The reason for this is that probably imaginative processes permeate every aspect of human life. Our imagination, like our memory, is a constitutive part of our sense of self. At the same time, imagination, like memory, operates at collective level, as "meaningful social forms" (Wagoner, 2012, p. 1053) that give us the sense of belonging to a collective and help us regulate everyday life. We feel that imagination is part of what we are, both individually and collectively. On the other hand, imagination is a mind tool that allows us to overcome the ethnocentric sense of what we are and to access the world of the alterity (Norton, 1996).

For its manifold and complex nature, the functions that have been attributed to imagination in Western thought are basically four:

The first is the formation of images, like the face of an absent friend; the second is resourceful problem solving, exemplified, for instance, by nonlinear thinking; the third is the falsification of some aspect of reality, as when we fantasize that the facts are other than they are; and the fourth is the mental exploration of what it would be like to realize particular possibilities, such as being very rich. (Kekes, 1993, p. 101)

Both the learned understanding of imagination and the commonsense one largely overlap. Nevertheless, this list must be integrated with two more functions, which have been presented in the course of philosophy. The first one is the imagination as arousal and excitement of mind, as in crowd behavior or in mystic experience (Black, 2000). The second is the function of creating intersubjectivity by accessing the other's mind (Norton, 1996). In the second part of the chapter, I will discuss the latter in detail, as I think it constitutes an important aspect of the contemporary conception of imagination.

The concept of imagination developed along with the history of ideas; it was called "*phantasia* and *eikasia* in Greek, *phantasia* and *imaginatio* in Latin" (Cocking, 2005, p. xiii). These terms referred to

the image-making capacity of human beings [which] manifests itself in a whole range of human experiences: in our ability to picture things which are absent, for instance, in dreams, fantasies and illusions, in artistic creativity and invention, in the ordinary person's power to envisage the possibility of a better world or to imagine other lives, as much as in the mystic's vision of a higher reality beyond the world of the senses. (Cocking, 2005, p. xiii)

By floating for a long time at the border between sense and intellect, only recently imagination has started to acquire some epistemological function that "can provide us with some special insight into the nature of truth" (Cocking, 2005, p. xiii).

In pre-Socratic philosophy and in Plato's work on imagination, the main problem was the external origin of the images that people have in their minds. Plato, for instance, argued that we experience just reflections, shadows, and diffractions of the light cast on objects, as in the myth of the cave. Thus we experience *eikasia*, the icons of the real objects. Only by means of rationality and reflection (again this term) we can imagine (form a secondhand idea or approximation) of the original. Whether the light comes from a divinity or a remote plan of absolute and pure ideas is a matter of taste. Thus, Plato provided the idea of *eikhasia* as the factory of food for rationality. By contrast, Aristotle was a theoretical empiricist. Though he never performed a single experiment (as far as we know), he elaborated a complex theory of animal and human psyche based on what we call today thought experiments. He developed a theory of mind based on two principles that originated and guided all of the following ideas on imagination: whatever is in intellect was originally in senses; and there is no thinking without images (*phantasma*).

For Aristotle, imagination was a motion that originates in sensation. *Phantasmas* are the product of the faculty—common to all animals—that he called *phantasia*. It is a strictly physiological process that goes from the senses to the creation of mental images, which though blurred and imperfect become more defined and memorized through repetition. Such images constitute the objects of thinking. Thus, we cannot think of something without first creating a mental image of it. As an attenuated form of sensation, the *phantasma* is not able to trigger the same full sensation of the real object. It rather becomes a diminished sensory experience (Schofield, 1992). On the other hand, Aristotle's theory of the animal soul states that there is more than one single type of *phantasia*, as he says in *De Motu Animalium* (Nussbaum, 1985). Another form of imagination works the other way around, from the inner mental work to external reality. It is a form of preparation to action in which organisms have an alteration of their normal states, experiencing an appetite for something. It is a kind of warming up (that Aristotle calls *phantasia aistetiké*) that the organism goes through before being ready for action. *Phantasia* is thus something in between reality outside and mental life. In the movement from the external world to the inner mental life, imagination is related to the senses: it is an attenuated *phantasma* of the sensation that lasts after the object has left its footprint on the mind. Thus, on the one hand, there is the idea of imagination as a *phantasmatic* representation of real objects, and on the other hand, it becomes a condition of internal exaltation of arousal and derangement of mental life. As a space in between, imagination is generated by the real world and can generate action in return. When these two processes are combined, we have the states of mental alteration as that of mystical ecstasy or delirium.

In Islamic culture, Avicenna and Averroes further developed Aristotle's ideas about the nature and potential power of imagination (Black, 2000). They started from the identification of a passive faculty that receives influences from the outside, from other people, authority, astral influences, or divine action, producing psychic images. Then they identified an active faculty that generates forms of communication that are able to influence other people. Avicenna connects imagination with a faculty called "estimative," that is, the capability to grasp nonsensible intentions associated with the object of sensation. Intentions are thus the extrasensible properties that an object presents to an animal or a person at the moment of perception. These intentions powerfully affect the perceiver; for instance, the negative feelings a sheep senses in perceiving a wolf or the positive feelings sensed in perceiving a friend or a child. The combination of formative imagination and estimation creates the material that will be retained in memory. This system of inner senses is constitutive of commonsense knowledge, which is largely sufficient for everyday activities but not enough to attain true knowledge. According to Averroes, the object of thought is composed of image and intention. So it is not the material object in its real form but as it is sensed, imagined, remembered, or elaborated by the intellect through the respective faculties of the soul: this is the mental object. Commonsense knowledge is always based on the power of imagination to generate strong collective feelings. Besides, the masses are not able to go beyond common sense to reach the true knowledge. The crowd thinks in terms of images and the feelings attached to them. But imagination, in Averroes, is also related to dreams, especially prophetic dreams, so that it connects the human soul directly to the universe or divinity. Thus, imagination has enormous political power. This is the reason rituals, images, and myths are able to generate strong passions in the lay, uneducated crowd.

Medieval tradition received Avicenna and Averroes conception of imagination (Black, 2000) and combined it with the Patristic tradition. Augustine had already started to use the Greek word *phantasia* and the Latin word *imaginatio* interchangeably (Cocking, 1984, p. 47). Imagination was placed at a lower level than understanding. He distinguished abstract knowledge from mental images that have no guarantee of truth. For Augustine, there is first "bodily seeing, which is sensation together with consciousness of sensation" (Cocking, 2005, p. 43), which forms the mental representation. At a second level, there is "'spiritual seeing' on its own, without sensation, which includes what we now call imagining and dreaming" (Cocking, 2005, p. 43). Finally, there is "'intellectual seeing' or understanding" (Cocking, 2005, p. 43). The overlap between *phantasia* and *imaginatio* creates a dangerous material, whose origin is uncertain with respect to senses. They can correspond to truth or falsity to the extent that the representation which mind presents to itself in the form of images is ethically suspect of evil origin. The capability of imagination to stir up people's passions, which we also find in Islamic philosophy, is compared to sorcery (Cocking, 2005). Interestingly, we will find again this idea of the relationship between imagination, excitement, and politics in the positivistic psychology of the crowd (van Ginneken, 1992). Imagination is suspected to be contagious because the performativity of the images can become a powerful tool of evil. The history of Christianity is full of episodes in which the Devil uses false images to tempt Christ and hundreds of saints in the desert. On the other hand, as humans cannot know God but can just achieve a partial intuition, the power of imagination remains a potential path of spiritual elevation. The "legitimate" suspicion toward imagination lasted for a long time throughout the Middle Ages. One can discern between true and false, evil and good images only by faith or by rationality. But which one to choose?

The Renewed Interest in Imagination Since the Renaissance

Two alternative solutions were provided during the Renaissance, which was perceived as "the golden age of the imagination given the level of pervasiveness and sophistication that characterized the debate on the nature of images and the imagination at the time" (Giglioni, 2013, p. 175). The first solution was that of Nicholas of Cusa (1401–1464), who developed the idea that we cannot attain any rational knowledge of divinity. In *De Docta Ignorantia* (1440/1990), he claims that ultimate truth can be achieved only by *intuitio*, the learned ignorance of the believer, who is aware of her limited understanding and relies upon an intuition of divinity that goes beyond rational understanding and language. The second solution to the problem of the relationship between imagination and knowledge is developed by Marsilio Ficino (1433–1499), who first outlined "the notion of imagination as the artist's creative faculty" (Cocking, 2005, p. 105). Humanism, as the birthplace of modern subjectivity, informed his view of the distinctive human faculties of invention, technical and artistic capability. People can use it for practical purposes to achieve extraordinary mastery over nature, like Ancient Romans, who were able to build roads, bridges, and machineries. But invention can also be used for playful activity, to find recreation and nurture the soul, as in artistic creativity and philosophy (see also Glaveanu, this volume). "Creativity in general is *ingenium*, just as poetic inventiveness was *ingegno*, and more specifically *alto ingegno*" (Cocking, 2005, p. 105). Ficino maintains the distinction between passive and active imaginative processes. Imagination synthesizes *in absentia* of the real object. Fantasy recognizes and combines different elements into a unitary presentation. Finally, intelligence understands (Cocking, 2005).

Another humanist, Gianfrancesco Pico della Mirandola (1469–1533), in his *De Imaginatione* (1501), develops some of the ideas of the more famous uncle Pico. For Gianfrancesco Pico della Mirandola, imagination is a fundamental psychological faculty of representation that mediates between senses and intellect (Caplan, 1930). "For imagination I thus mean the entire sensitive part of the soul, no matter how it is to be named by others" (De imaginatione, V, 40, as cited in Caplan, 1930, p. 41). In this sense, imagination is what links the body (with its appetites, needs, impulses) with the soul, so that every form of knowledge must pass through imagination before becoming an object of the intellect. Gianfrancesco Pico della Mirandola nevertheless describes imagination as the main psychological function on the border of the intellect, as it is still an animal faculty rather than a spiritual one. Pico also recognizes that the products of imagination can be culturally conditioned. For instance, he polemicized with Avicenna about the status of prophetic visions, saying that many could not have directly received their visions from God, but being influenced by the culture of their times, such as the case of Moses on the mountain. In sum,

> Renaissance philosophers saw the imagination as a mediator between the body and the soul, the intellect and the senses, the appetites and the will, between the animal and natural functions of the body, motion and rest, past and future, between memories, dreams and prophecies, between nature and culture. (Giglioni, 2013, p. 176)

Francis Bacon (1561–1626), in his *Advancement of Learning* (1605/2001), developed the idea of imagination as a mediator between senses and mind. Images are transmitted to reason, which interprets them in order to generate understanding. Imagination also mediates between the plan and the action. As a sort of preview or anticipation, the image or mental picture is translated into action in the real world (Cocking, 2005). Imagination can only elaborate within the limits of the raw material that is already been provided by senses and stored in memory images. The mechanist model of human psychology that was elaborated by empiricism had to frame imagination into the machine-like idea. We must understand also Thomas Hobbes' (1588–1679) position in the context of the scientific and technological revolution that was starting in that period. He developed a theory of psychic life organized around sense, imagination, and language. Sensation is a mechanistic process in which "pressure, by the mediation of nerves, and other strings, and membranes of the body, continued inwards to the brain and heart, causeth there a resistance, or counter-pressure, or endeavour of the heart, to deliver itself" (Hobbes, 1651, p. 9). This mechanism generates inner images, or fancies, that we call sense. On the other hand, human beings are not passive receptors but are moved by an "endeavour of the heart" that is "Appetite, or Aversion, to or from the object moving" (Hobbes, 1651, p. 9). This endeavor or conatus makes an object relevant and worth entering into the process of sensation. The sensations produced by objects, once internalized, so to speak, through the senses, become representations, as "all conceptions we have immediately by the sense, are delight, or pain, or appetite, or fear; so are all the imaginations after sense" (Hobbes, 1651, p. 9). Hobbes emphasizes the active nature of senses, that is, the inner motion of the subject to establish a relationship, to act upon the world. At the same time he stresses the role of imagination as a form of simulated preparation to action.

René Descartes (1596–1650) represented a "turning point in the history of imagination and formulated effective and memorable recommendations about the place of this way of thinking within a structure of mind" (Lyons, 1999, p. 302). Usually in Descartes philosophy, two different periods are acknowledged: a juvenile set of writings in which imagination seems to play a major role and a mature period in which he develops his extremely rationalistic theory. Descartes' theory of imagination is based on a corpuscular theory of sensation, in which the senses are receptors of the corpuscles transmitted from objects. Corpuscles reach the pineal gland, which mediates between the body and the pure dematerialized process of understanding (Galison, 1984). The pineal gland is the location of common sense and imagination, whose function is to elaborate the material from senses and present it to cognition, which is stored in memory for a later easier recall and reuse.

In one of his first works, the *Compendium Musicae* of 1618, Descartes describes the experience of music not as a single sensation but as a determination of proportions. After that, the role of imagination is that of producing a synthetic experience rather than the mere combination of sensations. This intermediate passage was necessary as "the precondition of abstraction and any manipulation of general quantities" (Galison, 1984, p. 321). Later, he will apply this concept to other fields, especially to mathematical thinking.

> Sensation gives us the data of the present, memory gives us the data of the past, but the ability to see relations in and between the data requires the synthesizing power of imagination, which sets the present situation against the background of the past and tries to generate new appearances necessary for grasping what is at issue, and ultimately for solving problems and answering questions of almost any type. (Sepper, 2013, p. 276)

Descartes applied this very principle to his own work when he related the new field of algebra to the old field of geometry, inventing analytic geometry. Though in his later works Descartes drew a neat autonomy of reflection from senses, imagination retains its practical utility, as for instance, in visually manipulating, building, and rotating geometric shapes: "every single idea that includes sensory perceptions is imaginary—then we realize that outside of metaphysics, theology, and pure mathematics all our thinking requires imagination" (Lyons, 1999, p. 311). This is the basic idea of imagination received by cognitive psychology, as Cornejo (this volume) has pointed out. Yet imagination had no role in abstract thinking and understanding, being, on the contrary, a source of error (Galison, 1984). In his later philosophy,

> Descartes despises fantasy and what comes to us through the senses, he discards history and tradition as a mass of popular nugacity, and believes only in the clear cold sense of the "honnete homme." He builds up nature mechanically, society atomistically. That is inevitable, since he is a mechanical abstractor, a mathematical machine producing only its own symbols. Deduction is an empty game when it is not preceded by the amplest of

inductions, covering all of our experience which starts with "fantasy"—an induction such as Descartes tyrannical precepts forbid. (de Santillana, 1950, p. 569)

Nicolas Malebranche (1638–1715) brings Descartes' ideas to their extreme conclusion. "His study of the imagination intended to defeat the errors that a high voltage imagination would generate in a human being of little mental capacity" (Fabiani, 2009, p. 25). Imagination is typical of those who lack a generous intellect. It is essentially made by strong sensations, vivacious images, and the ability to represent many different things. Imagination is a vestige of our finite nature (original sin and paganism), therefore is a source of erroneous beliefs, a projection of our appetites over the world.

In the golden age of Cartesianism, the philosopher, rhetorician, historian, and jurist Giambattista Vico (1668–1744) proposed an innovative theory of imagination, assuming a critical stance with respect to the dominant rationalism of the time that underrated imagination (Verene, 1991). As I have argued, one of the problems since Augustine was the epistemological status of imagination: to what extent it can be a reliable source of knowledge? Even Aristotle, elaborating on Plato, in Chapter 9 of his *Poetics* seemed to grant a role to imagination in knowledge.

> The difference between a historian and a poet is not that one writes in prose and the other in verse.... The real difference is this, that one tells what happened and the other what might happen. For this reason poetry is something more scientific and serious than history, because poetry tends to give general truths while history gives particular facts. By a "general truth" I mean the sort of thing that a certain type of man will do or say either probably or necessarily. That is what poetry aims at.... A "particular fact" is what Alcibiades did or what was done to him. (c. 330 BC/1970, p. 28).

The *verosimile* principle of Aristotle provides imagination with an epistemic status. The idea that poetic knowledge may not be true in the sense of being scientifically and historically accurate, but neither is it false, will be elaborated by Vico in the *verum-factum* principle (Vico, 1710/1988). Vico argued that knowledge of the relationship between psyche and civilization cannot be attained by referring to a nonhistorical generalization of human mind. To understand human mentality within a specific historical period is to access its specific form of elaborating experience and developing universal concepts. "There are abiding symbols in the imagination—in the semi-conscious mental processes of individuals and groups (some of which evolve at a different pace from others)" (Berlin, 1976, p. 56). These symbols are generalized images that constitute dynamic generalizations of basic human experiences, so that "certain images persistently recur in the history of mankind—such as salvation and resurrection, cataclysm and rebirth" (Berlin, 1976, p. 56). Therefore, studying the products of imagination (myths, rituals, symbols, etc.) is "the only historically possible way of describing their experience on the part of human beings at a given stage of linguistic, and *eo ipso* of social and psychological development" (Berlin, 1976, p. 56).

Vico's theory of imagination stressed the relationship between forms of knowledge, development in time, and language and social practices, which will become later one of the main assumptions of cultural psychology. His theory of mind echoes the development of civilization: it is a progressive distancing from the senses through the creation of images that grounds the construction of abstract concepts. Imaginative capability is based on three fundamental functions of the mind: *fantasia*, the capability to imitate and change; *ingegno*, the capability to create correspondence between things; and *memoria*, that is the capability to remember.

> All three appertain to the primary operation of the mind whose regulating art is topics, just as the regulating art of the second operation of the mind is criticism; and as the latter is the art of judging, so the former is the art of inventing ... And since naturally the discovery or invention of things comes before criticism of them, it was fitting that the infancy of the world should concern itself with the first operation of the human mind, for the world then had need of all inventions for the necessities and utilities of life, all of which had been provided before the philosophers appeared. (Vico, 1744/ 1948, p. 236)

Nevertheless, there is a fundamental anthropological difference between the primitive men who own these capabilities as a result of divine providence's farsightedness, and the contemporary human beings who developed rational thinking in the course of civilization. The historical forms of collective thinking developed in a given civilization cannot be understood unless we try to imagine the type of universals that civilization developed to make sense of experience and to regulate individual and collective behavior. In this way, what can be studied is the socio-psychological process of creation and development of universals instead of the universal *a priori* categories of thought, like in Kant. Imagination is a form of knowledge creation; therefore it can be used to grasp the distal mode of thoughts of the different civilizations, though we cannot have direct access to them.

> To discover the way in which this first human thinking arose in the gentile world, we encountered exasperating difficulties which have cost us the research of a good twenty years. [We had] to descend from these human and refined natures of ours to those quite wild and savage natures, which we can-

not at all imagine and can apprehend only with great effort. (Vico, 1744/ 1948, p. 89)

Imagination is thus not a form of insightful perception but requires a work of the mind, an exercise on something that "detaches it from the intricate circumstances of perception, and in this abstractive and simplified detachment releases it to a new positioning with respect to differential possibilities" (Sepper, 2013, p. 69). This would be similar to the work of archeologists, philologists, or ethnographers, who try to access the irreducible Otherness of a different civilization's mode of thought through the observation and recontextualization of cultural products such as language, iconography, architecture, myths, rituals, and such. Vico proposes a new kind of contextual metaphysics, understood not as a science of universals but as a science of how universals are created, developed and used in the different civilizations.

> For metaphysic, directing a history of human ideas from the beginnings of truly human thinking among the gentiles, has enabled us finally to descend into the crude minds of the first founders of the gentile nations, all robust sense and vast imagination. (Vico, 1744/1948, p. 5)

Thus, Vico's idea of imagination doesn't have anything irrational, mystical, or transcendental. It is a mundane epistemological tool to understand the relationship between mind and civilization from a historical perspective. This is one of the major differences with Goethe's conception of fantasy that Carlos Cornejo describes earlier in this volume. Vico's imagination applies only to human phenomena as a specific domain of knowledge, not entering the realm of natural sciences, to which he acknowledges a different epistemological status.

Another fundamental point of difference between Vico and Goethe is in the position attributed to the knower. In fact, while for Goethe positioning is universalistic and ethnocentric, as "he perceives the world only in himself, and himself only in the world," Vico is very aware of the historical situatedness of the forms of knowledge and civilization, as when he states that the goal of his new science is to study the "world of nations in all the extent of its places, times and varieties" (Vico, 1744/1948, p. 92). Finally, Vico introduces a clear cut in the relationship between humans and environment. Even though he says that the most primitive forms of embodied intellect are experienced without any mediation, like in the case of Goethe's intuitive perception, once language appears in the history of civilization, experience is mediated and shaped by cultural tools. This argument will be later developed by the Italian philosopher Carlo Cattaneo (1859–1866/2000), who first used the term *social psychology* to describe the mutual development of mind, artifacts, and civilization.

Elementism Versus Segmentationism

In the Western history of ideas there are at least two different approaches to imagination. I would call them "elementism" and "segmentationism." The first approach, typical of the empiricists' conceptions, understands imagination as a combinative faculty of the sensations. Like Lego bricks, imagination combines bits and pieces of information—the shadow representations of sensation—into different forms that are then presented to the intellect. Conversely, the "segmentationist" conception understands imagination as a synthetic form of apprehension, as the intuitive capability of immediately grasping wholes that only in a second moment are analytically segmented by rationality. I would ascribe Thomas Hobbes to the former group and Goethe to the latter. A similar destiny occurred to other higher mental functions (e.g., to memory, which from the very beginning is continuously overlapping with imagination, to the extent that the border between the two is very difficult to draw; Sepper, 2013). I also think that this fundamental difference in understanding imagination generated the thematic opposition between rationality and imagination. Paradoxically, romanticism, while trying to revalue imagination and to extend its "all-encompassing" role, nourished the contrast with rationality (Sepper, 2013), thus protracting this unfruitful thematic opposition, whose effects we can still see today. Both the tendencies nevertheless place imagination somehow in between sense and intellect. Whether imagination is only a factory that preworks the raw materials of senses for the kitchen of rationality, or it is a real higher mental symbolic function, is an open question to be addressed in the future. Yet it originated in the history of the concept that Cornejo (this volume) described and I tried to complement. Personally, I tend toward the second hypothesis, namely, that imagination is a higher mental function; thus, imagining is a process that requires work, not just an immediate insight. This requires addressing the role of imagination in the production of knowledge and in the construction of concepts, abstractions, and generalizations. If we follow Aristotle's suggestion in the *Poetics* (c. 330 BC/1970), both the particular and the general play a role in the construction of knowledge. This relationship is the object of Vico's study of myths and rituals, because he first understood that imagination can be the mental function that elaborates experience, both at the individual and collective levels, by relating the concrete images with the universal concepts.

> Imagining is the very act of placement and location of transient things ... of giving place, habitation, and name to things and their characters. Imagination is thus the placement and re-placement of thinking. It is active and ges-

tural; it indicates beyond itself its already-formed images as it reshapes their appearance. (Sepper, 2013, p. 51)

In the next section I will try to draw some theoretical suggestions to orient further research on imagination as higher mental function, relating individual and collective dimensions.

Imagination and Rationality

There is another very relevant point that must be taken into account: imagination is not only about images, it is about *figurae*. Imagination, from the very Greek philosophy is about thoughts-phantasmas, which can be iconic, linguistic, acoustic, and such (Sepper, 2013). This concept was common knowledge because it was one of the fundamentals of rhetoric. Quintilian in his *Institutio Oratoria* defines *figura* as any form in which thought is expressed. At the same time, *figura* has a second meaning, that is, configuration of elements in the discourse, what we know as rhetoric figures. From this idea we can deduce that thinking is related to configurations of signs, in which every linguistic sound carries an iconic function and every image has a linguistic aspect. For instance, Baroque art was treating visual representations with the same rules of rhetorical art of speech. Besides, all the contemporary branding and advertisement is based on this simple principle, like in the construction of lettering and products' logos. Aesthetics is quite aware of it but psychology too often seems to forget it, reducing imagination to mental manipulation of images.

> The divorce of rationality from imagination that has been a cultural commonplace for nearly three centuries would turn out to be illusory. Rationality itself, insofar as definition is in question, would have to be conceived as a power of reckoning in images seen and marked against the background of other (kinds of) images. Even logic would be an abstract but still imaginative marking system that tracks and shows with sharp distinction and important subset of the informing structures of language. (Sepper, 2013, pp. 485–486)

Imagination is a form of elaboration of experience that is not limited to emotional and perceptual processes but has to do with the mental manipulation of sign complexes, which have both iconic and linguistic content—it is a "rational imagining" (Sepper, 2013, p. 79). Once established that the opposition between imagination and rationality can be questioned, it is nevertheless necessary to define the specific features of the former, otherwise it would remain as too fuzzy a concept to have any heuristic power.

For Vico, imagination is the mental function that can synthetically elaborate the configuration of iconic and linguistic meaning, including the affective and ethical relationship to the object. Thus, imagination was not only a detachment from the immediate input of the senses, but was also a form of abstraction, namely, the elaboration of imaginative universals. In this sense, the image and the idea were in a metonymical relationship. It was at the same time a form of abstraction (detaching from the sensual experience), by distinction, analogy and replacement, and generalization. Metonymy is the rhetorical trope in which either one name is replaced by another or one part stands for the whole. It differs from metaphor, in which the replacement is made by creating a short circuit of meaning, and from analogy, in which two different objects are put together by similarity; in metonymy, the two ideas arbitrarily stand for each other. But this substitution is at the same time a relationship of identity and distinction. Thus, metonymy could be a general form by which metaphor and analogy represent special cases. In semiotics, one can say that sign and idea represented are in a metonymical relationship, as well as image and concept in rational imagining. For instance, the relationship between a religious icon and the divinity is metonymical, just like the relationship between a flag and a national identity. This relationship makes possible a wide range of sociopsychological phenomena, and I will argue that it is an imaginative process. One can worship a divinity into an icon, one can kill or die for a nation under a flag, but one can also develop a theory in physic of the atomic structure based on an iconic model of the solar system. This is what all iconoclastic movements were, and still are, always so afraid of (Kibbey, 1986): the immense epistemological and communicative power of imagination.

Metonymic Constitution of Reality

In the imaginative process, the two things that establish a metonymic relationship are the concrete and the abstract. Thus, imagination is not a simple mediator between sense and intellect, reality and mind, a sort of buffer in which representations from the external world are assembled to be scrutinized by rationality. It is not just a way of producing potential alternative courses of action, which are previewed before one goes into effect and the other disappears. Once established, the metonymical relationship in imaginative thinking becomes a self-regulatory system, which orients experience and identity construction. For instance, once the flag is related to the national identity, it creates a system of conventional logic in which both the statements "I am part of that nation therefore I will die or kill for the flag" and "I will die or kill for the flag therefore I am part of that nation" become equally true. Pushed to the extreme, even the *cogito ergo sum* principle can be understood as a form of imaginative rationality, in the sense that it establishes a metonymical relationship between one specific cognitive function and consciousness. Through imagination, the individual action is detached from the immediate experience and becomes a sign of identity. In return, the abstract concept is then naturalized as a collective action detached from the original cause, and it is again abstracted in a sign of identity at a higher hierarchical level. At this point something more emerges, a life-form of a nation (Simmel, 1918/2010) in which any new individual action of kill-or-die can be framed. Once imagination has created a sign that represents the cause of an event or a plan for future action, detached from the contingent experience of its presence, it can be used to self-regulate the behavior in different conditions and can be communicated to other people in different situations, becoming a hypergeneralized sign (Valsiner, 2014).

Imagination and Intersubjectivity

Zittoun and Cerchia (2013) propose an idea of imagination as a form of experiencing through meaningful scenarios. I think this is an important move toward an understanding of the complex nature of imaginative processes. In fact, evoking the scenario-type of imagination implies also the introduction of the different points of view or positions of the observer and the dimension of action. Think of yourself voting at the last elections (for those who still vote); you can see yourself putting a piece of paper into the ballot box. It is not a picture-like form of imagination. This involves memory as well as imagination. Now think about looking at someone else performing that action. And finally think about someone else looking at you while you vote. It seems that the same scenario-like imaginative process includes the possibility of changing the perspective of the person imagining. Thus, imagination is also imagining someone else's imagination, which is a form of access to intersubjectivity. Nevertheless, Zittoun's model still makes a too-sharp distinction between the "real" and the "imagined" worlds. In contrast, the voting example provides an argument in support of the idea of imagination as a complex semiotic dialogue between fantasy (in the classical sense, memory), perspective taking, perception, intersubjectivity and categorization (Sepper, 2013), through which we recontextualize the course of action, whether potential, inhibited, or performed.

Giambattista Vico put forward the idea that imagination is a way to access intersubjectivity and the irreducible otherness of different civilizations, adding a further epistemological function to it. The philosopher

David Norton developed this idea (Norton, 1996) by claiming that imagination is the function that allows people to reach an understanding of the other. In fact, he argues that people's relationship with the other is inevitably ethnocentric, in the sense that "as enculturated human beings we indeed can and commonly do interpret the words and conduct of the others 'by our own lights'" (Norton, 1996, pp. 44–45). But this is, according to Vico, a fundamental epistemological mistake (Vico, 1744/1948), or the "psychologist's fallacy." Understanding the other, indeed, "requires us to perceive the world and the other in his or her perspective" (Norton, 1996, p. 6). Thus, imagination is not only a form of internal knowledge (e.g., to elaborate alternative courses of action or to represent internal states) but also a form of external knowledge (e.g., to decentralize the ethnocentric perspective or to establish an affective, ethic, aesthetic, and cognitive relationship with the other).

It is now time to summarize the multifaceted view of imagination emerging from this historical overview and to draw some theoretical hints on the nature of imaginative processes that shall be empirically questioned.

CONCLUSION: A POSSIBLE DEFINITION OF IMAGINATION

We produce and reproduce signs as actions upon the world in order to make sense, through identities and distinctions, and manage uncertainty outside and inside us. From fairy tales to religious iconography to political propaganda, imagination has been used to promote specific valued behaviors or inhibit despicable ones, as well as dealing with otherness by promoting collective identity and differentiation processes. Sepper defines imagination as

> a (psychologically) evocative, anticipatory, abstractional-concretional activity that follows upon actual perception. It allows the imaginer to 1) dynamically (re)position herself and incipiently explore, place, vary, connect, and represent appearances originating within a field of concerns, 2) attend and mark the field's potentials, and 3) exploit those potentials by projecting them to other fields (possibly new) in abstracted/concreted appearances. (2013, p. 19)

This definition grasps several aspects of imagination presented so far, but is still too focused on the perceptual aspects, while neglecting the semiotic, affective, ethical, and collective dimensions. I have tried to argue that through the imaginative process, human activity creates universal and abstract representations of life starting from very situated individual actions. Such institutionalized representations of the world become traditions or life forms—the frameworks distanced from the individual's immediate experience within which the meaning of the experiences itself acquires sense in return. This continuous movement from concrete and situated to the general and abstract is a metonymical process. Through the semiotic substitution between the concrete and abstract we create those nonexisting objects that are the inhabitants of mental life. "Aspects of that 'external' world generated on the basis of firmly shared ecological-cultural background conditions tend to become objectified and acquire the status of social realities" (Rommetveit, 1992, p. 22). Santa Claus, the invisible hand of the market, Paradise, and Hell are all specimens of entities in which our fellow humans firmly believe without further ascertainment being required.

Georg Simmel (1918/2010) called this simultaneous movement oriented toward the future and transcending the actual experience "more-life" and "more-than-life." Thus, an object is never a thing *per se,* as it is always put forward into future-oriented sense-making and metonymically related to a general form of life that frames experience. The imaginative process plays a self-regulative function toward the ambivalent nature of experience and uncertainty of change during development. In my understanding, imagination is always part of experiencing as a way of semiotic elaboration of meaning in both linguistic and iconic forms. Therefore, I understand imagination as a fundamental higher psychological function that is devoted to the semiotic manipulation of complex wholes of iconic and linguistic signs. Through imagination we build things acting as they were abstractions, and build abstractions acting as they were real things, we generate identity and its opposite. Thus, the generalization-hypergeneralization process of sign use (Valsiner, 2014) is based on this metonymical work of imagination, which is the work of constructing meaning in a dialogue between fantasy, memory, reflection, affection, and idiosyncrasy. This dialogue is always imbued with ambivalences as it is oriented toward the uncertainty of the future.

Time has come for psychology to engage in an extensive multidisciplinary research program on imagination as a fundamental symbolic function (Tateo, 2016). Such a program should include the study of imaginative processes in everyday life experiencing within specific life-forms (e.g., art, architecture, education, cookery, religion, etc.). This also implies that we need a new methodology in order to grasp the developmental aspects of imagination and to focus on complex products of human activity. All the rest is left to our imagination.

NOTE

1. For instance, the Imagination Institute, based at the University of Pennsylvania's Positive Psychology Center, launched a $3 million grant competition a few years ago to award scholars "toward an Imagination Quotient."

REFERENCES

Aristotle (c. 330 BC/1970). *Poetics* (G. E. Else, Trans.). Ann Arbor, MI: University of Michigan Press.

Bacon, F. (1605/2001). *The advancement of learning*. Chicago, IL: Modern Library.

Berlin, I. (1976). *Vico and Herder: Two studies in the history of ideas*. London, England: Chatto & Windus.

Black, D. L. (2000). Imagination and estimation: Arabic paradigms and Western transformations. *Topoi, 19*(1), 59–75. doi:10.1023/A:1006399407731

Caplan, H. (1930). *Gianfrancesco Pico Della Mirandola on the imagination*. New Haven, CT: Yale University Press.

Cattaneo, C. (1859–1866/2000). *Psicologia delle menti associate* [*Psychology of associated minds*]. Rome, Italy: Editori Riuniti.

Cocking, J. M. (1984). Bacon's view of imagination. In M.Fattori (Ed.), *Francis Bacon: Terminologia e Fortuna nel XVII Secolo* (pp.43–58). Rome, Italy: Edizioni dell'Ateneo.

Cocking, J. (2005). *Imagination: A study in the history of ideas* (P. Murray, Ed.). London, England: Routledge.

de Santillana, G. (1950). Vico and Descartes. *Osiris, 9*, 565–580

Descartes, R. (1961). *Compendium musicae* [Compendium of music] (W. Robert, Trans.). Rome, Italy: American Institute of Musicology. (Original work published 1618)

Fabiani, P. (2009). *The philosophy of the imagination in Vico and Malebranche*. Florence, Italy: Firenze University Press.

Galison, P. L. (1984). Descartes's comparisons: From the invisible to the visible. *Isis, 75*(2), 311–326. doi:10.1086/353484

Giglioni, G. (2013). Phantasms of reason and shadows of matter: Averroes's notion of the imagination and its Renaissance interpreters. In A. Akasoy & G. Giglioni (Eds.), *Renaissance averroism and its aftermath: Arabic philosophy in early modern Europe*, (pp. 173–193). Dordrecht, The Netherlands: Springer Science+Business Media. doi:10.1007/978-94-007-5240-5_9

Hobbes, T. (1994). *Leviathan* (E. Curley, Ed.). Indianapolis, IN: Hackett. (Original work published 1651)

James, E. L. (2011). *Fifty shades of grey*. London, England: Vintage Books.

Kekes, J. (1993). *The morality of pluralism*. Princeton, NJ: Princeton University Press.

Kibbey, A. (1986). *The interpretation of material shapes in Puritanism: A study of rhetoric, prejudice, and violence*. Cambridge, MA: Cambridge University Press.

Lyons, J. D. (1999). Descartes and modern imagination. *Philosophy and Literature, 23*(2), 302–312. Retrieved from http://search.proquest.com/docview/750575554?accountid=8144

Nicholas of Cusa (1440/1990). *On learned ignorance*. Minneapolis, MN: Arthur J. Banning Press.

Norton, D. L. (1996). *Imagination, understanding, and the virtue of liberality*. Lanham MD: Rowman & Littlefield.

Nussbaum, M. C. (Ed.). (1985). *Aristotle's De Motu Animalium: Text with translation, commentary, and interpretive essays*. Princeton, NJ: Princeton University Press.

Rommetveit, R. (1992). Outlines of a dialogically based social-cognitive approach to human cognition and communication. In A. H. Wold (Ed.), *The dialogical alternative* (pp. 19–44). Oslo, Norway: Scandinavian University Press.

Schofield, M. (1992). Aristotle on the imagination. In M. Craven Nussbaum & A. Rorty (Eds.), *Essays on Aristotle's de Anima* (pp. 249–277). New York, NY: Oxford University Press.

Sepper, D. L. (2013). *Understanding imagination: The reason of images.* Dordrecht, Netherlands: Springer.

Simmel, G. (1918/2010). *The view of life. Four metaphysical essays with journal aphorisms* (J.A.Y. Andrews & D. N. Levine, Trans.). Chicago, IL: University of Chicago Press.

Tateo, L. (2015). Gulliver's eggs: Why methods are not an issue of qualitative research in cultural psychology. *Integrative Psychological and Behavioral Science, 49*(2), 187–201.

Tateo, L. (2016). What imagination can teach us about higher mental functions. In J. Valsiner, G. Marsico, N. Chaudhary, T. Sato, & V. Dazzani (Eds.), *Psychology as the science of human being: The Yokohama manifesto* (pp. 149–164). New York, NY: Springer.

Valsiner, J. (2014). *An invitation to cultural psychology.* London, England: Sage.

van Ginneken, J. (1992). *Crowds, psychology, and politics, 1871–1899.* Cambridge, MA: Cambridge University Press.

Verene, D. P. (1991). *The new art of autobiography: An essay on the life of Giambattista Vico, Written by himself.* Oxford, England: Clarendon Press.

Vico, G. (1710/1988). *On the most ancient wisdom of the Italians: Unearthed from the origins of the Latin language* (L. M. Palmer, Trans.). Ithaca, NY: Cornell University Press.

Vico, G. (1744/1948). *The new science of Giambattista Vico* (T. Goddard Bergin & M. H. Fisch, Trans.). Ithaca, NY: Cornell University Press.

Wagoner, B. (2012). Culture in constructive remembering. In J. Valsiner (Ed.), *The Oxford handbook of culture and psychology* (pp. 1034–1055). New York, NY: Oxford University Press.

Zittoun, T., & Cerchia, F. (2013). Imagination as expansion of experience. *Integrative Psychological and Behavioral Science, 47*(3), 305–324. doi:10.1007/s12124-013-9234-2

CHAPTER 3

REVIVING THE LOGIC
OF AESTHETICS

The Experience of Arts
in Cultural Psychology

Sven Hroar Klempe and Olga V. Lehmann-Oliveros

It is said that the Norwegian painter Henrik Sørensen once shared a dinner with the great Danish physicist Niels Bohr. The famous scientist enjoyed mingling with painters. He thought they were able to see the reality from different angles, which was certainly true for the modernists in art at that time. In fact, Bohr thought this coincided very much with his own theories about complementarity in physics (Sørensen, 2003). According to Bohr, cubism and quantum physics shared the understanding of reality as a composite that can be hardly understood with single and/or linear explanations. Precisely, this is the case of aesthetic experiences where intensity surpasses reality, while being deeply rooted in the reality itself.

In line with this, fantasy and reality interweave in an emotional sphere, both in the case of arts and in the construction of theories in science. This is an ignored aspect of science, but also an ignored aspect of Kant's philosophy. He is very much understood in terms of *The Critique of the Pure*

The Psychology of Imagination: History, Theory, and New Research Horizons
pp. 67–81
Copyright © 2017 by Information Age Publishing

Reason (Kant, 1781/2010) solely as is also the case in Cornejo's (this volume) understanding of him. Yet without mentioning it, Kant followed up Baumgarten's term *aestheticological truth* (Baumgarten, 1750/2007) in his *Critique of Judgment* by looking for the rationality in sensations and feelings (Nerheim, 1991). Baumgarten's term is fantastic for several reasons. First, it paved the way for a brand new understanding of art. Second, the term is derived from, and closely related to empirical psychology and how it was understood during the 18th century. Third, Baumgarten was driven by a genuine interest in poetry. Fourth, he had an unfulfilled attempt to bring aesthetic theory as a foundation for general science. And fifth, Kant's third critique can be regarded as a follow-up to Baumgarten's neologism. In the next sections, we will briefly expand these five aspects.

BOTTOM-UP AND TOP-DOWN PERSPECTIVES ON AESTHETICS: RECONCILING SENSATION AND COGNITION

Even if the understanding of beauty has changed over time, it is still a label depicting both great art as well as artistic experiences. Although the history of "aesthetics" is normally traced back to ancient Greece, it is a more modern term, primarily related to Alexander Baumgarten and the 18th century (Allesch, 2006). In this sense, the factor that unites the history of aesthetics is not the term but rather reflections on beauty in art.

Beyond identifying beauty, aesthetic experiences relate to a holistic comprehension of the process of sensemaking (Larraín, 2015). Nowadays, aesthetics points toward different directions, and it can be hard to conclude what precisely it is supposed to be about. One common definition would be "theories on art," and if so, these theories could tentatively be regarded from three different perspectives: (a) schematism and top-down approaches, (b) sensation and bottom-up perspectives, and (c) a path toward existence.

The question of whether anyone can refer to beauty in art is paradoxical, because even if a person agrees with another in the fact of having experienced it, disagreements appear when trying to generalize what beauty consists of. Moreover, since ancient times, this discussion has become also a search for truth and in this sense, an ethical question. After Kant, the exploration of the crossroads between rationality and aesthetics has been an important topic of the humanities, but paradoxically, the aesthetic nature of psychological phenomena and its implications for the understanding of imagination, fantasy, and creativity has not been sufficiently developed (Larraín, 2015; Glăveanu, this volume).

Bottom-up and top-down perspectives on aesthetics are examples of approaches to the understanding of cognition and affect, evidencing the challenges to appeal the interdependence of such processes within the social, cultural, and historical guidance of existence. The developing theories on imagination have acknowledged such tension between rational and sensorial processes (Tateo, this volume) and it is a challenge for psychology and other humanities to reconcile such interdependent processes.

Schematism and Top-Down Approaches to Aesthetics

Kant encountered many tensions in his attempt of theorizing the relationship between the intellectual and the emotional comprehension of the world, as it is evidenced in the differences between the *Critique of Pure Reason* and the *Critique of Judgment* (Rundell, 1994). Indeed, in Kant's first critique, schematism is related to a discussion of pure reason. Consequently, "in that case the judgment would not be made in relation to pleasure and displeasure" (Kant, 1790/2002, p. 104). When it comes to aesthetical judgments, or rather judgments about taste, using Kant's terms, the situation is completely different because the experiences of pleasure and displeasure are at the core, being subjective and distant from scientific explanations. However, even if the books discuss different topics, some perspectives of the theory of knowledge overlap, and *The Critique of Judgment* in discussions about theories of knowledge is often quoted as a rational approach. The postmodernists' discussion of the sublime is probably one of the many examples that have integrated Kant's arguments for the meeting points of rationality and sensation (Lyotard, 1984).

Kant was not as narrow-minded as it could seem from the *Critique of Pure Reason* (1781/2010). In fact, he investigated judgments in a broader perspective in his third critique, relating them to pleasure and displeasure. Therefore, schematism relates to Kant's attempt to define "pure science," an ideal that is partially achieved in connection with contemporary aesthetics, such as in the case of cognitive approaches to film studies. The American film critic David Bordwell is an example of this perspective, using a Popperian understanding of hypotheses to explain the interaction between the spectators and the film, rationality that guides the filmic perception and enjoyment (Bordwell, 1985). That is, decoding narration in film is based on a dialogue between the spectator and the film in terms of "perceptual hypotheses," which are confirmed or not: "After some interval, a perceptual hypothesis is confirmed or disconfirmed; if necessary, the organism shifts hypotheses or schemata" (Bordwell, 1985, p. 31). The term *perceptual hypotheses* is borrowed from Ulric Neisser (Bordwell, 1985). When it comes to the term *schemata*, he is referring to Frederic Bartlett, yet the term can rather be traced back to Immanuel Kant (Wagoner, 2016).

In *Narration in the Fiction Film* and *Making Meaning* (Bordwell, 1985, 1989, respectively), the author developed a very rational understanding of narration in fiction films. This perspective was supported by the philosopher Noël Carroll, who attacked different scholars in the psychosemiotic tradition, which, according to him, had "impeded research and reduced film analysis to the repetition of fashionable slogans and unexamined assumptions" (Plantinga, 2002, p. 17).

In filmic narrations, rationality is based (most of the time) on a sequential understanding. However, this is not necessarily embedded in the film itself but rather a result of the expectations and understandings of the spectators. A key notion related to this argument is "schemata," a standardized repertoire of preconceptions based on earlier experiences, but also physiological constraining factors like the eye inertia, which is the basis for experiencing the series of 50 still pictures per second as motion. This is an example of what is known as "phi-phenomenon" in gestalt psychology (Wertheimer, 1944), a tradition closely related with aesthetics.

However, when watching films we are often taken by intense sensations that bring us inside the script and, even if not understanding what is happening, we could affirm to be definitely involved in the movie. This fact, of course, cannot escape a historical guidance, and Walter Benjamin well affirms that films, as Dadaism, "aimed to ridicule and portray as absurd the modern world, and to emphasise the role of unpredictability in creativity. Dadaist [film] artists rearranged everyday and artistic objects and conventions to subvert dominant assumptions" (Robinson, 2014, p. 13). In this line of ideas, creativity, aesthetics, and poetry share the history of a project to empower a natural science of the soul (Cornejo, this volume). Cutting processes such as creativity, fantasy, and imagination from affect is impossible, but psychology of creativity has not sufficiently taken into account affective processes, as it has done with cognitive ones (Glăveanu, 2013).

The Ambivalence of Sensation and Bottom-Up Perspectives on Aesthetics

The American Wittgensteinian philosopher Stanley Cavell follows up Kant's third critique by bringing theory of knowledge very close to aesthetics. He emphasizes everyday experiences present in poetry, music, and film as a philosophical matter, as long as philosophy "concerns those necessities we cannot, being human, fail to know" (Cavell, 1969/2002, p. 96). In the same essay, Cavell remains ambivalent when discussing to what extent a poem can be paraphrased. It is this lack of conclusiveness that characterizes an aesthetic argument, which "rather than showing up an irrationality, shows the kind of rationality [aesthetic argument] has, and needs" (Cavell, 1969/2002, p. 86). Namely, it is almost impossible to derive general conclusions from the contextual situations where the aesthetic experience emerges. Indeed, recognizing ambivalence at the core of sensemaking of experience (Abbey & Valsiner, 2005) and existence (Lehmann Oliveros, 2015) cultural psychology is making the effort to develop theories and methodologies that are faithful to the tensions in which human life occurs.

According to Cavell, even Kant saw this tension between rational and irrational forces, as it is evident in one of his central formulations about art: "The beautiful prepares us to love something, even nature, without interest" (Kant, 1790/2002, p. 151). In line with this, Cavell says, a work of art "does not express some particular intention (as statements do), nor achieve particular goals (the way technological skill and moral action do), but, one may say, celebrates the fact that men can intend their lives at all" (Cavell, 1996, p. 122). In this sense, Cavell suggests the need for erasing the strong distinction between superior and inferior cognitive functions. Yet he remains in the intellectual sphere of top-down tendencies.

An aesthetician who follows a bottom-up perspective by focusing on sensation is Gernot Böhme. In the late 1980s he introduced a kind of "ecological aesthetics," which was announced as the "new aesthetics" (Böhme, 1993). This new approach stressed the sensorial aspects, which makes it different from traditional aesthetic thinking in three respects. First of all, "The old aesthetics is essentially a judgmental aesthetics" (Böhme, 1993, p. 114). This goes back to Kant and is a paradigm that has survived as a premise for discussions on art. Böhme is critical to the judgmental perspective because it is highly related to a question about approvals, which do not have to be included when art is at stake. In connection with the former, the second characteristic of old aesthetics is the dominant role of semiotics in theories on aesthetics, due to the central role given to language and communication.

In other words, Böhme questions the assumption that art is primarily about communication. If it is about communication, it neither has a certain message nor refers to something else, which a sign usually does. From this perspective, music is probably the best example of a discriminated form of art, primarily because in music there are no distinctions between the signifier and the signified as long as signification is embedded in the expression itself. Yet this might be true in figurative art as well. Böhme refers to Da Vinci's *Mona Lisa*, in which the model is completely uninteresting for the spectator (Böhme, 1993).

Thus, this second characteristic is crucial for the development of theories in cultural psychology that move on a semiotic basis. When recognizing affect at the core of sensemaking and decisionmaking (Valsiner, 2007), theories and methodologies need to address the bonds and boundaries of language, giving room to silence-phenomena (Lehmann Oliveros, 2015, in press) and finding the distinctions between communication and evocation, that the experiences of the beauty take into account (Lehmann Oliveros & Klempe, 2016). In the verses of *Arte Poética* (*Poetic Art*), the Chilean poet Vicente Huidobro (1916, p. 4) masters the distinction between evocation and communication: "Why do you sing the rose, oh poets!/Make it blossom in the poem."[1]

The third aspect that characterizes old aesthetics is "a strongly normative orientation" (Böhme, 1993, p. 115), which is traceable on three different levels. One is presented as having a social function in one respect or another. Then aesthetics can be also defined in terms of "theories of art," involving argumentative persuasive power as well as tacit requirements about genuineness and authenticity. The latter refers to the normative aspect on the third level. Although not all theories of art include the latter requirement, authenticity is very often a nonarticulated premise for evaluating art or the artist.

In fact, the notion of authenticity is closely related to Walter Benjamin and his understanding of the artwork's aura (Benjamin, 1936/1968). Böhme is obviously also influenced by him. However, both *aura* and *authenticity* are problematic terms, because they presuppose clear borders between the mass-produced and the unique artwork. Here, the ability of the artist to make the audience "feel" such uniqueness is a core gift, which claims for the emotional resonance of a masterpiece rather than the theorizations of it. A great example is Marcel Duchamp's *Fountain* from 1917, which on the one hand is a mass-produced standard urinal but on the other hand became a unique experience with a certain aura after all the controversies about exhibiting the urinal and the published picture of it in a journal. This demonstrated that even mass-produced art can represent a very unique experience, and it is hard to tell if the aura is there or not. On this background, Böhme introduces the term *atmosphere* to say something about aesthetical experiences (Böhme, 1993).

Böhme builds on the philosopher Hermann Schmitz who developed "atmosphere" as a generic term. Closely related to aesthetic experiences, atmospheric spaces are impossible to localize, as they have no physical borders but correspond to the emotional intensity of specific moments. This fact makes it hard to conceptualize the frames of the moods that people experience and is a great example of the fuzzy borders between inner and outer experiences. Although scholars in cultural psychology are dedicating efforts to understand the development of the borders of experience (Marsico, 2011), it is still a challenge to move from their structure toward their functions in sensemaking, as well as understanding the affective processes involved (Lehmann Oliveros, 2015).

These embodied resonances of emotions become crucial for sensational aesthetics, which refers not just to aesthetic experience but existential situations. On this basis, Böhme slightly changed the term *aesthetics* to *aisthetics (Aisthetik)*, defining it as general doctrine of awareness (Böhme, 2001). On the one hand, this highlights sensation, but on the other hand, there are no distinctions between sensation and thinking. Thus, "awareness" is probably the best English notion to emphasize the unity of higher and lower cognitive functions.

The notion of awareness involves an embryonic intellectual activity in terms of a certain amount of attention, which could include reflection as well. Yet on the other hand it points also to the almost opposite, specifically, a kind of subliminal registration of an indefinable and unspecific experience. Aware experiences are also linked to the processes of grasping values in terms of hypergeneralized affective levels (Branco & Valsiner, 2010; Valsiner, 2006), which are central and challenging topics for cultural psychology. In terms of Heidegger (1927/1980), awareness could be understood as the experiences of "being-in-the-world" (*dasein*) and "being-with" (*mitsein*), conduced toward an authentic existence, which is the responsible acceptance of ones finitude. In addition to these statements, when emphasizing human freedom of will, philosophy becomes existential and aesthetics paves the way to explore the incommensurable mysteries evoked by living.

Bottom-up and top-down trends in aesthetics, of course, reflect the tensions between affect and cognition in the construction of knowledge in psychology. The case of imagination, the main topic of this volume, is an example of this. Directions toward a psychology with soul (Cornejo, this volume) shall depart from acknowledging the dilemmatic nature of the tensions between different vectors rather than attempting to dissolve them. Precisely, imagination and fantasy have been attempts to reconcile the tensions between the logical and illogical qualities of human experience and existence.

A Path Toward Existence:
Being and Becoming Through Aesthetics

The notion of atmosphere is very strong in bringing into the scene existential aspects of aesthetic experiences. Although no one would assert that Theodor Adorno had any affiliations with existentialism, he wrote an important thesis about the founder of existentialism, Søren Kierkegaard

(Adorno, 1933/1998). In fact, his interest in the Danish philosopher was primarily motivated by the relation between aesthetics and authenticity. These aspects are at the core of discussions in the field of humanities, with the interest of understanding aesthetic experiences as an integrated part of everyday life and not as something extraordinary and unique. Indeed, an integrative focus on creativity, imagination, and fantasy shall deal with the affective processes related to daily experiences of the beauty.

Following this perspective, we suggest the notion of "poetic instants" used by Gaston Bachelard (1939/2013) and Octavio Paz (1956/1994) as a platform to reconcile aesthetic experiences with the sensational quality that is at the core of all perspectives on aesthetics described beforehand (Lehmann Oliveros & Klempe, 2016). From a logical perspective, the sensational represents the particular, so a sensational experience is by definition a unique experience and stands in direct opposition to theoretical considerations on generalizations. This is also a central argument for Kierkegaard's philosophy.

Kierkegaard struggled with separating and combining the three "stages": the aesthetical, the ethical, and the religious (Kierkegaard, 1845/1988). The religious stage is the world of ideas, while the aesthetic one refers to the "actual" or the sensational life. The ethical stage is in between. However, in his texts, he ends up including religious, aesthetic, and ethical statements altogether, which he himself describes as ridiculous (Kierkegaard, 1845/1988), but also reflects the fuzzy borders of human processes of sensemaking. This also corresponds to the presentation of the traditions in current aesthetics given here. For instance, strong rationalistic tradition exemplified by Bordwell (1985, 1989) ends up with great modifications, which Cavell (1969/2002) exemplifies.

The contradictory relationship between both sensation and thinking as well as the particular and the general has caused many problems. Language mirrors therefore a generality similar to thinking. The particular, on the other hand, is difficult to grasp through terms, and because of this, we have the old Latin proverb, which says that "*individuum est ineffabile*"—the particular is inexpressible. No one can say where this stems from, but it is often attributed to Aristotle, saying that the actual existence of an individual is not comprehensible from a scientific perspective (Borchert, 2010). However, the proverb was revitalized by Goethe, first of all by mentioning it in a letter saying that he could "derive a whole world of meaning" out of this proverb (Nikiforov, 2006, p. 140). He actually did so, especially in the Sturm und Drang novel *The Sorrows of Young Werther* from 1774, where he demonstrates a stylistic change from the classical characteristic of figures to the Sturm und Drang type by the formulation: "I will force myself to go into details" (*ich will mich zwingen ins Detail zu gehen*; Jannis, 1996, p. 27). Yet this is theoretically followed up by Wilhelm Dilthey, who emphasized that the "unique and singular is always the proper end of the sciences of the spirit (*Geisteswissenschaften* in German), thus for "Dilthey *Individuum est ineffabile*" (Hodges, 1944, p. 85, i.o.). By combining this Latin statement with a scientific approach, Dilthey almost dissolved the borders between aesthetics and science. In this sense, Goethe made a great contribution in bringing art and science closer to each other, although his terminology was still anchored in the enlightenment.

Poetry and Science

The tendency toward communion of arts and science has characterized many great scholars through history. Before Dilthey, Alexander Baumgarten tried to establish the foundation of a new scientific thinking through "modern aesthetics." This is proclaimed already in the first paragraph of the first volume of the Aesthetics: "Aesthetics ... is the science of sensitive cognition" (*Aesthetica ... est scientia cognitionis sensitivae*; Baumgarten, 1750/2007, p. 10/§1). The translation of this sentence is crucial, and this version is based on the Danish Philosopher Søren Kjørup, who highlights that Baumgarten's purpose was not to focus solely on sensation, but rather to combine the superior and the inferior aspects of cognitions (Kjørup, 1968).

For Baumgarten, poetry was a special field within the arts. This is why his first publication from 1735 was about philosophical considerations around the poem (Baumgarten, 1735/1968). The term *poetry* is used here in the original and broader meaning of the term: the Ancient Greek term *poïesis* (ποίησις), which is a verb that means "to make." This etymological root is also the reason why the composer Igor Stravinsky talked about "poetics of music" when he was challenged to lecture about the process of composing music (Stravinsky, 1956). Nevertheless, Baumgarten was actually focusing on poetry in a more narrow sense as well, just because this form of art gives direct access to the unbroken connection between the superior and inferior aspects of perception.

This is also how the term *beauty* fits in. It is not primarily a quality of the perceived object but rather the quality that appears by experienced congruence between the perceived object and the understanding of it. This implies that aesthetics has a much broader scope than just focusing on art. The search for beauty, in its ethical function, is an attempt for, and many times a success in, giving sense to the uncertainties of existence through the tensions of unbearable but necessary feelings of love and anguish, involved in human experience (Lehmann Oliveros & Klempe, 2016). Unfortunately, fantasy, phenomenon closely related to this aesthetic search, has been transformed into a representational and cognitivized process, as with most other fields of psychology (Cornejo, in this volume).

The "Aestheticological" Dimension of Human Being

The strong connection between thinking and sensation is also the background for the neologism *aestheticological*, which Baumgarten introduced. This refers to a kind of logic that goes beyond pure thinking, being derived from sensation. It refers to the ways in which the mind processes sensorial inputs in general, through the exemplar cases of experiences with art. Yet, this is not a call for empiricism but rather the opposite.

The experiential content of art evokes a sort of free association, in which different ideas and notions are combined in a way that does not follow the framework of formal logic. A deduction is linear; the premises are followed up by its consequences, which are given by necessity, and the one is following after the other. An association is vertical; the premises are immediately followed up with consequences that are not given by necessity. This has to do with the implications of the vertical aspects of the mind that provide widened explanatory frames, such as the case of musical polyphony. Following the example, the notion of polyphony allows scholars to understand the vertical coexistence of experiences.

However, the deeper meaning of the aestheticological cannot be explained just by referring to free associations ad hoc, but rather to the situation where a person has a more or less private experience of an immediate consistency between the formal and material aspects of an impression. For instance, a poem can be experienced as evoking the truth, through perhaps irrational linguistic and musical configurations. Another example is the creation of new chords that have never been heard before. In such cases an immediate concurrence is experienced because there is a complete compliance between what is articulated physically by means of the words or chords selected and what is meant. This compliance gives immediately an impression of an expression as "true" or genuine. Hence, Baumgarten even talks about "aestheticological truth" (Baumgarten, 1750/2007).

However, the aestheticological truth must be understood in line with German idealism that positions Baumgarten as a rationalist. He pointed at a phenomenon that goes far beyond German idealism in the 18th century, because the most important part of this term is the concurrence of the formal and the material, which implies that the general and the particular become united. This fundamentally contradicts Kant's attempts at defining "pure sciences," which isolates the formal from the material.

There are on the other hand a lot of links between the concept of aestheticological and the ideals of art in romanticism. Goethe's revival of the old *individuum est ineffabile* is due to the aestheticological in the sense that they both underline the inexpressible aspects of sense experiences. The aestheticological, though, does not imply any types of escapism as if art represents "a better world" compared to the real one. The 19th century's music for certain, but also novels that followed up Goethe's *The Sorrows of Young Werther* (1774/2005), made clear distinctions between this world as the place for grieving and sorrows on the one side and art and death as the gateway to a better world on the other.

The aestheticological concerns how we deal with the world here and now as living people, and as the term indicates, it aims at uniting the great paradox or even contradiction embedded in life, which is about the fundamental conflict between experiencing the sensorial world along with thinking. The unity of the particular and the general is probably one of the most important aspects of culture as well. This was exactly what Ernst Cassirer (1961) ended up with when he pursued the Kantian problem of defining objectivity in which subjectivity forms the inevitably point of departure. We may (or even have to) make distinctions between subjectivity and objectivity, but they are both embedded and present in culture without any demarcations or clear borders between them.

Values are a great example of these phenomena, which in reality include the most general ideas as well as the most concrete behavior or entities. Thus, culture reflects the human existential situation, which is characterized by ideas mixed up with actual behavior. This is captured in the paradoxical term *aestheticological*. However, it refers to an existential situation where there are no clear distinctions between essence and appearance, because the essence is appearance.

This is also why Böhme is highly skeptical of some aspects of semiotics (Böhme, 2001). When semiotics is defined in terms of a clear distinction between the signifier and the signified, it may reflect the same kind of distinction as we find between essence and appearance. Although both Baumgarten and Cassirer made a foundation for semiotics, both aestheticological and culture calls for uniting the signifier with the signified. Here we find a further challenge for the semiotic approaches of cultural psychology. In this sense, aesthetics complements other dynamics of discourse, such as the rhetorical and logical ones (Larraín, 2015, p. 141), but its implications transcend communicative dimensions, as long as the aesthetical experiences "evoke," inviting a resonance with the artistic object (Lehmann Oliveros, in press).

The field of music is reluctant to acknowledge the semiotic distinctions between signifier and signified because meaning in music is embedded in the way it is performed. Something similar occurs with poetry. The content of a poem is not what the words are referring to but rather the way the words are compounded and the meaningful experience it evokes. Furthermore, the meaning of a culture is first of all embedded in the interactions of all the elements that constitute a culture; it is never referring to something outside itself.

CONCLUSION

If we now bring in the experience the Norwegian painter Henrik Sørensen had with the Danish physicist Niels Bohr, we see that Bohr's thesis about complementarity in physics has something in common with the term aestheticological. As long as this type of logic does not refer to sequential and deductive reasoning, but rather to associations and verticality in thinking, this is comparable with competing theories that are applicable with explanatory power for the same physical phenomenon. However, to grasp these aspects of life and nature presuppose awareness and presence in the situation. In line with this, experiences of art are, according to contemporary aesthetics, characterized by awareness and presence instead of pure reflections. This demonstrates the exemplary role of aesthetics in science.

Both aesthetics and science are even more united in the broader term 'culture', which Cassirer (1961) demonstrated as representing the only solution to the subjectivity/objectivity problem. On this basis, culture represents the crucial point in the understanding of human beings as a whole. This was exactly what Wilhelm Wundt realized when he developed his folk psychology. The challenge here is to find the tools that bring psychology closer to culture. The term *aestheticological* in combination with the current discussions about aesthetics can represent some of the tools that are highly needed in this effort.

To bring into account the tension between the real and the possible involves both cognitive processes and the embodiment of memories and desires through diverse emotional intensities, which surpasses the capacity of language and recalls attention of psychology toward a more faithful comprehension of human phenomena. A faithful psychology, Freeman (2011) says, assumes responsibility toward the fact that

> We do of course know a good deal about feelings just as we know a good deal about lots of other important phenomena. But we generally do not encounter what might be termed the "life" of feeling in most contemporary psychological literature. (2011, pp. 389–390)

However, this was exactly what even Kant tried to explore when his investigation of the taste culminated with a rather astonishing focus on purposiveness in life and nature.

NOTE

1.   The authors translation of the original text in Spanish: "Por qué cantáis la rosa, ioh Poetas!/Hacedla florecer en el poema."

REFERENCES

Abbey, E., & Valsiner, J. (2005). Emergence of meanings through ambivalence. *Forum Qualitative Sozialforschung/Forum: Qualitative Social Research, 6*(1), Art. 23

Adorno, T. W. (1933/1998). *Kierkegaard. Gesammelte Schriften Band 2*. Darmstadt, Germany: Wissenschaftliche Buchgesellschaft.

Allesch, C. (2006). *Einführung in die psychologische Ästhetik*. Vienna, Austria: WUV Facultas Verlag.

Bachelard, G. (1939/2013). Appendix A. Poetic Instant and Metaphysical Instant. In G. Bachelard (Ed.), *The intuition of the instant*. Evanston, IL: Northwestern University Press.

Baumgarten, A. G. (1735/1968). *Filosofiske betragninger over digtet* (P. A. Brandt, Trans.) Copenhagen, Denmark: Poetik Bibliotek.

Baumgarten, A. G. (1750/2007). *Ästhetik, Band 1* (D. Mirbach, Trans.). Hamburg, Germany: Felix Meiner Verlag.

Benjamin, W. (1936/1968). The work of art in the age of mechanical reproduction. In W. Benjamin & H. Arendt (Eds.), *Illuminations* (H. Zohn, Trans., pp. 219–253). New York, NY: Harcourt, Brace & World,

Böhme, G. (1993). Atmosphere as the fundamental concept of a new aesthetics, *Thesis Eleven, 36*, 113, doi:10.1177/072551369303600107. Retrieved from http://the.sagepub.com

Böhme, G. (2001). *Aisthetik. Vorlesungen über Ästhetik als allgemeine Wahrnehmungslehre*. Munich, Germany: Fink.

Borchert, N. (2010). *Individuum est ineffabile. Veralgemeinerung ond Konkretisierung in der Philosophie*. Munich, Germany: GRIN

Bordwell, D. (1985). *Narration in the fiction film*. London, England: Methuen

Bordwell, D. (1989). *Making meaning. Interference and rhetoric in the interpretation of cinema*. Cambridge MA: Harvard University Press

Branco, A., & Valsiner, J. (2010). Towards cultural psychology of affective processes: Semiotic regulation of dynamic fields. *Estudios de Psicología, 31*(3), 243–325.

Cassirer, E. (1961). *The logic of the humanities*. New Haven, CT/London, England: Yale University Press.

Cavell, S. (1969/2002). Aesthetic problems of modern philosophy. In S. Cavell (Ed.), *Must we mean what we say? A book of essays* (Updated ed.). Cambridge, England: Cambridge University Press

Cavell, S. (1996). *The Cavell reader* (S. Mulhall, Ed.). Malden, MA: Blackwell.

Freeman, M. (2011). Toward poetic science. *Integrative Psychological and Behavioral Science, 45*, 389–396. doi:10.1007/s12124-011-9171-x

Glăveanu, V. P. (2013). *Affectivating environments in creative work*. Paper presented at Dialogue and Debate in the Making of Theoretical Psychology, Santiago, Chile.

Goethe, von J. W. (2005). *The sorrows of young Werther*. New York, NY: Modern Library. (Original work published 1774)

Heidegger, M. (1927/1980). *El Ser y El tiempo*. México: Fondo de Cultura Económica.

Hodges, H. A. (1944). *Wilhelm Dilthey: An introduction*. New York, NY: Oxford University Press

Huidobro, V. (1916). *Arte poética*. Retrieved from http://www.vicentehuidobro.uchile.cl/poema6.htm

Jannis, F. (1996). 'Individuum est ineffabile.' Zur Veränderung der Individualitätssemantik im 18. Jahrhundert und ihrer Auswirkung auf die Figurenkonzeption im Roman. *GoethezeitPortal*. Retrieved from http://www.goethezeitportal.de/db/wiss/epoche/jannidis_individuum.pdf

Kant, I. (1781/2010). *The critique of pure reason* (J. M. D. Meiklijohn & P. A. Hazleton, Trans.). State College, PA: Pennsylvania State University.

Kant, I. (1790/2002). *Critique of the power of judgment* (P. Guyer & E. Matthews, Trans.). Cambridge, England: Cambridge University Press.

Kierkegaard, S. (1845/1988). *Stages on life's way. Studies by various persons* (H. V. Hong & E. H. Hong, Ed. & Trans.). Princeton, NJ: Princeton University Press.

Kjørup, S. (1968). Baumgarten og æstetikens grundleggelse. In A. G. Baumgarten (Ed.), *Filosofiske betragninger over digtet* (P. A. Brandt, Trans., pp. 7–84). Copenhagen, Denmark: Poetik Bibliotek.

Larraín, A. (2015). The role of aesthetics in experience. In J. Cresswell, A. Haye, A. Larraín, M. Morgan, & G. Sullivan (Eds.), *Dialogue and debate in the making of theoretical psychology* (pp. 141–153). Ontario, Canada: Captus Press.

Lehmann Oliveros, O. V. (2015, August 2). Something blossoms in between: Silence-phenomena as a bordering notion in psychology. *Springer Link*. Retrieved from http://link.springer.com/article/10.1007%2Fs12124-015-9321-7#/page-1

Lehmann Oliveros, O. V. (In press). The oceanic resonance of instants: Extra-ordinary encounters with silence. In P. Marsico & L. Tateo (Eds.), *Ordinary things and their extraordinary meanings*. Charlotte, NC: Information Age.

Lehmann Oliveros, O. V., & Klempe, S. H. (2016). The centrality of aesthetics for psychology: Sciences and arts united through poetic instants. In J. Valsiner, G. Marsico, N. Chaudhary, T. Sato, & V. Dazzani (Eds.), *Psychology as a science of human being: The Yokohama Manifesto. Annals of theoretical psychology, Vol. 13*. London, England: Springer.

Lyotard, J.-F. (1984). *The postmodern condition. A report on knowledge*, Manchester, England: Manchester University Press

Marsico, G. (2011). The "non-cuttable" space in between: Context, boundaries and their natural fluidity. *Integrative Psychological and Behavioral Science, 45*, 185–193. doi:10.1007/s12124-011-9164-9

Nerheim, H. (1991). *Estetisk rasjonalitet. En analyse av konstitusjonsbegrepet I Kants Kritik der Urteilskraft* [*Aesthetic rationality. A study on the concept of constitution in Kant's "critique of judgment"*]. Oslo, Norway: Solum.

Nikiforov, V. (2006). *The collapse of philosophy and its rebirth: An intellectual history with special attention to Husserl, Rickert, and Bakhtin*. Lewiston, NY: Edwin Mellen Press.

Paz, O. (1956/1994). *El arco y la Lira*. Bogotá, Colombia: Fondo de Cultura Económica.

Plantinga, C. (2002). Cognitive film theory: An insider's appraisal/cinémas. *Journal of Film Studies, 12*(2), 15–37.

Robinson, A. (2014, June). An A to Z of theory | Walter Benjamin: Art, aura and authenticity. *CEASEFIRE*. Retrieved from https://ceasefiremagazine.co.uk/walter-benjamin-art-aura-authenticity/

Rundell, J. (1994). Creativity and judgment: Kant on reason and imagination. In G. Robinson & J. Rundell (Eds.), *Rethinking imagination* (pp. 87–117). London, England: Routledge.

Sørensen, S. O. (2003). *Søren. Henrik Sørensens liv og kunst*, Oslo, Norway: Andresen og Butenschøn.

Stravinsky, I. (1956). *Poetics of music in the form of six lessons* (A. Knodel & I. Dahl, Trans.) New York, NY: Vintage Books.

Wagoner, B. (2016). *The constructive mind: Frederic Bartlett's psychology in reconstruction*. Cambridge, England: Cambridge University Press.

Wertheimer, M. (1944). Gestalt theory. *Social Research, 11*(1/4), 78–99. Retrieved from http://thenewschoolhistory.org/wp-content/uploads/2014/06/wertheimer_gestalttheory.pdf

Valsiner, J. (2006). *The overwhelming world: Functions of pleromatization in creating diversity in cultural and natural constructions*. Paper presented at the International Summer School of Semiotics, Imatra, Finland.

Valsiner, J. (2007). *Culture in minds and societies*. New Delhi, India: SAGE.

CHAPTER 4

KANT *AND* GOETHE

The Connection Between Sensibility and Conceptuality

Bo A. Christensen and Steen Brock

In a conversation with his secretary Eckermann April 11, 1827, quoted here from Cassirer (1970, p. 61), Goethe is recorded as saying, "Kant never took any notice of me, although independently I was following a course similar to his. I wrote my *Metamorphosis of Plants* before I knew anything of Kant, and yet it is entirely in the spirit of his ideas." As Cassirer notes, this sounds like a curious remark, since Goethe and Kant have usually been depicted as polarities: Kant following Newton and emphasizing mathematics as a primary source of knowledge, versus Goethe attacking Newton, wanting to divorce any study of nature from the use of mathematics. But as Cassirer also notes, this appears so only when less attention is paid to the importance of Kant's third critique, *Critique of Judgment* (KdU), within Goethe's understanding of the Kantian philosophy (p. 64). The *Critique of Judgment* is significant in its emphasis on the intricate relationship between sensibility and cognition, without downplaying the role of sensibility, which often, and wrongly, is taken to be the case in Kant's previous first critique, *The Critique of Pure Reason* (KdRV), due to what is judged as its cognitive bias and formal epistemological architecture. The

The Psychology of Imagination: History, Theory, and New Research Horizons
pp. 83–101

supposed common spirit with Kant expressed by Goethe in the quote above, then, is based on evaluating the third critique as endowing sensibility with a central role akin to cognition in providing knowledge about the world. And as we will see in the following, this actually is the case in the first critique as well, though not as explicit as in the third critique.

This might seem like a surprise to a reader of Cornejo's chapter (this volume), which aims to reclaim the role of imagination against a highly rationalistic and cognitive psychology, and invoking Goethe against Kant in the endeavor. Our aim here therefore is *pace* Cornejo, to indicate a more nuanced view of the relationship between Kant and Goethe regarding imagination and its potential meaning for a cultural psychological perspective. Hence, we will underscore the continuity between Kant and Goethe in terms of their overall project, as well as their conceptions of the role of the imagination. We will furthermore stress a modern example of this in Rom Harré's thinking, especially on modeling. This is book-length stuff, one consequence being that our contribution will deal more with Kant than Goethe, focusing more on the similarities than differences against Cornejo's interpretation.

We will first describe what we take to be Carlos' project and the problem therein. In the light of this problematic, a description of Kant's first critique will be made in two rounds. We will first indicate a problem Kant himself encountered writing the first critique, namely, trying to provide a more active role for the imagination working within sensibility. Second, this means understanding what Kant terms *schematism* as the central notion in the first critique. The idea of schematism and its role in mediating between sensibility and cognition is also present in Rom Harré's thinking on modeling. Hence, we will end by making some comments on the relation between Harré and the role of imagination in a modern cultural psychology.

Goethe and Kant, According to Cornejo

Cornejo's effort in directing our attention to the overall problem with a too rationalistic and scientist-conceived psychology should be applauded: namely, because it tends to exclude psychologically phenomena-like fantasy, imagination, emotions, and such from having significance within a scientific psychological understanding. What we will take issue with here is his understanding of Kant and Goethe as exemplifying, respectively, a too rationalistic versus a more holistic understanding of the role of the imagination, as well as his claim that "We have to overcome Kant" (Cornejo, this volume, last page) to counterpoise this rationalistic tendency. But let us move onto Cornejo's interpretation of Kant.

According to Cornejo (this volume, p. 26ff), adopting the Kantian epistemology at the dawn of modern psychology resulted in a number of rationalistic tendencies. One example is the displacement of studies of imagination from psychology to other disciplines, like aesthetics, due to an increasing natural scientific study within psychology focusing on passive natural physiological conditions like perceiving, instead of activities done by the "creative mind." Another important tendency occurs because "Kant's epistemological interest is bounded necessarily to the knowledge capacities of the knower. Therefore the Kantian model of reason excludes the realm of feelings, emotions and moods of human being" (p. 29). When Kant investigates the conditions for knowledge to come into existence, and these conditions are deemed formal and *a priori*, then, according to Cornejo, the impact of feelings, emotions, and moods become only of a minor importance in the subsequent psychology based on this Kantian heritage. Two background implications exist for this.

First, Kant's thinking was based on a view of the world as ordered in a mechanical way (Cornejo, this volume, p. 30), with formal methods, predominantly mathematics and exemplified by Newton, providing the best modeling of the human soul. Against this, the Romantic Movement revolted, including the young Goethe, emphasizing passions, feelings, and creativity as a significant part of the human soul, and not capable of conforming to a pregiven and pure formal conceived rationality.

Second, this mechanical worldview is transferred, so to speak, into Kant's understanding of how the human mind works; namely, as a predominantly rational mind focusing on the cognitive functions as the most important, denigrating desires and feelings as human psychological capacities. Cornejo (this volume, p. 21) describes the functioning of the human mind according to Kant in his *Critique of Pure Reason* (1781/1787) as consisting of three faculties: sensibility, understanding, and reason. Sensibility is our capacity to have sensible experiences and operates actively by ordering the sensible data through the a priori forms of time and space. The understanding then brings additional order by subsuming these ordered perceptions under the conceptual categories (causality, unity, etc.) allowing us to perform judgments concerning our perceptions. Reason then has a guiding role in assuring us that a kind of unity prevails when all our judgments come together, that our worldview is harmonious, so to speak. This transcendental methodology corresponds to the Copernican revolution claimed by Kant, that "the constitution of the sensible objects depends on the structure of our own faculty of reason, and not the reverse, as was assumed by empiricism and rationalism" (Cornejo, this volume, p. 21). The transcendental method therefore seeks to understand and bring out what are the *a priori* conditions for our knowledge of the world to be possible.

But what is the role of the imagination, then? Well, according to Cornejo (this volume, p. 22),

> Kant's definition of *imagination* lacks any relation with feelings and organismic processes. For Kant, *imagination* has an intermediary role between sensibility and understanding: it is a force that produces synthesis in the form of sensible experiences, concepts and ideas. It satisfies therefore a function strictly intellectual and its possible grounding in feelings is plainly ignored or conspicuously minimized. (Emphasis in original)

Hence, imagination, in both its productive as well as reproductive aspects, is what helps tying the faculties making up the human mind together, making reason possible.

This Kantian psychology, then, expresses for Cornejo (this volume, p. 23) a model of man as a "cognizing subject rather than a person." That is, Kant's focus is on the epistemological subject, an abstract entity endowed with sensibility and reason, and not on persons, the concrete empirical entities doing what it is that humans do. According to Cornejo, this cleavage between epistemological subject and person, hence the cognitive bias towards human being, is manifested in Kant's view of the imagination as well, resulting in one of the main differences to Goethe.

Since for Cornejo's Kant, imagination is devoid of any genuine sensuous aspects—its role is only to make reason possible—nothing by Kant corresponds to Goethe's exact sensuous imagination, capable of leading to what Cornejo terms an *intuitive perception* (this volume, p. 6), or *Anschauung* in German. In contradistinction to Kant, Goethe therefore proceeds not from an abstract subject living at a distance to life, but assumes knowledge, including scientific knowledge, to be personal and based on lived experience, hence involving feelings as well as conceptions (p. 6). The aim of achieving knowledge for Goethe, then, is to understand archetypical phenomena (*Urphänomene* in German), that is, being able to intuitively perceive using this exact sensuous imagination, a phenomena in its complete actual and possible development. The primary example is the young Goethe's claim to discover a primordial plant (described in his *Italian Journey*), which is not a cause every plant can be derived from, but more an intuitive picture encompassing the developmental principles functioning in every plant. The primordial plant as archetypical phenomenon depicts variations of all plant's structural components, that is, branches, stems, flowers, and roots, thereby exhibiting an endless variety of actual and possible plants, and even some not existing in nature.

For Cornejo, perceiving an archetypical phenomena is impossible for Kant, because limits to human knowledge exist, and only a divine intellect could possibly "see" such a phenomena. However, and to start some of our reservations about Cornejo's interpretation, Cassirer (1970, p. 75ff) has emphasized, and in connection with the primordial plant, that a change occurred in Goethe's understanding of these archetypical phenomena. Initially the young and Italy-traveling Goethe thought he would be able to actually see and feel the plant with his hands. Returning home, meeting and discussing with Schiller, led Schiller to claim that what Goethe had discovered was not an empirical but an ideal plant, functioning like Kant's ideas of reason (Goethe 1988, pp. 19–20). The more mature Goethe eventually agreed with Schiller's Kantian understanding and claimed in 1830 that the archetypical phenomena "must not be interpreted too broadly; if we say it is rich and productive like an ideal, that is the best way to put it" (Cassirer, 1970, p. 76). The world of experience and the ideal is thus related for Goethe who claimed, "Time is ruled by the swings of the pendulum, the moral and scientific world by the oscillation between idea and experience" (Naturwiss. Schrf. 6, 354; Cassirer, 1970, p. 82), and "The highest wisdom would be to understand that every fact is already theory" (Maximen und Reflexionen, no. 575). The pairs of Ideas and experience, theory and fact, are thus at the outset related, and emphasizing only one part of these pairs is therefore failing to understand the complex nature of reality. So the cognitive abilities are also important for Goethe, and especially the role of the ideal.

According to Cassirer, Goethe therefore accepted Kant's claims about limits to human knowledge, and the archetypical phenomena expressed for Goethe "a limit not only to thought, but also to vision" (Cassirer, 1970, p. 83). Hence, the notion of exact in exact sensuous imagination connotes the concrete exhibiting of the relation between experiences of phenomena as well as ideas and concepts, and not a pure sensuous vision. As Goethe says "Merely looking at a thing can tell us nothing. Each look leads to an inspection, each inspection to a reflection, each reflection to a synthesis; and hence we can say that in every attentive glance at the world we are already theorizing" (1988, p. 159). This sounds similar to Kant's claim that "Thoughts without intuitions are empty, intuitions without thoughts are blind" (KdRV, p. B75). That is, both the possibility of there being objects of experience and experience as such is one and the same possibility. Our apprehending of things is equiprimordial (i.e., *ab initio*, occurring together as equally fundamental) with our apperception, that is, the empirical and discursive activity of the human mind are assigned to each other, and it is the task of reason to bring out the systematic nature of this relation. Common to both Goethe and Kant then was a view of absolute (divine) theoretical knowledge as being impossible for humans; instead, concepts and intuitions come together in human experience and make particular expositions of knowledge possible. To put it as Nassar (2014, p. 323) does, both Goethe and Kant claimed that "thinking must become perceptive and perceiving must become thoughtful." As an effort of making sense of the given, then, the possibility that we perceive things is already the possibility that whatever is presented to us is of such a kind that it is possible for us, meaningfully, to understand it using our cognitive capabilities (Brock, 2003, p. 22)

Now despite our claiming a certain similarity between Kant and Goethe here, this should not overshadow the differences between them. Especially that Kant was a philosopher using a logico-analytical methodology, and Goethe was a poet approaching science in terms of the arts. Hence their respective valuations of sensibility were also different: Kant describing the different relations in human experience necessary for knowledge to obtain, while Goethe was trying to reinforce an identity between thinking, perceiving, and the object perceived, the exact sensuous imagination. Nevertheless, as already indicated, and the following interpretation of Kant will show, this Goethean concept could and should be considered as more in debt to Kant's thinking than Cornejo claims.

To sum up Cornejo's (this volume, p. 23) interpretation of Kant, then, (a) there cannot be any understanding which is not of a nondiscursive nature, (b) Kant is more interested in the logico-formal conception of the transcendental categories connected with an abstract epistemological subject, and (c) imagination is not connecting sensibility or sensuousness with reason as in Goethe, but "provides images in a reproductive fashion (reproductive imagination) or imprints transcendental categories on sensorial data."

Now Cornejo's interpretation of Kant is actually in line with what he tries to argue against, namely, the predominance of a rationalistic understanding of human psychology. As Kukla (2006a) claims, there has been a tendency in the reception of Kant's philosophy, firstly, to downplay the role of third critique in Kant's philosophy. Secondly, too much emphasis has been put on certain parts the transcendental analytic (involving the understanding), while deeming the transcendental aesthetic (involving the sensibility) as well as the role of schematism in bridging sensuousness and reason as irrelevant. Cornejo seems to subscribe, probably unintentionally, to this highly rationalistic understanding of Kant's philosophy because he hardly mentions the third critique, and the role of the schematism, which Heidegger (1929), for example, claims is the most important aspect of the first critique, is not touched upon at all.

Not surprisingly, we will next present an interpretation of Kant indicating the importance of the schematism and the transcendental aesthetic, and how this presents a picture of the imagination, less rationalistic in Conejo's sense and more akin to Goethe's conception. We will, due to lack of space, dwell less on the third critique, but direct the reader's attention to Nassar's (2014, p. 8ff) analysis claiming that Kant, contrary to Cornejo's view, actually deals with organisms, thought as being both a "cause and effect of itself" (KdU, p. 370) and therefore "both an *organized* and *self-organising* being" (KdU, 1790, p. 374), thereby paving the way for our understanding of living beings and our ability to grasp them. Furthermore, as Kant claimed in a letter to Rheinhold, his intention with the third critique was to deal more specifically with the part of our experience revolving around the "faculty of feeling" (Guyer, 2000, p. xiv). So feelings are part of Kant's critical project, but touched upon mainly in the third critique and more implicitly, or presupposed as Kant says, in the first critique (KdRV, pp. A15–B29).

Another Kant I

If the above interpretation and our initial worries are significant, then more emphasis should be put on apprehending, firstly, as recent commentators on Kant have suggested (Förster, 2011; Kukla, 2006b; Nassar, 2014), the place of aesthetics within Kant's critical project, and secondly, the role of schematism as the point within Kant's system where sensibility and discursive understanding come together in an aesthetic sense (Heidegger, 1929; Schaper, 1964).

Now, it needs to be stressed that the sense in which Cornejo assumes Kant to be rationalistic has more to do with the sense in which Descartes and Newton were rationalistic. First, only cognitive structures and the discursive understanding matters when it comes to understanding how knowledge is procured, and second, this discursive understanding has a substantial (Descartes' *res cogitans*) character uncovering independent substances (*res extensa*). This is not Kant's position, which comes out when one attends more closely to the chapter called the transcendental aesthetics in KdRV (B33–34, A19–20).[1] In here, the fundamental category for people's relation to the world is described as involving what Kant terms *Gemüt* (DWDS, n.d.). This is usually translated as mind, but the etymological connotations of this concept are much broader according to the German digital dictionary, DWDS. It denotes a genuine openness on part of humans to be affected by the world in a sense involving both sensible and cognitive powers (what the dictionary terms *alle seelische kräfte*, all the powers of the soul). Through the *Gemüt* then, we are not uncovering the underlying substances of Descrates, this would be the thing in itself by Kant, but only appearances, or phenomena, and the different circumstances in which these phenomena are meaningful to us as sensible and cognitive beings. This is what Kant presupposed in the first critique in the chapter on the transcendental aesthetic, the *Gemüt*, denoting our basic relation to the world, which is worked out more explicitly in the third critique, as claimed in the end of the last section. We will leave the notion of sensibility in KdRV for now, but will return to it below (in the next section) where we will follow Schaper's suggestion of reading KdRV backwards from the chapter on schematism to the transcendental aesthetics (Schaper, 1964).

However, let us briefly return to what Kant's critical project is. Previous thinkers, for example Heidegger (1929), Cassirer (1918/1983), Gerhardt (2002) and Guyer (2005), have all emphasized Kant as not primarily a philosopher of science, but as a thinker trying to understand the diverse aspects of human experience. Correspondingly, Kant emphasizes the primacy of practical reason compared to theoretical reason. Practical in the sense that investigating the use of and relations between the different faculties is a way of expressing the interest and unity of reason (see Gardner, 2006). Hence, his critical project should be seen not as a metaphysics of science, but a metaphysics of experience, trying to overcome the "twin threats of humiliating scepticism and hubristic dogmatism" (Kukla, 2006a, p. 4). Hubristic dogmatism in the sense of a complacent conventionalism assuming truth is already realized. Humiliating skepticism in the sense that when we have to give up the dream of our total epistemic mastery of the world, as Kant claims, then accepting that we will never understand things as they are in themselves, unconditioned by our own epistemic activities, will not lead to a skepticism of our understanding not being able to grasp and make sense of that world. Kant's project, then, is arguing that despite the fact that our different experiences of the world contain human elements that cannot be eliminated. In other words, these elements (viz. sensible and cognitive) will always help establish the order they encounter, these experiences, and the judgments based upon them, are still directed toward objects in a world not of our making and therefore "answerable for their correctness to the way these objects are" (Manning, 2006, p. 62). Justifying this, that our experiences are actually about what they purport to be about, is what culminates in the famous transcendental deduction. This is probably what gives *The Critique of Pure Reason* (Kant, 1781/1787) the rationalistic touch Cornejo builds his interpretation on. Kant, however, encounters the following problem, as Kukla (2006a) has emphasized, internal to his argumentation, which leads to the idea of schematism, as well as a reappraisal of sensibility and the imagination.

Recall that Kant claimed the separation of three faculties—sensibility, understanding, and reason—with sensibility initially receiving impressions. Ordering these within the *a priori* forms of time and space as intuitions was a result of the understanding subsequently reflecting on and determining these intuitions. The understanding effectuates this by categorizing what it receives from the sensibility in terms of the concepts it possesses, it subsumes the sensible particulars as intuitions under concepts—I see a particular dog right here and now, and claim "There is a dog." That the impressions received in sensibility have the *a priori* forms of space and time entails, however, that these impressions in addition are conditioned by the cognitive faculty of understanding. So, strictly speaking, Kant ends up here with a dualism of a passive sensibility and active understanding, without being able to actually understand how these are connected in an equal manner. That is, how objects of experience and experience as such are expressions of one and the same possibility.

This forces him to introduce the imagination as that which is capable, at the level of the sensible particular, of performing a prediscursive synthesis of the manifold. He denotes it a figurative synthesis, a kind of intuitive representation of the manifold as combined. As in the above example of the dog, the sensible manifold must be put together in such a way that different dogs must be recognizable even though they, as dogs, also must be subsumable under the general concept *dog*. However, refusing to grant too much autonomy to a nondiscursive capability, Kant claims this prediscursive synthesis, and the work of the imagination, still is "an action of the understanding on sensibility" (KdRV, p. B152). So the imagination is here more of a servant of the understanding than a partner, readying the manifold "for understanding's rule *according to the latter's own discursive principles*" (Kukla, 2006a, p. 10). According to Kukla, this poses a problem for Kant, which he recognizes at the end of the deduction (KdRV, pp. A133–B172), and though he doesn't put it exactly his way, his intention can be put as the following: our general rule-like capacity to subsume the sensible manifold under the correct concepts, cannot itself be governed by conceptual rules, because the right application of these rules, then, must be governed by other rules for their right application, and these must afterwards be governed by other rules as well, and so on. This will eventually end in an unacceptable regress (Malpas, 2003; Margolis, 2013; McDowell, 1994).

Hence, Kant needs to accord a more fundamental role to the imagination not as a pure formal and discursive capacity, and here the chapter on schematism in KdRV becomes important. Schematisms cannot be guided by conceptual rules only because their role is to enable the connection of concepts with the sensible manifold, so schematism must be governed in another way, but how?

Another Kant II

First, though, let us consider what a schemata is. Well, a schemata at the time of Kant was something like a plan or a diagram. An architectural plan for constructing a bridge, for example, would stand between a general idea of a bridge and its particular construction. To put it another way, schemata functions like models with a guiding role for understanding the world. According to Schaper (1964, p. 274f) two points need to be emphasized if we want to understand the role of the schematism in Kant. First, that schemata are exhibited by the productive imagination, and not by either of the faculties, that is, sensibility, understanding, or even reason. Second, that Kant (KdRV, p. B184) thought of the schemata as time-determinations. Accepting these two points, means settling with the "orthodox" interpretation of Kant, what Schaper terms *constructionalism*, that the mind imposes some sort of structure on matter, that "structure in every sense is contributed by and derivable from the interest and activity and make-up of the experiencing subject" (Schaper, 1967, p. 276). Understood this way, the job of imagination would be molding the sense-manifold so it can be submitted to the conceptual apprehension of the understanding, eventually leading to the regression described above.

According to Schaper (1964), instead, we should think about the relationship between sensibility and understanding as one of mutual entailment, as connected at the outset through the activities of the imagination. She finds textual evidence in *inter alia* KdRV (p. B181) and (p. A124), where Kant claims that the schematism is an "art concealed in the depth of the human soul" and that the imagination conditions all knowledge. That is why we must read KdRV backwards, for what Kant initially starts by separating, namely, the different faculties, we must know understand as connected from the outset through the imagination. For example, Kant claims in KdRV (p. A124), "The two extremes, namely sensibility and understanding, must stand in a necessary relation to each other." But is this not just a new form of "constructionalism?" No, Schaper answers, because as the second point stated above, schemata are time-determinations, entailing that "though it is true that we construct, we construct not as minds, or intellects, not by being mind but by being in time" (Schaper 1967, 281) So what the chapter on schematisms shows us is that human nature is temporal nature. This implies that human nature is not confronting a separate manifold and then structuring it, but is, rather, already standing in relation to this manifold, through the openness of the *Gemüt*. Remember, this is not a passive receptivity but some sort of basic activity involving all human powers. We can now see that this fundamental relation is internal to the world, and that is why the chapter of the schematism leads us back to the notion of aesthetics. The message of the schematism, in Schaper's interpretation, is worth quoting at length:

> not that man imposes what he is himself (to a certain extent he obviously does), but that he discovers, via the schemata as underlying the possibility of

things for him, his own nature and the nature of that in which he is, his being-in-the-world. (Schaper, 1967)

To put it in a slightly different way, the schemata are not mirroring the world but are expressions of our engaging and arranging the world. Different schemata, then, disclose different aspects of the world. To use the example we started with, different architectural plans for making bridges are ways of arranging the world, and as such provide us with knowledge of the world and our relation to it (that bridges have to be constructed differently, in terms of materials, calculations, design, etc., according to whether they are for people walking or for carrying trains). Different plans for the same bridge can be presented through an ordered sequence in time, plan 1, plan 2, and such showing a development in our knowledge of this particular bridge as a pattern in space-time. Furthermore, as examples of engaging the world, bridges are signs of the times: they exhibit different interests and experiences in time; for example, the difference between Tower Bridge in London and the seven-mile bridge in Florida. What the imagination does then, is that it exhibits the amenability of the given to the joint operation of sensibility and understanding from within time. It is the imaginative ability to hold the discerning power of the understanding together with the play of the senses, akin to what Goethe terms *exakte sinnliche Phantasie*. Schematizing is the way the imagination can exhibit the exactness, without this schemata being some sort of involuntary invention, which would be an inexact fantasy, for example, a daydream or an inaccurate plan or model incapable of being realized, hence incapable of guiding the human experience and succeeding in this. Remember, Kant claimed, "Thoughts without intuitions are empty, intuitions without thoughts are blind." (KdRV, p. B75). Schematas are neither empty nor blind, as expressions of the relationship between sensibility and understanding they are historical and instructive. Blueprints, for example, have developed historically as media for constructing buildings and have been instructive in different ways as well.

Schematas, then, are the result of the activity of the imagination; they are exhibitions exhibiting different modalities of experience (as relations between sensibility and understanding) as different articulations of human temporality. Schemata therefore

> can be seen as the conditions under which men are active and formative in many different ways. The schematic suggestions ... provide directions and frames also for non-discursive modes of insight, of social and creative coming to terms with the life we are living and making. (Schaper, 1967, p. 290)

Schemata are not restricted to cognitive or even linguistic expressions, then, but are more akin to Cassirer's symbolic forms, the *in media res* of human experience, the media through which sensibility and our conceptual capacities come together in a modal sense (the schemata actualize something through the media, e.g. blueprints through traditions of blueprint making, and they make something possible, both the construction of a building and the development new blueprint making techniques). One modern example of this understanding of schematas, we will suggest, is Harré's understanding of modeling, as exploring the human *umwelt*. The plausibility of this comes out of quoting Harré (2004, p. 104) "As Kant had it and contemporary psychology confirms, our experience is a product of schematic ordering." This was written in 1981 and revolves around understanding how creativity and imagination is part of science within Harré's working out a realist theory of science (Harré, 1986) and developing adequate methodologies and theories for the social sciences (e.g., Harré 1990)

Before moving on to Harré, however, let us reiterate briefly. *Pace* Cornejo, we have indicated that Kant's view on imagination is somewhat more complicated than conceiving it as being the hireling of discursivity. The chapter on schematisms shows the imagination as more akin to Goethe's exact fantasy, and the schemata as time-determinations opens up a conception of humans as epistemological subjects, as well as subject to historical conditions, that is, persons engaging in concrete endeavors using symbolic tools according to norms. Furthermore, we have indicated that Goethe and Kant have more in common than what separates them, or at least that it is wrong to conceive their relationship in such antagonistic ways as Cornejo and others often do.

One last common thing between Kant and Goethe concerns the notion of idea with regard to Goethe's claim that the primordial plant is an ideal plant. Corresponding to Kant's schematism is Goethe's notion of a morphology (Cassirer, 1970, p. 68) exemplifying a genetic view of nature culminating in the theory of metamorphosis. What ties different forms of plants together, as well as describing their development in both a linear and analogical fashion, is what Kant terms the regulative use of reason. Ideas like the world, God, and the primordial plant are not principles constituting objects of knowledge. Instead they are ideas regulating our work in achieving knowledge by helping us correct errors and reaching a more comprehensive knowledge. The function of an idea is to reach a unity among the diversity of forms/schematisms, an idea is "a moment, a factor in the process of experience ... it is necessary for the use of experience itself, completing it and giving it a systematic unity" (Cassirer, 1970, p. 74f). Implied in being a regulative use is a continuous search in light of changing circumstances, and involving the integrated doing of sensibility and understanding, for a more comprehensive survey of the diverse forms/schematisms, capable of functioning as a provisional ground for further series of integrated doings.

Harré and Models

We will end this chapter with an additional indication of how the above interpretation of Kant has implicitly, and sometimes explicitly, been carried over into the *oeuvre* of Rom Harré. As any reader of Harré will know, his writings are very impressive, encompassing studies covering diverse subjects from chemistry over physics to social psychology, and always with the aim of creating some sort of perspicuous representation of human life as expressed within and through these sciences. Harré's work, and especially Harré (1986, 2004) is furthermore filled with references to schemata, models, and the use of imagination. So the idea of modeling occupies a central place, particularly as a common denominator for understanding what it is the sciences exploring the human *umwelt*, that is, the personal, social, and natural world (Harré, 1990), actually do.

Three things will end our comment here: first, the move from a first to a second cognitive revolution, namely, moving from a Cartesian view on mind as ultimately independent of the world it thinks and feels about, to a view of mind as embedded in contexts and basically related to it. Second, a short description of some models, or schemata, in natural as well as social sciences, exemplifying a way of bridging our openness to the world through sensibility, emotions, and discursivity. Discursivity for Harré is not related internally to the mind, rather it encompasses public discourses serving as the basis of which persons understand themselves, their social relations, as well as their relation to the natural world. Third, what this shows of the overall thinking about imagination and the use of models/pictures.

Let us first note the similarity between imagination conceived as schematizing above, that is, exhibiting the temporal character of human nature, understood as different cultural forms on the basis of which people understand themselves, each other, and the surrounding world, and what Harré (1992; Harré & Gillett, 1994, pp. 18–37) terms the *second cognitive revolution*. We could describe this as moving from a predominantly internal view of the mind focusing on processes internal to the mind, to an external view, focusing on how the mind must be conditioned by external cultural and natural historical factors, to understand what goes on inside our minds.

The first cognitive revolution occurred with the shift within psychology moving from behaviorism to the study of cognition. Here, mental processes were understood as occurring behind people's sayings and doings, functioning as a kind of cluster of modules processing information. The metaphor used was the mind as a computer, with cognitive processes being akin to the program running in a computer. Hence, two processes actually occur: what we do and the mental processes going on behind our actions.

Moving to the second cognitive revolution, according to Harré (1992, p. 6), took place when certain insights from sociologist and philosophers were incorporated into psychology, arguing against the first revolution. Harré's main examples here are Wittgenstein and Vygotsky, illustrated through two points. First, doing arithmetic calculations on paper and within one's head are autonomous processes. Using the pencil doing these calculations does not involve the occurrence of a similar process of calculation in the mind, only the practice of actually doing the calculation matters. Nothing is gained but confusion by splitting the process into two, one mental and one physical. Second, Wittgenstein warned against making "use of an unjustified and misleading generalization of a grammatical model to explain all the uses of a psychological word" (Harré, 1992). Instead we should become aware of the multiple ways in which psychological concepts are used, like saying "I love you" does not necessarily mean the same thing, psychologically, when said to one's children, one's spouse, or one's parents.

The important insight from the second revolution, then, is not that cognitive processes do not occur, but rather that they are immanent to our practices and involve relations to both sensibility and emotions. There are not two different "things" or "processes" connecting with each other; they must be connected from the outset to understand what separates them in the first place. Accepting Vygotsky's famous claim that one learns to do privately only what one has learned to do publicly is precisely not creating a mind separate from the practices it participates in. On the contrary, "both private and public cognition are of the same kind, symbolic procedures, according to certain norms" (Harré 1992, p. 6). This pertains to emotions as well. Hence, a display of an emotion is not so much a bodily response to a stimulus as it is a symbolic act embodied in a physiological state. Using the positioning theory associated with Harré, then different positionings come with different, correct or incorrect, displays of emotion. Laughing at a funeral in Denmark would be incorrect as an indecent display of emotion, but laughing might be an acceptable way to display sorrow somewhere else. So, the production of psychological phenomena such as emotions, decisions, attitudes, and such "depends on the skill of the actors, their moral standing in the community, and the story lines that unfold" (Harré & Gillett, 1994, p. 27). To model, according to Harré (2004), then, is to capture these different symbolic procedures and norms guiding the cognitive, sensible, and emotional aspects of our relating to the world, other people, and ourselves. This of course is different within natural and social sciences. Different models apply, but modeling itself, as a way of understanding what goes on in the natural, social, and personal world, is part of the schematic ordering of, or modeling, our experience as scientists, natural and social.

Implied here is Harré's (1986) three-realm theory, where different models pertain to these three realms. Briefly put, Realm one consists of the domain of fairly unassisted experience of beings, that is, everyday objects as well as objects the sciences have helped make visible like protuberances or asteroids. Realms two and three consist of the beings not observed but which either could be observed using new equipment and models, like the electron microscope, enabling the visibility of viruses, or as in Realm three, beings which will never be observed, like charges, quantum states, or social structures, which we infer through their observable affordances. All three realms overlap: objects from Realm two can eventually become part of Realm one, for example, bacteria, and as a whole, that is, as the ontological background of scientific inquiry, they amount to the world but as "being used *regulatively*" (Harré & Krausz, 1995, p. 20). Through the use of models (like an experiment or using dramaturgy as a model of social interaction),[2] exploring the human *umwelt*, the space available to the human species and human exploratory equipment and only a part of world as a whole, different and related aspects of the three realms are expressed. Inquiries done using optical telescopes and radio telescopes disclose different aspects of the same space and rely on different models for explaining these aspects. Put together, however, they indicate a more comprehensive understanding of what it is they are modeling.

Two examples will suffice here. The first example used by Harré and Gillett (1994, p. 62f) concerns why physicist like Maxwell and Bolzmann postulated molecules as significant parts of their model of the constitution of gases when they weren't observable. The answer was that they framed it within an overall Newtonian theory and conceived molecules as tiny particles whereby the physicists "helped themselves to the law of Newtonian mechanics as at least part of the cluster of laws that could be used to describe their imagined world of molecules" (Harré & Gillett, 1994, p. 63) Hence, using a model in this sense involves relating what is observed to what is not observed, that is, inferring from the phenomena observed by us the unobservable processes responsible for, or affording these phenomena. As an act of imagination then, "The model allows us to infer that observed pressure is caused by the impact of the moving molecules, without our needing to observing them!" (Harré & Gillett, 1994, p. 63). And as with Goethe, it allows us to infer, using our imagination, future possible states or models of the constitution of gases. The second model revolves not around unobservable entities but the interrelations between people and how to model these. Harré (2004, pp. 235–242) uses here one model of conversation as role/rules to capture how people relate to each other and themselves. Rules should here not be thought of as causes of but rather as guides to action. They help to characterize people, not as conforming to pregiven rules but by guiding people in writing their own history, as a form of lived narrative whereby people are coming into character. Rules, then, "express norms of intelligible and warrantable conduct. They are not causes of regularities in behaviour." (p. 240). The next step is considering the positioning triangle, where one imagines a normative order within which people allocate to each other a variety of duties, rights, and tasks. Here the different social positions, the narratives connected herewith, and the rules guiding our behavior come together. Events within this order are then seen as relating to a narrative in which certain acts, linguistic and nonlinguistic, make sense through people positioning themselves and each other within this order. Modeling through this triangle is therefore modeling a dynamic of change of social interrelations instead of a fixed social structure. And we should note, there is a projective dimension connected herewith as well. Modeling positions, narratives, and concrete acts in connection is also a way of conceiving what is yet to come. As Rothbart (2004, p. xi) puts it, "The projective aspect of narratives, and models, is essential for revealing unobserved, but observable events." The force of modeling by social scientists is immense, according to Harré (2004, p. 111), because by the creative use of imagination, it is possible to

> create an icon [a model] whose close simulacrum of a real world is so potent that people will live their lives within its framework, hardly ever suspecting that the framework is no more than a theory for making the messy, unordered flurry of day-to-day life intelligible, and so meaningful and bearable.

Both examples then show us that a model such as Harré conceives it, is not a representation of a pregiven structured reality, but a model of reality. Our use of a model is both showing something about the world we are in, and exhibiting our understandings as beings in time, as we are exploring the unobservable realms of molecules as well as actual and projected plans for future human action. The second cognitive revolution presents us with a way of understanding what this being in time means, namely, that discursivity or conceptuality and emotionality are connected to pregiven (historical) symbolic structures of diverse kinds, which guides us in our individual and common thoughts and feelings. And as schemata are models presenting our particular guidance, as involving particular relations between discursivity and sensibility, models by Harré try to capture how we develop practices dealing meaningfully with observable as well as unobservable natural processes, and the dynamics of social relations within the human life as a whole. What we have tried to indicate here, then, is that Kant might be of more relevance than Cornejo thinks, and not just as a historical precursor, but one who is seriously engaged with by authors informing cultural psychology like Cassirer or Harré.

CONCLUSION

So we have argued against Cornejo's view of Kant, trying to describe how the relationship between Kant and Goethe is much closer than usually understood, especially when we pay attention to the completed character of Kant's entire work and the role of the imagination within Kant's aim of providing a metaphysics of experience. Addressing the imagination and connecting this with the schematism, we ended up with features similar to Goethe's concept of an *exakte sinnliche Phantasie*. Bringing this idea up to a modern psychological understanding, we pointed toward Rom Harré's notion of modeling and its connection with what Harré terms a *second cognitive revolution*. The first cognitive revolution pictured the mind's activities as some sort of information processing, modeled on a computer with a highly discursive and rationalistic program running. Cornejo's interpretation of Kant comes close to this, depicting the understanding (*Verstand* by Kant) as the "central processing unit," reacting to the separate surrounding world. Instead, separating human beings with their cognitive processes from the world surrounding them, the second cognitive revolution, in the spirit of Wittgenstein and Vygotsky, claims that what goes on in the mind of somebody must have been a matter of what one has learned publicly in the first place. Hence, there is a plain connection between private and public cognition, which is exhibited in many different historical ways through language, signs, gestures, norms, and the like and in many different fields like art, law, religion, and such. To study this, in a cultural psychology, is to study all sorts of symbolic manipulations and formations as Harré claims, and his way of using models and comparisons between these is a modern way of understanding what Kant's schematisms and Goethe's exact sensible fantasy is all about.

NOTES

1.   See also KdU, §75, pp. 270–271, where Kant says "For it is quite certain that we can never adequately come to know the organised beings and their

internal possibility in accordance with merely mechanical principles of nature."

2. Other models would be the positioning theory he helped develop and lately he has been working on the development of a hybrid psychology, combining biological and social sciences as a model for investigating discourse.

REFERENCES

Brock, S. (2003). *Niels Bohrs' philosophy of quantum physics*. Berlin, Germany: Logos Verlag,

Cassirer, E. (1918/1983). *Kant's life and thought*. New Haven, CT/London, England: Yale University Press

Cassirer, E. (1970). *Rousseau, Kant, Goethe*. Princeton, NJ: Princeton University Press.

Das Digitale Wörterbuch der deutschen Sprache (DWDS). (n.d.). *Gemüt*. Retrieved August 18, 2015, from http://www.dwds.de/?qu=Gem%C3%BCt

Förster, E. (2011). *The twenty-five years of philosophy*. Cambridge, MA: Harvard University Press.

Gardner, S. (2006). The primacy of practical reason. In G. Bird (Ed.), *A companion to Kant* (pp. 259–271) Oxford, England: Blackwell.

Gerhardt, V. (2002) *Immanuel Kant. Vernunft und Leben*. Stuttgart, Germany: Reclam Verlag.

Goethe, J. W. (1982). *Italian journey, 1786–1788*. London, England, Penguin Books.

Goethe, J. W. (1988). *Scientific studies* (D. Miller, Ed. & Trans.). New York, NY: Suhrkamp.

Guyer, P. (2000). Editor's introduction. In P. Guyer & E. Matthews (Eds.), I. Kant, *Critique of the power of judgment* (pp. xiii–lii). Cambridge, MA/New York, NY: Cambridge University Press

Guyer, P. (2005). *Kant's system of nature and freedom*. Oxford, England/New York, NY: Clarendon Press.

Harré, R. (1986). *Varieties of realism*. Oxford, England: Blackwell.

Harré, R. (1990). Exploring the human umwelt. In R. Bhaskar (Ed.), *Harré and his critics*. Oxford, England: Wiley-Blackwell.

Harré, R. (1992). The second cognitive revolution. *The American Behavioural Scientist, 36*(1), 5–7

Harré, R. (2004). *Modelling. Gateway to the unknown*. Amsterdam, The Netherlands: Elsevier.

Harré, R., & Gillett, G. (1994). *The discursive mind*. Thousand Oaks, CA/London, England/New Delhi, India: SAGE.

Harré, R., & Krausz, M. (1995). *Varieties of relativism*. Oxford, England/Cambridge, MA: Blackwell.

Heidegger, M. (1929). *Kant und das Problem der Metaphysik*. Frankfurt, Germany: Klostermann.

Kant, I. (1781/1787). *Critique of pure reason* (KdRV) (P. Guyer, Ed., 1998). Cambridge, MA/New York, NY: Cambridge University Press.

Kant, I. (1790). *Critique of the power of judgment.* (KdU) (P. Guyer, Ed., 2000). Cambridge, MA/New York, NY: Cambridge University Press.

Kukla, R. (2006a). Introduction. Placing the aesthetic in Kant's critical epistemology. In R. Kukla (Ed.), *Aesthetics and cognition in Kant's critical philosophy* (pp. 1–31) New York, NY: Cambridge University Press

Kukla, R. (2006b). *Aesthetics and cognition in Kant's critical philosophy.* New York, NY: Cambridge University Press.

Malpas, J. (2003). *From Kant to Davidson.* London, England/New York, NY: Routledge.

Manning, R. N. (2006). The necessity of receptivity: Exploring a unified account of Kantian sensibility and understanding. In R. Kukla (Ed.), *Aesthetics and cognition in Kant's critical philosophy* (pp. 61–84) New York, NY: Cambridge University Press

Margolis, J. (2013). The regress argument in Kant, Wittgenstein, and the Pittsburgh "pragmatists." *Washington University Jurisprudence Review, 6*(1), 121–146

McDowell, J. (1994). *Mind and world.* Cambridge, MA/London, England: Harvard University Press.

Nassar, D. (2014). Sensibility and organic unity: Kant, Goethe, and the plasticity of cognition. *Intellectual History Review, 25*(3), 311–326.

Rothbart, D. (2004). General introduction. In R. Harré (Ed.), *Modelling. Gateway to the unknown* (pp. vii–xiii). Amsterdam, The Netherlands: Elsevier.

Schaper, E. (1964). Kant's schematism reconsidered. *Review of Metaphysics, 18*(2), 267–292.

CHAPTER 5

THE *SINNLICHKEIT* OF PANORAMIC EXPERIENCE

Jaan Valsiner

When we look at mountains, whether from far or near, and see
their summits, now glittering in sunshine, now surrounded in
mists or wreathed in storm-tossed clouds, now lashed by rain
or covered with snow, we attribute all these phenomena to the
atmosphere, because all its movements and changes are visible
to the eye. To the eye, on the other hand, shapes of the
mountains always remain immobile; and because they seem
rigid, inactive and at rest, we believe them to be dead.

—Johann Wolfgang Goethe in 1786 (1962, p. 11)

Nobody can escape the weather—be it good or be it bad. Yet nature has
no weather, the specific states of here-and-now atmospheric perturbations
become translated into weather by our poetic meaning-making minds. In
its totality (*Ganzheit*) as an ephemeral-but-real abstraction, "the weather"
is a prime example of how the human psyche operates in its instant poetic
productivity. Not only do we instantly create the notion of "weather," but
from the outset this meaning is affective. It is an all-inclusive relationship
between our bodies and the atmospheric conditions—once created we
cannot eliminate it ("the weather is so bad today let us throw it away").

The Psychology of Imagination: History, Theory, and New Research Horizons
pp. 103–120

Other generalized all-inclusive meanings can lead to eliminative actions ("this is garbage, let us throw it away"), the weather cannot. Neither can it be differentiated within the structure of the body of the meaning-maker, whose nose (actually exposed to "the elements") and toes (which are likely to be protected by appropriate footwear) are subject to the same "weather" that their master, the mind, has created. They only differ in the potential kinds of clothing options to "protect" the particular body part from "the weather" or let it be exposed to it for some purpose. And the notion of protection is an example of a similar *Ganzheit*-kind abstraction as is weather. The human mind creates such abstract affective clouds in abundance.[1]

For cultural perspectives in psychology, the phenomenon of "the weather" constitutes an interesting theoretical puzzle that precultural psychologies from Wundt to Kahnemann failed to grasp. Cornejo (this volume), returning to the epistemological roots of psychology in the *Naturphilosophie*, points to the need to return to some of the premises of Goethe's poetic science that can be helpful to make psychology once again appreciative of the processes of human experiencing ("the Yokohama Manifesto"; Valsiner, Marsico, Chaudhary, Sato, & Dazzani, 2015). But how can this be done within a discipline that has become theories-phobic in its recent past (Smedslund, 2016; Toomela & Valsiner, 2010)? Solution here is not theoretical but metatheoretical. The key here seems to be to move to the axiomatic standpoint of the primacy of the whole (Diriwächter & Valsiner, 2008) and focus on the sense-making processes (Salvatore, 2015) as the human being is involved in the constant relating with the *Umwelt* (Chang, 2009) in the making of the past out of the imagined futures (Zittoun et al., 2013). The totality of experience is the starting point, its further divisions into specifics—an outcome of the general differentiation and hierarchical integration processes (Valsiner, 2005; Werner, 1948).

The Panoramic Nature of Human Experience

We live in complete perceptual fields—visual, acoustic, tactile, and haptic. Each of these constitutes an all-inclusive arena—a panorama which is experienced from the body outwards. Panoramic experience is total. Even if its borders may be visible—as in paintings put into frames—the panoramic experience remains a *Ganzheit* as the focus of attention moves across the panorama (Figure 5.1).

The totality of the whole scene is what we experience, with temporary moments of focusing guided by the artist's imagination[2] encoded into the

Figure 5.1.   *Der Watzmann* by C. D. Friedrich (1825–1826).

picture. In terms of landscape painting as art, in Friedrich's rendering, a viewer wanders over the landscape with a sense-making gaze

> while the peak and the outcrop retain a convincing degree of realism through their singularity of shape, the painting itself is invested with a sense of order and structural symmetry which *elevates the particular to the universal.* Friedrich's success lay in his unique ability to combine the specific and the universal without forsaking a sense of reality *or reducing the sense of divine power.* As in most of his works, here too an extreme vividness of detail is combined with the subtle compositional rhythm. Through a momentum that builds gradually from the pyramidal shape of the outcrop through the swelling middle hill to burst forth exaltedly in the peak itself, the viewer *is made to feel a moment of enlightenment.* (Mitchell, 1984, p. 459, added emphasis)

The process captured here is that of abstraction through symbolic exemplification introduced by Susanne Langer (or presentational abstraction; Innis, 2012, p. 54). The artistic image is created so as to embody patterns of tensions which may be maintained or resolved in an act of subjective synthesis (as emphasized by Vygotsky; Valsiner, 2015). In both cases, maintenance and synthesis, the tension involved in presentational abstraction sets the work of art apart from affective tensions of everyday life where abstraction is secondary to action. By such separation—inclusive one—art retains its symbolic role in guiding everyday life rather than succumbing to the social norms of everyday living.[3] The painting of landscapes in the latter part of the 18th century was built on the social representation of spirituality through the depiction of natural scenes—trees, rivers, mountains,[4] and any other parts of nature. Its central interlocutor among the sciences was geology, up to the emergence of photography (1820s–1830s), wherein all depiction of geological objects of investigation proceeded through drawings. The issue of authenticity of the details of such paintings was crucial for science, whereas for the purposes of the artists' expression of their creative messages it was the deviation from the real depiction that motivated their taking on painting of imaginary real[5] landscapes.

Panoramas: The Whole of a View

The capacity of human beings to relate to the totality of experience was exploited in late 18th century for commercial purposes—to create artificial environments for viewing of which a person would pay a fee. The "all-embracing view" was created by

> a circular room whose walls are entirely covered by a continuous, painted canvas lit from above. The spectators entered the room using an underground passage suitably darkened to enhance the effect when they emerged onto a central island from which they could view the scene. (Bigg, 2007, p. 73)

Possibly it is the views from hot air balloons—of fascination in the 18th century—that led to the proliferation of panoramic image promotion. Looking at the totality of a view from an elevated point would guarantee the dominance of the panoramic scene over a viewer's own reference frames. Experiencing a panorama in the late 18th century for a fee provided an experience of full immersion in the field.

Commercial panorama constructors of the 18th and 19th centuries created a 3-dimensional experience of space on the basis of 2-dimensional images covering all of the visual field, wherever the viewer might look. In contrast, landscape painters represented landscapes within picture frames and in 2 dimensions, reconstructing the image of a 3-dimensional object in the drawing on the canvas. The picture frame circumscribes the field (Tarasov, 2011). It sets up the borders that guide our experience. Yet, in the case of panoramic experiences, the borders are set by our own limits of the perceptual field. We are immersed in the totality of experiencing—total *Ganzheit*. An artist trying to convey that experience is limited by the borders of the canvas.

Theory of Pleromatization and Schematization

The artist's capacity of creating a *Ganzheit* based on details, combined into a "subtle compositional rhythm," is demonstrated by Friedrich also in the opposite version of the totality of feeling, exemplified also by the cover of the present book and in the rest of his paintings (Beenken, 1938). Here the subtlety of the rhythm is taken to the extreme of the lack of details, with the imposing contrasts of fuzzy contours guiding the viewer's emergence of feeling. It is both through focus on details and making that focus fuzzy that the affectivating process proceeds. This equifinality is granted by the active role of the sense-maker whose affective feeling-into the environment (*Einfühlung* in terms of Theodor Lipps) guides the cognitive follow-up of the meaning-making.

The ways in which such feeling-into-environment takes place is conceptualized by the dual process of pleromatization and schematization (Figure 5.2). The two processes operate in mutual relation—each feeds into the other, and the result of such mutuality is generalization and eventually hypergeneralization of the experience. Both abstracted categories (point-like signs X) and sign fields (field X) are present in any of human meaning construction. Only their relations may vary. Thus, in the extreme case of maximum rational abstraction (e.g., in case of mathematical terms), it is the schematization that is in full dominance in meaning-making. In contrast, in any situation where a person lets oneself float on the waves of overwhelming sensuality, it is the pleromatization that leads the meaning-making. Deep feelings of some overwhelming kind, be it describable as "love," "hatred," "depression," or "boredom," are examples of complete dominance of the pleromatization processes that are not reducible to point-like schemas. All panoramic experiences in human lives are of such kind.

Pleromatization processes are primary in the *Aktualgenese*[6] of meaning, leading into schematization (Valsiner, 2006, 2014). On many occasions, schematization is made hard, if not impossible. The meaning of "things"—the ultimate goal for schematization—can be countered by the ephemerality of the objects of classification. Some objects defy efforts to classify them:

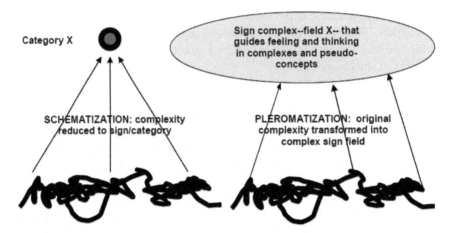

Figure 5.2.   Meaning construction through parallel processes of schematization and pleromatization.

> Are clouds things? If yes, is fog, air, cold? If clouds are things, they are surely things different in kind from stones and sticks, and the twinkling stars are again different. Air? The breath, the "pneuma," the "spirit" has thing-like qualities.[7]... A fog we see creeping up the mountain valley has a thing-like quality similar to that of clouds, but a fog that makes our ocean liner reduce speed and sound its piercing horn is not thing-like at all, as little as the mist from which we emerge when we climb a mountain. (Koffka, 1935, p. 70)

Again, it is the perceived uncertainty of the events that fascinated the young amateur meteorologist Goethe watching the weather on the mountaintops; that feed into the core of psychological phenomena, subjective processes in the person-environment relations. It is here where the science of psychology, an 18th century invention that became an autonomous discipline in the 19th century, developed in liaison with landscape painting.

Romantic Roots of Psychology

Psychology today has much to learn from the German Romantic "school" of painting that emerged and flourished in the first decades of the 19th century. First, what was presented by artists as real was meant to be hyperreal, in the sense of generalized values encoded into the iconic images (Scholl, 2015). Secondly, the encoding of these values was delegated to the totality of the picture—independent of whether there existed a central figure or not, the picture as a whole was meant to get the viewer to lead oneself in a particular affective direction. This focus on *Ganzheit* antedated the efforts by psychologists to capture the generalized nature of the whole by about a century (Diriwächter & Valsiner, 2008). Of course the artists' credo at the time was in synchrony with the up and coming *Naturphilosophie*, which later became extinct due to the avalanche of the *Naturwissenschaften* over the latter part of the 19th century (Valsiner, 2012). Philosophy and *Wissenschaft*[9] have both been separating from each other over the last two centuries, but they were not disunited at the time of the "Romantic Era." Thirdly, the psychological focus of the Romantic painting was based on the efforts to save the primacy of religious sentiment in the middle of rapidly secularizing societies of the era, which at first romanticized the French Revolution and later suffered through the atrocities of Napoleonic dominance. One of the directions of social ideas was promoted in the painting of religious ideas through the depiction of realist scenes—the Nazarene school of young German artists in Rome (Reiter & Schröder, 2015). The other—the romantic extrapolation of nature scenes—dominated the Dresden painting traditions of the beginning of the 19th century.

Last, but not least, the German Romantic painting tradition was directly related to the emerging psychology as a discipline. Started by Christian Wolff in 1732 and brought into German universities by Johann Friedrich Herbart in 1806, the painting and psychology traditions converged in the work of Carl Gustav Carus (1789–1869). Carus linked psychology (with a main focus on feelings) with his hobby of landscape painting together with his fascination with the *Naturphilosophie* of Goethe and landscape physiognomics of Alexander von Humboldt (Böhme, 1999).

Carus wrote a series of nine letters about landscape painting expressing his credo for its functions. In Letter VI he specified the imperative to landscape painters to go beyond the representation into the affective presentation:

Any painter who attains true knowledge of the life of nature must find the purest and most sublime subject matter on every side. *With what eloquence and power the history of the mountains speaks to us*; how sublimely it *makes of man a thing divine*, in direct relation to God, by sweeping away all the vanities of his transient, earthly existence; and how clearly that history speaks to us *in certain stratified formations and mountain outlines:* so clearly as to *suggest even to uninitiated that such history exists!* (Carus, 2002/1824, p. 115, added emphasis)

The goal orientations of the landscape painters of the Romantic era were clearly ideological (religious), yet the promotion of the religious feelings was accomplished through the forms of nature. Friedrich Schiller's ideology of poetics was crucial in the landscape painting (Gaiger, 2000). Landscape painting that in previous centuries had been the least valued genre of painting—no competition with religious imageries, portraits of aristocracy, or depiction of battlefield—became suddenly the most valued genre at the turn of the 18th–19th centuries. It conveyed spirituality not via religion but via nature, enriching it with poetic sentiments. The pleromatic nature of the landscape scenes supports their use in the promotion of spiritual feelings, a goal that is present in the institutional efforts of all religious systems of the world. They need work out their ways to gain access to the innermost feelings of persons, who are usually protected against direct ideological interventions. Creating overwhelming experiences via *Ganzheit* in panoramic views or musical or ritual involvement is a major step toward reaching that goal.

Carus' lectures in psychology (Carus, 1831) are one of the first systematic courses in the discipline that became institutionally established in the German language room in the 1820s (Valsiner, 2012). These were followed up with books on human soul (Carus, 1856, 1858) and comparative psychology (Carus, 1866). Together with Johann Fridrich Herbart and Rudolph Herman Lotze, Carus was one of the creators of psychology as an integrative discipline of *Geistes-* and *Naturwissenschaften*, before their enforced splitting into opposites at the end of the 19th century in the hands of Wilhelm Wundt and Wilhelm Dilthey.

From Gestalt Principles to *Ganzheit* Negotiations

Observing landscapes defies most of the Gestalt principles. Although being standard items in psychology textbooks to introduce Gestalt (usually Berlin school) ideas, four of the laws (law of proximity, law of similarity, law of closed form, and the law of good contour; Katz, 1950, pp. 26–27) are subordinated in the case of panoramas to the overwhelming totality of experience. The laws of Gestalt, formulated on the basis of the scientific credo of the Berlin School (with focus on vision), represent the schematization focus of meaning construction. In contrast, landscapes and their paintings guide our visual meaning-making to the opposite, feeding into the pleromatization process (Valsiner, 2006, 2014). Panoramic experience renders schematization processes secondary to the "capturing the scene" with one's "full feeling." Schematization can only partially cover the fullness of the scene, either emphasizing some detectable features (e.g., "the houses in front"—Figure 5.3) or attempting to put into words the wider view (e.g., "the enormity of the view"—Figure 5.3). Words (and other schematizing devices) fail when the fullness of the panoramic experience is lived through.

Figure 5.3.   A real panorama of Danish landscape—a view from Ribe Cathedral.

As a *Ganzheit*, a landscape (as well as a painting that, as if, represents it) sets the stage for various images to emerge, as well as resistances to gaining clarity of the meaningfulness of the *Aktualgenese* of the percepts. Instead of the percept moving toward a "good Gestalt," our *Einfühlung* with the depicted view keeps wandering across the canvas, now concentrating on some discernible parts (the top of the mountain or the geological formations in the foreground—Figure 5.1), yet failing to create one particular whole. Or the wide panorama of a real landscape (Figure 5.3) captures the whole of the perceptual field leading to pleromatized generalization.

Independent of whether we experience a painting, a sculpture, a natural mountain scene, or a panorama of a Danish real landscape (Figure 5.3), our experiencing comes in the form of affectivated *Ganzheit* (Cornejo, Marsico, & Valsiner, 2016). Human beings feel-into their environments, and that feeling feeds forward into the cognitive construction of the explicit meanings which may then be attributed to the environment. Finding a panorama of a mountain range, in real life or on an artist's canvas, "breath-taking" projects the agency to the environment (it is the sight out there that "takes" my breath), rather than accepting one's own subjectivity ("I take my own breath through exposing myself to this sight" or "I create you (my deity) to control me"; Valsiner, 1999). Or the perception of confined-yet-large spaces can lead to subjective feeling of "capture";

> A recent visit to the gardens of the Palace of Versailles ... afforded the same [walled in] experience. In each square-shaped garden, dead-straight pedestrian avenues were lined on either side by high walls of trees, and led to enclosed groves with statues or mountains. I felt, in these gardens, an overwhelming sense of claustrophobia. (Ingold, 2016, p. 109)

The movement through a particular environment is an act of feeling-with it, from the personal perspective. Furthermore, creating the spaces for moving through, be these the gardens of Versailles (explicitly constructed to communicate the royal power and its totality to the powerless visitor—all visitors were expected to follow the given route through the gardens in the 19th century) or the Nazi marching grounds in Nuremberg (Macdonald, 2006) are oriented toward social guidance of such feeling-in (*Einfühlung*) processes. Our constant feeling-into anything we pass by—perceived centrally or peripherally—is the affective process through which human beings constantly negotiate the domains of as-is and as-if.

Reaching Out Toward Infinities: Two Interdependent Processes

The examples of landscapes and landscape paintings emphasize what William Stern back in 1935 considered to be the meeting place of two infinities—"inner" and "outer" (Stern, 1935; see also Figure 5.4). The feeling-into the environment as a whole feeds further into the intrapsychological (equally total) search of the person's inner feelings, with further feed-forward to the exploration of the outwards horizon, and so on. In addition to this Person <> Environment relationship process that Stern emphasized (*Aktualgenese* of the reflection upon the self and exploration of the world), what is at stake is the person's negotiating one's past and future infinities (Figure 5.4). In the present negotiation of the inner and outer infinities it is the guidance from imaginary past (reconstructed memories) together with anticipated future (imaginatively constructed) that structures the immediate present feeling and acting.

Why Landscape Painting is an Innovation?

> A tapestry hanging on the wall decorates that wall; it does not destroy the vertical plane. A landscape painting on the wall, however, has the effect of

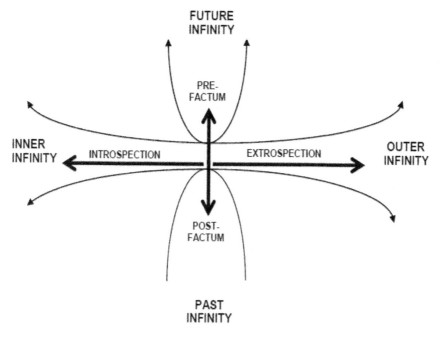

Figure 5.4.   The human psyche coordinating two parallel processes between infinities (after William Stern).

opening a window through which a person can penetrate the vertical plane and direct his gaze outward to the horizon. The walls of Italian villas of the Renaissance period were painted with landscapes, not only that their owners could boast the extent and variety of their estates, but also that they could enjoy the illusion of expansive vistas. (Tuan, 1974, p. 135)

Treating landscape paintings as windows—or paintings of religious themes on the ceilings as "doors" to the heaven—was an act of transcending the conventionalized horizons of the *Umwelt*. The structure of *Umwelt* includes partitions that are real (bona fide boundaries) and others that are constructed as if real (*fiat* boundaries; Smith, 1999). The borders where the two kinds of boundaries enter into relations with each other are the demarcations of the functional end of the to-be-perceived (or to-be-acted-within) fields from the external field—the unreachable (all that stays beyond the horizon as perceived) or conventionally dismissible (all that stays beyond the picture frame in a museum). The perception of the horizon by human vision is an example of a 1-dimensional fiat boundary demarcating the interior of the visual field and simultaneously the external boundary of what can be seen and what stays beyond (e.g., Figure 5.3 above). More specifically,

> the boundary of the visual field is a complex, subtle, ever-changing ... patchwork of physical surfaces and other components. The patchwork is "open," topologically speaking: its external boundary is not a part of the visual field itself (as death is not an event in life). The patchwork is organized further in terms of an opposition between entities ("figures") in the focus of attention, which characteristically manifest determinate boundaries, and entities which have indeterminate boundaries and which are experienced as running on (as "ground") behind them. (Smith, 1999, p. 324)

Mereotopology (as exemplified by the discussion of boundaries by Smith) remains an ontological field where the bona fide and fiat boundaries are seen as separate categories and where the formation of the figure (Gestalt) is given precedence to the role of the ground ("entities with indeterminate boundaries"). When seen from the nonontological—dialogical—perspective, each border (fiat or bona fide) sets up the conditions of tension that may lead the person to move beyond the current border. The desire to travel to the (current) horizon to see what is beyond—unattainable in practice—has motivated many travelers and inventors. The tension around the imaginary borders of the Future and Past infinities (Figure 5.5) are arenas for human development (in this sense, death is an event in life). Furthermore, the negotiation of the bona fide and fiat boundaries is built deeply into human lives, starting from the borders created on and around the human body (Figure 5.5). The ornamentation of transitions between the covered and noncovered portions of the presented parts of the body— across all layers of clothing layered over one another—is a vehicle for creating the meaningful *fiat* border (of "beauty," or "seduction," or "self-care," etc.) on the basis of bona fide transition zones between separated parts of the whole.

Similarly to Goethe's description of the phenomena of the weather around the mountain contours, human beings create complex border regions at the transition arenas between the skin and the immediate clothing—affectivating the gaze of the observer (who is, first of all, the wearer of the clothes, her- or himself).

It is the uncertainty, similar to the weather on the Alpine mountain tops described by Goethe, that becomes the arena for creating new meaning-based border zones linking inner infinity dynamically with its outer counterpart (Figure 5.3). Particularly in the case of socially important but at the same time socially constrained areas of human activities such uncertainty becomes the arena for personal dialogues with oneself, through acting upon the world. Thus, young Canadian women

Figure 5.5.   Panoramas as replicated in microscale on the ornamentation of clothing.

articulate persistent tensions between sexual agency and desire and the disciplining effects of regulatory norms, which operate within intrapsychic tracks always inflected by gender difference. Registers of shame and anxiety attach to gender-marked bodies and subjectivities. These attachments shape desire and agency around warding off allegations of promiscuity as a key exigency. Pursuit of sexual pleasure and performance alternately appears and recedes. (Gurevich, Vasilovsky, Brown-Bowers, & Cosma, 2015, p. 525)

The move between the inner and outer infinities in the dialogue of "myself as that kind of a woman" (Nedergaard, Valsiner, & Marsico, 2015) is explicated in a self-statement about clothing:

I am very open about it [sexuality]. I am wearing this shirt and most people would tell me I should not wear a shirt that looks like this and I specifically put on a tan-colored bra so that you question is she wearing a top or not, like I throw people off with stuff like that. I will show my cleavage, I will be sexy if I want to be sexy and still cover myself up if I want to cover myself up, you know. I just wear what I feel like wearing, I do what I feel like doing and you know often I will get "Wow, you're asking for it, you're asking for it" and

I was like "No I do not ask for anything," if that idea runs through your mind or the feeling you think you can grab my arm and pull me to you or try to talk to me, you think you can do that, that's all you, that's all you and I'm not asking for anything, like I can give two shits about what anyone thinks about me and it's always been this way because I've always had people talking. (Gurevich et al., 2015, p. 525)

Creating uncertainty in the inner<>outer infinities meeting point is the locus for freedom of action, exemplified by flexibility of change of goal orientations. Constraining, by self and others, leads to freedom of the self (and of others). Shift between goal orientations and actions is based on the primacy of affect ("I feel that I want X!"). Sensuality is the starting condition for relating with the world.

Human panoramic experiencing is sensual in its fullness, out of which the sexual ideations and conduct episodically becomes assembled (Valsiner, 2003). When we observe the far-away panorama—a mountain range on the horizon, a stormy ocean bounded by the horizon, or our own body—in mirror or by haptic exploration, we are involved in the same basic process of meaning making through the totality of immersion in the object of our focus. Yet that immersion does not equate fusion; we retain the active subject role even in the closest relation to our object (our own bodies), not to speak of the landscapes "out there."

GENERAL CONCLUSIONS: WHAT DOES "GOING FORWARD WITH GOETHE" IMPLY?

Cornejo's (this volume) suggestion to return to the poetic nature of human conduct, emphasized by Goethe and his contemporaries but subsequently eliminated from psychology as a science, has far-reaching implications for turning psychology from an imitating science[10] into a real one. A real science is true to its object of investigation. Chemistry became one once it left behind its alchemical constructions and concentrated on the analysis of chemical synthesis. In an interesting twist, psychology needs to leave behind its efforts to get rid of the poetic nature of human living and turn the ways of creating such nature into the object of investigation.

Extrapolating our anticipation of the imaginary landscapes into the future is an important feature of human relating with environments. City planners building visual images of the panoramas of future cities operate with landscapes that are (at the moment) observed by the planners' inner infinities projecting into the future feeling into human living in the imaginary urban future environment (Jansson & Lagerkvist, 2009). All of our contemporary social discourses about future "ecological catastrophes" and diagnosing the climate changes of today are of similar kind. The inevitable totality of human dependence upon the environment-in-transition sets up the imperative for the human mind to operate at the level of *Ganzheit*—uniting the general and the particular—in the move toward future development.

ACKNOWLEDGMENT

The preparation of this chapter has been supported by the Niels Bohr Professorship grant by *Danske Grundforskningsfond*. Suggestions by the editors of this book for improving the previous draft are gratefully acknowledged.

NOTES

1. Add to this list security, love, justice, democracy, fairness, and many others.
2. The given painting—quite unusual in the artist's portfolio in its seeming realism and large-size canvas—was created by Caspar David Friedrich without ever experiencing the actual mountain in Bavaria, but is based on the image drawn by his student August Herrmann (died in 1822). It reflects the geognostic focus (knowledge of the eternal through empirical exploration of geological formations) of the late 18th century German natural sciences as well as treating nature as representation of religious sentiments (see analysis in Mitchell, 1984). Two other artists, Ludwig Richter and Johann Christian Dahl, painted parallel presentations of the Watzmann in the same years (1824–1826), also through their imagination rather than from nature itself. The realistic images of the Romantic painters of the obvious were deeply nonobvious; evocation of feelings was encoded in the painted surfaces on the canvas.
3. The tension involved in such inclusive separation is exemplified by the episodically reemerging traditions in different societies to cover the genitals of classic Greek human figures by fig leaves. The objects of art, framed by their presentation in a museum context, are being interpreted as if ordinary life figures to which the local social norms apply ("indecent exposure").
4. In the words of Anton Büsching, one of the German originators of the "geognostic" (intuitive knowledge though geological forms—all, of course, assumed to be divine creations) mountains "are an ornament of the earth's surface and provide the most beautiful vistas" (written 1766–1769, as cited in Mitchell, 1989, p. 657). The focus on geological forms was affectivated from the outset, which is an example of inclusive separation of the aesthetic and the mundane.

5. Aside of *Der Watzmann* being built on Friedrich's imagination, the geological formations in the foreground are a realistic but unreal (in terms of the real Watzmann) symbolic message to the audience about the divine judgment operating through the creation of the magnificent natural forms.

6. This German term has usually been translated into English as *microgenesis*. Yet the German version is accurate, independent of the level (micro or macro), it entails the process of constructing the image of the actual state of affairs.

7. Likewise, core terms invented in psychology to characterize some aspects of conduct—personality, character, intelligence, etc.—are assumed to take on the form of a thing (entity) to which then causal powers are attributed: compare "the spirit of the ancestors causes X" with "personality type Y causes X." Creating things out of the fog creates certainty instead of making sense of the lingering uncertainty.

8. I prefer to use the German term as its meaning—*knowing*—is closer to the goals of science than its English counterpart.

9. A discipline that attempts to become a science by imitating the practices of other, already recognized, sciences.

REFERENCES

Beenken, H. (1938). Caspar David Friedrich. *The Burlington Magazine, 72*(421), 170–175.

Bigg, C. (2007). The panorama, or La Nature A Coup d'Ceil. In E. Fiorentini (Ed.), *Observing nature-representing experience: The osmotic dynamics of romanticism, 1800–1850* (pp. 73–95). Berlin, Germany: Reimer Verlag.

Böhme, G. (1999). Die Physiognomie einer Landschaft. *Geographische Zeitschrift, 87*(2), 98–104.

Carus, C. G. (1831). *Vorlesungen über Psychologie*. Leipzig, Germany: Verlag von Gerhard Fleischer.

Carus, C. G. (1856). *Erkenntnis der Natur und des Geistes*. Leipzig, Germany: Brockhaus.

Carus, C. G. (1858). *Symbolik der menschlichen Gestalt*. Leipzig, Germany: Brockhaus.

Carus, C. G. (1866). *Vergleichende Psychologie*. Wien, Germany: Baunmüller.

Carus, C. G. (2002/1824). Letter VI. In C. G. Carus (Ed.), *Nine letters on landscape painting* (pp. 113–116). Los Angeles, CA: Getty Foundation.

Chang, R. S. (Ed.). (2009). *Relating to environments: A new look at Umwelt*. Charlotte, NC. Information Age Publishers

Cornejo, C., Marsico, G., & Valsiner, J. (Eds.). (2016). *"I activate you to affect me." Annals of cultural psychology, Vol. 2*. Charlotte, NC: Information Age.

Diriwächter, R., & Valsiner, J. (Eds.). (2008). *Striving for the whole: Creating theoretical syntheses*. New Brunswick, NJ: Transaction.

Gaiger, J. (2000). Schiller's theory of landscape depiction. *Journal of the History of Ideas, 61*(1), 115–132.

Goethe, J. W. (1962). *Italian journey (1786–1788)*. London, England: Penguin.

Gurevich, M., Vasilovsky, A. T., Brown-Bowers, A., & Cosma, S. (2015). Affective conjunctions: Social norms, semiotic circuits, and fantasy. *Theory & Psychology, 25*(4), 513–540.

Hartmann, G. W. (1935). *Gestalt psychology: A survey of facts and principles.* Westport, CT: Greenwood Press.

Ingold, T. (2016). The maze and the labyrinth. In E. Schraube & C. Højholt (Eds.), *Psychology and the conduct of everyday life* (pp. 99–110). Hove, E-Sussex, England: Routledge.

Innis, R. E. (2012). Signs of feeling: Susanne Langer's aesthetic model of minding. *American Journal of Semiotics, 28*(1/2), 43–61.

Janson, A., & Lagerkvist, A. (2009). The future gaze: City panoramas as politico-emotive geographies. *Journal of Visual Culture, 8*(1), 25–53.

Katz D. (1950). *Gestalt psychology: Its nature and significance.* New York, NY: Ronald Press.

Koffa, K. (1935). *Principles of Gestalt psychology.* London, England: Routledge & Kegan Paul.

Macdonald, S. (2006). Words in stone: Agency and identity in a Nazi landscape. *Journal of Material Culture, 11*(1/2), 105–126.

Mitchell, T. (1984). Caspar David Friedrich's Der Watzmann: German romantic landscape painting and historical geology. *The Art Bulletin, 66*(3), 452–464.

Mitchell, T. (1989). Johann Christian Reinhardt and the transformation of heroic landscape, 1790–1800. *The Art Bulletin, 71*(4), 646–659.

Nedergaard, J. I., Valsiner, J., & Marsico, G. (2015). "I am not that kind of …": Personal relating with social borders. In B. Wagoner, N. Chaudhary & P. Hviid (Eds.), *Integrating experiences: Body and mind moving between contexts* (pp. 245–263). Charlotte, NC: Information Age.

Reiter, C., & Schröder, K. A. (Eds.). (2015). *Welten der Romantik.* Wien, Germany: Albertina.

Salvatore, S. (2015). *Psychology in black and white.* Charlotte, NC: Information Age.

Scholl, C. (2015). *Caspar David Friedrich und seine Zeit.* Leipzig, Germany: Seemann.

Smedslund, J. (2016). Why psychology cannot be an empirical science. *IPBS: Integrative Psychological & Behavioral Science, 50*(2). doi:10.1007/s12124-015-9339-x

Smith, B. (1999). Truth and the visual field. In J. Petitot, F. J. Varela, R. Pachoud, & J.-M. Roy (Eds.), *Naturalizing phenomenology* (pp. 317–329). Stanford, CA: Stanford University Press.

Stern, W. (1935). *Allgemeine Psychologie.* Den Haag, Germany: Martinus Nijhoff.

Tarasov, O. (2011). *Framing Russian art: From early icons to Malevich.* London, England: Reaktion Books.

Tuan, Y.-F. (1974). *Topophilia: A study of environmental perception, attitudes, and values.* New York, NY: Columbia University Press.

Toomela, A., & Valsiner, J. (Eds.). (2010). *Methodological thinking in psychology: 60 years gone astray?* Charlotte, NC: Information Age.

Valsiner, J. (1999). I create you to control me: A glimpse into basic processes of semiotic mediation. *Human Development, 42*, 26–30.

Valsiner, J. (2003). Sensuality and sense: Cultural construction of the human nature. *Human Affairs* (Bratislava),*13*, 151–162.

Valsiner, J. (Ed.) (2005). *Heinz Werner and developmental science*. New York, NY: Kluwer Scientific/Plenum.

Valsiner, J. (2006, June 12). *The overwhelming world: Functions of pleromatization in creating diversity in cultural and natural constructions*. Keynote lecture at the International School of Semiotic and Structural Studies, Imatra, Finland.

Valsiner, J. (2012). *A guided science: History of psychology in the mirror of its making*. New Brunswick, NJ: Transaction.

Valsiner, J. (2014). *An invitation to cultural psychology*. London, England: SAGE.

Valsiner, J. (2015). The place for synthesis: Vygotsky's analysis of affective generalization. *History of the Human Sciences, 28*(2), 93–102.

Valsiner, J., Marsico, G., Chaudhary, N., Sato, T., & Dazzani, V. (Eds.). (2015). *Psychology as the science of human being*. Cham, Switzerland: Springer.

Werner, H. (1948). *Comparative psychology of mental development*. New York, NY: International University Press.

Zittoun, T., Valsiner, J., Vedeler, D., Salgado, J., Gonçalves, M., & Ferring, D. (2013). Human development in the life course. *Melodies of living*. Cambridge, England: Cambridge University Press.

PART III

THEORETICAL APPROACHES AND DEVELOPMENT

CHAPTER 6

RUINS AND MEMORIALS

Imagining the Past Through Material Forms

Zachary Beckstead

Our modern landscapes are saturated with ruins of different varieties, from ancient buildings in Europe and Central and South America to modern-day cities like Detroit, Michigan. Some of these ruins are carefully preserved and maintained in the case of the former and stubbornly present in the case of the latter. Similar to memorials and monuments, ruins are clear illustrations of the way the past becomes objectified and populates our present and future worlds through our imagination. Georg Simmel's ideas about material relics, ruins, and ruination, in particular, provide an interesting starting point to look into the intimate connection between imagination and feelings. Much inspired by Goethe's *Naturphilosopie* tradition, Simmel discusses two cosmic tendencies: nature, which is related to brute matter and mechanical aspects of life, and spirit, which reaches upwards and reflects human striving. These dual tendencies interpenetrate and exist in sometimes discordant and occasionally harmonious relationship. With ruins, however, we see a separation of these forces and the eventual ascendance of nature or matter over spirit. According to Simmel, the aesthetic experience of encountering a ruin is affected by the materiality and composition of the ruin as well as its com-

The Psychology of Imagination: History, Theory, and New Research Horizons
pp. 123–136
123

plex temporality. This chapter investigates how Simmel was influenced by and adopted some of Goethe's notions embodied in his *Naturphilosopie* as well as the relationship between materiality, imagination, and feelings by drawing on current strands of thought in cultural material studies in sociology, anthropology and archeology.

Materializing the Past

The past and the present, the living and the dead, mingle together in complex and deeply felt ways. Past events, individuals, and communities may "intrude" into the present through the stories we retell and reconstruct for each other. These often repeated stories about the past orient our modern lives and present us with possibilities for preadapting to the future and becoming intertwined with our present beliefs and ritual activities. Likewise, the past might be objectified by "capturing" it through photos and videos or it may be represented through other media such as commemorations and memorials. The latter have become ubiquitous in our modern environments, from memorials of war to memorials recalling the persecution of "witches," and this memorializing impulse seems to have increased over the last century (Doss, 2010; Everett, 2002; Santino, 2006; Winter, 2006). Indeed, this proliferation of remembrance can be witnessed in academia and in the wider culture (Winter, 2006). Transforming our material environments to recollect and preserve the past for the future has become a common activity by not only states and nationalities, but also individuals who wish to honor and remember loved ones killed in tragedies such as auto or bicycle accidents (Beckstead, 2015; Santino, 2006).

Accordingly, the past, or at least its echoes, reverberates into the present. It is apparent and almost quotidian that only certain aspects of a past event or deceased person are retained and maintained for current purposes while other aspects of the past are forgotten in part or in total. Thus, the past is dynamically alive, revisited by every generation, and the act of selective preservation and restoration go together with forgetting and destruction. For example, some sites of tragedy, such as the World Trade Center in New York City, the Alfred P. Murrah federal building in Oklahoma City, or the location where John Lennon was murdered, become sites that are preserved and sanctified—set apart as places of deep veneration (Foote, 2007). On the other hand, the field where United Airlines Flight 93 crashed on September 11, 2001, in Pennsylvania has been largely neglected, at least in comparison to the attack sites in New York City and Washington, DC, and the house where John Wayne Gacy murdered and buried the bodies of his victims has been razed to the ground (e.g., Foote, 2007). The processes of remembering, renovating, memorializing, and forgetting unfold against the backdrop of human beings grappling with the significance of the past and its relevance for the present and future.

These material traces of the past in the present provide situated activity contexts for the development of the higher psychological functions—microgenetic changes become transformred into ontogenetic changes through situated and socially guided activities (Valsiner, 2007, Ch. 7). Through the internalization/externalization process, our moment-by-moment experiences at memorials become guided through the built-up environment and might lead to personal transformations, including an internalization or reorientation of values (Beckstead, 2012; Beckstead, Twose, Levesque-Gottlieb, & Rizzo, 2011). Critical to these processes, memorials and monuments also provide settings for the emergence of the imaginative faculties of human beings as individuals relating to and going beyond the here-and-now setting. Indeed, it is the nature of memorials and other material traces to evoke deep affect and to facilitate a sense of wonder, respect, peace, hope, and imagination (e.g., what may be) that lead to moving and occasionally personally transformative experiences (Beckstead, 2012). The capacity of a place connected with the past to evoke rich flights of the imagination can be observed in Gordon Mill's account of Werner Heisenberg and Neils Bohr's visit to the Kronberg Castle in Denmark.

> Isn't it strange how this castle changes as soon as one imagines that Hamlet lived here. As scientists we believe that a *castle consists only of stones*, and admire the way the architect put them together. The stone, the green roof with its patina, the wood carvings in the church, constitute the whole castle. *None of this should be changed by the fact Hamlet lived here, yet it is changed completely.* Suddenly the walls and the ramparts speak a different language. The courtyard becomes an entire world, *a dark corner reminds us of the darkness of the human soul*, we hear Hamlet's "To be or not to be." (Mills, 1976, emphasis added)

Bohr observes that, on the one hand, the castle is just a material object composed of stones but yet at the same time it is somehow saturated with meaning. Thus, the detached and objective mode of relating to the castle does not do justice to the lived experience of the castle. Furthermore, this experience illustrates the interplay of materiality, senses, and the imagination. Stories and objects—here a place that is anchored in the past, even if it is, in part, a fictional past—become fused and allow for an opening into imagined worlds. In other words, the story of Hamlet and the castle with its tangible, material characteristics interpenetrate and recursively feed into each other so that one is immersed in the particular settings, but one also goes beyond this setting as the past mingles and becomes unified in the present. Everything changes because it is Hamlet's castle (not in the ontological sense, of course), and thus I would argue that the materiality is not secondary but rather it is intrinsic to the experience of the visitors and how it links to the imagination. To put it differently, the natural world is not a neutral tableau upon which human beings project their emotions and imagination. Rather, the very materiality of what we commonly refer to as objects or things are intimately connected with the psychological functions such as fantasy and the imagination. The nonhuman realm of things and objects are therefore key but often neglected participants in the dramas of the psyche.

The critical role of the materiality of "things" in relation to inter- and intrapsychological functions has recently been explored by a diverse array of social scientists (e.g., Boivin, 2008; Fuhrer, 2004; Gonzalez-Ruibal, 2012; Ingold, 2004; Law, 1999; Olsen, 2003; Tilley, 2004). This trend has been referred to as "return to things" and a "turn to the nonhuman." While there is certainly diversity in this movement, two general goals have been to critique humanist and anthropocentric approaches to understanding human—object relationships—and faithfully follow the implications of the notion that things and objects "act and have a performative potential" (Domanska, 2006, p. 339). Drawing on Heidegger's distinction between an object (i.e., a material entity approached from a detached or present-at-hand mode of engagement) and a thing (i.e., a material entity approached from an intimate, ready-to-hand mode of engagement), these scholars have explored how things function as a site of gathering or conjoining of different elements or parts into a larger whole (Webmoor & Witmore, 2008). For example, eyeglasses gather together basic physical materials—ovens, fire, technologies and knowledge systems (i.e., optics)—and the transactions between these human and nonhuman actors. Eyeglasses reflect an accomplishment "which involved transactions between various entities and which occurred at a distance in space and linear time" and that become "folded into things" (Webmoor & Witmore, 2008, p. 65).

Objects or things, therefore, are said to have agency, an idea which is controversial and easy to misunderstand. What these scholars, like Bruno Latour, are positing is not that things have intentions and consciousness (Domanska, 2006; Latour, 2008), but rather that they have some capacity to enact, configure, and impose certain ways human beings relate to it and to each other. According to Gonzalez-Ruibal, we are material beings living in a material world and thus

> materiality is in a privileged position to regulate social and individual action. It promotes, inhibits, or sets the pace of certain actions and opera-

tional sequences.... A pot with a hand forces us to hold it in a particular way and throwing a spear involves a different bodily gesture than using a bow and arrow. A mosque imposes a bodily behavior and a mental attitude. Wearing a toga and wearing trousers preclude and allow different sets of actions and prescribe a different bodily hexis. (2012, p. 137)

While this approach toward things may be seen as a recent turn, some of the most salient ideas of this movement can be brought into dialogue with the much older ideas of Georg Simmel in order to further explore and illuminate the relationship between the materiality of things and the higher psychological functions of feelings and imagination. As I examine in what follows, Simmel's investigation into ruins offers social scientists and especially cultural psychology a fruitful approach for understanding how the imagination and feeling become integrated and how past, present, and future are unified through the material traces of the past.

Simmel and Goethe

Simmel's general philosophy and his analysis of ruins in particular reflect his engagement with the ideas of Goethe. As Cornejo (this volume) has illustrated, Goethe can be seen as a forerunner of modern cultural psychology who espoused a holistic and developmental approach to Nature. Thus, Goethe's *Naturphilosopie* was in direct contrast to the dominant deterministic and reductionist ideas and approaches flowing in the scientific stream of his day. For Goethe, nature was living, dynamic, changing, and made up of myriad parts interwoven together—a totality of poetic complexity—that was to be understood by not a passive and objective observer but rather a fully immersed and subjective observer. Goethe called for the work of the scientist to go beyond breaking down and analyzing the separate parts of Nature from our abstract and conceptual frameworks to recognizing relationships and therefore synthesizing the parts into a larger whole. Hence, our concepts and theoretical frameworks are derived and rooted in our lived experiences and so it is a living, feeling being that the scientist must gain access to this sensuous world through their intuitive capacities. Thus, the scientist must ground their approach through their very corporality and commitment or fidelity to the phenomenon. Yielding insight into the whole of Nature requires the totality or unity of the scientist—reason as well as their feeling and imaginative faculties—and anything that distances the scientist from Nature is to be eschewed (Cornejo, this volume).

Goethe's breakthrough in understanding of color is illustrative of this *Naturphilosopie*. First, his "discovery" of the laws of light came not from a laboratory but from his personal experience as he looked once more at a prism before returning it to a colleague who had lent it to him. His careful attention to the phenomenon and his dedication to his senses led to the realization that colors derived from the dynamic relationship between light and dark and that "colors ... do have effects on man's inner nature, those being sensorial, moral, and aesthetic" (Cornejo, this volume, p. x). Importantly, as it relates to Simmel's ideas, Goethe argued that the range of colors stemmed from their polarity and intensification. By polarity Goethe is positing that there is a state of attraction and repulsion between the active and passive properties of light and this tension can also be observed in other dualities (e.g., "We and the objects/Light and dark ... Spirit and matter/God and the world ... Sensuality and reason ... Being and yearning" (Cornejo, this volume, fn iii). Intensification, on the other hand, refers to an upward thrust and striving found in the whole of nature (e.g., the unfolding of a seed into a stem and then a leaf), including human beings. This striving is then held in an unceasing, oscillating tension. A commitment to understanding Nature as a whole and from a very interested and subjective orientation as well as an employment of Goethe's notions of polarity and intensification can be observed in Simmel's reflections on ruins.

Simmel and Ruins

Georg Simmel was influenced by and wrote extensively about Goethe in many of his works (e.g., Bleicher, 2007; Simmel, 2003). Like Goethe, one of the seminal events in Simmel's intellectual life was his visit to Italy and the ancient city of Rome (Simmel, 2007, p. 30). Many of the themes discussed in Simmel's reflections of Rome (i.e., beauty, unity, wholeness, and multiplicity) can be observed in his analysis of ruins—Simmel uses some of the ruins in Rome in his paper to elucidate his thoughts (see below). Broadly speaking, Simmel situates his exploration of ruins against the backdrop of two cosmic tendencies in the universe. Echoing Goethe's ideas about polarity and intensification, Simmel posits that there is the upward striving of the spirit and downward pull of nature and that these cosmic tendencies or laws are universal to all of nature, of which human beings are part. Spirit and matter, spirit and nature, upward striving and downward pulling, creation and destruction, activity and passivity, and other dualities or polarities operate in tense, oscillating relationship to each other and their existence and movement can be found regulating both human life and the natural world.[1]

Simmel eloquently describes ruins as buildings in decay and slow dissolution and as manifestations of the coexistence between the striving, upward lifting spirit and the resisting, necessary material of nature. Buildings draw on the materiality of the natural world in the service of the will and human intentions and goals. Thus, buildings are constructed for particular purposes—shelter, organizing home life, conducting business activities, leisure, religious practices and rituals, and much more. The form of the building has particular meanings, functional and aesthetic, and they emerge out of the striving spirit looking to impose its will and transcend the environment. This harmonious relationship between spirit and nature collapses as the building is abandoned and intentionally left to decay. As this occurs, the relationship of spirit over nature reverses as nature reasserts her primordial dominance. As the abandoned building starts to decay, it "destroys the unity of form, nature and spirit separate again and reveal their world-pervading enmity" (Simmel, 1958, p. 379–380). Furthermore, as decay sets in, the church[2] is no longer a place for a community of believers to visit, offer sacrifices, sing hymns, take communion or otherwise practice their religion. Yet there is a new meaning and object forged in this reversal—the ruin—with a new unity or constellation of parts emerging. In contrast to the purpose for which the building was created, the ruin is no longer an instrumental or purposive object but, according to Simmel, its new meaning is rooted "in that depth where human purposiveness and the working of non-conscious natural forces grow from their common root" (1958, p. 380). Of course ruins may become inhabited and used by various passers-by (e.g., travelers looking for temporary shelter, lovers searching for privacy) or those seeking more permanent refuge (e.g., the homeless). However, this use has the tendency to destroy the harmony between the conflicting tendencies of nature and spirit and strike us as unbearable and unsettling (Simmel, 1958, p. 381).

Simmel's analysis of our response to ruins bears the marks of Goethe's influence and discussion of wholeness, intuition, and the imagination. While Simmel distinguishes between nature and spirit and sets them in a relationship of tension and opposition, humans are striving beings that find nature not only externally but also within themselves. Additionally, not only do human beings strive to fulfill their inner propensities but so does nature. Thus "the whole history of mankind['s] ... mastery over nature" (Simmel, 1958, p. 379) is always tentative and never complete since the cosmic tendencies of spirit and nature, upward striving and necessity constitute a nonreducible unity, in spite of the illusion of human transcendence. Hence, when we encounter a ruin (or an alpine mountain whose form has been shaped by the upward thrust of volcanic eruptions and other elements leading to batter and shape it, per Simmel) it resonates with us:

In this form, we thus feel the vitality of those opposing tendencies—and instinctively sensing these antitheses in ourselves, we notice, beyond everything formal and aesthetic, the significance of the configuration in whose serene unity they have their synthesis. (Simmel, 1958, p. 381)

Here we can see that the ruin is not primarily a text to be read, decoded, and analyzed. Nor can we understand our response to ruins simply through the laws of association; instead, the ruin is immediately and intuitively understood through our senses and because of the resonance between the ruin and our human nature, which involves the tension between the upward striving of the soul and the downward pull of nature. Indeed, spirit and nature are parts of the larger whole that constitutes the human being and constantly mingling and interrelating. It is this dynamic interplay that, according to Simmel (1958), determines the "form of our soul" (p. 384). Yet the reversal of the order of spirit and nature (with nature taking the lead) embodied in a ruin reveals the limits and constraints of the spirit and the upward and incessant striving of human beings. While we continue to build, cultivate, develop, and master our worlds, these projects do not last forever and come to an end. Yet this situation should be viewed more than as a nihilistic cliché about the finitude of life. Explicitly borrowing from Goethe, Simmel refers to this reversal as a return to the "good mother" and the ruin becomes a liminal object, existing between the past and future. As Simmel expresses, "Between the not-yet and the no-longer lies an affirmation of the spirit whose path, it is true, now no longer ascends to its peak but, satiated by the peak's riches, descends to its home" (p. 382). The themes of "passivity," "noninstrumentality," and "unity" run throughout Simmel's analysis of the ruin. Therefore, a ruin is not a "thing" in the Heideggerian sense of something to be used (present-to-hand); instead, the significance of a ruin is largely to be found in its noninstrumental nature. Ruins then are a product of the destruction of human beings or nature, but ultimately it is the restraint of human beings, or the "positive passivity, whereby man makes himself an accomplice of nature" (p. 380). We can view the ruin as a liminal object, or perhaps alternatively, we can understand the ruin as a reminder (a sort of memorial) of our constant liminality (i.e., we are unfinished, constantly developing and living in-between past and future). Accordingly, ruins have the potential to briefly break our illusions of mastery and control (since it is not something to be used) and assumed separation from nature; both cosmic tendencies of "striving upward and the sinking downward" are brought together simultaneously in the ruin and seem to be working in harmony (p. 383). Illustrative of this point, the ruin becomes integrated into the surrounding environment—the ruin becomes inseparable from landscape (Hetzler, 1988, p. 54). This suggests that the meaning or meanings of a ruin cannot be found exclusively in the ruin, but instead in the relationship between the ruin and the person encountering the ruin. Nevertheless, the sensuous qualities and composition of the mirror are central to one's experience and the ethical-aesthetic effect the ruin evokes.

Materiality and the Ruin

Simmel's analysis of the ruin, while guided by an understanding of the cosmic tendencies of the universe and their interrelationship, is still rooted in the lived experience of the person encountering the ruin, the material aspects and composition of the ruin. Ruins are works of art and are experienced with the whole of human senses. In short, the material qualities and the ruin as an organized whole are primary instead of secondary characteristics of how the ruin is experienced. As Simmel elaborates, there must be a balance between the two poles of the universe (i.e., cosmic tendencies) and this is expressed, in part, through the way these are materially manifested.

> The aesthetic value of the ruin combines the disharmony, the eternal becoming of the soul struggling against itself, with the satisfaction of form, the firm limitedness, of the work of art. For this reason, the metaphysical-aesthetic charm of the ruin disappears when *not enough remains of it to let us feel the upward-leading tendency*. The *stump of the pillars of the Forum Romanum are simply ugly and nothing else, while a pillar crumbled—say, halfway down—can generate a maximum of charm.* (Simmel, 1958, p. 384, emphasis added)

Through this interplay of striving and eternal becoming and downward limitedness of embodied in the composition of the abandoned building there is an intensification of affect and aesthetic value. Moreover, ruins are not objects that are distinct and ultimately detached from their environment, like any human-made building, and therefore must be appreciated in their relationship to their surroundings. Through the work of the natural forces or elements such as rain and sun and the growth of plants surrounding the ruin, the ruin becomes integrated into the surroundings as it takes on the appearance of the natural environment. The contrast between spirit embodied in a man-made edifice and nature meld into a "peaceful unity of belonging" (Simmel, 1958, p. 383). Thus, the boundary between ruin and nonruin, human-made and nature is irrevocably blurred. Drawing on the example of the castle of Siegfried de Rachewiltz in Italy, Hetzler notes that the ruin extends beyond the castle to include the clouds, the animals grazing, the work of the farmers in the field, and even the path and walk up to the castle (Hetzler, 1988, p. 52). Thus, the ruin is a material object that unites and holds in relationship the cosmic tendencies of the universe, transformed by nature and the positive passivity of humankind and therefore uniting with the surrounding environment. As Hetzler comments, ruins cannot be moved to another location since their very essence depends on its surroundings. Ruins are thus objects that reflect, manifest, and conjoin a sense of wholeness between nature and spirit, aesthetic and ethical, and inner and external realms. Borrowing on the Heidegerrian notion, as discussed above, ruins can be considered objects that gather together seemingly disparate elements in relationship to each other. In this sense, we need to consider the temporality of ruins and how they are relics of the past that are part of our present and immediate future.

Ruin Temporality

Ruins are objects that provoke fascination and heightened affect because they exist in the present but belong to a time period that has come and gone. An ancient column, abandoned house, or decaying building connect and gather together different aspects of the past: that of natural elements (e.g., rain, snow, wind, etc.), human knowledge and value systems (e.g., art and science), and technology (Hetzler 1988, p. 51). Indeed, ruins have what Hetzler describes as ruin time. Ruin time includes the span of history when the ruin was first built to the beginning of its decay and also includes the vegetation, animals, and insects in the environment; the cosmological time of the stars, sun, and moon; as well as the subjective time of the person who visits and encounters (i.e., what time of day they visit) (Hetzler, 1988). All of these factors are gathered together in the ruin's materiality—tangible and intangible traces or indices of the past constitute the ruin as an object manifesting the past as irrevocably past. Yet the ruin stands and exists in the here-and-now. Simmel observes that the ruin

> is the site of life from which life has departed.... In the case of the ruin, the fact that life with its wealth and its changes once dwelled here constitutes an *immediately perceived presence*. The ruin creates the present form of a past life, not according to the contents or remnants of that life, but according to its past as such (Simmel, 1958, pp. 384–385, emphasis added).

To emphasize once more, the ruin is not a text to be decoded by the perceiver but instead bears the marks of the past (indexical signs) and is similar to the form that once stood (iconic sign). Unlike a model of a past village, for example, the past in its specificity is not re-created or represented; but rather there is a general sense of the past that is invoked and immediately perceived. We might even be able to claim that the generality of the past that is evoked allows for the play of the imagination—the past is present and it guides, constrains, but leaves room for the individual to be affectively drawn into the setting in the here-and-now and to go beyond it and to imagine what life was like for those who lived, worked, loved in, around, or near the building that has become a ruin.

Interestingly, Simmel draws the analogy between the ruin and an antique or relic. Antiques are common today, but we can image how prevalent antiques were during Simmel's lifetime as archeological digs uncovered the treasures of lost civilizations during the 18th, 19th, and early 20th centuries. For Simmel, questions of authenticity of an artifact, which preoccupy so many, are not of central importance. Whether the antique is "real" or is only a "copy" of the original artifact is insignificant to our experience of it since we have at our fingertips the entire history of the artifact as "the past with its destinies and transformations has been gathered into this instant of an aesthetically perceptible present" (Simmel, 1958, p. 385). Like the ruin, the antique is a sensuous object that presents us with the past. However, with the ruin we can imagine that in the not-so-distant future the building will be completely decayed and effaced as it continues in its destined course. Not only are the contrasts of past and present fused together, but past, present, and future become united and the relationship between the object and the "energies of our soul" that are brought to the encounter of the ruin or antique dissolve any distinction between perception and thought— "psychic wholeness is at work in this encounter" (Simmel, 1958, p. 385).

CONCLUSION: RUINS AS STRANGE AND FAMILIAR

Simmel was deeply inspired by Goethe's philosophy, and we can trace this influence by examining his ruminations on ruins. Ruins continue to be sites of fascination and places that provoke heightened affective responses. On the one hand, they bear and gather together the traces of the past. Yet ruins simultaneously belong to the past, present, and future. It is an object in transition, a quintessential liminal object that blurs the boundaries human beings construct to separate temporal periods and also objects from their surroundings. The ruin emerges out of a multiplicity of contradictory forms, elements, and cosmic tendencies. Ruins evoke this strong feeling in human beings because they, on the one hand, are strange and reflect an encounter with otherness. Yet there is also a sense of familiarity since there is a resonance between the person who encounters the ruin and the ruin itself—ruins and humans have much more in common than we (the person encountering the ruin) might suppose at first reflection; each consists of a constellation of spirit and nature in dynamic, oscillating tension. Ruins manifest a particular configuration of this constellation, one in which there is a reversal of nature over spirit. Accordingly, ruins both interrupt, at least momentarily, our quest for dominance and transcendence and reveal the fundamental unity between human beings and their environment and nature. Thus, while buildings may be seen as the culmination of the spirit and will, ruins act to decenter human will and consciousness from their central positions. In this sense, ruins and the passivity involved in their emergence can be contrasted with memorials that serve to retrieve, establish, and create a static representation of the past. The existence of ruins is fundamentally tenuous and reminds us of the limits of our own existence.

Simmel's reflections on ruins also relate to and have implications for our understanding of feeling and imagination. Does the imagination "invest" the ruin with meaning, or do the ruin and its materiality spark the imagination? While often evoking a sense of nostalgia or sense of tragedy, ruins are also often perceived as beautiful (Hetzler, 1988), and Simmel viewed ruins as originating in our artistic impulses (1958, p. 379). Similar to our perceptions of ruins and the feelings they evoke (e.g., peacefulness), our perception and experience of beauty is rooted in the unity of thought and feeling or "psychic wholeness." Thus, speaking of beauty, Simmel posits that perceiving beauty is an act of grace.

> Perhaps the most profound appeal of beauty lies in the fact that beauty always takes the form of the elements that in themselves are indifferent and foreign to it, and that acquire their aesthetic value only from their proximity to one another. The particular word, colour fragment, building stone, or sound [Ton] are all lacking on their own. The essence of their beauty is what they form together, which envelops them like a gift that they do not deserve by themselves. Our perception of beauty as mysterious and gratuitous—something that reality actually cannot claim but must humbly accept as an act of grace—may be based on the aesthetic indifference to the world's atoms and elements in which the one is only beautiful in relation to the other, and vice versa, in such a way that beauty adheres to them together but not to any one of them individually. (Simmel, 2007, p. 31)

Imagination and fantasy, according to Goethe and Simmel, are human faculties that are always constituted through and anchored in our (bodily) experience with the world. As such, the material world is more than a prop for the imagination (a secondary element); rather, the material may often be considered as a necessary part of the process of imagining. Instead of viewing each as fundamentally separate and giving primacy either to our imagination or to our environments, it might be more beneficial to explore their interdependence. Thus, the question of whether ruins give rise to the imagination or are constituted by the imagination, or if it is the imaginative faculties of the person that organize the multiple elements into a whole or if the whole gives impetus to the imagination seems to be invalid and misleading. It is through our experience of ruins and through grace that psychic wholeness is enabled and all of the multiplicity of elements becomes unified, connected, and gathered together. We thus experience peace, longing, equanimity, resolution, hope, and other feelings, and we imagine what might be or may have been.

NOTES

1. While it might be tempting to view these dualities as Cartesian dichotomies that need to be rooted out, it is perhaps more helpful to make sense of these dualities as reflecting separate yet interdependent forces, tendencies, and movements. Here the notion of inclusive separation (Valsiner, 1998) may be helpful since it provides a way forward, beyond the problems of dualism and attempts to eradicate all boundaries (see Abbey, 2007). Instead, it allows for an analysis and synthesis of the parts of the whole.
2. The building has not yet been described as a church, so this is a bit sudden. Best reword somewhere along the line.

REFERENCES

Abbey, E. (2007). From dualism to duality: A cultural psychological approach to cognition. *Anthropological Psychology, 18,* 14–17.

Beckstead, Z. (2012). Value internalization on the move: The revivification of faith along the pilgrims' path. In A. Branco & J. Valsiner (Eds.), *Cultural psychology of human values* (pp. 87–112). Charlotte, NC: Information Age.

Beckstead, Z. (2015). Marking the past for the future: Roadside shrines and recursivity. In Z. Beckstead (Ed.), *Cultural psychology of recursivity* (pp. 219–239). Charlotte, NC: Information Age.

Beckstead, Z., Twose, G., Levesque-Gottlieb, E., & Rizzo, J. (2011). Collective remembering through the materiality and organization of war memorials. *Journal of Material Culture, 16,* 193–213.

Bleicher, J. (2007). From Kant to Goethe: Georg Simmel on the way to leben. *Theory, Culture & Society, 24*(6), 139–158. doi:10.1177/0263276407078716

Boivin, N. (2008). *Material cultures, material minds: The impact of things on human thought, society, and evolution.* Cambridge, England: Cambridge University Press.

Domanska, E. (2006). The material presence of the past. *History and Theory, 45,* 337–348.

Doss, E. (2010). *Memorial mania: Public feeling in America.* Chicago, IL: University of Chicago Press.

Everett, H. (2002). *Roadside crosses in contemporary memorial culture*. Denton, TX: University of North Texas Press.

Foote, K. E. (2007). *Shadowed ground: America's landscape and tragedy*. Austin, TX: University of Texas Press.

Fuhrer, U. (2004). *Cultivating minds: Identity as meaning-making practice*. London, England/ New York, NY: Routledge.

Gonzalez-Ruibal, A. (2012). Archeology and the study of material culture: Synergies with cultural psychology. In J. Valsiner (Ed.), *The Oxford handbook of culture and psychology* (pp. 132–162). New York, NY: Oxford University Press.

Hetzler, F. M. (1988). Causality: Ruin time and ruins. *Leonardo, 21*(1), 51–55.

Ingold, T. (2004). Culture on the ground: The world perceived through the feet. *Journal of Material Culture, 9*(3), 315–340.

Latour, B. (2008). *Reassembling the social: An introduction to actor-network theory.* New York, NY: Oxford University Press.

Law, J. (1999). After ANT: Complexity, naming and topology. In J. Law & J. Hassard (Eds.), *Actor network theory and after.* Oxford, England: Blackwell.

Mills, G. (1976). *Hamlet's castle: The study of literature as a social experience*. Austin, TX: University of Texas Press.

Olsen, B. (2003). Material culture after text: Re-membering things. *Norwegian Archeological Review, 2*(36), 87–104.

Santino, J. (2006). *Spontaneous shrines and the public memorialization of death*. Houndsmills, Basingstroke, Hampshire, England: Palgrave Macmillan.

Simmel, G. (1958). Two essays. *The Hudson Review, 11*(3), 371–385.

Simmel, G. (2003). Goethe. In O. Rammstedt (Ed.), Georg Simmel Gesamtausgabe (Vol. 10, pp. 2–270). Frankfurt, Germany: Suhrkamp.

Simmel, G. (2007). Rome. *Theory, Culture & Society, 24*, 30–37.

Tilley, C. (2004). *The materiality of stone: Explorations in landscape phenomenology*. Oxford, England: Berg.

Valsiner, J. (1998). *The guided mind*. Cambridge, MA: Harvard University Press.

Valsiner, J. (2007). *Culture in minds and societies: Foundations of cultural psychology*. New Delhi, India: Sage.

Webmoor, T., & Witmore, C. (2008). Things are us! A commentary on human/ thingsrelations under the banner of a 'social' archaeology. *Norwegian ArchaeologyReview, 41*(1), 1–18.

Winter, J. (2006). *Remembering war: The great war between historical memory and history in the twentieth century*. New Haven, CT: Yale University Press.

CHAPTER 7

FANTASY AND IMAGINATION

From Psychoanalysis to Cultural Psychology

Tania Zittoun

> The waters hissed, the waters rose,
> The Fisherman alongside,
> Quietly gazing at his rod,
> Cool at heart, inside.
> And as he listens, as he sits,
> The waters split and rise:
> Out of the flowing waters hiss
> A mermaid meets his eyes.
>
> —From the *Fisherman,* Goethe, 1778
> (Goethe, 2012, p. 105)[1]

THE FORGOTTEN PART OF PSYCHOLOGY

In his impressive historical chapter, Cornejo proposes to explore the major contributions to the study of fantasy before a new, modern psychology reduced it to mere reproductive imagination, losing much of the depth of the initial notion. Fantasy was forgotten by psychology, he

The Psychology of Imagination: History, Theory, and New Research Horizons
pp. 137–150
Copyright © 2017 by Information Age Publishing
137

argues, and left to other disciplines emerging at the 19th century, such as psychoanalysis and phenomenology. In Cornejo's reading, Goethe plays an important role, giving a full and new status to fantasy as part of his whole developmental reflection on light, aesthetics, and mind. In that frame, fantasy appears as a fundamental, embodied mode of experiencing the world and knowing through it: "fantasy represents the faculty to fully feel this world, that is, to see nature's inner relationships and not merely the superficial ones." (Cornejo, this volume). Cornejo also highlights Vico's contribution to the notion, which pursues a similar line, when he considered fantasy or imagination as the key capacity to accede to other people's lives, in distinct time and spaces, where the method of fantasy

> seeks its proofs not in the external world but *within the modifications of the mind of him who meditates it*. For, as we have said above, since this world of nations has certainly been made by men, it is within these modifications that its principles should have been sought. (Vico, 1725/1948, para. 374; emphasis added; as quoted in Cornejo, this volume)

Vico also encourages adults and educators to support imagination in children with the use of various symbolic resources; hence, imagination can complete their first learning of both things to be memorized and understood, so as to render them lively and meaningful (Vico, 2004; Zittoun, 2015b). Vico had not only a theory of the role of imagination in ontogenesis, he also saw it functioning in the microgenetic emergence of ideas, and at a sociogenetic level. There, he claimed, in ancient times, people's fear of the unknown forces of nature led them to imagine gods and creatures acting behind these; the universe thus populated with imagined creatures became much more familiar and understandable (Granatella, 2015; Vico, 1993). Culture, thus, is the result of the work of imagination rendering the world meaningful.

As Cornejo underlines, such understandings are lost after Kant's divisions between a productive and reproductive imagination, which will then be flattened out by later authors in forms of relatively passive functions of mind, with a rather great mistrust in psychology for a creative imagination—the latter being anyway considered as inaccessible scientifically (but see Tanggaard & Brinkman, in press; Zittoun, 2016).

It is to note that in current psychology, very few approaches have developed an understanding of an embodied, emotional imagination, binding experience and insight into a way to know into, or through, the world, partly because psychology in general has given little consideration to emotions and embodiment as part of understanding or development.

In what follows, I will first come back to some work that Cornejo considers outside of psychology but that, in my understanding, is still part of its attempt to understand human mind in society, that is, psychoanalysis. I then try to integrate the old intuitions highlighted by Cornejo in our current effort to develop a sociocultural and integrative model of imagination.

Fantasy and Imagination in Psychoanalysis

Psychoanalysis is a domain of investigation developed by Sigmund Freud (1865–1939) at the beginning of the 20th century. Trained as a medical doctor and neurologist, Freud found himself progressively dissatisfied with the existing theories able to explain a great number of patients' suffering. Called "hysterical," these persons seemed to fight with imaginary physical pain or be haunted by fears or forces blocking their intelligence or relation to the world in very selective ways. Freud progressively formulated a new model of psychic life, in which unconscious dynamics play a main role.

In very simplified terms, his idea was that human emotional and embodied experience needs, in order to come to consciousness, to be associated to traces of experiences which themselves can be linked to traces of words or socialized signs. Once semiotized, these can become part of the train of our consciousness. However, internalized social rules or unprocessed emotional experience can create barriers to such flow of consciousness, and thus some part of our experience simply never become part of our awareness. Intrinsic to the psychoanalytical enquiry is thus the idea that an important part of human experience, deeply emotional and embodied, is partly decoupled from the demands of reality (Freud, 1940, 1978).

Freud very early in his work used the German term *Phantasie* to designate this component of psychic experience, first in a sense close to the common sense, and from 1897 as a concept (Roudinesco & Plon, 2011, p. 432). In an 1897 letter to his friend Fliess, his main interlocutor in these years, Freud writes,

> Phantasies arise from an unconscious combination, in accordance with certain trends, of things experienced and heard. These trends are towards making inaccessible the memory from which the symptoms have emerged or might emerge. Phantasies are constructed by a process of amalgamation and distortion analogous to the decomposition of a chemical body which is compounded with another one. For the first sort of distortion consists in a falsification of memory by a process of fragmentation in which chronological relations in particular are neglected. (Chronological relations seem precisely to depend on the activity of the system of consciousness). A fragment of the visual scene is then joined up with a fragment of the auditory one and

made up into the phantasy, while the fragment left over is linked up with something else. In this way it is made impossible to trace up an earlier connection. (Freud, 1897/1966, p. 252)

Such initial theorization will then be expanded and refined in Freud's subsequent work. However, before going there, it is interesting to examine what relation such hypothesis has with Goethe's understanding of *Phantasie*.

Freud was a very well-read man, with a deep interest in literature and the arts. He was knowledgeable of Goethe's work both as a poet and as a theoretician. Goethe is often quoted and mentioned in Freud's writing, with different statuses and purposes. First, in his adolescent writings, Freud quotes Goethe in a letter to a friend to underline the need to be true to oneself, as a guidance toward self-knowledge (Bernat, 2009, p. 297). Many commentators will underline this role of internal mentor or guide that Freud finds in Goethe (e.g., Holt, 2013; Jaimes, 2014; Schneider, 1999). Second, as a consequence, Freud uses Goethe's writings to define an epistemological stance, a will to go beyond the obvious and look for hidden explanations, with the risk of making great yet risky discoveries. For instance, in one of his 1897 letters to Fliess, Freud interprets one of his dreams in the light of a poem by Goethe; the dream itself is about the wish to find the deep source of inspiration of his theory, as Goethe once did (Freud, 1966, p. 262). Reversely, he will mock his colleague Breuer's fear to go deep enough in the psyche of Anna O., only himself having the Faustian courage to do so (and hence founding psychoanalysis) (Personal communication, Freud-Zweig, February 6, 1932, as quoted in Bernat, 2009, p. 298). Third, Freud very often completes or underlines his thinking through examples taken from poets, including from Goethe. In the *Interpretation of Dreams* (Freud, 2001b), Freud adds three extracts of Goethe's poems as footnotes or in the text to his interpretation of his or other people's dreams; he mentions his interpretation of Shakespeare, as well as the origin of his inspiration.

Fourth, and more interestingly for us here, in his attempts to understand mind, creativity, and imagination, Freud mentions Goethe's creative process. Hence, as he is at the beginning of defining the modalities of work of the unconscious, and just after having defined *Phantasie* in 1897, in a further letter to Fliess Freud analyzes Goethe's creative process as a variation of the process of phantasy:

The mechanism of poetry [creative writing] is the same as that of hysterical phantasies. For his *Werther* Goethe combined something he had experienced (his love for Lotte Kästner) and something he had heard (the fate of young Jerusalem who died in his own hand). He was probably toying with the idea of killing himself and found a point of contact in that and identified himself with Jerusalem, to whom he lent a motive from his own love-story. By means of this phantasy he protected himself from the consequences of his experience. (Freud, 1966, p. 256)

Hence, although it is beyond my role and my capacities here to explore how much Freud knew about Goethe's theory of phantasy itself, it is clear that Freud was deeply knowledgeable and an admirer of the man and his work. The search for a truer understanding of mind, the risk-taking attitude to make hypotheses about its deep unity and mysteries, as well as the developmental posture of Freud can be seen as pursuing a project that Freud saw exemplified in Goethe's work. In addition, man of his time, trained as scientist and not as poet, Freud has a deep pragmatist epistemology, which allowed him to constantly confront his speculations with empirical and clinical facts, and to revise these in the light of their explanatory and pragmatic power (Zittoun, 2015a).

This being said, Freud's investigation of what he initially called phantasy took many ways. His analysis of people's symptoms, of works of art, of his own life and dreams and of others' dreams allowed for the creation of a very complex model of psyche, accounting for the many ways by which thoughts are generated and transformed, blocked, and distorted. This led to two interdependent evolutions. On the one hand, Freud saw the origin of phantasy in very basic and early needs and drives, which he called sexual and are deeply rooted in early relationships, and connected to hunger, sensual pleasure, or intellectual curiosity. Depending on their satisfaction or repressions, these give rise in the infant to various basic unconscious phantasies about one's place in the world or the structure of relationships; these, to some extent, remain as organizers of the adult's psychic life. In Freud's work, the term *phantasy* came thus to designate the imaginary scenario at work in all layers of mind, more or less conscious, and which underline its various semiotic productions. On the other hand, the processes defined as resulting from Phantasy above will progressively be refined in Freud's analysis of dream. What was initially "amalgamation and distortion" will be more subtly analyzed in the basic processes of displacement, condensation, and figuration of various contents on diverse semiotic material (Freud, 2001a, 2001b; Zittoun & Gillespie, 2016). These processes of the "dream work" are the semiotic transformations that allow thoughts, embodied experiences, and emotions to take a semiotic form that one can become aware of, or socially shared. The same processes will be identified by Freud in dreams, daydreaming, and artistic and scientific creation (Freud, 1959).

Altogether, Freud tried to understand both the origin of phantasies and their effects. Although dreams, daydreaming, or human creations are not phantasies themselves, these are the expressions of deep underlying scenarios organizing people's lives—desires, longings, impossibilities (see also Laplanche & Pontalis, 1967, pp. 152–157). Yet as a whole, this constitutes the phantasmatic life, which confuses temporalities and causalities and allows people to feel the many layers of their lives as concatenation of all their past experiences buzzing in the background of the present.

Interestingly, and although there is no proof that Freud had actually read Vico (Verene, 1997, p. 502), their understanding of the role of imagination in human life and society have similarities as well. One can for instance quickly recall Freud's attempts to explain the creation of Gods and civilization, where inside fears and drives are the leading forces behind the projection of imaginary powers in the world (Freud, 1913).

Fantasy and Imagination After Freud

The term *Phantasie* had various fates in the psychoanalytical tradition, progressively losing its contact with Goethe's intuitions still present in Freud's work. For instance, one core debate in psychoanalysis, since Freud and after him, has been whether psychic life and more specifically neurosis and symptoms were only defined by phantasmatic scenarios, independently of any connection with true, real events experienced by people (for a short introduction, see Roudinesco & Plon, 2011, pp. 432–437). Depending on psychoanalytical schools' positions, more or less attention has thus been given to phantasies.

For instance, in the British school following Melanie Klein's work, infantile unconscious phantasies play a major role (Klein, 1975); these are quite clearly defined (it is about very basic instinctual moves) and distinguished from more conscious fantasizing. Hence, after this work, two terms have been defined: phantasy with *ph* to designate unconscious basic scenarios, and fantasy with *f* to designate a more general imagination involved in creativity and daydreaming (Segal, 1991). In the French tradition, Jacques Lacan's work took a different stance, defining a different role for fantasy, an organizing principle of mind, clearly distinct in its function from what he called the imaginary (a presemiotic range of experiences), itself distinct from the symbolic, understood as the range of experiences that come subsumed into language (e.g., Lacan, 1978).

More interestingly for contemporary cultural psychology, the independent British psychoanalyst Donald W. Winnicott proposed to distinguish three zones of experience: that of inner life (with its fantasmatic scenarios, unconscious life, emotional and embodied, etc.), the zone of contact with the real and its demands (social and material), and the zone of imagination, which is at the meeting of inner life and the real. Winnicott made a distinction between fantasizing which is self-enclosed, for instance as a form of rumination, and imagining, which occurs in such a contact zone. Imagination, according to him, occurs in the zone of cultural experiences, and it allows one to work through, or elaborate new psychic contents, which enriches human experience in a creative way (Colombi, 2010; Kuhn, 2013; Winnicott, 2001; Zittoun, 2013). In that sense, this rich experience, combining inner and outer life and adding to it in a novel way, is closer to Goethe's propositions than we could have expected.

Theorizing Imagination in Cultural Psychology Today

Imagination was once seen as a core, uniquely human faculty, part both of our ability to deeply experience our environment and our life with others, and to create our cultural environment. Part of this richness precisely was to be found in its emotional and embodied nature (Cornejo, this volume).

As recalled above, Carlos Cornejo suggests that the richness of the psychological study of fantasy was lost at the end of the 19th century. So far, we have seen how it has been addressed by psychoanalysis. In psychology at-large, for different reasons linked to the evolution of occidental thought and techniques, human and social science progressively reduced imagination to a poor version of reason, versatile if not dangerous. On the individual level, imagination was mainly considered and treated as acceptable as long as it was temporary, or linked to a state of exception or marginality, such as in children, artists, or the mentally ill. On the collective side, imagination has often been seen as the threatening power of irrationality, likely to bring crowds and societies to the worst abominations. As a consequence, imagination has often been reduced to a flat version of representation, a subpart of rational decision, or accepted when leading to socially recognized, that is, ultimately marketable, creativity (for an overview, see Zittoun & Gillespie, 2016). However, imagination has not totally disappeared from the project of a more general psychology. Independently from psychoanalysis, yet compatible with its attention to the semiotic, embodied, and emotional nature of imagination (Zittoun, 2011), cultural psychology is currently reexpanding the notion of imagination.

Cultural psychology has developed with a triple inspiration in the work of Vygotsky and other Russian authors, the American pragmatist traditions, and the rediscovery of the *Ganzheit* German tradition of psychology (Bruner, 1990; Cole, 1996; Diriwächter & Valsiner, 2008; Valsiner, 2012, 2014). From this triple anchorage, it has become a psychology which is deeply historical and developmental, aiming at understanding phenomena in the wholeness, which implies examining people's location and participation within a role of culture and with a focus on sense-making. These aspects make cultural psychology compatible not only with the project of psychoanalysis, but also with both Goethe's project (Cornejo, this volume) as well as Vico's visions of a new science (Brinkmann, 2015; Zittoun, 2015b).

More specifically, there has also been recently in cultural psychology a movement of rehabilitation of fantasy or imagination, anchored in these foundational authors, yet attentive to integrating other advances in psychology and the social sciences. Authors have thus drawn on Vygotsky's strong intuitions about the role of imagination (Vygotsky, 1931, 1933) and have expanded and actualized these ideas in the light of empirical material (Jovchelovitch, 2010; Pelaprat & Cole, 2011; Zittoun & Cerchia, 2013; Zittoun et al., 2013). This has led to theories of imagination which continue both Vico and Goethe's visions of imagination and fantasy (although this is not the term used in English) yet have also complemented them.

A first specificity of these approaches over previous works up to Kant is a shift from topological models to processual models. For Goethe, for instance, fantasy is a Faculty of mind. Other works in psychology (still) consider imagination as a part of the mind, a place in the brain, or a specific module. In contrast, cultural psychology conceives of imagination as a specific dynamic in the flow of an ongoing thinking stream.

More precisely, inspired by Vygotsky (1931, 1933), but also drawing on William James, Donald W. Winnicott, Georges H. Mead, as well as Freud's work, we have recently proposed an integrative model of imagination (Zittoun & Gillespie, 2016). Imagination for us designates a specific range of semiotic process, or a specific movement within the stream of consciousness. We have called it the "loop" of imagination.

> Imagination, we propose, is the process of creating experiences that escape the immediate setting, which allow exploring the past or future, present possibilities or even impossibilities. Imagination feeds on a wide range of experiences people have of, or through the cultural world, through diverse senses, now combined, organized and integrated in new forms. Imagination can either be more or less deliberate; it can be enjoyed in itself (such as in a daydream) or be part of a more deliberative process of creation. Imagination is a process, in the sense that it only exists in the making, which we call a looping dynamic. In other words, we are not interested in an abstract capability for imagination that exists independently of the real-time process of imagining, or in the stable outputs of imagination sometimes called "the imaginary." Imagination, we maintain, is a social and cultural process, because, although it is always individuals who imagine, the process of imagination is made possible by social and cultural artefacts, it can be socially allowed or constrained, and because the consequences of imagina-

tion can be significant changes in the social world. (Zittoun & Gillespie, 2016, p. 2)

In that sense, imagination includes experiences such as remembering yesterday's events, wondering how it would be to hike through the Gobi Desert, or planning the transformation of the road system into an electric one. Indeed, all these experiences demand the momentary abandonment (at least in one's dominant stream of thought) to explore (i.e., construct) another sphere of experience, distant in time or space, or simply not responding to the usual rules of social life, time, and causality.

Second, as many authors before us, we have attempted to distinguish the variety of shapes and outcomes of imagination. However, rather than theorizing different capacities, or senses, or zones of mind, we have proposed a vectorial model—a model of a 3-dimensional space, organized around dimensions that create an infinite space of possible occurrences (Zittoun, 2014; Zittoun & Gillespie, 2016, Ch. 3). We have proposed to organize this theoretical, vectorial space, along the dimensions of time, generalization, and plausibility. Hence, as intentional activity, imagination can have different temporal aboutnesses: imagining can be oriented toward the past of the imaginer, or the future, or some alternative present. Imagining can then be defined about specific events or occurrences, or in general terms. Finally, imagining can take shape or be about things that have some chances to become actual in a given sphere of experience, or that are highly unlikely to ever become true or be socially acknowledged. Visually, this means that the loop can be represented as a loop, or a bubble, leaning toward a temporal dimension, more or less flatly, or with more or less depth. For instance, imagining a fisherman meeting a mermaid, as Goethe does in his *Fisherman* poem, is oriented in a parallel present, both quite general and rather implausible (see Figure 7.1).

Note also that an important aspect of such a loop is precisely that it ends, bringing back the person to the here-and-now of a socially situated activity. Only this looping-out has now changed, even minimally, the person's experience, bringing relief, an aesthetical experience, or a good idea. Hence, imagining fishing in the shadow of trees along a mountain river on a very hot day, one can feel slightly cooled down.

Third, this looping model expands Goethe's idea, highlighted by Cornejo, of the emotional and experiential roots of imagination. In effect, according to our model, the movement of the loop is nourished by all available semiotic material, within or around the person, or available in her semiosphere. Hence, imagining mermaids demands drawing on specific symbolic resources—paintings or movies or stories about mermaids. Also, imagining fishing and meeting a mermaid demands drawing on much more personal experiences. Writing a poem about mermaids,

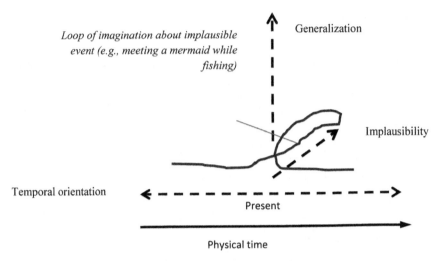

Figure 7.1.   Implausible imagining in a 3-dimensional space.

daydreaming or escaping from one's prison cell, one can imagine fishing. In all cases, imagining draws on one's embodied experiences, such as sitting still, smelling the water, hearing the flow of the water and the murmur of the leaves blowing in the wind, feeling the humidity and the sun on one's skin. These experiences are sensual, perceptual, embodied, and emotional. Yet, like any other, such experiences are likely to leave mnemonic traces, especially if they have become object of our attention. Then these can be, as any other semiotic resources, used to construct new experiences in the intimacy of our embodied mind, or shareable in a poem or in a painting. And these experiences are configured in new, unique ways, through processes that can be described using Freud's term *displacement*. As such, these can both use cultural resources or acquire a symbolic, sharable form, yet they also have a unique emotional and embodied resonance.

The fourth specificity of our understanding of imagination is specifically rooted in the sociocultural perspective. In effect, from such a view, any experience of imagining is, even the most private one, deeply sociocultural. Not only are some of the resources used to imagine usually cultural in their origin, such a stories about mermaids, the semiotic nature of imagining as well as the sociocultural location of that activity (like any other) make it inherently sociocultural. One implication of this is, for instance, that the development or shape of the loop is in effect seen as enabled and constrained by the semiotic material we have internalized, and by the actual condition of our living, symbolic as well as material. It is not the same to imagine a mermaid while writing a plausible conclusion for a school essay, to daydream in one's hammock on holidays, or to imagine while in jail so as to keep some sanity (Cohen & Taylor, 1992).

Altogether, this type of theorization thus pursues intuitions developed by Goethe and Vico, refines these analyses through the confrontation to empirical material, as done by psychoanalysis, and socializes them in the light of more social and cultural understanding of human experience. This allows then to develop an actionable model, that is, a model that allows us to account for conditions in which people cannot imagine, for instance, when they are taken in administrative or political relationships that do not fully acknowledge them, or reduce their access to resources (Marková, in press), or to create conditions for children to imagine better (e.g., Hilppö, Rajala, Zittoun, Kumpulainen, & Lipponen, 2016), or also, to better understand the conditions in which a society could face major crises (Wagoner, Jensen, & Oldmeadow, 2012; Zittoun & Gillespie, 2016, Ch. 7).

TO CONCLUDE: *A MERMAID MEETS HIS EYES …*

Fantasy and imagination are the mermaids of psychology—always hidden under the surface and ready to jump out of the flow. Like careful fishermen, most psychologists have avoided the apparent dangerous seduction of this figure of the depth. A few braver authors, poets, visionaries, as identified by Cornejo, or ambitious scientists and especially psychoanalysts, as recalled here, have tried to give a space, if not to capture, the range of phenomena designated by the terms fantasy and imagination.

More modestly, and thanks to the important work of authors in various fields, we can now look more carefully at this strange creature. By understanding imagination as individual and cultural process, we may perhaps find new ways to understand learning and development in the life course, and also, allow for the transformations of our societies' imaginative horizons (Crapanzano, 2004). In effect, although many irrationalities of our current world might be attributed to the dangerous powers of irrationality and fantasy, it needs perhaps even more individual and collective imagination to accompany the emergence of new societal pathways.

NOTE

1.   Trans. A. S. Kline (2004), http://www.poetryintranslation.com/PITBR/German/Goethepoems.htm

REFERENCES

Bernat, J. (2009). Freud et la 'fonction Goethe.'? *Revue Internationale de Philosophie*, *249*(3), 295–323.

Brinkmann, S. (2015). Imagining cultural psychology. *Culture and Psychology, 21*(2), 243–250.

Bruner, J. S. (1990). *Acts of meaning*. Cambridge, MA: Harvard University Press.

Cohen, S., & Taylor, L. (1992). *Escape attempts: The theory and practice of resistance to everyday life* London, England: Routledge. (Original work published 1976)

Cole, M. (1996). *Cultural psychology. A once and future discipline*. Cambridge, MA/ London, England: Belknap Press of Harvard University Press.

Colombi, L. (2010). The dual aspect of fantasy: Flight from reality or imaginative realm? Considerations and hypotheses from clinical psychoanalysis. *The International Journal of Psychoanalysis*, *91*(5), 1073–1091.

Crapanzano, V. (2004). *Imaginative horizons: An essay in literary-philosophical anthropology*. Chicago, IL/London, England: University of Chicago Press.

Diriwächter, R., & Valsiner, J. (Eds.). (2008). *Striving for the whole: Creating theoretical syntheses*. Somerset, NJ: Transaction.

Freud, S. (1913). *Totem and taboo and other works* (Vol. 13, J. Strachey, Ed.). London, England: Karnac Books.

Freud, S. (1940). *An outline of psychoanalysis* (New Ed). Penguin Classics.

Freud, S. (1959). Creative writers and day-dreaming. In J. Strachey (Ed.), *The Standard Edition of the Complete Psychological Works of Sigmund Freud* (Original German publication 1907, Vol. 9, pp. 141–154). London, England: Hogarth Press and the Institute of Psychoanalysis.

Freud, S. (1966). Extracts from the Fliess papers (1950 [1892–1899]). In J. Strachey (Ed.), *The standard edition of the complete psychological works of Sigmund Freud* (Vol. 1, pp. 172–280). London, England: Hogarth Press and the Institute of Psycho-analysis.

Freud, S. (1978). *Five lectures on psycho-analysis* (Reissue). New York, NY/London, England: Norton.

Freud, S. (2001a). On dreams. In *The complete psychological works of Sigmund Freud* (Vol. 5, New ed., pp. 631–714). London, England: Vintage Classics. (Original work published 1901)

Freud, S. (2001b). *The interpretation of dreams* (Vols. 4–5, New ed.). London, England: Vintage.

Goethe, J. W. V. (2012). *Poems of Goethe: A selection with introduction and notes by Ronald Gray* (R. Gray, Ed.). Cambridge, England: Cambridge University Press.

Granatella, M.-G. (2015). Imaginative universals and human cognition in the new science of Giambattista Vico. *Culture & Psychology, 21*(2), 185–206.

Hilppö, J., Rajala, A., Zittoun, T., Kumpulainen, K., & Lipponen, L. (2016). Interactive dynamics of imagination in a science classroom. *Frontline Learning Research*.

Holt, R. R. (2013). Freud's occupational choice and the unconscious: Reverberations of Goethe's 'on nature.' *The Psychoanalytic Review*, *100*(2), 239–266. Retrieved from http://doi.org/10.1521/prev.2013.100.2.239

Jaimes, J. J. R. (2014). Goethe y Freud: Confluencias. *Revista de Psicoanálisis, 72*, 201–223.

Jovchelovitch, S. (2010). The psychology of imagination and social development reflections from Rio's Favelas. *UNESCO.* Retrieved from http://www.psych.lse.ac.uk/undergroundsociabilities/pdf/presentations/Imagination-SocialDevelopment-Cambridge.pdf

Klein, M. (1975). *Envy and gratitude.* London, England: Hogarth Press and the Institute of Psycho-Analysi.

Kuhn, A. (Ed.). (2013). *Little madnesses: Winnicott, transitional phenomena and cultural experience.* London, England: Tauris.

Lacan, J. (1978). *Le moi dans la théorie de Freud et dans la technique de la psychanalyse, 1954-1955* (J.-A. Miller, Ed.). Paris, France: Editions du Seuil.

Laplanche, J., & Pontalis, J.-B. (1967). *Vocabulaire de la psychanalyse.* Paris: Presses Universitaires de France.

Marková, I. (in press). *The dialogical mind: Common sense and ethics.* Cambridge, England: Cambridge University Press.

Pelaprat, E., & Cole, M. (2011). 'Minding the gap': Imagination, creativity and human cognition. *Integrative Psychological and Behavioral Science, 45*, 397–418. Retrieved from http://doi.org/10.1007/s12124-011-9176-5

Roudinesco, E., & Plon, M. (2011). *Dictionnaire de la psychanalyse* (3rd ed.). Paris, France: Fayard. (Original work published 1997)

Schneider, M. (1999). Freud, lecteur et interprète de Goethe. *Revue Germanique Internationale, 12*, 243–256. Retrieved from http://doi.org/10.4000/rgi.758

Segal, H. (1991). *Dream, phantasy and art.* London, England: Routledge.

Tanggaard, L., & Brinkman, S. (in preparation). Imagination—Methodological implications. In T. Zittoun & V. P. Glaveanu (Eds.), *Oxford handbook of culture and imagination.* New York, NY: Oxford University Press.

Valsiner, J. (2012). *A guided science: History of psychology in the mirror of its making.* New Brunswick, NJ: Transaction.

Valsiner, J. (2014). *An invitation to cultural psychology.* London, England: Sage.

Verene, D. P. (1997). Freud's consulting room archaeology and Vico's principles of humanity: A communication. *British Journal of Psychotherapy, 13*(4), 499–505. Retrieved from http://doi.org/10.1111/j.1752-0118.1997.tb00335.x

Vico, G. (1993). *L'Antique sagesse de l'Italie (1710)* (B. Pinchard, Ed., J. Michelet, Trans.). Paris, France: Flammarion.

Vico, G. (2004). *Vie de Giambattista Vico écrite par lui-même (1728)* (D. Luglio, Ed., J. Michelet, Trans.). Paris, France: Allia.

Vygotsky, L. S. (1931). Imagination and creativity of the adolescent. Retrieved July 22, 2010, from http://www.cddc.vt.edu/marxists/archive/vygotsky/works/1931/adolescent/ch12.htm#s02

Vygotsky, L. S. (1933). Play and its role in the mental developmental of the child. Retrieved July 22, 2010, from http://www.cddc.vt.edu/marxists/archive/vygotsky/works/1933/play.htm

Wagoner, B., Jensen, E., & Oldmeadow, J. A. (Eds.). (2012). *Culture and social change: Transforming society through the power of ideas.* Charlotte, NC: Information Age.

Winnicott, D. W. (2001). *Playing and reality.* Philadelphia, PA/Sussex, England: Routledge.

Zittoun, T. (2011). Freud and cultural psychology. In S. Salvatore & T. Zittoun (Eds.), *Cultural psychology and psychoanalysis: Pathways to synthesis* (pp. 67–86). Charlotte, NC: Information Age.

Zittoun, T. (2013). On the use of a film: Cultural experiences as symbolic resources. In A. Kuhn (Ed.), *Little madnesses: Winnicott, transitional phenomena and cultural experience* (pp. 135–147). London, England: Tauris.

Zittoun, T. (2014, January–April). Three dimensions of dialogical movement. *New Ideas in Psychology, 32,* 99–106. Retrieved from http://doi.org/10.1016/j.newideapsych.2013.05.006

Zittoun, T. (2015a). Compatibility between early psychoanalysis and pragmatism. In P. J. Rosenbaum (Ed.), *Making our ideas clear: Pragmatism in psychoanalysis* (pp. 23–42). Charlotte, NC: Information Age.

Zittoun, T. (2015b). From Vico to the sociocultural imagination. *Culture & Psychology, 21*(2), 251–258. Retrieved from http://doi.org/10.1177/1354067X15575796

Zittoun, T. (2016). Studying 'higher mental functions': The example of imagination. In J. Valsiner, G. Marsico, N. Chaudhary, T. Sato, & Dazzani (Eds.), *Psychology as a science of human being: The Yokohama Manifesto* (Vol. 13). Cham, Switzerland: Springer.

Zittoun, T., & Cerchia, F. (2013). Imagination as expansion of experience. *Integrative Psychological and Behavioral Science, 47*(3), 305–324. Retrieved from http://doi.org/10.1007/s12124-013-9234-2

Zittoun, T., & Gillespie, A. (2016). *Imagination in human and cultural development.* London, England: Routledge.

Zittoun, T., Valsiner, J., Vedeler, D., Salgado, J., Gonçalves, M., & Ferring, D. (2013). *Human development in the lifecourse. Melodies of living.* Cambridge, England: Cambridge University Press.

CHAPTER 8

HOPE AS FANTASY

An Existential Phenomenology
of Hoping in Light of Parental Illness

Ditte Alexandra Winther-Lindqvist

> The development of a creative individual, one who strives
> for the future, is enabled by creative imagination
> embodied in the present.
>
> —Vygotsky (2004, p. 88)

In most psychological theorizing on fantasy and imagination, imagining is explained as the creative ability to form mental images, to bring to present that which is in fact not present, that is, not directly perceivable, not tangible, nor factual. Often the metaphor of drawing an image of one-self through mental construction and representation is at the center of description. The experiential status of the "imagined" and the relation between imagining and the real are ongoing discussions in theoretical psychology (Valsiner, 2014). The attempts to come to grips with both what imagination is, how fantasy and imagining relate to reality, and the functions that imagination serves for us, not to mention its process, many forms, and how these develop, is a quest in recent theorizing in cultural

The Psychology of Imagination: History, Theory, and New Research Horizons
pp. 151–173

psychology (Valsiner, 2014). This quest is reflected in the present volume, as well as elsewhere (Glåveanu, Gillespie, & Valsiner, 2015; Zittoun et al., 2013).

The theme of this chapter is hope as a reaction to parental somatic illness. In my analysis of teenagers, who are possibly or likely to lose a parent, their imagining often finds its form in hoping: Hoping for the doctors to be wrong, for the next treatment to be successful, hoping for a cure, for a miracle to occur, for more time, or in some cases hoping for death to come sooner than later. I recognize hope as a form of imaginative activity and practice, because hope is formed in light of an uncertain future, and rests upon imagined scenarios of what could be. Hope, like imagination, remembering, and many other central psychological phenomena, typically is theorized as a mental and private matter of the mind; however, aligned with a shared ambition among cultural psychologists, I aim to take hope out "of the head" and analyze it as a constructive process of situated and meaningful practice, motivated by a particular personal lifeworld (Wagoner, 2012, p. 1035).

In this chapter, I will analyze hope as fantasy and practice, and focus on its function for the one who hopes. I will provide an analysis and phenomenological description of hope as imaginative activity, spurred as a reaction to parental illness in teenagers. The empirical basis for this analysis is comprehensive interviews with 35 teenagers, who are asked about their current lives and concerns, hopes and challenges when living with a parent who is ill. I argue that fantasy (when involved in hope) is a meaning-making effort intrinsically interwoven with (changed by and itself changing) everyday life of the family. Such a way of analyzing hope as fantasy, makes it impossible to separate hope, that is, the hoping from the particularities of the hardships of living with parental illness as a teenager in all its varied circumstances. However, hoping (and the imagining involved), as well as serious illness has essential features that cut across the many individual differences. I will try to elucidate these through an analysis inspired by basic principles from cultural psychological ontology and secondarily congruent ideas in existential phenomenology: namely, that persons are intentional responsive agents who are future oriented, that life is a developmental process taking place in irreversible time, and that being is essentially always being-with-others in cultural historical practices (Cornejo, 2008, this volume; Heidegger, 2014; Merleau-Ponty, 2012; Valsiner, 1998; Vygotsky, 2004, 1998).

Taking Vygotsky's theory of imagination as a point of departure, I engage in a critical discussion of the recently suggested loop metaphor (Zittoun, this volume) in order to argue that imagination is such an intrinsic quality in a wide range of different phenomena, as well as an in-built feature in all meaning-making (including perceiving, knowing, feeling, believing, and experiencing) that we are in need of more than one meta-phor (i.e., the loop) for imagining. In order to avoid too much conceptual confusion, I will talk of imagination as the creative process proper (*Einbil-dungskraft*) and only deal with it in the form of its "products" in imagining and fantasy. When we imagine, we imagine something; what it is that a person is imagining is connected to that someone's current situation, con-cerns, interests, and projects. I will argue that hoping serves as a meaning horizon, a *gegenstand* (object against a background) for developing and maintaining practices and adjusting to the ongoing challenges that living with illness imposes on the families. Hoping is an imaginary backdrop, against which events and tasks, moods and impressions are experienced and evaluated, and thus the fantasies involved in hoping becomes consti-tutive for experiencing. I apply Vygotsky's experiential view of imaginary activities to the phenomenon of hope as a fantasy and a practice, with ref-erence to philosophical and anthropological insights into this issue. This is done in order to illustrate that hoping is a meaning-making effort that, in the event of illness, protects the hoper from despair.

On Imagination and Experience

In Vygotsky's theorizing, imagining is always based on prior experi-ence. This is his first developmental principle. However, for the purposes of this chapter, the second principle is an equally important point in Vygotsky's thinking: "If, in the first case, imagination is based on experi-ence, in the second case experience itself is based on imagination" (Vygotsky, 2004, p. 17). He explains this mutuality via the intimate rela-tions between emotion, mood, evaluation, and imagining. According to Vygotsky, our emotional state is influential in regard to which elements from reality are emphasized and recombined in associative transforma-tions. Imagining is an internal expression of our feelings: "determined from within by our mood, and not from without by the logic of the images themselves" (Vygotsky, 2004, p. 12). In that way, the whole state of being of a person colors his/her perception and experience of events going on. "Every construct of the imagination has an effect on our feelings, and if this construct does not in itself correspond to reality, nonetheless the feel-ings it evokes are real feelings, feelings a person truly experiences" (Vygotsky 2004, pp. 19–20). Vygotsky's thinking here is aligned with exis-tential phenomenologists like Heidegger and Merleau-Ponty. Heidegger (2014) regarded understanding as fundamentally related to mood, and Merleau-Ponty understood perceiving and imagining as a tightly woven fabric on a basis of faith or belief (Morley, 2003). We cannot therefore meaningfully make any clear separation between a literal and objective

experience of reality on the one hand and our ongoing imaginary tran-
formations of experience on the other. What we take to be factual is so
through our meaning-making efforts and thus implies that imagination is
constitutive to the reality of facts (Boesch, 2012, p. 353). This is also a fundamental insight in Carlos Cornejo's (this volume) pragmatist and phenomenological archaeology of the way fantasy has been theorized in
prescientific psychology, that is, as a faculty of knowing. Our moods and
interpretations of what we are in the midst of and where we think we are
heading are forming constituents of our experience of the now. Or as
Jaan Valsiner (2014) puts it, "We act in our real worlds (AS-IS) in ways that
are fuelled by the non-existing world of AS IF" (p. 296).

Imagining and Future-Orientation in the Present

Vygotsky argues that it is the creative activity of our imagination that
enables us to be future-oriented, explore the potentialities of what may
come, through a creative reworking of impressions and experiences in the
present (Vygotsky, 2004). Vygotsky regards imagination as a developmental achievement, which takes different forms of expression during ontogenesis and which increases both in scope and kind as a function of
expansion of lived experience. However, he makes the general assumption that play in childhood and fantasy in adolescence has the same origin
in unsatisfied desires (Vygotsky, 2004). In line with the idea of imaginative
activity as motivated, it serves as an active dynamic mechanism, in which
the "protective and wishful nature of imaginative activity operates so that
the individual transforms himself and recasts his relation to the world"
(Valsiner, 1998, p. 213, citing Stern, 1938, p. 330). As this quote reflects, I
am interested in the way in which imaginative activities, in this case hope,
play a part in how people steer their lives into the future, as well as how
they have their present world. Imagining can be more or less fantastical in
its relation to what is in fact experienced as realistic and rendered possible
to the best of our knowledge. Hope is a central phenomenon to study in
this regard as it is formed through a scenario of a future anticipated and
its contents range from far-fetched fantasies (i.e., a miracle) to much more
mundane imaginings of estimative probabilistic possibilities.

Experiencing As-Is, As-If, and What-If

Noting that imagination creates real feelings, feelings truly experienced, and that experiencing itself cannot be completely separated from
as-if and what-if transformations, is not the same as claiming that imag-

ined and actual experiences are identical. In fact, it is a crucial indicator of mental health that we can make distinctions between what we imagine and what we perceive as actually happening. We can bring ourselves to tears by imagining the loss of a loved one; however living through the actual loss, with all its countless and unanticipated implications in our social, emotional, relational, and material world is a very different story. "Imagining is like perceiving, but in the mode of in-actuality. When I imagine something … it is as if I perceive it, but not quite" (Jansen, 2013, p. 68). Here it is crucial whether imagining serves us presently (in solitary playing or wishful fantasizing for the excitement of it now), or if it serves us in anticipating a possible future event. It also makes a difference whether the imagined is shared among people or held privately. Jansen discusses imagining as it serves herself in the now, and she provides the example of herself imaginatively walking through a meadow in the summer, enjoying the sounds of birds and the sensation of grass beneath her feet (where she is in fact in her office and also knows that she is in the office). The qualitative difference between experiencing as-if and as-is is fundamental to uphold, If the imagined scenario was identical to the real thing, there would be no incitement to actually ever take a walk in the meadows if we had only done it once, because we might as well relive it in our imagination. Experiencing as-if has real qualities, but is far from identical to what's experienced as real. I think the case is different when imagining serves us with regard to anticipating possible future events, because here there is no reality to assess our imagining against; only further imagining is available to us, when it regards the not-yet-reality to which we are confronted more or less inevitably.

The principle of uncertainty of the next moment is countered by our efforts of stabilization, enabling us to imaginatively apprehend what is possibly going to happen in the future, involving as-if constructions created in dialogue with the perceived present events of what-is (Valsiner, 2007, p. 352). I suggest in activities like playing or wishful fantasizing we recognize its as-if qualities, and when we are aroused by the feelings evoked by these experiences we assess it in situ and in retrospect tell ourselves, It was just a nightmare, a wishful fantasy, or just part of the play. Such assessment with regard to something known and recognized is impossible to make toward possible future events, which Valsiner recognizes as a process of abduction, a concept suggested to describe the semiotically mediated transcendent quality of imagination (Valsiner, 1998, p. 245). When we imagine scenarios of possible future events, the imagined what-if and its accompanying experiences cannot be validated against anything but further imagining of experiences with yet new as-if qualities, and thus imagination becomes constitutive in a different way. When anticipating something possible, likely, or impossible, our imagining of it (as dreaded, desired, ambivalent, hopeful, or hopeless) becomes constitutive for how we experience what in fact is. I think this temporal structure is crucial to keep in mind when discussing the complex relation between the real and imaginary, as more or less separate or merged in our experiencing.

Critical Comments on the Metaphor of Imaginary Loops

Understanding imagination as an act of expansive distancing is prominent in recent cultural-psychological theorizing by Zittoun and colleagues (Zittoun & Cerchia, 2013), although not in an entirely consistent way (see e.g., Zittoun, this volume). Imagining or fantasizing is both described as an expansion of experiencing, a distancing from, an excursion from, and a disconnection from the ongoing flow of experiencing. "Imagination is a process unfolding in time: In a person's current apprehension of reality, something triggers imagination, imagination develops on its own, and eventually the person comes back to reality, usually having gained something from that excursion" (Zittoun & Cerchia, 2013, p. 313). This excursion is suggested to take place in imaginary loops. The imaginary process is illustrated as a loop, disconnected from the person's unfolding experience of the "real" world, a real world to which the person eventually returns, when back from the loop (Zittoun & Cerchia, 2013, p. 305). I find it hard to comprehend what is meant by imagination developing on its own but guess that it is the looping (as a disconnection) that the authors are referring to, and I find this idea of paralleling imagination as disconnected looping problematical for a number of reasons.

With reference to Vygotsky, imagining is the capacity to take distance from one's awareness of the unfolding reality. "From this perspective, the semiotic function, the capacity of using signs, allows humans to take distance from experience" (Zittoun & de Saint-Laurent, 2015, p. 60). I cannot find in Vygotsky's developmental theory on imagination, any justification for privileging distancing, or disconnection, when it comes to the experiencing of imagining. The way imagination serves us as a generic activity is that it broadens or deepens experiencing (Vygotsky, 2004, p. 22). He argues that the process of imagination is one of dissociation and disconnection, as well as association and reconnecting in a unified process of the altered elements. This could be recognized as a loop, but distancing, or dissociation, association, and reconnection is the prereflexive microprocess, below the level of awareness in Vygotsky's thinking. At an experiential level, imagination is a movement from one concrete toward a new concrete (Valsiner, 1998, p. 240; Vygotsky, 1998, p. 163). Even more importantly, I do not find the disconnecting looping to be a phenomenologically adequate description for a wide range of imaginative activities (like hoping). The person who hopes probably does not experience a disconnection from reality, a reality to which she returns when she's finished hoping. Rather, someone who hopes is in the world in ways altered by his/her hopes and has the world colored by his or her hoping. I should say the same holds for children in playing. Zittoun and colleagues (Zittoun & Cerchia, 2013, Zittoun & de Saint-Laurent, 2015) suggest the looping to be a general metaphor for exploring potential worlds, however I argue that it extrapolates a particular form of imaginary activity (something like daydreaming) to be indicative of imagination proper.

Critical Questions Regarding Time and Space in the Loop Model

Otherwise sympathetic with the project by Zittoun and colleagues, I am rather puzzled by the loop metaphor and its suggested embodied, temporal as well as spatial implications, even when only applied to cases of daydreaming. Zittoun and de Saint-Laurent (2015) propose seeing imagination as "loops by which the person disconnects from the on-going flow of experience and explores an alternative or potential world" (p. 62). Does exploration of alternative worlds entail a disconnection from the flow of experiencing? Or is it rather in itself a flow of experience, just with a possible (future) imagined scenario as center of awareness? According to Zittoun and de Saint-Laurent, imagination involves a looping away from the "real" world, to which the person then can return: "Finally, as a loop, it allows the person to come back to the 'real' starting points, yet changed by that imaginary episode" (p. 62). Or in Zittoun and Cerchia (2013), it is formulated that imagination creates loops out of the present, and a working hypothesis is suggested in which imagination is triggered "by a temporary disjunction or misfit, or rupture, between the given of one's experience of the world … and one's on-going flow of thinking" (p. 307). To these descriptions we may ask, what happens with embodied experience unfolding in time, while in the loop? Is there a split between experiencing the world and one's ongoing flow of thinking? What kind of time is there to return to when coming back from the loop? Can one put time on hold, loop out, and return to the same starting point? "Of course, in such a model, 'leaving' reality and coming back to it does not imply literally a change of space; we do not consider imagination as 'place'" (Zittoun & Cerchia, 2013, p. 313). But in leaving and coming back, looping and distancing are essentially temporal and spatial concepts, and one might ask of these descriptions, If the loop is not a "place," then how can we return from it? And from where do we loop (the unaltered objective reality?)?

The imaginary loop metaphor creates, I think, against its declared intentions, problems regarding the embodied temporal structures of existence as unfolding in irreversible time, as well as provides us with a blurred grip on the experiential qualities of the imagined, as a mental disconnection from the "real" embodied ongoing flow of experiencing.

A Focus on Lived Experience in Social Practice

I suggest that we are in need of more metaphors for imagination and fantasy than a disconnecting loop which starts, unfolds, and ends as a parallel event in time, at least when we are interested in lived experience. The dispute raised here only illustrates the difficulties in accounting for the complexities of the experiential status of the world as-is, and the world of as-if and what-if. This is an issue still unresolved, and one I doubt can be solved in a singular general model. Instead I suggest approaching imagining and fantasy as part of lived experience in cultural practices and activities, each practice calling for different theorizing of its many forms (playing, drawing, writing, daydreaming, wishing, hoping, remembering, falling in love, etc.) and each intrinsically connected to the involved persons concerns, desires, and situations at-large. In this particular case, I will explore the phenomenology of hope as a way of handling the hardships of living with parental illness as a teenager. I find that hope as imagining in fact enables the hoper to connect with and relate to the reality of the situation, which only highlights that imagining potentially serves us very broadly, and that there is no reason to privilege disconnection and distancing as experiential qualities of imagining. In addition, I argue that hoping, rather than running parallel to, becomes constitutive for how the hoper has the present, in the flow of experiencing. In line with the suggested strategy, hope is its own phenomenon requiring its own theorizing, to which we turn to now.

Things Could Be Different:
Hoping Practices in Light of Hostile Events

Hope becomes relevant whenever there is a realization of a potential possibility envisioned regarding the future (Steinbock, 2003, p. 17). This potential novelty is central, as there cannot be hope if one cannot imagine that things could be different from one's present situation or circumstance (Wentzer, 2015, p. 77). Hope is based on this openness of possibility in a future sense. Hope we ascribe to the welcomed scenario regarding some future state or event and thus hope is countering dread, fear, and anxiety (although on intimate terms with those at the same time, because hope is relevant when the hoped for end is uncertain in its realization). Steinbock (2003) describes hope as an engaged possibility, which transforms the experience of impossibility into a sustained practice with at least an implicit ground for what one hopes for. Hoping then, rather than a single (mental) act, is an ongoing practice unfolding in irreversible time, constitutive for how events, tasks, and situations are experienced, and thus crucial to how people prioritize in their daily affairs and carry out their daily activities. Hope then cannot be theorized independently of the perceived event or situation of possibility (that which could be different) and the emotional status of it.

In the case of parental illness—the new of the what-if possibilities is a hostile event—which is characterized by Wentzer (2015) as an event putting an end to some, or all of our agency, as its powers are beyond our control. An event which arrests our ideas of a future and one in which instead of being subjects we find ourselves subjected to our situation (Wentzer, 2015, p. 84). So when we hope in light of hostile events, we hope to minimize the impact of the expected as well as striving to minimize our actual dreading through a fantasy of what might happen otherwise. However, the relationship with agency is paradoxical in hope, including when we hope in light of some positive possibility. We hope when our own powers alone will not suffice (Steinbock, 2003). For example, when someone falls ill, the fate of the ill person is out of our hands, yet, despite bad prognostics and even despite an announced average living-dying interval, there is always the chance that in this particular case things could turn out otherwise. This chance for survival or cure, no matter how probable, is what hoping holds on to, and for some this hope is upheld to the very end. As Steinbock puts it, "When I live through the experience of hope I do not negate a current reality by positing a different reality, I implicitly acknowledge both the negative and positive possibilities, and live the hoped for event as sustainable" (2003, p. 15). The ambiguity in knowing is in-built in hope and particularly clear when hope is formed as response to an unpredictable illness. Its presence casts a shadow of nothingness into everyday life, because it is potentially lethal; however through hoping practices this threat is avoided, and in the act of avoidance there is a preconscious knowledge of its existence as well (Merleau-Ponty, 2012, p. 83). Hope enables living with many imagined scenarios for what is to come, also when these scenarios rest on illogical or inconsistent premises, exactly because hope is imaginative and transcending: it reaches beyond what's present and probable, through which the hoper gains belief, faith, and a sense of agency.

Hope and Agency

Imagining usually and in normal circumstances serves us well; however, as Kierkegaard (1963, pp. 88, 93–94) and Vygotsky (2004, p. 31) have pointed out, the protective and wishful nature of imagination has its dangers. These dangers are related to the constructive activity or agency as propelled or paralyzed by fantasies. This aspect also finds its version in the imagining involved in hope:

> Wishful hopers generate hopes that are fanciful insofar as they are not grounded in any real understanding of how they will be realized; they are simply the direct output of desires and undisciplined by knowledge of the world. Moreover, because wishful hopers have a high dependence on external powers for bringing their hopes about, this generates a kind of passivity with respect to invoking their own agency for realizing hoped-for ends: wishful hopers await their future goods; they do not constructively work toward them. (McGeer, 2004, p. 14)

This citation both points toward the dangers in fantasy as well as to the more general complex and paradoxical interplay between agency and hope: On the one hand "we hope in situations where our own agency is irrelevant to the occurrence of the hoped for end" and yet "hoping involves sustaining our investment despite a recognition of that what is hoped for may not be realized despite our best efforts" (McGeer, 2008, pp. 244–245). McGeer argues that hoping serves a regulative role in our psychic life and agency, exactly as a means for imaginatively exploring the constraints on our own and other's powers of agency (McGeer, 2008, p. 246). This exploring, I will argue, for the most part serves us well, and even when it does not, we seem to hope and imagine anyway. Regardless of what it is that we hope for, it affects how we experience the present (as more or less prosperous, critical, ambivalent, etc.), and therefore also for how we feel inclined to act. "Novelty is bound to a person's capacity to conceive of himself or herself in terms of open possibilities and active participation in life" (Wentzer, 2015, p. 84). The relation between agency and hope is thus a central concern. In the case presented below, hope propels a sense of agency, on a background of an otherwise powerless situation (where it is entirely out of one's hands). Although it may be on far-fetched grounds, that one finds agency in hope is the overarching role of preventing despair in the realization of a possible and likely permanent loss of the parent in death. On this basis we turn to the hoping as a practice of caring and exploration of one's powers to cope in the case of the hostile event of parental illness.

Modes of Hope

Hope is connected to wishing, willing, and knowing (Lynch, 1965). It may be highly unsustained by realistic assessment compared to the invested efforts (like in the wishful hoping person), nonetheless hoping is distinguishable from a wish exactly because it does not lose sight entirely with what is in fact possible, to the best of our knowledge. The philosopher Darren Webb has suggested analyzing hoping in three modes: (a) hoping resolutely, (b) hoping estimatively, and (c) hoping globally (Webb, 2007). These modes correspond well to the features of wishing, willing, and knowing as more or less prominent characteristics in each of the suggested modes of hoping.

1. **Resolute hoping** involves most extensive fantasizing and wishing, where what is hoped for overrides the probabilities of its realization, even to the extent of a counter-conviction on the verge of illusion (i.e., a firm disbelief in the doctor's opinion).

2. **Estimative hoping** relies heavily on knowing and cannot be maintained against what authorities (like medical opinions) predict and expect. Estimative hope then is a processual piecemeal kind of hope, which engages with quite concretely formulated expectations, probabilities, and risks (i.e., let us see what the next scan says).

3. **Global hoping** is more open-ended and relies mostly on willing and knowing, in its realistic outlook, with a faith in the good (i.e., no matter what happens we still have each other and are to spend our time well).

Most cases reflect all modes of hope at different times during the process of illness, closely connected to its developments (e.g., ups and downs) and how it reverberates into the family as a whole. Also, these modes of hope do not rule out one another, but on the contrary seem to fill in for each other so that when one hope ceases, another hoped-for-scenario takes its place and prominence, sometimes changing the mode of hope. For instance, an estimative hoping mode is eventually given up, because yet another treatment fails and thus survival through current treatments available is rendered unsustainable; instead of despairing completely, a more resolute hoping takes form, and what is hoped for instead is a miraculous new treatment and cure to be invented within time. Or a more global hope takes form where the illness is realized as a permanent companion, and death may be at the end of it, but that this life with the illness can be a good life too, and for as long as there is time, that time is to be spent well together.

Analyzing Case Material: Method and Aims

In the following I will provide an analysis of the case material consisting of 35 interviews with teenagers who are living with an ill parent at home. Interviews were conducted in 2008–2013 in the Danish Counselling and Research Centre for Grieving Children, Teens and Young Adults (DCRC). The interviews were carried out according to a semistructured guide, which among other things asked of ways of coping, experiencing the illness and evaluating its severity, analyzing resources, and mapping out current challenges, changes, and developments. There is no single way that illness affects a child's life and development, and no single way in which their hoping takes form and functions for them. However, through a careful phenomenological analysis of the material in its entirety, carried out in light of the principles provided by cultural psychology and insights from existential phenomenology, I shall provide generalizable trends into hope as fantasy and practice as central to lived experience. The general analysis of hope as fantasy in relation to parental illness as presented below is structured around how hope as a phenomenon is formed and experienced, and subsequently further substantiated by a particular case. Emily's case story illustrates how she in the process of losing her father, forms various hopes in practices of caring for the relationship, threatened by illness. It becomes apparent how hope draws on intensive imagining and fantasizing, which seems to function in ways that prevent her from despairing. Emily's case then substantiates the general claims in concrete ways: Returning to the initial discussion about the experiential status of imagination and its relation to the real, Emily's case serves to illustrate that imagining in the form of hoping is constitutive for how she experiences her situation, and that her hoping efforts is as much a way of connecting with and handling the illness situation as it is a way of getting away from it, or disconnecting from it. Also the case shows how hoping is lived as a practice of caring rather than a mental looping out of an otherwise unaltered real reality. However, let us begin with the general empirical analysis.

Describing Hope as Reaction to Parental Illness

Inspired by Martin Heidegger's analysis of fear in his *Being and Time* (2014, §30, p. 168), we can ask the same essential questions to the analysis of the phenomenon of hope in relation to parental illness: What is it that hope is facing? What is it to hope? And what is it that hope hopes for? I will answer these questions based on the general analysis of the interview material in order to unpack the structure of hope and its essence in order

to understand what hope enables from the point of view of lived experience as a teenager with an ill parent. I will try to purify these answers in
congruence with the ontological cornerstones in cultural psychological
theorizing of lived experience below and thereupon illustrate and solidify
their descriptive validity with reference to the case of Emily as a more in-
depth empirical example.

Hope is Faced With a Threat to What One Cares About[1]

When hope is achieved in relation to the hostile event of illness, it is
also formed by the essence of illness. Being next of kin to someone ill is in
its essence to be brought into the uncertainties of the potential loss, as
well as the uncertainties of the illness itself, that is, its duration, its potential impact on the parent and the family, and its outcome in surviving or
dying (Winther-Lindqvist, 2014). It is the ultimate threat of losing a parent to death and thus also losing the life of oneself as one knows it. However, to many, the nothingness of death is not the most prominent,
compared to all the changes in the parent's abilities to take part in activities and relationships as before, due to pains, exhaustion, depressed
moods, hospitalizations, and so on. In chronic conditions this is the most
prominent concern, and hoping relates to easing the pains or incapacities
of the parent. Hope is on intimate terms with despair, just as hope is the
foundation for hopelessness (i.e., when what is hoped for is experienced
as an impossibility, one cannot hope; Steinbock, 2003, p. 13).

What Is It to Hope?

The motivational structure for hope is care. To hope is to care for a
future. Only one who cares also hopes in the face of a threat toward that
which is cared for. H. Frankfurt (1988) suggests that it is a fundamental
quality of personhood to care and that people are inclined to invest themselves in matters (relationships, causes, projects) that they care about.
Care can be for the self (self-care), toward a particular other person (other
care), and toward the world (world care). All these forms of care are often
involved in teenagers' hoping, and often self-care is indistinguishable
from the care for the other.[2] Self-care and other care are complexly connected when it comes to our most intimate relationships. In those, the
other's misfortune or happiness is my concern to an extent where the we-
ness of our connection in effect is the only one relevant. As one informant
explains to us, "It is my mother who is sick, but we all have the illness."
Despite this prominent we-ness, it is meaningful to uphold a separation of
self-care and other care, as they are not always aligned and because they
can be internally contradictory. For instance, sometimes caring for the
other may result in a gradual annihilation of caring for oneself. That our
lives are future oriented means that our relationships are too; our rela-

tionships are based on an expected future together, because we are not only social but rather intertwined in living with our important others (Winther-Lindqvist, in press). I think that this is a defining character for intimate relationships, that they hold a promise of future together. When this future is threatened, like when a parent falls ill, that future (as so far taken for granted) becomes arrested and turned into a painful what-if-uncertainty (Winther-Lindqvist, in press). Caring is as much a practice between people, outplayed and materialized in encounters and gestures in shared life as it is an emotional connection (Mattingly, 2010). Hoping is thus not (only or primarily) a private imagining, but also sustained through interaction in the here-and-now (Mattingly, 2010). However, sometimes there is discongruence and disagreement between family members on what to hope for and then hoping can remain or become a private or secret matter. However, hoping is recognized as a practice of self-/other care when related to parental illness, which threatens a continuation of the relationship cared for.

What Is it That Hope Hopes For?

This question is quite indicative of how hope is experienced and the functions it serves psychologically for the person who hopes as it relates to the situation, which brings about hope in the first place. Hope hopes for a continuation of, or a new future for which one cares, in estimative, resolute or global modes. Hope looks different in each individual case, but often there is a hoping for the whole thing to be a mistake, or second best, for the illness to be cured. In cases of chronic conditions it is a hope for keeping the hardships of the condition at bay and minimizing its impact on the families and parent's freedom and ability to live as they desire. So what hope hopes for is entangled with the illness, its progression and prognosis, and how its severity is perceived, as well as with the caring relationship threatened. The caring qualities of the relationship colors what is hoped for, as well as reflects the areas of life that have changed or are made impossible due to the illness, such as going on a vacation, having friends over, talking about what's on your mind, turning the music up loud, not having to worry about the ill parent, not having to worry about the other parent or siblings, or just enjoying a light and joyful atmosphere at home. In some families, caring for one another is not the most prominent characteristic of the relationship. Sometimes the illness has driven family members apart and sometimes care was never a very prominent part of the relationships in the family. This determines what it is exactly that hope hopes for. Some teenagers hope for a situation where their parent in effect is out of the picture, one way or the other, and some even hope for the parent to die sooner than later, due to immense exhaustion, or in a few cases due to a deterioration of what they used to care for in their parent. In these cases, self-care is the most prominent form of care; growing old enough to move away from home and leave the family and the illness could then be what one hopes for. However and most often, self-care and other care are indistinguishable in the parent-child relationship when its continuation is threatened.

Hope as *Gegenstand* When Faced With Uncertainty

Although hope, and its counterpart in despair, plays a central role, somehow to all teenagers in the material, it is not so that they find themselves invested in hoping explicitly all the time. Rather their hopes create a form of resistance, or taking a stand against the threats of the illness. The hoping acts as a reaction to the hostile event and often painful state of affairs (the subsisting permanent loss as well as the parents suffering). The act of hope resists, or stands against, this risk of the parent dying from the illness, as well as makes the painful suffering of the parent a temporary matter. In this way we can regard the hoping effort as a functional *gegenstand* (Valsiner, 2014). The function I think of here is that the hoped-for scenario provides a temporary yet highly functional stand against the dreaded uncertain, by creating a distinct time frame and content to which one concerns him/herself (Let us see what the next scan says!). Through hoping, there is a slicing up of relevant temporal durations, and constraining of relevant aspects of the condition (the next scan) to pay attention to, in ways where hoping provides momentary time-outs from worrying intensely, in the midst of the uncertain (e.g., where we can feel that we are standing on a slope, gradually sliding, except when we get a hold of something to prevent us from falling further). Hope is structurally future oriented and thus uncertain, but not future oriented in endless indefinite terms; for example, let's see how things turn out when the next treatment starts, or when she/he has had the operation. Benchmarks, footholds or handles are added or fitted into the flow of events. In these ways the hoped-for scenarios serve the function of keeping the anxiety and despair of the finality of it all at bay, leaving room and space in mind to think of and also engage in other matters, while also at the same time gradually committing to and realizing its impact and prospects as well. Or one could say that it is through hope as *gegenstand* that a hopeful practice of everyday life becomes possible. Elsewhere I have argued that transitional states between incidents of what to hope for now are particularly vulnerable times for the teenager because the perplexity of what to hope for entails a barrier-breaking state that altogether brings to the forefront the despair of the ultimate dread of losing the parent anyway. This experience of the presence of the absent (nothingness) of the parent dying is what hope seems to keep at bay and prevent in its resolute and estimate forms (Winther-Lindqvist, in press). Only in global hope, hope is sustained, despite realizing that one is in fact losing the parent at some point anyway. Hope then is formed through enjoying qualities of the relationship, often on a day-by-day basis, choosing to do well with the time that is left. In any case of hope, the teenagers also are able to continue building a future for themselves despite the risk of losing the parent.

Further Analysis: Emily's Case

The particular case of Emily is chosen among the 35 interviews analyzed more generally above because it vividly illustrates all three modes of hope in Webb's terms and also shows the process of shifting and changing between hopes (not all cases display all modes of hope this clearly). The resolute hoping resonates with the ideas of fantasy as a gut-feeling way of knowing, and intuitive conviction and belief, which Carlos Cornejo's (this volume) description of Goethe's account suggests. I shall show what it looks like in Emily's case and try to depict its functions in a spectrum of ways. In this, as many other cases, the fantasy is formed on a basis of illusion, yet it still serves as a *gegenstand*, enabling a steering out of despair. Although presented through a single case, I aim at substantiating the general suggestions that imagining, when involved in hope, becomes constitutive for how one perceives and experiences the present, and that hoping as a practice of care, serves us in upholding a future to desire.

Emily's Resolute Hope

Emily, now aged 16, lives with her mother (and until recently an older sister). Her father was diagnosed with cancer when she was 10, just after the parents' divorce, where he moved to another town with a new partner. The doctors estimated that he would survive only 6 months so Emily's hope was faced with a death-threat, ruling out a continued future with her father, whom she cares so much for. Emily never believed in this death verdict and at the time of the interview her father has survived 6 years. So Emily's hope has also been faced with his continuous survival, which has sustained her resolute hoping efforts. Emily believed that her hope and conviction in his survival had a curative effect on his health, she says,

> I don't know how it started, but I thought I had done something wrong, for him to get ill, and I also thought that if I was good, he would get better ... Also, maybe as a child, it is so hard to believe in something you've just been told. I could not tell by looking at him. He did not look ill—what you see is easier to believe.

So Emily relies on her imaginary-real, as gut-feeling and simultaneously she makes a connection between her own actions to affect the course of the illness, an illness she also, at the same time, refuses to admit the existence of. Merleau-Ponty's (1968) point about the imaginary-real distinction as based fundamentally on belief or faith is quite striking here. In the beginning her hope indeed is a private one. Her hope is her own conviction about her father's strength and her caring for him, and her ability to keep him alive through her care and belief. However, hope is also a practice on her part, involving right-out refusal of engaging with the illness topic through talking about it, not crying over it (when her sister cries), and leaving the room whenever others keep on talking about it.

Emily's Estimative Hope

Emily gradually reaches a perplexed realization of the truth of the illness and over the years she also allows herself to engage in estimative hoping. However, in her case the estimative hoping alone cannot function as a *gegenstand*, as it is so confusing what to believe and hope for next. So she never entirely leaves her resolute hope, only she holds on to it in less rigid ways than in the beginning. She explains,

> It is just, no one knows. It makes it hard to believe. First of all because I protect myself from the evil, but second of all because then they promise something, or they don't promise, but they say what they believe, and then that turns out not to happen, but what I thought was true instead happens and then, even if I tell myself I don't have too high hopes for this next treatment, then I actually deep inside have these high hopes, although I will not admit to it, because I get so sad, when it turns out that this treatment fails too.

Her hope is tied to her own actions and she oscillates between guilt and confusion (when he worsens) and reassurance and faith (when he gains strength). Hoping is paradoxically risky and monitoring her mood and feelings toward her hopes is a hassle. In the last year her father has been increasingly marked by the illness: he is exhausted and also now looks very ill. Many of her statements regarding present time reflect that she knows he is in fact going to die from it eventually:

> It is hard, because in one way it is just another Monday, like in the past, but it is also a Monday in the progression of the illness process and that is hard … it is not just the illness, it is time itself that we are up against and even if we spent that time well, it'll run from us eventually … that is scary.

Emily's hope is faced with a lethal illness, which she gradually takes in as a reality that will eventually separate her from her father. In this time,

Emily is engaging in both estimative and resolute modes of hope so that when one estimative hoped-for end ceases, the resolute hope as conviction takes prominence and keeps her from paralysis and despair.

Emily's Global Hope

The contours of a global mode of hope are taking form in her narrative of their last year together, which is spent with her visiting as much as she can, but not entirely enough because her conduct of everyday life does not permit her seeing her father as often as she wishes. So she battles a constant bad conscience and doubt as to how she makes best use of her time and their time together. However, the global mode of hope, which is best described as a shared practice of caring for one another, shows in how they are with one another when together. Without extensive talking about his illness and his eventual dying from it, they try to keep their relationship intact and unpolluted by the situation, however on a backdrop of knowing that time is limited. This requires steering out of situations where his weakness becomes too apparent and yet in the same moment, exactly through the effort of avoiding it, admitting to its existence as well. Emily says,

> We have so little time together; we both know that ... it is not like a façade we put up, it is more like a sorting ... so that we have the best possible time together. He also does a lot to show that he is still the same; you know, he cracks jokes, he plays the guitar, we turn up the music loud and sing. So he protects me in that way, but whenever I disappear for a while, like I turn around to go down the stairs, then, without him noticing, I see him, and I can tell that he is tired. I think we look after one another in that way ... I also concentrate on making shortcuts for him, so that things are easier. I say, "You don't have to come up kissing me good night, I'll fall fast asleep you know." Then he doesn't have to climb the stairs and I don't have to see him catching for his breath, because I know he would do that for me. The things we always did, but that he doesn't have the strength for anymore. In fact, I think that when you have an ill parent, then there are many things you don't have to say. What's the use? It does not make him or me any happier. I think we both know this. I always end the day by saying: "See you tomorrow." It is like my insurance that he is indeed there in the morning, and it is for him to: "You know that we'll see each other in the morning, so don't go get worse or anything."

Emily and her father are reenacting their relationship by continuing to do the things that they used to enjoy and avoid direct confrontation with all those things that they are not able to repeat doing (like the father climbing the stairs to say goodnight). The limitations of the illness they put on hold when playing this game, which is hopefulness in action by pretending that things are not that bad. They take a rest together when in that game and thereby maintain and relive their relationship. However, the fact that he is dying is a constant signifier, the backdrop of these interactions and as such the presence of the absent (death) is embedded in it all. It is a situation of an ambiguous presence of the absent (Winther-Lindqvist, in press). This is quite similar to Merleau-Ponty's (2012, p. 83) point, when he discusses the phantom limb as loss, and describes a preconscious knowledge of it through attempts to avoid confrontations with it. Emily struggles to comprehend and grip the irreversibility of time—a time running out (no matter what she does), but also a time that has proven much longer than predicted and one she insists on spending well. This she connects to her hoping for his day-to-day survival ("See you tomorrow.") and thus she fills the gap of dread with her convictions of choosing right and monitoring her actions. Time spent right involves pretending that the illness is not what's central to their relationship, so that the illness is kept (effort-fully) momentarily out of the picture.

Emily's Perplexed Existence

Emily comments on her own story in the following way: "I don't know if you can tell, but every time I say one thing, I also say another thing." She is rather hyperreflexive and also suffers a lot from ambivalence and perplexity. She feels stressed and often finds herself in doubt regarding her decisions about how to prioritize it all. However, she does maintain her youth-life and practice of self-care by attending school, doing her homework, attending parties, seeing her friends and boyfriend, and so on, which is also other care as her father wishes explicitly for her to continue her own projects and enjoying herself. While attending to her doings, she however describes the illness as a shadow.

> It is a little mean, because you can try to flee your shadow, but it always follows you. It is there. But sometimes you don't see it, because it is behind you, but it always comes in front of you at some point during the day.

Again the ambiguous presence of the illness is there, also when it is not. And so she insists on keeping up a habit of writing him goodnight, every day, and makes sure to stay in touch. This balancing is exhaustive and the shadow of the illness, constrains her everyday life in various ways, as it sets a "mean" mood of an inescapable companion to what she otherwise does, feels up to, and thinks about. It also comes in conflict with how she regards life more generally: "I suppose I just think that you cannot always get to it all tomorrow, right? Then I prefer to get it done today." Emily's hope is thus an indistinguishable part of her perplexed existence on the verge of losing her father. It is intrinsic to how she acts in her world, how she has relationships, and how she perceives herself and experiences events, options, possibilities, and situations and how she prioritizes and steers her ways in these. She is in her world and has her world colored by the meaning horizon of her hope.

General Comments

Irreversible time is the inescapable enemy of intertwined lives, and teenagers like Emily seem to come to realize this particularly clearly when confronted with critical parental illness. What hope hopes for changes over the years, but mostly in ways where one hoped-for end is given up and a new one is formed and where one mode of hope takes primacy over another mode of hope, without entirely ruling out the other. In every case hope proves a *gegenstand* toward what is dreaded. What otherwise is an indefinite principally endless and multidirectional future of options and opportunities for the self in movement with others, the teenager's life world turns into one with quite a concrete path toward losing a parent at some point in the near (or more distant) future. This indefinite definiteness constrains the appreciation of the present, as well as the other possibilities floating in the dynamical system of imagined future possibilities. Emily, along with many other adolescents in the studied cases, has at times formed hopes which were mostly based on wishes in the form of fantasies (he cannot be ill in reality; or if I am only good, then nothing bad can happen). This hope is definitely on the verge of illusion. But the hoper still engages with whatever there is to know and also enters a more realistic yet confusing mess of estimative hope in the case of an unpredictable progressive illness process (Rolland, 1999). In any case, hope, even when it is illusive, seems to have helped these teenagers steer out of complete despair and has further helped them keep up self-care in their own activities regarding other spheres of their lives.

SUMMING UP

When imagining is involved in a phenomenon like hoping, it entails transformation of the entire attitude or meaning horizon for the hoper. Here perception of the real and the imagined merge in forming experience. This I suggest points back to the knowledge status of possible future events, because no one knows about the future (like we know about a daydream, a play episode, a fantasy, etc.). With regard to the future, we can only form beliefs about what happens. In some logical way, the future only subsists, as it is not yet here; however it is already here in how we experience our present situation, altered by our beliefs and faith in what awaits.

This simultaneity of protention and presence warns us against upholding a clear distinction between the real and imaginary (Morley, 2003). It also warns against dividing and privileging some reality from an imagined version that we can create in our minds, loop into, and return from. A phenomenological reading of Vygotsky's theory of imagination, inspired by existential phenomenological questions (what hope is facing, what hope is, and what hope hopes for) enables a concept of hoping as a meaning horizon which is an ongoing achievement, upheld by numerous practices and efforts in an everyday life with illness in the family. I am arguing that fantasy, in the case of hoping, is a way of in fact connecting with and getting into a current situation (rather than an act of distancing), which recasts the person's relation to the world. Hoping efforts provide a *gegenstand*, a settling upon a relevant time frame to which one concerns him/herself. All these efforts are maintained because the essence of hoping is caring for the future—in this case of a hostile event of illness, caring for a threatened, yet possible continuation of intertwined lives between a child and his/her ill parent. In that way hoping and its imaginings is rather a particular way of engaging with and connecting to a real-life situation, enabling a sense of agency amidst an ambiguous, uncontrollable, and unpredictable uncertainty.

ACKNOWLEDGMENTS

I thank the Danish Counseling and Research Center for Grieving Children, Teens and Young Adults (DCRC) for funding this research project on teenagers living with critical parental illness. I also thank my colleague and friend Allan Køster, for being a steady and stimulating partner of dialogue in the attempt at integrating existential phenomenology into my cultural psychological research and theorizing.

NOTES

1. Central to the concept of a person (as distinguishable from other agents), is that persons are respondents, who act in and interpret their world in terms of what matters to them (Taylor, 1985); or in Harry Frankfurt's words: What matters, is that of which we care about (Frankfurt, 1988).
2. World-care takes the form of a more general inclination, for making a difference to others (many wish to become doctors, scientists, or nurses in their adult life).

REFERENCES

Boesch, E. (2012). Culture: Result and condition of action. In J. Valsiner (Ed.), *The Oxford handbook of culture and psychology* (pp. 347–356). New York. NY: Oxford University Press.

Cornejo, C. (2008). Intersubjectivity as co-phenomenology: From the holism of meaning to the being-in-the-world-with others. *Integrative Psychological and Behavioral Science, 42*(2), 171–178.

Frankfurt, H. (1988). *The importance of what we care about. Philosophical essays*. Cambridge, England: Cambridge University Press.

Glâveanu, V., Gillespie, A. & Valsiner, J. (Eds.). (2015). *Rethinking creativity: Contributions from social and cultural psychology*. London, England: Routledge.

Heidegger, M. (2014). *Væren og Tid [Being & Time]*. Aarhus, Denmark: Klim.

Jansen, J. (2013). Imagination, embodiment and situatedness: Using Husserl to dispel (some) notions of off-line thinking. In R. T. Jensen & D. Moran (Eds.), *The phenomenology of embodied subjectivity* (pp. 63–83). New York, NY: Springer.

Kierkegaard, S. (1963). *Samlede værker*. Bind 15. Sygdommen til døden/collected works. Oslo, Norway: Gyldendal.

Lynch, W. (1965). *Images of hope—Imagination as healer of the hopeless*. Paris, France: University of Notre Dame Press

Mattingly, C. (2010). *The paradox of hope—Journeys through a clinical borderland*. Berkeley: University of California Press.

McGeer, V. (2004). The art of good hope. *Annals of the American Academy of Political and Social Science, 592*(1), 100–127.

McGeer, V. (2008). Trust, hope and empowerment. *Australasian Journal of Philosophy, 86*(2), 237–254.

Merleau-Ponty, M. (2012). *Phenomenology of perception*. New York, NY: Routledge.

Morley, J. (2003). The texture of the real: Merleau-Ponty, imagination and psychopathology. In J. Phillips & J. Morley (Eds.), *Imagination and pathologies* (pp. 93–108). Cambridge, MA: MIT Press.

Rolland, J. (1999). Parental illness and disability: A family systems framework. *Journal of Family Therapy, 21,* 242–266.

Steinbock, A. (2003) Hoping against hope. In C-F. Cheung, I. Chvatik, I. Copoeru, L. Embree, J. Iribarne, & H. R. Sepp (Eds.), *Essays in celebration of the founding of the organization of phenomenological organizations*. Retrieved from http://www.ipjp.org/images/e-books/OPO%20Essay%2023%20-%20 Hoping%20against%20Hope%20-%20By%20Anthony%20J.%20 Steinbock.pdf

Taylor, C. (1985). *Human agency and language—Philosophical papers* (Vol. 1). Cambridge, England: Cambridge University Press.

Valsiner, J. (1998). *The guided mind. A socio-genetic approach to personality*. Cambridge, MA: Harvard University Press.

Valsiner, J. (2007). Human development as migration: Striving towards the unknown. In L. M. Simão & J. Valsiner (Eds.), *Otherness in question: Labyrinths of the self* (pp. 349–378). Charlotte, NC: Information Age.

Valsiner, J. (2014). Functional reality of the quasi-real: Gegenstandstheorie and cultural psychology today. *Culture & Psychology, 20*(3), 285–307.

Vygotsky, L. (1998). *The collected works of L.S. Vygotsky* (Vol. 5). New York, NY: Plenum Press.

Vygotsky, L. (2004). Imagination and creativity in childhood. *Journal of Russian and East European Psychology, 42*(1), 7–97.

Wagoner, B. (2012). Culture in constructive remembering. In J. Valsiner (Ed.), *The Oxford handbook of culture and psychology* (pp. 1034–1056). New York, NY: Oxford University Press.

Webb, D. (2007). Modes of hoping. *History of the Human Sciences, 20*(3), 65–83.

Wentzer, T. (2015). The eternal recurrence of the new. In S. Liisberg, E. Pedersen, & A. Dalsgård (Eds.), *Anthropology & philosophy—Dialogues on trust and hope* (pp. 76–90). New York, NY: Berghahn Books.

Winther-Lindqvist, D. (2014). Uncertainty as organizing principle of action. Teenagers living with a critically ill parent. *Journal of Illness, Crisis, and Loss, 2*(22), 95–115.

Winther-Lindqvist, D. (in press). Time together—time apart: Nothingness and hope in teenagers. In J. Bang & D. Winther-Lindqvist (Eds.), *Nothingness: Philosophical insights in psychology*. Edison, NJ: Transaction.

Zittoun, T., & Cerchia, F. (2013). Imagination as expansion of experience. *Integrative Psychological and Behavioral Science, 47*(3), 305–324.

Zittoun, T., & de Saint-Laurent, C. (2015). Life-creativity: Imagining one's life. In V. Glâveanu, A. Gillespie, & J. Valsiner (Eds.), *Rethinking creativity: Contributions from social and cultural psychology* (pp. 58–76). New York, NY: Routledge.

Zittoun, T., Valsiner, J., Vedeler, D., Salgado, J., Goncalves, M., & Ferring, D. (2013). *Human development and the Life course: Melodies of living*. Cambridge, England: Cambridge University Press.

CHAPTER 9

FROM FANTASY AND IMAGINATION TO CREATIVITY

Toward "Psychology With Soul" and a "Psychology With Others"

Vlad Petre Glăveanu

> I no longer want to be anything except what who I am. Who what am I? My answer: I am the sum total of everything that went before me, of all I have been seen done, of everything done-to-me. I am everyone everything whose being-in-the-world affected was affected by mine. I am anything that happens after I've gone which would not have happened if I had not come. Nor am I particularly exceptional in this matter; each "I," every one of the now-six-hundred-million-plus of us, contains a similar multitude. I repeat for the last time: to understand me, you'll have to swallow a world.
>
> —Salman Rushdie, *Midnight's Children*

Rushdie's inspired remark applies both to the fate of a person or a nation as much as it does to that of a discipline or a concept. It resonates greatly as well with Goethe's own developmental and holistic perspective. And it

The Psychology of Imagination: History, Theory, and New Research Horizons
pp. 175–187

also reminds us of the great challenges of understanding someone or something in a truly contextual and historical manner.

Carlos Cornejo's (this volume) discussion of fantasy gives us a great example of how the challenge of contextualization can be dealt with in a very scholarly and thoughtful manner. He not only delves deep into history but also tries to reconstruct the world at the time, at least in its conceptual dimensions. Writing a cultural history of any psychological concept is a difficult task, particularly when this concept is "fantasy," and Cornejo is certainly able to stand up to the challenge. His reflections are important for cultural psychology as well as "the cultural psychology of creativity" (Glăveanu, 2010).

Creativity is an old/new area of interest for cultural psychologists (see Glăveanu, Gillespie, & Valsiner, 2014). It is a new concern because our community traditionally focused, as Cornejo's text vividly exemplifies, on the topic of fantasy and imagination rather than creativity, and for some good reasons. First of all, the concept of creativity itself is a much newer addition to our vocabulary (despite the fact that, of course, ideas about "creation" are very old). Second, this notion has been greatly appropriated by mainstream cognitive and nowadays neuropsychological approaches that conceive creativity and study it as a property of the person, of the mind, of cognition, personality and, not least, of the brain. Finally, creativity became today a very popular concept that we come across virtually everywhere: in educational debates about whether schools harm children's creativity, in organizations where creative leaders and employees are in high demand, in economic discourses about the GDP contribution of creative industries, and in politics where it is rhetorically used to argue for a nation's intrinsic resources. Rarely are any of the people producing such discourses able to define what they actually mean by creativity, contributing thus to the risk of turning it into an "empty signifier." The reasons above can, understandably, make cultural psychologists suspicious and reluctant to engage with creativity; on the other hand, each of these reasons should, in my view, motivate us even more to study creativity. A cultural psychological approach can make us aware of the fact that the debates we have today about creativity are not new and, in fact, emerge out of a long and complex cultural, social, and economic history. Cultural psychology can substantially contribute to socializing current conceptions of creativity, without losing sight of the individual, and also add a critical perspective to the social representation of creativity (not least by understanding it, among others, as a social representation).

There is yet another reason for which we should look more toward creativity and it has to do precisely with our regained interest in fantasy and imagination. For better or worse, as Cornejo demonstrates, fantasy and imagination are less popular concepts today than they were in Goethe's time. Many of their associated meanings have not been lost though, but transformed and integrated into the growing literature on creativity. This is why it makes a lot of sense to participate in this literature and contribute to it in ways that turn creativity from a purely psychological into a psychosocial and cultural phenomenon. Understanding the history of this concept and how it relates to older histories of intuition, fantasy, and imagination, is of key importance in this process. But so is bringing these histories to bear on modern and contemporary research, in this case, research on creativity.

My aim in this commentary is to do precisely this, picking up the historical analysis from where Cornejo ended it, "before the establishment of scientific psychology" and in particular the establishment and growth of a scientific psychology of creativity. In doing so, my general argument is twofold. On the one hand, I will argue that while it is certainly more than worthwhile to focus on cultural history and on recovering old meanings and theories, we should also keep in mind the fact that these meanings were then and are now a double-edged sword. In fact, a lot of the Romantic conception of what it means to create is still alive and well in the psychology of creativity but the consequences of this legacy are not always positive. Second, I want to point to the fact that a focus on the way great historical figures dealt with important dualisms should not prevent us from discovering that, in some cases, the same dualisms are much better dealt with at present than they were a few centuries ago. Of course, old and new solutions can and should be integrated. Cornejo argues, from the perspective of history and his focus on fantasy, that we should recover a "psychology with soul." From the standpoint of present-day creativity studies, I will add to this the pressing need to construct a "psychology with others."

"The Past Is a Foreign Country, They Do Things Differently There"

Hartley's witty remark applies well to the cultural history of fantasy proposed by Cornejo. His lead chapter also persuasively argues that this foreign country is well worth a visit. In this section I will raise three questions that I find important in light of this "invitation."

Why should we be concerned with how Goethe, Vico, or Nicholas of Cusa theorized intuition, fantasy, or imagination? Because their ideas, often forgotten, are nevertheless present, in many implicit ways, in how we do or understand things today. Cornejo makes the point that modern psychology displaced or transformed many of the old meanings and debates surrounding them. I agree that it does use much less some of the concepts above and, when it does, it narrows or changes their (historical) definition. Moreover, researchers nowadays show little interest in the history of these terms. But the universe of meanings they carried, including their relation to the senses, to experience, to the body, is not lost. Cornejo mentions in passing psychoanalysis and phenomenology; these are only two traditions that aim to recover this conceptual universe. Cultural psychology is certainly a third one. More recent developments within cognitive science and the philosophy of mind are equally starting to expand their view of human cognition from localized and intracranial, to distributed, embodied, embedded, and enacted (see Rowlands, 2010). This might seem like the same "country," but the way things were done (thought about) then and the way they are done (thought about) now can be very different indeed.

The second important question becomes then, Are we able to recover the older meaning of intuition, fantasy, and imagination and do justice to it in our present times? Of course we can access old texts and we can read and interpret them but in any interpretation we necessarily consider them from the perspective of the present. The risk of understanding the past in terms of modern values and concepts—presentism—is not to be dismissed here. This is something alluded to by Rushdie as well when we reminded us that, in order to understand a person, we need to swallow up a whole world. Cornejo's (this volume) discussion of fantasy aims to take this broader "world" into account. He writes,

> Words acquire their meanings only in a specific sentence; sentences in texts. In their turn, texts can only adequately be interpreted in the sociocultural context in which they are produced. A specific scientific term makes sense only within the entire language used by a discipline to approach its knowledge domain. Consequently, by following the historical course of a technical term such as *fantasy* we obtain not mere anecdotal facts, but valuable information on the implicit cosmological and anthropological models extant through the European societies where it was used.

These models made perfect sense in their historical context and, just as this context has been constantly changing, so did the meaning and value of intuition, fantasy, and imagination, including the relation between them. Cornejo's text refers to both continuities and shifts in meaning, which he makes great efforts to contextualize for us. We learn, for instance, that there is a clear trajectory linking Nicholas of Cusa's (1440/ 1990) conception of *intuitio* as a form of "wise ignorance"; Vico's (1744/ 1948) use of *fantasia*, often translated as imagination, and his revolt against rationalism; and later on, Goethe's (1810/1998) attempt to integrate the knowledge we gain from sensuality and fantasy with that of reason. But at the same time, there are also some deep differences in this history that spans several centuries. Take for instance the two big figures

framing the interval we are focusing on. Nicholas of Cusa separated intuition from imagination and defined the latter in rather narrow, representational terms (not unlike modern cognitive science), as the "chamber" in
the mind where the images produced by our senses are brought back to
life. Goethe, on the other hand, made of the integration between fantasy
or imagination and reason the very condition of any form of intuitive perception. In many ways, Goethe's project is closer to us, cultural psychologists, both conceptually and historically, a "foreign country" that is less
foreign than the mystical and theological approach of Nicholas of Cusa.
As historical times, with their social, economic, and political arrangement, change, so does the world of ideas. It is thus not surprising that two
centuries after Goethe we are in a different place still. The third key question is, Is this place better, worse, or just different?

   This is a rather difficult issue because it not only asks us to "swallow"
the whole world of the past, in Rushdie's terms, while being grounded in
the present, but also runs the risk of making the present more homoge-
neous than it is. Change is intrinsic to history and, in itself, it is neither
good nor bad. But change seen from the perspective of different people
and different communities does gain a clear moral value. This is what
Cornejo is keen to emphasize in his title, where he refers not only to cultural history but also a moral for cultural psychology. In his view, and jus-
tifiably so, the neglect of intuition, fantasy, and imagination in modern
times has negative consequences for our understanding of human beings
and their society. He also shows us this neglect was not the norm in centuries past. But if we are to play devil's advocate, we can argue that, in times
when discussions of intuition flourished, such as Nicholas de Cusa's
period, ideas about "wise ignorance" and the value of not knowing
served, in different ways, the church's ambitions to subjugate the masses
and bring them under its uncontested authority. Conversely, the Age of
Reason, for all its shortcomings, did open up new possibilities of thought
and action specific for modernity. I am not trying here to defend either
side but, in a manner specific for pragmatism, point to the fact that each
of these conceptions benefited some areas of our life while being profoundly damaging for others. In this sense, the past is neither better nor
worse than the present. They are both good and bad at the same time.
The important thing is to understand in which ways and, in order to do
this, I will take the example of creativity, arguably one of the main succes-
sors, in modern science, of intuition and fantasy.

The (Re)Birth of Creativity

   Scholarly interest for creative action, people, and outcomes predates
the word *creativity* itself in the Western world (see Glăveanu & Wagoner,

2016). The Latin verb *creare* meant bringing forth, making or producing, emphasizing the relation between creating and generating something new, an underlining feature of creativity up to this day. While Chaucer is credited by some with using the verb *create* as early as 1393 (Albert & Runco, 1999, p. 18), the noun *creativeness* was used in the English language by the end of the 18th century, preceding the noun *creativity* by almost a century (Mason, 2003, p. 10). In any case, creativity was not widely talked about until about 1950, when it also gained much of the positive value we attach to it as a hallmark "of our modern, secular, democratic, capitalistic society" (Weiner, 2000, p. 1). The psychological study of creativity intensified in fact after the first half of the last century and, since then, the scientific definition of this notion consistently included two dimensions: novelty/originality and utility/value.

The study of creativity, in psychology at least, has been dominated from its early beginning by the use of psychometrics. It was the development of creativity tests, mostly tests of divergent thinking in fact, that gave the pioneers of this field a chance to claim scientific credit for their work (Barron & Harrington, 1981; Guilford, 1950). Adopting a traditional approach—that of trying to differentiate constructs by actually differentiating their measurement—creativity researchers started first to analyze closely the correlations between intelligence and creativity (Meer & Stein, 1955). They were relieved to find, statistically, that intelligence and creativity are not the same thing. This opened a new class of questions about the relation between creativity and another important construct that, fortunately, had a long tradition of testing: personality.

Unsurprisingly, this line of research has consistently shown a strong correlation between creativity and openness to experience (less and less exciting if we look more closely at the similar way in which these constructs are operationalized). From the 70s until today, under the influence of the cognitive revolution in psychology, a new dominant stream of research emerged: creative cognition (Finke, Ward, & Smith, 1992). The emphasis was now placed on creative thinking, creative decision-making, and creative problem-solving. More recently, due to the development of new technologies for the study of neurological processes, old questions about creativity and the brain became popular once more (Fink & Benedek, 2014). Thus, by and large, it is reasonable to conclude that the psychology of creativity was and continues to be written in individualistic terms, prioritizing the study of intraindividual variables at the expense of more social and cultural understandings (Amabile, 1996). This conceptualization however is increasingly challenged today, something I will return to in the next section.

For now it suffices to say that Cornejo's (this volume) criticism about how scientific psychology abandoned or transformed historical concepts that challenged reason or intellect-based understandings of human beings seems to hold. Indeed, there is little talk today in the field about imagination and creativity (for a notable exception see Vygotsky, 1991, 2004), little less about fantasy or intuition, at least outside of a cognitive redefinition of these terms. However, the Romantic legacy still plays an enormous role in the creativity literature, underpinning many of its key lines of research. One of the obvious ones is the investigation of genius. Cornejo listed genius under the "forgotten words" of psychology but reality contradicts this claim. In fact, a new journal dedicated entirely to genius and creativity was recently launched (*Journal of Genius & Eminence*, edited by Mark Runco). Moreover, some of the classic texts in the psychology of creativity deal with understanding the exceptionality of the genius; we can think here about Gardner's celebrated book *Creating Minds* from 2011. While certainly interesting in its own right, this line of research often ends up glorifying the genius at the expense of everyday-life creativity. The Romantic ideal of the troubled artist and its focus on special qualities of perception and intuition, achieved or possessed only by a few, still dominates our imagination of what it means to be a (truly) creative person. Among its negative consequences we have a persistent image of disconnection between creators and their society, the idea that creative people often need to struggle in order to create, to fight the conformity of their peers and the conservative forces of their culture (Montuori & Purser, 1995). An elitist and essentialist account of creativity is thus set in place, one that is reflected, to this day, in the long-standing interest in the relation between creativity and pathology, among others.

This brief example illustrates the fact that old concerns that seem displaced today by an excessive focus on measurement and individual differences are not actually gone but transformed. Also, this transformation has both positive and negative consequences and we should be sensitive to both when considering the broader implications of old scholarship. This is not to say of course that Goethe himself directly contributed, through his writing, to the disconnection between creators and their environment. If anything, he advocated for personal engagement in knowing and understanding the world. His developmental and holistic approach is greatly needed today in the psychology of creativity as a counterbalance to the widespread use of static and disjointed categories such as person, process, product, and press (Rhodes, 1961; for a critique, see Glăveanu, 2013). Even studies of the creative process suffer in psychology from an excessive focus on stages and their segmentation rather than an understanding of creativity as an integrated, situated act (see for instance Wallas's, 1926, old but still popular typology of preparation, incubation, illumination, verification). In this regard, Goethe reminds us that

> if I look at the created object, inquire into its creation, and follow this pro-
> cess back as far as I can, I will find a series of steps. Since these are not actu-
> ally seen together before me, I must visualize them in my memory so that
> they form a certain ideal whole.... At first I will tend to think in terms of
> steps, but nature leaves no gaps, and thus, in the end, I will have to see this
> progression of uninterrupted activity as a whole. (Goethe, 1785/1998, p. 75)

Creativity in the making, creativity as a forward movement, creativity as the action of the whole person—these are just a few insights creativity scholars would gain from a close reading of Goethe. But this reading will not suffice if it takes us back only to the person of the creator and his/her perception and action. There is a second, crucial theoretical step to be made toward understanding creativity as a relational phenomenon, grounded in the dynamic between self and other. This concern has reemerged in creativity studies in the last 2 to 3 decades and it is this fea-ture that most radically sets apart old conceptions of intuition and fantasy from contemporary, sociocultural thinking about creativity.

Creativity and the Other

Despite the strong tradition of individualization referred to before, cre-ativity theory also benefited, in time, from the growing appeal it has for psychologists working in the social, organizational, and educational fields. What these applied domains brought to the fore was a profound dissatisfaction with a view of creativity as something that happens (pri-marily) inside the mind. The reality of creating is, in fact, that of people and groups collaborating with each other. This need to take other people into account was the basis for Amabile's (1996) social psychology of cre-ativity. Unfortunately, the largely experimental approach to the social constructed it in this case essentially as a set of external variables (e.g., surveillance, rewards, and punishments) that condition creativity (by act-ing on the intrinsic motivation of the creative person). Group creativity studies share the same social cognition legacy and often end up focusing on people and outputs rather than interaction and communication. Is this the only way to understand the role of others in creative expression?

Decidedly, no. Systemic and sociocultural approaches place the other not at the periphery but at the very center of creativity. A cultural psychol-ogy account of creativity needs to start from this relational basis and con-ceptualize creative action not within a space of subjectivity but one of intersubjectivity (Glăveanu, 2014; for a broader discussion, see Cornejo, 2008). Novelty itself always depends on the comparison term we use and, when it comes to creativity, this comparison term is always social. Not only is it the case that we wouldn't be able to recognize or validate creativity in the absence of social agreement (Csikszentmihalyi, 1988), but no creative action is ever possible outside of collaboration and division of labor (Becker, 2008). More than this, if we adopt the developmental perspective Goethe advocated for, we find self/other interactions (between child and caregiver) at the origin of the very first forms of creative expression. The capacity to symbolize and its development in pretend play are both achievements of decentration and thus grow out of understanding and engaging with otherness (see Piaget & Inhelder, 1966; Vygotsky, 2004; Winnicott, 1971).

As I mentioned above, there are many things present-day creativity theories can learn from Goethe's developmental and holistic perspective. The emphasis on the senses and the lived experience of creating, as well as the necessity of reuniting fantasy and reason, are of key importance and have often been neglected in contemporary research, including within the sociocultural tradition. There are signs of progress though in this regard. Cognitive and psychometric approaches tend to think nowadays that both divergent and convergent thinking are required for creative production (Lubart, 2003), building bridges between the imaginative and the more "rational" (analytical) sides of the creative act. In addition, the sociomaterial perspective on creativity (Tanggaard, 2013) brings to the fore not only the material world but also the senses and the body as key channels for creativity.

Conversely, present-day theories of creativity rooted in the long cultural tradition developed, among others, by Goethe, also make what I consider great steps forward compared to older theories of fantasy. While the latter focus our attention on the human "soul" and its capacity for relating to the world in both intuitive and rational ways, they rarely consider the self/other relation as critical for acquiring, developing, and enacting these capacities. The discussion of fantasy in Cornejo's lead chapter, following historical sources, is equally focused on the individual and his or her use of fantasy. Vico was perhaps the closest one to address the dynamic between self and other when he related imagination to our ability to empathically understand the experience of others, including their experience of making or creating. But for Vico, this ability applied mainly to grasping the social world, its history, including the history of different social groups (Tateo, this volume). His version of perspective-taking requires imagination, but, moving this line of argument further, we can notice that all forms of imagination and, by extension, creativity, are in fact grounded in perspective-taking, achieved through social interaction Glăveanu (2015). This insight invites us to consider not the self but the self/other relation as a central unit for fantasy and creativity. And this shift in perspective (pun intended) is expressed in much more clear terms in the last century both within (e.g., George Herbert Mead's symbolic interactionism) and outside psychology (e.g., Mikhail Bakhtin's dialogism).

My main critique of old conceptions of fantasy, for as much as I understand them, is that they invite us to imagine, as Cornejo very nicely put it, "a psychology with soul" but not necessarily a "psychology with others." Goethe and, further back, Nicholas of Cusa, started from the individual because their reflections engage mainly with the question of the production of knowledge through experience, so central for centuries past and still important to this day. Using contemporary sociocultural theory to socialize even further their conception would, I believe, lead to a much more productive dialogue between past and present. Many meanings have been lost or transformed in our understanding of fantasy, as Cornejo notes, but some things might have changed for the better. One of the main modern-day incarnations of fantasy, creativity, can be taken as an example. Fantasy directs our attention to psychological processes; creativity reunites these processes with interpersonal and material forms of action. In doing so, it can even help us transcend many of the historical dichotomies that scholars like Goethe struggled with.

Cornejo's lead chapter often refers back to such polarities (Goethe himself was guided by the principle of polarity, including in his theory of color; see Goethe, 1810/1998). On the whole, if on one side we have reason, logic, intellect, and scientific measurement, on the other (the "forgotten" side) we find empathy, physiognomic properties, sensibility, intuition, fantasy, aesthetics, poetic imagination, and so on. Creating sharp distinctions between these two "poles" quickly becomes problematic, and this is something Goethe argued against. He proposed the union of opposites within intuitive and poetic forms of understanding the world. What we need is to place this union in the intersubjective space created by self and other and to study dichotomies in (inter)action; this, if nothing else, is the present-day lesson of creativity.

Toward a Critical Cultural Psychology

I began this commentary by raising three questions that seem essential to me in relation to the arguments put forward by Cornejo in his chapter (see the first section). I would like to end with a fourth, more general one, that relates to the discipline of cultural psychology and its future. Cornejo eloquently makes the point that we should pay closer attention to the past, including what seems to be a distant and forgotten past. In his words,

the fate of fantasy in psychology is a fractal reflection of the fate of the whole dimension of internal experience: abandonment or transmutation.

> The challenge for cultural psychology is to recover the forgotten dimensions of the human being.

This is the moral that such a cultural history of fantasy brings to bear on our discipline as a whole. I wholeheartedly agree with this type of exercise and welcome the new light it sheds on past and present debates about fantasy and reason, rationalism and empiricism, materialism and idealism; they are, in many ways, at the core of cultural psychology as a reflective discipline. The question is though, where do we go from here? Clearly, and I am certain this is not Cornejo's intention, we cannot go back. The definition of fantasy Goethe or Vico used can and should be considered a valuable reference point but they grew out of a world (including a world of ideas) that is considerably different from the one we inhabit today. It is rather on this world, of today, that we might decide to focus, and particularly its (dis)continuity with conceptual histories of a much longer duration. But what would this focus help us achieve in practical terms? Gergen (1973) some time ago made the very pertinent point that social psychology is history, a form of history in the making. This resonates with Cornejo's observation that, "from a wider point of view, modern psychology looks more like another chapter of the large book of the human studies; neither the first one, nor the last." It is because there are always more/new chapters to come that we have a collective responsibility, as psychologists, for how they are written. In this sense, looking toward the past is a scholarly practice with great future-making potential.

Is it enough to point, as cultural psychologists, to the fact that contemporary psychological science constructs reality in ways that skew our understanding of what it means to be human (in this case, by downplaying the role of fantasy in our life) and reduce our possibilities of being/acting in the world? Or should we go further? We can, in our writing and research, look at things differently, and we often do. But does this make a real difference for the lives of those we study, observe, or consider co-participants in our work? Achieving such difference requires a critical cultural psychology, one that moves comfortably from construction to deconstruction and action. It is a kind of psychology that is both "with soul" and "with others"; much more than this, it is also a "psychology for others."

ACKNOWLEDGMENTS

I would like to express my deep gratitude to Constance de Saint-Laurent for discussions that shaped the ideas presented in this chapter. Also my gratitude goes to the participants at the 3rd Annual Niels Bohr lecture at Aalborg University for their feedback and many constructive comments.

REFERENCES

Albert, R., & Runco, M. (1999). A history of research on creativity. In R. Sternberg (Ed.), *Handbook of creativity* (pp. 16–31). Cambridge, England: Cambridge University Press.

Amabile, T. M. (1996). *Creativity in context.* Boulder, CO: Westview Press.

Barron, F., & Harrington, D. (1981). Creativity, intelligence, and personality. *Annual Review of Psychology, 32,* 439–476.

Becker, H. S. (2008). *Art worlds* (Upd & exp. ed.). Berkeley: University of California Press.

Cornejo, C. (2008). Intersubjectivity as co-phenomenology: From the holism of meaning to the being-in-the-world-with-others. *Integrative Psychological and Behavioral Science, 42*(2), 171–178.

Csikszentmihalyi, M. (1988). Society, culture, and person: A systems view of creativity. In R. Sternberg (Ed.), *The nature of creativity: Contemporary psychological perspectives* (pp. 325–339). Cambridge, England: Cambridge University Press.

Fink, A., & Benedek, M. (2014). EEG alpha power and creative ideation. *Neuroscience & Biobehavioral Reviews, 44,* 111–123.

Finke, R. A., Ward, T. B., & Smith, S. S. (1992). *Creative cognition: Theory, research, and applications.* Cambridge, MA: MIT Press.

Gardner, H. (2011). *Creating minds: An anatomy of creativity seen through the lives of Freud, Einstein, Picasso, Stravinsky, Eliot, Graham, and Gandhi.* New York, NY: Basic Books.

Gergen, K. J. (1973). Social psychology as history. *Journal of Personality and Social Psychology, 26*(2), 309–320.

Glăveanu, V. P. (2010). Principles for a cultural psychology of creativity. *Culture & Psychology, 16*(2), 147–163.

Glăveanu, V. P. (2013). Rewriting the language of creativity: The five A's framework. *Review of General Psychology, 17*(1), 69–81.

Glăveanu, V. P. (2014). *Distributed creativity: Thinking outside the box of the creative individual.* Cham, Switzerland: Springer.

Glăveanu, V. P. (2015). Creativity as a sociocultural act. *Journal of Creative Behavior, 49*(3), 165–180.

Glăveanu, V. P., Gillespie, A., & Valsiner, J. (2014). *Rethinking creativity: Contributions from social and cultural psychology.* London, England: Routledge.

Glăveanu, V. P., & Wagoner, B. (2016). Memory and creativity: Historical and conceptual intersections. In J. Valsiner, G. Marsico, N. Chaudhary, T. Sato, & V. Dazzani (Eds.), *Psychology as a science of human being: The Yokohama manifesto* (pp. 67–83). New York, NY: Springer.

Goethe, J. W. (1785/1998). Excerpt from "Studies for a physiology of plants." In D. Miller (Ed.), *Goethe: The collected works, Vol. 12, Scientific studies* (pp. 73–75). New York, NY: Suhrkamp.

Goethe, J. W. (1810/1998). Theory of colors. In D. Miller (Ed.), *Goethe: The collected works, Vol. 12, Scientific studies* (pp. 157–298). New York, NY: Suhrkamp.

Guilford, J. P. (1950). Creativity. *American Psychologist, 5,* 444–454.

Lubart, T. (2003). *Psychologie de la créativité.* Paris, France: Armand Colin.

Mason, J. H. (2003). *The value of creativity: An essay on intellectual history, from Genesis to Nietzsche*. Hampshire, England: Ashgate.

Meer, B., & Stein, M. I. (1955). Measures of intelligence and creativity. *The Journal of Psychology: Interdisciplinary and Applied, 39*(1), 117–126.

Montuori, A., & Purser, R. (1995). Deconstructing the lone genius myth: Toward a contextual view of creativity. *Journal of Humanistic Psychology, 35*(3), 69–112.

Nicholas of Cusa (1440/1990). *On learned ignorance*. Minneapolis, MN: Arthur J. Banning Press.

Piaget, J., & Inhelder, B. (1966). *The psychology of the child*. London, England: Routledge & Kegan Paul.

Rhodes, M. (1961). An analysis of creativity. *Phi Delta Kappan, 42*, 305–311.

Rowlands, M. (2010). *The new science of the mind: From extended mind to embodied phenomenology*. Cambridge, MA: MIT Press.

Tanggaard, L. (2013). The sociomateriality of creativity in everyday life. *Culture & Psychology, 19*(1), 20–32.

Vico, G. (1744/1948). *The new science*. Ithaca, NY: Cornell University Press.

Vygotsky, L. S. (1991). Imagination and creativity in the adolescent. *Soviet Psychology, 29*(1), 73–88.

Vygotsky, L. S. (2004). Imagination and creativity in childhood. *Journal of Russian and East European Psychology, 42*(1), 7–97.

Wallas, G. (1926). *The art of thought*. New York, NY: Harcourt-Brace.

Weiner, R. P. (2000). *Creativity and beyond: cultures, values, and change*. Albany: State University of New York Press.

Winnicott, D. W. (1971). *Playing and reality*. London, England: Routledge.

PART IV

THE SCIENTIFIC IMAGINATION IN PSYCHOLOGY

CHAPTER 10

THE DYNAMICS OF "NECESSITY" SHAPING OUR IMAGINATIVE LIVES

A Preconceptual Account of Discriminative Word Usage

John Shotter

> Psychology embraced the Kantian model of man, which paradoxically enough was never a description of a human being, but rather a prescription of *"what mind had to be like* to make the certainty of Euclidean geometry and Newtonian science possible.
>
> —Kaufmann (1980/1998, p. 94; emphasis in the original, quoted in Cornejo, this volume)

> Human choice, by its nature most uncertain, is made certain and determined by the common sense of men with respect to human needs or utilities, which are the two sources of the natural law of the gentes. Common sense [*sensus communis*] is judgement without reflection, shared by an entire class, an entire people, an entire nation, or the entire human race.
>
> —Vico (1968, paras. 141–142)

The Psychology of Imagination: History, Theory, and New Research Horizons
pp. 191–220

> For nature is the motion by which things are composed, live,
> and are dissolved ... Bodies near other bodies never stop
> changing their position. They flow in and out all the time. This
> is the life of things, just like the river that seems the same, yet
> is forever the flowing of different waters.
>
> —Vico (1988, p. 82)

Carlos Cornejo (this volume) concludes his brilliant survey of our European cultural history by outlining our need to place our productive imaginations (Kant, 1781/1998) once again at the center of our mental lives—his accounts of Goethe's and Vico's explorations of the primacy of our poetic forms of thought are especially striking. We have for too long been "bewitched" (Wittgenstein, 1953, might say) by a felt authoritative demand to exercise only our reproductive imaginations (Kant) in an effort to obtain a "geometric certainty" (Descartes) in relation to our actions in the world—along with, I might add, the urge to assume that thinking in terms of concepts (e.g., see Vygotsky, 1986, Ch. 6), is the only kind of advanced thinking that is up to the task we face in making sense of the social practices at work in our conduct of our everyday lives together. Indeed, following on from Descartes (1637/1968) claim, in his *Discours* of 1637, that everything can come to be known by those "long chains of reasoning, quite simple and easy, which geometers use to teach their most difficult demonstrations" (p. 41)—such a view takes it that reality "works," so to speak, not simply in terms of forms, but in terms of ideal forms, precise theoretical spatial shapes that "things" in reality correspond to. In other words, knowledge in this form, literally, is at the center of everything that we do in our lives.

As Cornejo (this volume) realizes, the task we now face in conducting our future inquiries in cultural psychology, is that, he says, of recovering "the forgotten dimensions of the human being, whose roots connect psychology to anthropology rather than to epistemology," that is, to the epistemological concerns of Descartes and Kant that have almost totally occupied our attention in modern times.

But to change the very nature of our encultured ways of life, the everyday methods (Garfinkel, 1967) by which we make sense of each other's actions and utterances, entails, as Charles Taylor (1995) puts it, "overcoming epistemology" (p. 1). This is not at all easy to do. As Taylor notes, by beginning our inquiries in our reflections, in our deliberate thinkings rather than with our feelings, there is

> a temptation here to a kind of self-possessing clarity, to which our culture
> has been almost endlessly susceptible. So much so that most of the enemies
> of Descartes, who think they are overcoming his standpoint, are still giving

primacy of place to epistemology ... They are still practising the structural idealism of the epistemological age, defining their ontology, their view of what is, on the basis of a prior doctrine of what we can know. (p.viii)

In other words, it is still only too easy for us all to think of our "inner lives" as working in terms of inner depictions of an outer reality, for us to talk of our "ideas" as being basic to our "doings" out in the world. Whereas, as we will see—if it really is the case that, as Vygotsky (1966) puts it,

the relations between the higher mental functions were at one time real relations among people ... and, if we want to trace the [original] function of the word in the behaviour of the personality, we must consider its former function in the social behaviour of people. (p. 41)

Then we will find that it is our social activities, our utterances (speakings) and other bodily expressions out in the world, that are the primary source of what later, mistakenly,[1] we come to talk of as occurring within us. Indeed, if these relations are of a very limited or even of a reductive or humiliating kind (see Shotter, 2004), then we will in fact find the inner imaginative lives of those growing up under these conditions, full of felt political and felt ethical tensions to do with how we ought to act in being a proper kind of person (Geertz, 1983) in our culture.

Indeed, the relations of authority among us can both shape and constrain the movements of feeling occurring within us, for not just any ways of acting are afforded (Gibson, 1979), permitted, or made available to us within our current *sensus communis*; various "civilizatory orders" set the horizonal boundaries of legitimate conduct. And, as Cornejo (this volume) outlines,

"By the end of the 18th century, the French revolution and the industrial revolution seemed to converge in the suggestion that a more promising civilizatory order was beginning. In the new worldview, rational planning according to scientific theories occupied a central role. The conception that a mechanical order susceptible of mathematical modeling governed the whole cosmos became commonsensical for the European intellectual world. (pp. xx–xx)

But as Sir Isaiah Berlin (1981) noted long ago, "The history of thought and culture is ... a changing pattern of great liberating ideas which inevitably turn into suffocating straitjackets, and so stimulate their own destruction by new, emancipating, and at the same time enslaving, conceptions" (p. 159). And the time has now come, when the limitations of the civilizatory order promised by the current mechanical, rationalistic worldview, have become more and more clear. In excluding all that is changeable or without a prior foundation in unquestionable axioms, the particular historical processes by which we came to be as we now are, are closed off from us.

Our task now is thus to seek to understand what we experience and perceive only in terms of what we experience and perceive, to understand it in terms of itself, rather than in terms of another, external, eternal, perfect, hidden world, in fact, of our own creation—to explain what is real for us only by what is real for us, and the situated and time-bound only by the situated and time-bound. That is, to talk from within our actual lived and living lives, rather than from an illusory "ideal" place outside them. Somehow, we need to grasp, once again, a way of thinking and talking that does not merely elaborate how we already think, but which can open up to us new, previously unthought-of ways of thinking that can have their beginnings in incipient activities already at work out in our current everyday lives together. As we will see, instead in our thinkings and reflections, such a new way of thinking must begin with our feelings or sensings, as Cornejo (this volume) suggests, a whole new approach which requires a whole new program for the conduct of research in a rethought cultural psychology. In the next section, I want to set out some preliminary indications of much already existing work of relevance to this aim.

Moving on From Cornejo's Account: Preliminaries to Bringing the Practices at Work Within Our "Civilizatory Orders" to Light

In introducing his geometric and mechanistic world, Descartes (1968) said that he had resolved to speak, "only of what would happen in a new world, if God were to create, ... enough matter to compose it, and if he were to agitate diversely and confusedly the different parts of this matter, ...and afterwards did no more than to lend his usual preserving action to nature, and to let her act according to his established laws" (p. 62). Thus here, he establishes the view (which we now take for granted) that the subject matter of our investigations can be analyzed into a set of externally related, separate, self-contained atomic parts, subject to a certain set of laws or principles governing how they combine into larger wholes—an essentially cause and effect, mechanistic view of reality as a lifeless systematic whole exhibiting a single order of connectedness. But as Cassirer (1960) pointed out, this mathematical and mechanical view of things is "a *terminus ad quem*, not a *terminus a quo*—an end, not a beginning ... It achieves its true aim only by disregarding the world of self and other" (pp. 103–104).

Indeed, further, it leaves us in ignorance of the fact that, although the world made us, and not we it, we have no idea of how we have come to develop, not into many different living species, but into a single living species with so many different ways of being in the world, with so many different cultures and languages—and neo-Darwinianism has come up with absolutely nothing by way of an answer to this question of human cultures (see Ingold & Palsson, 2013, p. 5).[2]

Life Within a Holistic, Still Developing World

What if, instead, we resolved to imagine and to speak of a very different world, a world in continual movement, an indivisible, holistic world, containing within itself many continuously flowing strands of intra[3]-mingling activity? And what if, within the dynamics of their intratwining with each other, they spontaneously create, within the intraplays occurring within the regions and moments of their meetings, new forms, new "time-shapes," "flow-forms," or "dynamic stabilities"—like the vortices, swirls, or eddies created when two or more streams of water flow into a river. And further, what if, instead of merely being a spectator of such a fluid world from a distance, we are active, living, embodied participants within it, and whether we like it or not, we have to live out our lives immersed within the many intratwining flows of many such different, unceasing activities which, like many seasons of the year, or the winds and waves, and so on, occurring naturally, and in fact involve all the other people around us. Then in such a world, just as we cannot flatten the waves or still the winds, we would have to accept that the activities we are immersed in affect us much, if not more, than we can affect them.

Such a dynamic world of continuously emerging forms, instead of being a world merely of Being, of already determined forms, is a world of Becoming, a world in which various dynamic forms would come into existence, perhaps remain in existence (or not) for a while and then, perhaps, also pass out of existence again, in many different ways or styles.[4] Indeed, as creatures initially created in primordial times by the world processes at work in those times, just as much as the other animals and plants, we are also participant parts within the world's coming-into-being—as Merleau-Ponty (1968) puts it, we are clearly just as much "of it," as "in it" (p. 100).[5]

Descartes' world is a world of intrinsically unrelated things, of things which are not internally related to each other as participant parts of a larger, indivisible whole; to form a whole, they must be "glued" or "screwed" together somehow by third entities extrinsic to their own essential nature. It is a world to which we are, related only as spectators at a distance, not as involved participants.

Whereas, in a holistic, flowing world, a world in which every "thing" is always in movement, in both senses of the word—as always moving along within a larger movement, as well as moving within ourselves—we find ourselves buffeted by the wind and waves of the social "weather" around us, "movements" to which we must continually respond if we are to sustain ourselves in existence as who we take ourselves to be. Thus, we cannot be external observers within such a world; we cannot get outside of it; we must always work from within it. In other words, our task is to seek to understand what we experience and perceive only in terms of what we experience and perceive, to understand it in terms of itself, rather than in terms of another, external, eternal, ideal but hidden (mathematical) world of, in fact, our own creation; that is, we must talk from within our lives, rather than from an illusory place outside them.

If we are concerned to understand, not only how our current, rationalistic ways of thinking and acting came about, but also how we can "move on" from them, we need a developmental or a historical, cultural psychology that focuses, not simply on the contents of our "minds," but on our actual "doings," our socially contextualized, bodily expressions and gestures out in the world. As Wittgenstein (1980b), for example, expresses the issue: "The origin and primitive form of the language game is a reaction; only from this can more complicated forms develop. Language—I want to say—is a refinement, 'in the beginning was the deed' [Goethe]" (Wittgenstein, 1980b, p. 31), and elsewhere, he goes on to comment: "But what is the word 'primitive' meant to say here? Presumably that this sort of behaviour is pre-linguistic: that a language-game is based on it, that it is the prototype of a way of thinking and not the result of thought" (Wittgenstein, 1981, p. 541).[6] Vico (1968) too, as we shall see, also makes it very clear, that "minds" do not give rise to "language," but emerge and are structured as our communicative expressions also emerge and come to be structured in one way rather than another.

But what Vico also makes clear that Wittgenstein doesn't, is that there is a kind of necessity involved, a social necessity for the group to come to a grasp of a startling experience. But how? Vico's (1968) answer is that we do it by making use of what is already familiar to us. Indeed, he notes how many of our basic images are formed "by metaphor from the human body and its parts, and from the human sense and passions" (Vico, 1968). This is because, although

> rational metaphysics teaches that man becomes all things by understanding them, [my] imaginative metaphysics shows that man becomes all things by *not* understanding them; ... for when man understands, he extends his mind and takes in the things, but when he does not understand, he makes the things out of himself and becomes them by transforming himself into them. (para. 405)

For, as Vico puts it, "the early gentile people, by a demonstrated neces-sity of nature, were poets who spoke in poetic characters" (para. 34).[7] Wittgenstein (1980b) too remarks: "I think I summed up my attitude to philosophy when I said: Philosophy ought really to be written only as *poetic composition*" (p. 24); Austin (1962) also draws our attention to what he called performative utterances, utterances which may seem to be "describing" or "reporting" something factual, but are in fact a part of, "doing an action" (p. 5).

In other words, in understanding "things" poetically, or imaginatively, people sense them as being like other "things" already familiar to them; and when they cannot make such "outside" comparisons, they must find a likeness "from within themselves." So, while sensing identities of form is central to the doing of Logic (A = A; B = B, etc.), as we shall see, imagi-natively sensing similarities is both a central and a very basic human capacity for Vico (as it is also for Wittgenstein) in coming to an under-standing of the emergence of our communicative expressions.

Indeed, what seems so special about us as human beings, is our still indeterminate, unfinished nature; the fact that so much of what is of importance to us exists not *only* in relation to what else is around us, as well as our sense that there is always a something more beyond that. We are what we are as persons (in Geertz's sense), because of our immersion within our social institutions. But these are not wholly knowable to us; the nature of our institutions, as Vico (1968) puts it, "is nothing more but their coming into being (*nascimento*) at certain times and in certain guises" (para. 147).[9]

As living embodied beings, surrounded by such a world of flowing, dynamically changing forms, we cannot not be spontaneously responsive to the changes continually occurring around us. Thus, both to understand how to move on from our current, rationalistic ways of thinking and acting, instead of a focus on the separate things around us, on their merely spatial (picture-able) relations—"things" we can theorize and conceptualize (see discussion in a later section)—our focus must shift to a study of the "move-ments of feeling" occurring within as a result of our immersion within the flowing activities around us and within us. We must become concerned with, as Gadamer (2000) puts it, not so much with "what we do or what we ought to do, but what happens to us over and above our wanting and doing (p. xxviii). We need, so to speak, in discerning articulations occurring within the world, to repeat, to direct our investigations "not towards phe-nomena, but ... towards the 'possibilities' of phenomena. What that means is that we call to mind the kinds of statement that we make about phenom-ena" (Wittgenstein, 1953, p. 90) with the aim of bringing to light, so to speak, the "ontological landscape" (Merleau-Ponty, 1968) of incipient alternatives for other ways of being currently open to us.

Finding the "Roots" of Possible New Ways
of Being in Current Forms of Talk

So, while already well-developed Western intellectuals, already living within a more or less peaceful social order, may begin their inquiries with wonder, Vico, as we shall see, saw the initial socially shared task of the first peoples as being that of assuaging their otherwise incapacitating fears; fears aroused in them by the sheer turbulence and occasional violence of the natural world around them. They thus faced the need to create among themselves shared activities aimed at alleviating the intense feelings aroused by startling or frightening events occurring in shared moments or circumstances—pervasive feelings that would otherwise, so to speak, "sit within them," allowing them no respite in the rest of their lives to focus on other things. But it was only by beginning to come to an imaginative grasp of such intense experiences in terms of images already familiar to them, that they could begin to try out possible ways of acting that might ameliorate them. In other words, was by the metaphorical move of responding to such events, suggests Vico (1968, para. 191), as if occasioned by the anger of gigantic beings similar to ourselves, and by doing in relation to these imagined beings what we would like done to ourselves in response to our own anger. Thus it was, he suggests, that we brought into existence between us, divinities,[10] invisible but strongly felt influences at work within us, limiting and shaping all our social activities together.

Thus, social processes are based, Vico claims, not in anything preestablished either in people or in their surroundings, but in socially shared similarities[11] of feeling that they themselves create within the flows of activity occurring between them. He calls these similarities of feeling, "sensory topics"—"topics" (Gr. *topos* = "place") because they give rise to "commonplaces," that is, to shared moments or to the "dynamic stabilities" (Shotter, 1984) occurring within a flow of social activity which afford a "moment of common reference" (Shotter, 2009, 2013), and "sensory" because they are moments in which shared feelings for already shared circumstances are aroused. It is these similarities of feeling, he claims, that constitute the prelinguistic origins of a social order, the paradigms or prototypes from which more organized forms of communication may be derived; and it is the hermeneutical-dialogical-developmental nature of these preconceptual, particular "imaginative universals" (Vico, 1968, e.g., #381, para. 460) making such similarities possible, that I want to explore more extensively below.

But in emphasizing in these preliminary comments that the primary source of what later we come to talk of as occurring within us, is to be found first in our utterances (speakings) and in other bodily expressions, out in the world among us, I want to suggest that (a) by further exploring, on the one hand, the "inner political" dynamics at work in shaping our imaginative lives, I think Cornejo's (and Taylor's) account of why Cartesian influences still exert a hegemonic hold on our academic lives, constraining and channeling what it is possible for us (easily) to think within them, can be extended and further articulated to reveal why this is so. While, on the other hand, (b) explorations of how an "inner ethical dynamic," that must still be at work within them, can bring into rational-visibility these incipient processes, thus to open up the possibility of imagining "again a psychology with a soul."

For, as I see it, in line with the comments already made above, prior to any concern to do with what goes on within us when we do what we call "imagining," is a concern with how, as a member of a social group, we can come to distinguish in people's activities out in the world between, say, the sense of seeing something before our eyes (simply seeing), seeing something as a possibility (imagining), and the sense of seeming to see something before our eyes that no one else sees (hallucinating). In other words, when we talk of "simply seeing," "imagining," or of "hallucinating," we are already doing a kind of after-the-fact talking; that is, we are talking as someone well-versed in the use of a language, able to judge[12] what words to apply in describing an activity after it has occurred. Whereas, if our task is to understand how it is that we can come to make such distinctions in people's behavior (and our own) out in the world, then we will need what we might call, a before-the-fact account (Shotter, 2014, 2016).

In other words, in taking a Wittgensteinian (1953) approach to distinguishing between these different uses of the words "see" or "seeing" in our everyday speaking, we need to be able to describe how, in relation to the shared "civilizatory order," as Cornejo (this volume) puts it,[13] currently at work in shaping our everyday ways and methods of spontaneously acting and communicating with each other, they "show up," so to speak, within that order. In short, we need a psychology that seeks to study, not what goes on inside people's heads now, but what people's heads have gone on inside of in both the distant and recent past such that we can—after we have, as children, grown "into the intellectual life of those around [us]" (Vygotsky, 1978, p. 88)—easily make such judgments as to appropriate word use, spontaneously.

But to do this entails our entering, like an anthropologist, into the "inner landscape" of our own actual everyday world to get to see, in the imaginative sense, the overall nature of the background "norm[s] of description," as Wittgenstein (1969, p. 167) calls them, at work in our shared, commonsense ways and methods of making intelligible sense of events occurring around us. His use of this phrase occurs in a remark in which he asks us to think of chemical investigations and of Lavoisier concluding that certain changes occur when an event all call "burning" happens:

> He doesn't say that something different might happen at another time. He has got hold of a definite world-picture (*Weltbild*)[14]—not of course one that he invented: he learned it as a child. I say world-picture (*Weltbild*) and not hypothesis (*Hypothese*), because it is the matter-of-course foundation for his research and as such also goes unmentioned. (p. 167)

His concerns here are ontological rather than epistemological ones, to do with our ways-of-being-in-the-world as the kind of persons we are.

Indeed, to go further into the nature of his efforts to show people around, as he put it, the "details of an immense landscape which they cannot possibly know their way around" (Wittgenstein, 1980b, p.56), that is, the details of what we show as spontaneously influencing our actions and utterances in our daily lives together. A task essentially, it is not going too far to say, is like that of an anthropologist or ethnographer (see Hacker, 2010), and as such, is just as difficult, if not more so. From originally thinking that his investigations into *logic* (Wittgenstein, 1922) would reveal the essential structure of the world to us, he came to realize that what had appeared to be that essential structure was actually the structure (grammar) of the terms in which we talk of the world. But about his work in the *Tractatus*, in his later work he went on to say, "One thinks that one is tracing the outline of the thing's nature over and over again, and one is merely tracing round the frame through which we look at it" (Wittgenstein, 1953, p. 114).

But this means that the task is not now that of arriving at a small number of basic axioms; it becomes instead the vast task of trying to arrive at a unitary sense of "a landscape which language presents us with in countless fragments," said Wittgenstein (1980a), and "piecing them together is too hard for me. I can only make an imperfect job of it," (p. 78) he went on to remark, but that was, perhaps, because, as we will see, it now becomes essentially a hermeneutical task which, by its very nature, is always open to further developments and inner articulations, and can never be completely finalized. To complete it or to perfect it, would be to falsify utterly its living nature.[15]

So, if we are to find the "roots" connecting psychology to anthropology rather than to epistemology, as Cornejo (this volume) suggests, what might the task of the anthropologist searching for those roots look like, and what might be the nature of the methods required in trying to achieve it? As I see it, in the Wittgensteinian approach I am taking here, we will find those roots is our usages of language and our other communicative expressions.

IMAGINATIVE WORD USAGE, EXPRESSING SIMILARITIES (AND DIFFERENCES), AND NOTICING DISTINCTIONS

> Vico … asks a completely new epistemological question. He does not ask how the mind functions in relation to the object to produce knowledge … Vico asks how the mind comes to have something before it at all.
>
> —Verene (1981, p. 81)

Perhaps what is amazing about language (perhaps I should just say about *our* language, English, as I want to speak from personal experience), is not just that we have so many different words for drawing so many subtle distinctions, but what we can, seemingly, make countless such distinctions with so few words—indeed, Wilhelm von Humboldt (1863), in his famous but rarely studied introduction to general linguistics, expressed the view that a language "makes infinite use of finite means"—a phrase that Chomsky (1972, p. 17) was fond of quoting in support his Cartesian, after-the-fact claim that it is our innate grasp of the rules of syntax that makes such an infinite use possible.[16]

But Chomsky's (1965) Cartesian account of syntax works, of course, in terms of forms, in fact, only in terms of innate ideal forms, which represent, he says, people's "*knowledge* of the language that provides the basis for actual use of language by a speaker-hearer" (p. 9, my italics). And he is quite adamant that he has nothing to say "about how the speaker or hearer might proceed, in some practical or efficient way" (p. 9) to make use of such knowledge. "These questions," he says, "belong to a theory of language use" (p. 9). And this rationalistic approach now continues apace in "cognitive psychology," and in so-called cognitive science— essentially "geometric" forms of thought are still at the heart of these kinds of inquiry. We still feel that we must begin with the formulation of concepts and with theories—how else can we begin?

But to quote Cornejo (this volume) again here,

> Psychology began its scientific path by making an ontological redefinition of its subject matter: the discipline is not about all that people *experience*, but instead about the *rational* aspects of such experiences. From then on, psychology pursues epistemological rather than anthropological aims. (p. xx, my italics)

To reverse this, instead of studying like Chomsky patterns of already spoken words, we need to begin our anthropological inquiries by studying what happens in actual events of words in their speaking, we need to go out into the everyday world of living people, and to study the "countless different *kinds of use* of what we call 'symbols,' 'words,' 'sentences'" (Wittgenstein, 1953, p. 23, my italics). Rather than with thinking and reflecting, we need to do some noticing and describing. For instance, as Wittgenstein (1953, pp. 48–53) points out, given that there are many different ways in which a 3x3 arrangement of colored squares (red, white, and black) might be described, we need to focus on which one is used and why, thus, he says, "In order to see more clearly, here as in countless similar cases, we must focus on *the details of what goes on*; must look at them from close to" (no. 51, my italics).

> If I had to say what is the main mistake made by philosophers of the present generation … I would say that it is that when language is looked at, what is looked at is the *form of words* and not *the use* made of the form of words. (Wittgenstein, 1966, p. 2, my italics)

Thus, like Wittgenstein (1953), our anthropological task now—our task of not only entering into other cultures different from our own, but also of entering into our own culture, as a culture that we still do not wholly understand—is that of looking at the details of what goes on within them.

But what is entailed in our doing that? What can we make use of in guiding ourselves in doing the kind of looking needed? The Cartesian thinker is straight away tempted to say, The issue here is a matter of how we conceptualize or theorize the phenomena involved. While on the other hand, the Wittgensteinian thinker and looker, having already put aside any prior theorizing or conceptualizing, begins their inquiry in an imaginative fashion, by seeking similarities to the phenomenon before them. Doing this, they may very well, as indeed Wittgenstein (1953) did, see the task before them as not unlike that faced by young children learning their first language.

In other words, we cannot take it for granted that, even as adults with a mastery of our own first language, our task is merely that of learning how to translate our own everyday ways of talking into our professionalized ways of talking. For even as professionalized adults, we still need to learn how to "pick out" from the indeterminate flows of activity occurring around us, the unique "time-shapes"[17] of either already well-recognized "things," or of previously unencountered "things"; that is, even as professionalized adults, we still need to learn how to make judgments as to "what" in fact is occurring before us in ways similar to the judgments made by the everyday people we are studying (see Note 5). And we need to do this by noticing and learning to respond to such events in the same way as they respond to them—a task that, as we will see below, entails us coming to an awareness of the embodied structure of anticipations we share with them.

The "Moving" Power of Words in Their Speaking

This is why I have taken as the organizing motif for this chapter, Vygotsky's (1966) claim, to repeat, "that the relations between the higher mental functions were at one time real relations among people" (p. 41). But to it here, I want to add his claim that

> all the higher psychic functions are mediated processes, and signs are the basic means used to master and direct them. The mediating sign is incorporated in their structure as an indispensable, indeed the central, part of the total process. In concept formation that sign is the word, which at first plays the role of means in forming the concept but later becomes its symbol. (1962, p. 56; this paragraph is missing from 1986 translation)

And the question is: In what way does the voicing of a word, or the expression of another kind of sign, act as a "means" in forming what we call a "concept?"

Unnoticed in the background and spontaneously at work in all our communicative relations with each other is what we might call a relationally responsive kind of talk and understanding—a spontaneous form of talk and understanding much more basic than the representational-referential kind of talk and understanding which, as individuals, we are consciously aware of, and which we make use of in our more deliberately considered talk. As Bakhtin (1986) puts it,

> when the listener perceives and understands the meaning (the language meaning) of speech, he simultaneously takes an active, responsive attitude towards it. He either agrees or disagrees with it (completely or partially), augments it, applies it, prepares for its execution, and so on. And the listener adopts this responsive attitude for the entire duration of the process of listening and understanding, from the very beginning—sometimes literally from the speaker's first word. (p. 68)

And the speaker also is expecting such an active responsive understanding:

> [The speaker] does not expect passive understanding that, so to speak, only duplicates his or her own idea in someone else's mind (as in Saussure's model of linguistic communication). Rather, the speaker talks with an expectation of a response, agreement, sympathy, objection, execution, and so forth. (p. 69)

But to go further:

> The word in living conversation is directly, blatantly, oriented toward a
> future answer-word; it provokes an answer, anticipates it and structures itself
> in the answer's direction. Forming itself in an atmosphere of the already
> spoken, the word is at the same time determined by that which has not yet
> been said but which is needed and in fact anticipated by the answering
> word. Such is the situation of any living dialogue. (Bakhtin, 1981, p. 280)

And as we will see, the anticipatory nature of our talk—the way in which
certain of our expressions can get us ready for the happening of an
event—can orient us, so to speak, toward how the others around us will
respond to certain events occurring in our shared circumstances, and is a
crucial aspect of our coming to an embodied capacity to make judgments
as they make them.

Indeed, as I noted above, in discussing the different uses of the words
"see" or "seeing" (simple seeing, imagining, or hallucinating), it is clearly
a matter of judgment as to whether the application of such words is
appropriate; but it is also an imaginative matter. For we cannot be working here in terms of simply visibly seeing identities, that is, a formal same-
ness; we are sensing likenesses, that is, using words metaphorically—no
wonder that when Wittgenstein (1953) faces the task of saying what a language is like, he comes up with the metaphors of a city, a toolbox, or with
words being like the different controls of a locomotive (all seeming to be
similar to each other, although serving different uses, because of being
designed for use by our hands), while overall, choosing the metaphor of a
game (without saying precisely, what game in particular he has in mind).

In the past, with our assumption that "science-like" thought is the only
proper, reliable form of thought, we have allowed ourselves to be ruled
over in our more self-conscious, deliberate ways of thinking and speaking,
by what I have called (1) geometric, mechanistic, or Cartesian forms of
thought and talk, in which we commit ourselves to using a "framework,"
"perspective," "theory," or "model," that we take as corresponding with
reality, and through which we then perceive and act in the world around
us, what elsewhere I have called aboutness-thinking (Shotter, 2010) working in terms of identities. Here, in line with my overall concern with the
imaginative nature of our mental activities, I want to compare these ways
of thinking with what I will call (2) poetic, imaginative, or Wittgensteinian
ways of thinking, in which people make use of already existing particular
kinds of understanding—what Wittgenstein (1953) called "*objects of comparison*" (p. 130)[19]—that, in relation to such understandings, enable them
to have a sense of both the similarities to them, as well as the differences
from them.

In this kind of thinking, that elsewhere I have called withness-thinking
(Shotter, 2010), people may feel free to use a whole set of such "poetic
comparative devices" without feeling committed to any one of them. For

our task now is to explore unique possibilities, the anticipation of a possible next step in a practical circumstance (a before-the-fact matter of inquiry), rather than that of establishing general facts (as the result of an after-the-fact form of inquiry). Consequently, instead of seeking the hidden "mechanical workings" (mechanisms) presumed to be produced the phenomena we can observe, our task now is the hermeneutical one of piecing together, somehow, the countless fragments our language usages present us with, in our spontaneous use of words and other forms of communicative expressions in our everyday, practical circumstances. As Wittgenstein (1953) puts it,

> We feel as if we had to see right into phenomena: yet our investigation is directed not towards phenomena, but rather, as one might say, towards the "possibilities" of phenomena. What that means is that we call to mind the kinds of statement that we make about phenomena. (p. 90)

This, as I noted above, is essentially a hermeneutical, ethnographic, or anthropological task (Hacker, 2010).

Originally, hermeneutical methods were developed in relation to the task of arriving at the meaning of a text. As we read a text, we do not begin with a preestablished, theoretical order or set of abstract concepts to which the first words we encounter need to be assimilated, hoping to explain them as particular instances of something more general, with all their uniqueness lost. Nor are we concerned with arriving at factual knowledge, with finished and finalized objective understandings, that can be represented by (pictured in) purely spatial forms. The process begins with our immersion within the as yet indeterminate text, as a whole in its full individuality, as the unique text it is, known to us only globally as situated within a particular genre (as a novel, textbook, instruction manual, etc.). We then proceed, as we sequentially read each fragment of text, to conduct a step-by-step movement, from part-to-whole and back again, gradually specifying or internally articulating it as a unique, imaginative, global unity with its own unique meaning—I say (a) unique in the sense of being distinct from all other such unities; (b) imaginative in the sense of providing an inexhaustible landscape of possibilities related to the unity in question; and (c) global in the sense of our being able to make use of it as a source of possible likenesses and differences, in our many spheres of our everyday life's activities—all features making it quite distinct from an abstract generality or general concept. But something more is needed in moving from making sense of already written texts, to trying to understand the still-developing cultures of living peoples.

"Objects of Comparison"
in an Anthropological Hermeneutics

In seeing Wittgenstein's approach to anthropology as essentially a her-meneutical one, I was also pleased to note anthropologist Clifford Geertz's (2000) acknowledgment that Wittgenstein's later works "had an enormous impact upon my sense of what I was about and what I hoped to accomplish" (p. xi). What in particular impressed him, in his anthropo-logical endeavors, were Wittgenstein's admonishments, and other atten-tion-directing phrasings, such as "Don't' look for the meaning, look for the use," "A picture held as captive," "Back to the rough ground," and so on. For as Geertz noted—in relation to his concerns with "ferreting out the singularities of other people's lives" (p. xi), and with "the fine detail of lived life" (p. xi)—Wittgenstein's critique of inquiries aimed at only at dis-covering generalities and ideals, "narrowed the gap between [such inqui-ries], and going about in the world trying to discover how in the midst of talk people—groups of people, individual people, people as a whole—put a distinct and variegated voice together" (p. xii). Going out into the every-day world rather than doing experiments in the specially controlled con-ditions of the laboratory, is OK after all!

I mention Geertz (1983) here in particular because, rather trying by "empathy" to translate their ways of acting into the conceptual framework of the "rather peculiar idea" we have ourselves and of our ways of acting (see Endnote 11), he suggests that "The ethnographer does not, and, in my opinion, largely cannot, perceive what his informants perceive. What he [or she] perceives, and that uncertainly enough, is what they perceive 'with'—or 'by means of,' or 'through' ... whatever the word should be" (p. 58); and he continues by suggesting that "the concept of the person is, in fact, an excellent vehicle by means of which to examine this whole ques-tion of how to go about poking into another people's turn of mind" (p. 59)[19]—for how proper persons should act, in different situations in differ-ent cultures, is very revealing of the kind of world in which they take themselves to be living.

What is of special interest here, is the method Geertz (1983) employs in "ferreting out the singularities of other people's lives," that is, in coming to grasp of the overall inner landscape of what he calls their "experience-near concepts" (p. 58) that they use "spontaneously, un-self-consciously, and as it were colloquially" (p. 58) in almost seamlessly conducting their everyday lives. In outlining the nature of his method, he suggests that we must first

> notice the characteristic intellectual movement, the inward conceptual
> rhythm, in each of these analyses, and indeed in all similar analyses ...—

namely, a continuous dialectical tacking between the most local of local detail and the most global of global structures ... Hopping back and forth between the whole conceived through the parts which actualize it and the parts conceived through the whole which motivates them, we seek to turn them, by a sort of intellectual perpetual motion, into explications of one another. All this is, of course, but the now familiar trajectory of what Dilthey called the hermeneutic circle, and my argument here is merely that it is as central to ethnographic interpretation, and thus to the penetration of other people's modes of thought, as it is to literary, historical, philological, psychoanalytic, or biblical interpretation. (p. 69)

But what is special about Geertz's (1983) use of it—for he is not using it to arrive at the meaning of a written text, but at the "inner landscape" of a people's mentality—is his thinking of the role of the most global of global structures involved in the relevant hermeneutical movement as being played by "those experience-distant concepts theorists have fashioned to capture the general features of social life" (p. 58).

In other words, we can come to a grasp of concepts[20] which, for another people, are experience-near, says Geertz (1983), by placing them "in illuminating connection with those experience-distant concepts" (p. 58)—an activity about which I will have much more to say later.

Again, we can see Wittgenstein's (1953) use of "objects of comparison" as he calls them, at work here. By his use of other possible ways of talking, other "language games" both actual and invented, and such, like Geertz, he is trying "to throw light on the facts of our language by way of not only similarities, but also dissimilarities" (p. 130); he is seeking to produce

> just that understanding which consists in "seeing connections" (no. 122). For, by noticing how what occurs in a distinctive way, is both similar to, and different from, what we otherwise would expect (anticipate), such comparisons can work, he notes, to establish "an order in our knowledge of the use of language: an order with a particular end in view; one of many possible orders; not the order. (p. 132)

This would be a hermeneutical understanding (as we shall see) that is arrived at in a way quite different from that of imposing a particular theoretical or conceptual framework on the phenomena in question.

A BACKGROUND LANDSCAPE OF PARTICULAR, HERMENEUTICAL UNITIES—THE POSSIBILITY OF CONSTITUTIVE FORMS OF TALK

> Vico ... asks a completely new epistemological question. He does not ask how the mind functions in relation to the object to

produce knowledge ... Vico asks how the mind comes to have
something before it at all.

—Verene (1981, p. 81)

Synthesis *finds* truths, analysis *makes* them—Imagination is the
eye of ingenium, judgment the eye of understanding.

—Vico (1988, p. 98, my italics)

Above, following Vico (1988), we assumed that nature "is the motion by
which things are composed, live, and are dissolved ... This is the life of
things, just like the river that seems the same, yet is forever the flowing of
different waters" (p. 92). But in starting to do this, we have not only to try
to make ourselves aware of all the many of the well-established Cartesian
notions we so easily take for granted—in order to prevent ourselves from
drawing on illusory ideals—but we now also have to try to reinstall ourselves[21] within this forever-indeterminate "flow of experience," a flow
which is both currently at work within us on us, and within which and
upon which we are also currently at work; a flow of experience still open
to yet further inner articulation. It is from within our own unique situation within this flow that we can begin to notice unique features, occasional dynamic stabilities to which we can then try to give some
expression, to try to say what they are like. This, however, is clearly, not at
all easy to do. For it is unclear to us "where" should we start, and "where"
to stop; we feel we need to place some boundaries somewhere.

Someone who long ago wrote on the indeterminacy of the flow of experience was William James (1912/2003). About our fields of experience he
wrote, "[They] have no more definite boundaries than have our fields of
view. Both are fringed forever by a more that continuously develops, and
that continuously supersedes them as life proceeds. The relations, generally speaking, are as real here as the terms are" (p. 37)—where this
"more" can be seen as the openness to further articulation I mentioned
above.

In other words, such experiences are not bounded entities with a clear
beginning and a clear end, and never can be, but as James put it (1890/
1950) long ago, they are "feelings of tendency, often so vague that we are
unable to name them at all" (p. 254)—even as they occur, they are on the
way to somewhere else. Further, along with such a feeling

goes the sense of its relations, near and remote, the dying echo of whence it
came to us, the dawning sense of whither it is to lead ... We all of us have
this permanent consciousness of whither our thought is going. It is a feeling
like any other, a feeling of what thoughts are next to arise, before they have
arisen. (pp. 255–256)

In other words, they have a unique and distinctive time-shape to them. So although we cannot name them at all, such feelings can, nonetheless, function, James says, as "signs of direction in thought of which we have an acutely discriminative sense, though no definite sensorial image plays any part in it whatsoever" (p. 253). And as such, such feelings can function as "standards" in the "mental background" to our imaginative attempts to say what they are like.

There is, thus, something very special about our speakings, about our "moving" bodily expression of our speech, and about the back-and-forth, dialogically structured nature of the flow of social intra-activity within which it occurs. Uniquely new understandings, appropriate to the circumstances of their occurrence, are continually created within that flow of intra-activity—understandings which we cannot, as individuals, be said to have caused. They just happen, they emerge, and the tangled nature of the process of their emergent production cannot easily be untangled. This because the components or units into which they would need to be analyzed are determined by those within the unfolding process according to the contingencies of the moment.

So, although it is the case as Bakhtin (1986) points out that

> each individual utterance is a link in the chain of speech communion. It has clear-cut boundaries that are determined by the change of speech subjects (speakers), but within these boundaries the utterance, like Leibniz's monad, reflects the speech process, others' utterances, and, above all, preceding links in the chain (sometimes close and sometimes—in areas of cultural communication—very distant). (p. 93)

Each individual utterance has its own unique relational nature in accord with its "place" within a particular dialogue as a whole. We thus now need to turn to the hermeneutical nature of the process within which, gradually, we come to articulate the unique nature of each particular dialogical circumstance of significance to us.

Earlier, I quoted Wittgenstein (1953) as remarking that, "if language is to be a means of communication there must be agreement not only in definitions but also (queer as this may sound) in judgments" (p. 242). But now we must also note that Vico (1968) remarked, "Providence gave good guidance to human affairs when it aroused human minds first to topics rather than to criticism, for acquaintance with things must come before judgment of them" (para. 498). In other words, before we can make any judgments of similarity, we must be able, imaginatively, to bring two or more "somethings" to mind to subject them to such a comparison. We thus need to ask, What might the nature of these "different somethings" be like, such that some of their features (but not all, else we would see them as identical, and would be doing logic) are seen as amenable to being described verbally as identical, for such judgments of similarity to be possible?

Here, we seem to be touching on a very, very basic human capacity. The modern view is that criticism leads to the growth of knowledge: wrong hypotheses are eliminated in a kind of neo-Darwinian process of evolution toward the truth (e.g., Popper, 1972). But, as Vico (1988) saw it, this is to fail to

> pay attention to the proper faculty of knowing ... mother wit, the creative power through which man is capable of recognizing likenesses and making them himself. We see it in children, whom nature is more integral and less corrupted by convictions and prejudices, that the first faculty to emerge is that of seeing similarities. For example, they call all men fathers and all women mothers and they make likeness: "They build huts, hitch mice to little wagons, play odds and evens, and ride on a great hobby horse of a stick"[23] (p. 102)

But here, we also seem to be touching on another a very, very basic human capacity: Vico (1988) called it *Ingenium*: "the faculty that connects disparate and diverse things" (p. 96), the faculty which, in his *Scienza Nuova* (1968), he calls an "imaginative universal," which as I mentioned above, although each one is a quite particular universal, it qualifies as such due to the "copious"[23] nature of the meanings we can draw from each one of them. Here, as I see it, the many different, holistic unities of meaning we come to construct, as we gather a significant fragment of here at this moment, and another there at that moment, are not only like the fields of view (James, 1890/1950) we constrict as our eyes flick and drift from one point of fixation to another, but also like those particular unities of meaning we construct, hermeneutically, in our reading of a particular text (but not a textbook), for the particular *Weltbild* (Wittgenstein) or ontological landscape (Merleau-Ponty, 1968) it portrays.

For clearly, we do not begin our reading with a preestablished set of abstract concepts to which the first words we encounter need to be assimilated, hoping to explain them as particular instances of something more general, with all their uniqueness lost, as when we are deriving a theorem in geometry. Nor are we concerned with arriving at factual knowledge, with finished and finalized objective understandings that can be represented by (pictured in) purely spatial forms. We begin by immersing ourselves within a particular indeterminate whole as the unique whole it is, known to us only globally as situated within a particular genre (as a mystery or detective story, as a historical or fictive novel, etc). We then proceed, as Geertz (1983) outlined above, to conduct a step-by-step movement, from part-to-whole and back again, gradually internally articulating it as a living sequential order adapted to the undistorted accommodation of all the particular, discernible details of significance in the original global whole. Vico (1988), in railing against then-current efforts "to recommend the use of geometrical methods into public speaking," in noticing that "Cicero is [now] dismissed as imprecise, disorderly, and all mixed up," goes on to remark that

> Yet the world's most learned men have all, till now, admired the order and cogency that they have noticed in his work; this is such that what he says first opens itself in a certain way and embraces what he says next; so that what comes later in the speech seems not so much to be asserted by him, as to emerge from and flow out of the facts themselves. (p. 99)

Clearly, the particular unities of meaning we constitute here are not at all like abstract generalities, defined in terms of the few distinctive features common to many instantiations; they are particular unities of, in fact, unmerged particularities that are all intralinked with each other without losing their particularity.

But as I needed to note above in relation to Geertz's (1983) reference to the hermeneutical movement, he feels involved in arriving at an account of the "inner landscape" of a people's mentality, more is involved than arriving at the meaning of a written text:

> Only when you have seen," he writes, "as I have, a [Javanese] young man whose wife—a woman he had raised from childhood and who had been the centre of his life—has suddenly and inexplicably died, greeting everyone with a set smile and formal apologies for his wife's absence and trying, by mystical techniques, to flatten out, as he himself put it, the hills and valleys of his emotion into an even, level plain. (p. 61)

Then we ask ourselves, What are the social necessities (à la Vico), the everyday practical concerns that are not only at work within this young man impelling him to act like this, but also, seemingly, making all apparent alternatives to his particular course of action, in relation to all his fellow Javanese, unthinkable for him? Although seemingly at first inaccessible to us, as Geertz makes clear, without trying to bring out the hidden special process going on hidden inside a person's head, we can, by attending to the distinct things he or she says and does out in the world in relation to their circumstances—as well as what led up to and what consequentially followed the focal events in question—come make sense of their actions; we can distinguish their doings from purely logical, syntactical, or mechanical activities. And then further, once one has collected them into a meaning unity, trying to find an "instructive" way of bringing the attention of others to their nature by telling them what they are like in ways already familiar to those others.

CONCLUSIONS: FROM CONCEPTS AND THEORIES TO IMAGINATIVE AND INDICATIVE WAYS OF TALKING

> As I was studying the origins of the Latin language, I noticed that [the origins of] many words were so learned [i.e., wise ~ js] as to seem derived from some inward learning rather than from the vernacular usage of the people.
>
> —Vico (1988, p. 37)

> The essence of life is its continuously changing character; but our concepts are all discontinuous and fixed, and the only mode of making them coincide with life is by arbitrarily supposing positions of arrest therein ... When we conceptualize, we cut out and fix, and exclude everything but what we have fixed ... Conceptually, time excludes space; motion and rest exclude each other; ... unity excludes plurality; independence excludes relativity; "mine" excludes "yours"; this connexion excludes that connexion.... whereas in the real concrete sensible flux of life experiences compenetrate each other so that it is not easy to know just what is excluded and what not.
>
> —James (1912/2003, pp. 253–254)

The overall theme I have been pursuing in this chapter, is, as Vico (1988) puts it above (and as I quoted Vygotsky (1966) at the beginning as saying), that the "things" we currently think of as ending up as "cognitive mechanisms" hidden inside individual people's heads, both start out, and are sustained in existence, by what goes on out in the world among them, their "languaged activities," that is, within those activities in which the "moving power of words in their speaking" is at work in organizing and shaping them. Thus our research task in cultural psychology is not that of rationalistically discovering those supposedly hidden, causal mechanisms, but that of anthropologically studying (à la Wittgenstein and Geertz) how such forms of talk, so to speak, "show up" within certain behavioral sequences of languaged, and "do" their organizational work.

As an aid to our noticing and attending to what matters to the participants in such activities, we also, to repeat Wittgenstein's (1980) felt need for poetic forms of talk, need what we might call "orientational" forms of talk, talk that, again as Wittgenstein (1953) puts it, helps us both to know our "way about" (p. 123), and also how we might "go on" (p. 154), in relation to the behavioral sequences in question. Thus, my task now is to say a little bit more about the nature of the talk needed.

As James (1912/2003) comments above, our modernist, rationalistic, Cartesian forms of conceptual thought and talk, along with our current scholarly training in "scientized" academic disciplines, orient us away from conducting our inquiries from within Vico (and James') flowing, holistic realities within which we also, in fact, live our lives. Instead, they orient us toward seeking a set of already determined ideal entities, along with the relations between them, which we need to think of in separation from how we actually live our everyday practical lives. Instead of seeing that the meaning of our speakings is "in" our speaking, "in" our unfolding, expressive bodily activity, we seek it in the "content" of what is said; and this is where we meet all the trouble of academic ways of working. For each discipline has its own subject matter—the what of its member's inquiries. "How shall we define it?" they say; "How can we conceptualize it?" they also say. And this is how they take meanings out of the everyday lives of ordinary people; this is how they disconnect it from the lives in which it has its proper home; this is how they/we create a fantasy world, which for us as academics, is more real than the everyday world of ordinary people.

But the trouble with conceptual talk is that in working "from outside" a circumstance of concern, talk of concepts is "preemptive" in the sense of decreeing ahead of one's inquiries, the basic entities one is going to discover;[24] thus they work in an after-the-fact manner to decree the what-ness (ontology) of what we have already observed as having happened in a situation or circumstance. Indeed, we see the world only through them, as corresponding to definitions of our own devising, and as such, they work only in terms of samenesses, "identities" even. By defining ahead of time a discipline's subject matter, they also work to put a boundary around its field of study. Further, to the extent that their power is supposed to be in their general nature, true for all time, and all places, "in our interest" of explaining events solely in terms of their causes, they are thus decontextualized and thus inflexible in relation to the context of their use. Finally, in only having currency within the vocabulary of those specially trained within an academic discipline, ordinary people experience themselves as lacking in this special expert knowledge, while at the same time experiencing it as lying outside of what matters to them. Thus such knowledge can all too easily work to disable just those who are in fact already perfectly well enabled in the very activities that academics are meant to be explaining to them.

Is there an alternative? Yes there is: in our ordinary, everyday, nonconceptual, contextualized, difference making speakings. In working from within a shared-sensed circumstance of concern to internally articulate it into a more richly structured landscape of possibilities, they work, not only to leave that circumstance open to yet further development, but also, to work continually in a before-the-fact manner to point out possible next steps in our exploratory efforts, aimed at determining, along with all the others around us, what collectively we will come to call the facts of the matter. Working in this way means, of course, that we cannot define in any precise way the nature of the shared-sensed circumstance ahead of time—but, noting James' (1890/1950) comment above, that "we nevertheless have an acutely discriminative sense" of the "signs of direction in thought" it provides us with, we can (by the use of images and metaphors, and other carefully crafted ways of talking, say very precisely what they are like so that all concerned can relate themselves to its nature.

But further, in not placing any boundaries on the fields of our inquiry, we are always left with a sense of there being a something more that we might bring out into the light of day in our later inquiries. Most importantly, in working, not in terms of identities, but in terms of similarities (and differences[25]), thus to produce, to repeat the point made above, an internally articulated landscape of possible ways forward, inquirers are enabled to inquiry into this, that, or some other particular situation in terms of itself, in terms of features within it of relevance to the concerns of those living within that circumstance. Such difference making talk works on listeners by pointing out features in the listener's surroundings to which we can attend—features that they themselves may not yet have responded to. But what is most crucial here, though, is our choice of words, for our words can have both an ethical and a political function, in that different words can arouse different anticipations as to what might and/or should happen next—ethically in our ways of responding to a particular individual, and politically in our being sure that all concerned in the circumstance have had an equal say in determining its nature. Finally, in the musical or gestural qualities of our speakings, in how we voice our utterances, in our pausing, pacing, and different intonations, we indicate our own relations to our own words, whether we are confident, hesitant, offered, demanding, or what.

In other words, to repeat, our task is to seek to understand what we experience and perceive only in terms of what we experience and perceive, to understand it in terms of itself, rather than in terms of another, external, eternal, perfect, hidden world, in fact, of our own creation—to explain what is real for us only by what is real for us, and the situated and time-bound only by the situated and time-bound. That is, to talk from within our lives, rather than from an illusory place outside them.

So our conclusion here is not a conclusion at all, but merely a sketchy introduction to a whole new program of research for cultural psychology. Central to it is the importance of our imaginative difference making forms of talk, along with relinquishing the still in fact unfulfilled and, as I see it, forever unfulfillable dream of gaining the very general results we have desired in our more rationalistic inquiries, and to be content with the limited, partial, and situated results we can in fact obtain, which, in the end, will, I believe, perhaps surprisingly, turn out to be of far greater practical use and value to us.

Working in this limited, situated manner, then, will be aimed at achieving agreement among human beings about what to do, at bringing about consensus on particular ends to be achieved in particular circumstances, and the means to be used in achieving those ends. As such, the imaginative or poetic speech-based, hermeneutical form of inquiry proposed above, will give rise to a whole new set of expectations, a new horizon of future goals and endeavors, quite different from our more instrumental, theory-driven, discipline-based approaches in the past. But as I indicated at the very beginning of this chapter, our words or wordings matter, for they are not at all neutral, in shaping how we go out toward one or another future world of our own making, they can have both ethical and political consequences of how we come to treat both our own fellows, as well as all those who are strangers to us.

NOTES

1. I say "mistakenly," for we think of these events as "inner occurrences" because they seem to be "hidden" from us; but this is not because they reside inside our heads somewhere, but because, as we shall see, they emerge or come into existence as shared events "we" undergo in the course of the dynamic unfolding of our practical, everyday meetings with the others around us—these shared undergoings are not within us, individually, but within our relatings. As such, they have an ephemeral, dialogical-hermeneutical structure to them as a temporary stability, shared like a musical phrase, structured almost wholly in the temporal sequencing of their unfolding.

2. See also, Vico (1968): "There remains, however, the very great difficulty: How is it that there are as many different vulgar tongues as there are peoples? To solve it, we must here establish this great truth: ... by virtue of the aforesaid diversity of their natures they have regarded the same utilities or necessities of human life from different points of view, and there have thus arisen ... as many different languages as there are nations" (para. 445).

3. I say, *intra*- rather than *inter*mingling, as clearly, no strands of activity within a holistic flowing medium can have a separate existence from all the other strands in the flow; they are, of necessity, all internally related to each other and owe their character to the dynamic "intraplays" occurring among them all.

4. Such a world is not wholly unfamiliar to us. Whorf (1956) described the world of the native American Hopi thus: "The Hopi microcosm," he wrote, "seems to have analyzed reality largely in terms of EVENTS (or better

'eventing') ... [Where] events are considered the expression of invisible intensity factors, on which depend their stability and persistence, or their fugitiveness and proclivities. It implies that existents do not 'become later and later' all in the same way; but some do so by growing like plants, some by diffusing and vanishing, some by a procession of metamorphoses, some by enduring in one shape till affected by violent forces. In the nature of each existent able to manifest as a definite whole is the power of its own mode of duration: its growth, decline, stability, cyclicity, or creativeness. Everything is thus already 'prepared' for by the way it now manifests by earlier phases, and by what will be later, partly has been, and partly is in the act of being so 'prepared'" (p. 147).

5.   "The openness upon the world implies that the world be and remain a horizon, not because my vision would push the world back beyond itself, but because somehow he who sees is of it and is in it" (Merleau-Ponty, 1968, p. 100).

6.   Here, we could also add Mead (1934): "Mind arises through communication by a conversation of gestures in a social process or context of experience—not communication through mind" (p. 50).

7.   "This discovery," he says, "which is the master key of this Science, has cost us the persistent research of almost all our literary life, because with our civilized natures we moderns cannot at all imagine and can understand only by great toil the poetic nature of these first men" (Vico, 1968, para. 34).

8.   Later, in the section on hermeneutical unities, I will discuss Vico's (1988) account of *Ingenium*, as the basic "faculty that connects disparate and diverse things" (p. 96), here I will just mention Wittgenstein's (1953) remark on our need for "just that understanding which consists in 'seeing connections'" (p. 122).

9.   See also para. 346, in which Vico (1988) outlines the task of his new science as that of describing "the origins of institutions, divine and human ... [to] reach those first beginnings beyond which it is vain curiosity to demand others earlier."

10.   "Fear first created gods in the world" (Vico, 1968, para. 191). Later, when we turn to Bakhtin's (1986) work, we will find him also commenting: "When consciousness appeared in the world ... the world (existence) changed radically ... a new and major character in this event appears for the first time on the scene of earthly existence—the witness and the judge ... a *supra-existence* has emerged ... all existence exists in it and for it" (p. 137).

11.   His emphasis on similarities rather than identities, as we will see, will turn out to be important, for identities can be established by the "pattern matching" of static and fixed forms, an essentially mechanical activity; while seeing likenesses (and the consequent sensing of differences) is an imaginative activity. As Wittgenstein (1953) remarks, unlike mere sensing, seeing a likeness between two or more things—what he calls "noticing an aspect" (p. 193)—"demands imagination" (p. 207).

12. As Wittgenstein (1953) remarks, "If language is to be a means of communication there must be agreement not only in definitions *but also* (*queer as this may sound*) *in judgments*" (p. 242, my emphasis).

13. Or our shared common sense, or *sensus communis*, as Vico (1968, para. 141–142) puts it.

14. As Genova (1995, p. 25) points out, Wittgenstein distinguishes here between two very different kinds of world-pictures, between a *Weltanschauung* (an after-the-fact "view" invented by an individual inquirer), and a *Weltbild* (a before-the-fact a "view" gained by listening carefully to uses of language within a form of life, to discover the nature of the *sensus communis* spontaneously at work within it, determining a people's ways or methods of making sense of events happening around them.)

15. Indeed, Wittgenstein (1980b) is well aware of the open, always incomplete nature of this task: "Mere description is so difficult because one believes that one needs to fill out the facts in order to understand them. It is as if one saw a screen with scattered colour-patches, and said: the way they are here, they are unintelligible; they only make sense when one completes them into a shape.—Whereas I want to say: Here is the whole. (If you complete it, you falsify it)" (vol. 1, p. 257).

16. In a moment below, I will offer an alternative before-the-fact account, in terms both of the directedness of our sensings, that is, the fact that they provide us with action guiding anticipations, and also, the fact that we have an acute sense of their uniqueness in relation to the requirements of our current circumstances—again, the issue here is a matter of sensing likenesses and making connections.

17. I will explain the use of this term later.

18. "We can avoid ineptness or emptiness in our assertions only by presenting the model as what it is, as an object of comparison—as, so to speak, a measuring-rod; not as a preconceived idea to which reality must correspond. (The dogmatism into which we fall so easily in doing philosophy)" (Wittgenstein, 1953, p. 131).

19. And as Geertz also goes on to note (very much in line with Cornejo's comments quoted above), "The Western conception of the person as a bounded, unique, more or less integrated motivational and cognitive universe, a dynamic centre of awareness, emotion, judgment, and action organized into a distinctive whole and set contrastively both against other such wholes and against its social and natural background, is, however, incorrigible it may seem to us, a rather peculiar idea within the context of the world's cultures" (p. 59).

20. In the next section, I will—in relation to the epigraph quotation from William James (1912/1996)—want to raise the whole question as to whether what we call "concepts" are in fact relevant to the developmental, historical task we face in attempting to come to an understanding of, from within a holistic, essentially indeterminate, continuously flowing reality, it becomes possible for us to, as Wittgenstein (1953) puts it, to find our "way about" (p. 123), to come, so to speak, "to feel at home" in initially strange surroundings.

21.   As Bergson (1946/1974) puts it, "Not only may we thus complete the intellect and its knowledge of matter by accustoming it to install itself within the moving, but by developing also another faculty, complementary to the intellect, we may open a perspective on the other half of the real" (p. 344).

22.   Quoted by Vico (1968) from Horace, *Satire* 3, II, 247–248—written by the Roman poet, probably in 35 BC and at the latest by 33 BC.

23.   See, for example, Vico (1968, paras. 437, 446, 454).

24.   "The world of the [laboratory] experiment seems always capable of becoming a man-made reality, and this, while it may increase man's power of making and acting, even of creating a world, far beyond what any previous age dared to imagine in dream and phantasy, unfortunately puts man back once more—and now even more forcefully—into the prison of his own mind, into the limitations of patterns he himself created" (Arendt, 1958, p. 261).

25.   As Ferdinand de Saussure (1959/1966) remarks about the unfolding, sequential structure of our speech: "Everything that has been said up to this point boils down to this: in language there are only differences [the making of distinctions]. Even more important: a difference generally implies positive terms between which the difference is set up; *but in language there are only differences without positive terms*" (p. 120, my italics). See also Jakobson, Fant, and Halle, (1951) for an account of distinctive features in speech analysis.

REFERENCES

Arendt, H. (1958). *The human condition*. New York, NY: Doubleday Anchor Books.

Austin, J. (1962). *How to do things with words*. London, England: Oxford.

Bakhtin, M. M. (1981). *The dialogic imagination: Four essays by M. M. Bakhtin* (C. Emerson & M. Holquist, Trans.). Austin, TX: University of Texas Press.

Bakhtin, M. M. (1986). *Speech genres and other late essays* (V. W. McGee, Trans.). Austin: University of Texas Press.

Bergson, H. (1974). *The creative mind: An introduction to metaphysics*. New York, NY: Kensington. (Original work published 1946)

Berlin, I. (1981). Does political theory still exists? In H. Harvey (Ed.), *Concepts and categories philosophical essays* (pp. 158–159). Harmondsworth, England: Penguin Books.

Bortoft, H. (1996). *The wholeness of nature: Goethe's way toward a science of conscious participation in nature*. Hudson, NY: Lindisfarne Press.

Cassirer, E. (1960). *The logic of the humanities* (C. S. Howe, Trans.). New Haven, CT/ London, England: Yale University Press.

Chomsky, N. (1965). *Aspects of the theory of syntax*. Cambridge, MA: MIT Press.

Chomsky, N. (1972). *Language and mind* (Enl. ed.). New York, NY: Harcourt Brace Jovanovich.

de Saussure, F. (1959/1966). *Course in general linguistics* (C. Bally & A. Sechehaye, Eds.). New York, NY: McGraw-Hill.

Descartes, R. (1968). *Discourse on method and the meditations* (F. Sutcliffe, Trans.). London, England: Penguin. (Original work published 1637)

Gadamer, H.-G. (2000). *Truth and method* (J. Weinsheimer & D. G. Marshall, Trans.). New York, NY: Continuum.

Garfinkel, H. (1967). Practical sociological reasoning: Some features in the work of the Los Angeles suicide prevention center. In E. Shneidman (Ed.), *Essays in self-destruction* (pp. 171-186). New York, NY: Science House.

Geertz, C. (1983). *Local knowledge: Further essays in interpretative anthropology*. New York, NY: Basic Books.

Geertz, C. (2000). *Available light: Anthropological reflections on philosophical topics*. Princeton, NJ/Oxford, England: Princeton University Press.

Genova, J. (1995). *Wittgenstein: A way of seeing*. New York, NY/London, England: Routledge.

Gibson, J. J. (1979). *The ecological approach to visual perception*. Boston, MA: Houghton Mifflin.

Hacker, P. M. S. (2010). Wittgenstein's anthropological and ethnological approach. In J. P. Gakvez (Ed.), *Philosophical anthropology: Wittgenstein's perspectives*. Frankfurt, Germany: Ontos Verlag.

Ingold, T., & Palsson, G. (Eds.). (2013). *Biosocial becomings: Integrating biological and social anthropology*. Cambridge, England: Cambridge University Press.

Jakobson, R., Fant, G., & Halle, M. (1951). *Preliminaries to speech analysis: The distinctive features and their correlates*. Cambridge, MA: MIT Press.

James, W. (1890/1950). *Principles of psychology, Vols. 1 & 2*. New York, NY: Dover.

James, W. (1912/2003). *Essays in radical empiricism*. New York, NY: Dover.

Kant, I. (1998). *Critique of pure reason*. Cambridge, MA: Cambridge University Press. (Original work published 1781)

Kaufmann, W. (1980/1998). *Goethe, Kant and Hegel: Discovering the mind, Vol. 1*. New Brunswick, NJ: Transaction.

Mead, G. H. (1934). *Mind, self and society*. Chicago, IL: University of Chicago Press.

Merleau-Ponty, M. (1968). *The visible and the invisible* (C. Lefort, Ed.; A. Lingis, Trans.). Evanston, IL: Northwestern University Press.

Popper, K. (1972). *Objective knowledge: An evolutionary approach*. Oxford, England: Oxford University Press.

Shotter, J. (1984). *Social accountability and selfhood*. Oxford, England: Blackwell.

Shotter, J. (2004). The manufacture of personhood, and the institutionalization of mutual humiliation. *Concepts and Transformations, 9*(1), 1–37.

Shotter, J. (2009). Moments of common reference in dialogic communication: A basis for unconfused collaboration in unique contexts. *International Journal of Collaborative Practices, 1*(1), 1–23.

Shotter, J. (2010). *Social constructionism on the edge: 'Withness'—Thinking & embodiment*. Chagrin Falls, OH: Taos Institute Press.

Shotter, J. (2014). From 'after the fact' objective analyses to immediate 'before the fact' living meanings. *Culture & Psychology, 20*(4), 525–536.

Shotter, J. (2016). Undisciplining social science: Wittgenstein and the art of creating situated practices of social inquiry. *Journal for the Theory of Social Behaviour, 46*(1), 60–83. doi:10.1111/jtsb.12080

Taylor, C. (1995). *Philosophical arguments*. Cambridge, MA: Harvard University Press.

Verene, D. P. (1981). *Vico's science of the imagination*. Ithaca, NY/London, England: Cornell University Press.

Vico, G. (1968). *The new science of Giambattista Vico* (T. G. Bergin & M. H. Fisch, Eds. & Trans.). Ithaca, NY: Cornell University Press.

Vico, G. (1988). *On the most ancient wisdom of the Italians* (L. Palmer, Trans.). Ithaca, NY: Cornell University Press.

Von Humboldt, W. (1836). *Über die Verschiedenheit des menschlichen Sprachbaues und ihren Einfluss auf die geistige Entwickelungdes Menschengeschlecht*. Berlin, Germany: Ferdinand Dümmer.

Vygotsky, L. (1962). *Thought and language* (E. Hanf-mann & G. Vakar, Trans.). Cambridge, MA: MIT Press.

Vygotsky, L. S. (1966). Development of the higher mental functions. In A. N. Leontyev, A. R. Luria, & A. Smirnov (Eds.), *Psychological research in the USSR* (pp. 11–46). Moscow, Russia: Progress.

Vygotsky, L. S. (1978). *Mind in society: The development of higher psychological processes*. Cambridge, MA: Harvard University Press.

Vygotsky, L. S. (1986). *Thought and language* (Newly Rev. ed.; A. Kozulin, Trans). Cambridge, MA: MIT Press.

Whorf, B. L. (1956). *Language, thought and reality: Selected writings of Benjamin Lee Whorf*. Cambridge, MA: MIT Press.

Wittgenstein, L. (1922). *Tractatus logico-philosophicus*. London, England: Kegan Paul.

Wittgenstein, L. (1953). *Philosophical investigations* (G. E. M. Anscombe, Trans.). Oxford, England: Blackwell.

Wittgenstein, L. (1966). *Lectures and conversations on aesthetics, psychology and religious belief*. Oxford, England: Blackwell.

Wittgenstein, L. (1969). *On certainty* (D. Paul & G. E. M Anscombe, Trans.). Oxford, England: Blackwell.

Wittgenstein, L. (1980a). *Remarks on the philosophy of psychology, vols. 1 & 2*. Oxford, England: Blackwell.

Wittgenstein, L. (1980b). *Culture and value* (P. Winch, Trans.). Oxford, England: Blackwell.

Wittgenstein, L. (1981). *Zettel* (G. E. M. Anscombe & G. H. V. Wright, Eds.). Oxford, England: Blackwell.

CHAPTER 11

AMERINDIAN PSYCHOLOGY

Cultural Basis
for General Knowledge Construction

Danilo Silva Guimarães

This chapter addresses the challenge of cultural psychology to recover the forgotten dimensions of the human being, whose roots connect psychology to anthropology rather than to epistemology (Cornejo, this volume). For most of the Amerindians peoples, knowledge is not related to deciphering the world, as it were in Mesopotamia, Greece, or in the second wave of Enlightenment in the modern sciences (Gadamer, 1981/2010). The notion of deciphering, in modern sciences, was constructed out of the abandonment of nonrational human dimensions. Deciphering addresses precise and correct content that corresponds to the supposed true image of the world. Therefore, vital forces, empathy, physiognomic sensibilities, intuition, and fantasy, among others, had to be excluded in the process of constructing true knowledge, mainly because these ways of apprehending the environment do not fit classical logic.

Instead of stabilizing the knowledge through the supposed universal images of the truth, that is, toward general categories, opposed to unreal, fantasied/fictional images/categories, diverse cultures proposed that the process of knowledge construction is permanent and generative of multi-

The Psychology of Imagination: History, Theory, and New Research Horizons
pp. 221–238

ple categories that become acceptable due to a sensory education of the body.

I argue that sensory education consists in the acquisition of clues, not ciphers, and that [Amerindian] songs and stories—including stories of how animals respond to the presence of the hunter—give shape to a perception of the world guided by this education. (Ingold, 2000, p. 10)

the cipher is centrifugal, allowing the novice to access meanings that are attached ("pinned on") by the mind to the outer surface of the world [the correct representation], the clue is centripetal, guiding him towards meanings that lie at the heart of the world itself, but which are normally hidden behind the facade of superficial appearances. (Ingold, 2000, p. 23)

In this chapter, we assume that the clues vindicated in the Amerindian talks guide a process of knowledge construction. As an open-ended process, it is more general than the knowledge understood as ciphers, which remains as a fixed image of the world delivered by any dominant culture. Instead of stabilizing the knowledge in universal images of the truth, opposed to unreal, fantastic images, Amerindian basis for knowledge construction, or epistemology, implies a sort of subject-subject relationship (cf. Viveiros de Castro, 2006), a permanent negotiation concerning the topics of investigation culturally guided.

Throughout the following pages, we will reflect on how scientific knowledge builds its generality as an outcome of the rational—deductive, inductive or abductive—elaboration of a narrative and mythic experience of the world. If we depart from a different narrative and mythological socially constructed realities, and proceed to the rational, methodic elaboration of these realities, we are able to develop, as an outcome, distinct knowledge, which can be relevant to the cultural field from which it originates Historical and anthropological data will be selectively focused in order to discuss the viability of an Amerindian psychology, as a sort of reflexive attitude that can emerge aligned with and from the cosmological tradition of autochthon peoples of the Americas. Finally, we argue that the Amerindian path of knowledge construction is linked to a broader, universal process of argumentative elaboration that is not only restricted to the Amerindian context.

CONSTRUCTING THE SUPPOSED TRUE KNOWLEDGE FROM LEGENDARY IMAGES OF THE OTHERS IN WESTERN SOCIETIES

Many philosophers, scientists and art makers have already discussed the issue of mutual misinterpretations in the first meetings of the Europeans and Amerindians more than five centuries ago, in the period of the invasion. Tzvetan Todorov (2010), for instance, asserted that meeting Amerindian peoples was "the most surprisingly meeting in our history" (p. 4). Nevertheless, its consequences have not yet been completely understood: as the Amerindian peoples were not completely vanished, they also were not assimilated in the contemporary Western global world. A scientist would say that the cipher that would give us the perfect understanding of these societies was not yet discovered, or, for a certain kind of mechanist thinking whose vestiges remain from the 19th century, these people were not yet fixed in the intelligible order susceptible of mathematical modeling of the scientific minds.

The issue of alterity, as the nonapprehensible dimension of the other, remains as a necessary fuel for disquieting experiences growing fantasies and knowledge construction. In this sense, knowledge construction includes the sensible, intuitive perception, fantasy, and sensuousness as integrated dimensions in science and art production, because they are culturally situated and symbolically guided by the active craftsmanship of the scientist and artist.

The fertilization of fictional ideas about the others has had a historical function in Western societies since ancient times. It was especially useful to ideologically protect some commercial routes. For instance, Phoenician's legends about monsters more or less like human beings worked as semiotic barrier (Boesch, 1991) to the commercial interest of the other peoples living in the Mediterranean. The supposed presence of these fantastic and terrible creatures, as sirens and cyclops, worked as a sort of customs agency to terrified naïve navigators (Melo Franco, 1937/2000). A profusion of fictional beings continued to increase during all classical antiquity and postclassical ages, filling with fantastic images the ignorance about the lands abroad and their people. When the Europeans reached the American lands, the surprise was not because of the difference or the beauty of the landscape, but because they found there similar human beings.

> When it comes to European encounters with hitherto unknown peoples, there were always multiple ways in which they could be potentially categorized according to familiar templates. The kind of image of the Others that came to be constructed, on the basis of real of alleged "facts" about them, will have been dependent on the prior background of ideas and values of the perceivers; and if these varied, so did the result of assimilation to the "familiar." It is only after images have become culturally conventionalized that more uniformity can be expected. (Jahoda, 1999, p. 11)

The ignorance about the cultural basis of epistemology led philosophers, artists, and scientists to construct very convincing justifications presented as truth knowledge, which ended supporting the Eurocentric racism in the 19th century (Jahoda, 1999). Contemporary historical analysis shows that most of this knowledge was grounded in very ancient, myth-based, assumptions about the foreigners in Eurocentric cosmology. These assumptions, impregnated in the mythological and ritual texture of Western societies, are culturally transferred and ignore rational proofs, constituting the emotional basis of people belonging to these societies. Such emotional basis, within the academic world of philosophical, artistic and scientific knowledge, let their vestiges as bricks in the large buildings of the *Naturwissenschaft* and *Geistenwissenchaft*.[1]

Images of Fantasy as Opposed to the Reality, the Illuminated Truth, and Scientific Knowledge

For ancient Mesopotamians (Assyrian and Babylonian peoples), an image had an indexical nature, "it functioned through a relationship of contiguity to the signified" (Bahrani, 2008, p. 51). Images and statements were considered not as copies, but as part of reality with power and capacities, substituting their agents. At that time, the ground rules of the war adopted practices of abducting images of gods and kings during battles and carrying off monuments with the aim of destroying representations of the enemies. Mesopotamians apprehended the world as a text that had to be deciphered. The work of deciphering in the Mesopotamian divination involved a ritualized exegetical reading, mainly conducted by clergypersons, following previously established codes supposed to be embedded in nature (Bahrani, 2008).

In contrast, the semiotics of ancient Greeks constructed a distinction between the copy and the original. The intellectual mental activity (*Noûs*) started to be considered the most elevated way in which the truth was revealed (Gadamer, 1981/2010). Taking into account the Aristotelian analogical and substitutive theories of metaphor, there is, in fact, a construction of a detached representation of the real allowing the possibility of grasping meaningful similarities underlying a signifer (Aristotle, 1992). The logos, in opposition to the myth (an originally Greek word with the meaning of discourse, proclamation, announce, or news), had the function of systematizing the narrative discourse (myth) in clear and demonstrable arguments.

In the 5th century B.C., the Myth and the Logos become detached genders of discourse, which opposed the invented stories to the enumerable, demonstrable truth. Nevertheless, Aristotle recognized the truth in the roots of what is narrated and/or invented: "The Myth is, in all cases, the already known, the announcement that is spread without determining its origins or certification" (Gadamer, 1981/2010, p. 67).

To the Mesopotamian and Greek cosmology, the world and its images should be deciphered in order to apprehend the real meaning of things. In both cases, there is a basic, tacit or explicit understanding that the landscape and/or the writings have encoded meanings to be deciphered. Through contiguity or through representation of the world, there is a quest for the correspondence, for the correct image of the world, which reveals the real underlying the appearance. The images that supposedly correspond to the real started to be classified as knowledge (*epistéme*), and the images that do not correspond to the real entered in the realm of fiction (i.e., fantasies created by human imagination).

Gadamer (1954/2010) emphasized that Christianity, through the New Testament, radicalized the criticism to the mythological images of the world. The gods, belonging to the different peoples (paganism), were confronted by the God enlightened in the Christian messages, which reunited the multiplicity around the unity of a universal principle, originated in a transcendent dimension. The falsification of the supposed false ideas in the pagan cultures paved the way to the development of the modern sciences, at least promoting the emergence of a cultural ground that no longer accepted the multiple mythical conceptions of the world.

Modern sciences started to be developed few centuries before the milestone foundation of the first laboratory on psychological research by Wundt, in Leipzig, 1879, when Europeans were suffering the psychosocial impacts out of their encounter with a novel sort of diversity of things and peoples around the world (Figueiredo, 1992). The relatively stable life around small territory with small villages became ruptured by unknown variations and novelties; the well-known local population and language were invaded by foreigners' dialects and accents; the social hierarchies started to be questioned; the clear distinction between center-periphery was confused; as well as the well-defined notions of regularity and order.

Instead of a world plentiful of meaning and integrity with durable personal and collective identities, as the Christianity vindicated in the medieval period, the new emergent sociocultural field brought the diversity and the complexity of unusual ways of being human. The dissolution of internal borders and the meeting of external borders allowed the emergence of new ethnic mixtures, linguistic hybridism, transformations in the religiosity, and the like. The Renaissance was not only a period of openness to ancient European history, but also allowed the meeting of otherness and their ways of life beyond the borders of each feudal territory within Europe, including lands overseas.

Different strategies emerged, along centuries, as efforts to reorganize the chaos in this complex sociocultural field. Until the 18th century, a series of transformations took place in the pool of intellectual life: the religious reformation; the construction of consistent philosophical systems, in which rigorous rational deductions were in the core of the environment explanation; the strengthening of empirical studies, from Galileo to Newton and so on. Cosmological formulas emerged along this historical moment as a solution to the gaps and uncertainties of unbalanced natural and social world (cf. Cassirer, 1994).

In this sociocultural context, Francis Bacon (1980) criticized what he considered epistemological obstacles for scientific knowledge construction. His empiricism presupposed the possibility of understanding phenomena through observation, minimizing the participation of false ideas—so-called idols. Nevertheless, empirical observations lacked strong theories for interpretation of nature. The positivism of Comte (1978) addressed the knowledge history, asserting that science would be the most advanced stage of law formulations about the real, once it was able to regulate imagination, to be pragmatically used and more precise in describing the nature of phenomena. Science should also have the capacity to organize society, avoiding metaphysical and religious tendencies. Positivist ideals guided efforts in the development of verification criteria of meaning, which divides reality from fantastic ideas relegated to the space of artistic creation, or madness.

The quest for validation criteria aiming to find the correct knowledge is remarkable from the experimental model of Galileo and posterior philosophical epistemological debate addressing the attainment of empirical data and theoretical formulation. The presupposition was that the correct knowledge should be unique. The idea of universality in science can be associated to Western cosmological-philosophical conception of the ontological unity of the cosmos (cf. Fausto, 2008). From this basic presupposition emerged devices for controlling symbolic-cultural elaborations, in conflict with the so-called mythological and fictitious ideas of other cultures (cf. Stengers, 2002). When some fictional discourses produced in the scientific grounds become more than fiction, they can be turned into a representation of "bidding system of reality" (Boesch, 1991, p. 276).[2] It somehow encapsulates firm and unquestioned ideas of reality, its reasons, and consequences. As such, these discourses acquire a cultural-mythological function. A scientific discourse is converted into myth when it works as a crystallized and unquestionable formula.

The Constructivist Alternative

According to Duran (2004), both constructivist and positivist epistemologies are similar in that they consider reality as something that exists.

One difference is that while for positivism, the knowledge of reality is something possible to be reached because the organism has access to the reality through its sensible organs, for constructivism, knowledge of reality is something impossible, because we just have access to some experiences of reality: valid knowledge is that which finds internal consistency, intersubjective agreement, and viability for the continuity of human life. For positivism, knowledge is a sort of copy or representation of reality; the validation of knowledge is made through comparison between the representation and empirical phenomena, while for constructivism it is an organization of experience.

Considering that there are different kinds of constructivism (cf. Neymeyer, 1997), when discussing it in an epistemological level, there are some convergences that allow us to integrate different theories in a meta-theoretical umbrella. For instance, in the constructivist epistemology, the organism (a person, a subject) is understood as an active system in relation to its environment:

> The organism experiences its environment in an interactive and continuous process, adjusting and changing itself, letting impacts in its epigenetic system, in its genome as well as in its environment. These impacts are left to the subsequent generations. So, there is not any separation between development and evolution. The organism takes an active part in the process of its own development, as well as in the evolution of its ecological community. (Almeida & Falcão, 2008, p. 529)

From this, there is no biological or sociological determinism over the organism. Instead, it considers the role of self-regulatory processes and self-reproductive agency of the person-subject in relation to its exteriority. New psychological functions emerge from the relation of the organism/subject in the world, as functional organizers of these relations (Valsiner, 1994, p. 250). That is, the organism/subject is able to act persistently over disquieting experiences in the world, organizing it and addressing a less tensional state; for instance, through the creation of meaning for these experiences and devices to overcome difficulties.

So, from the epistemological viewpoint, constructivism is defined in contrast with objectivism (cf. Neymeier, 1997). Additionally, from the ontological viewpoint, it is defined in contrast with idealism (Duran, 2004). Therefore, constructivism can be situated in the intersection between the realism and the subjectivism: there is a reality, but we just have access to the experience of the reality. The Figure 11.1 shows some key points of rupture between objectivist epistemologies and subjectivist epistemologies.

Historically, in the field of psychology, distinct versions of constructivism were developed through the elaboration of consistent metaphors for the

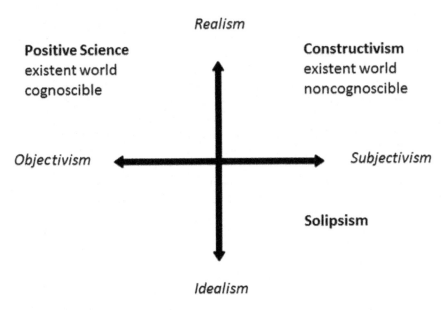

Source: Adapted from Duran (2004).

Figure 11.1.   Coordination system of constructivism.

understanding of knowledge construction. In these versions, consensus and viability as criteria to knowledge validation in constructivism, have a functional relevance in the adaptation to the social and natural world, intertwining the cultural preconceptions and novel intellectual elaborations. Therefore, the culture, from which a science is a part, is something that "belongs to the relating of the person and the environment ... a process of internalization and externalization or mutual constituting between person and the social world ... elaborated in terms of appropriation, guided participation or mastery" (Valsiner, 2007, p. 22).

The members of a culture guide their actions according to a small number of values that they are not usually aware of (Descola, 1998). These values can be found in the myths and ideologies socially reproduced in different ways by the members of any society. Myths are constantly reaffirmed by each community, spreading "a pattern of intelligibility that allows the articulation of understandings about the world, society and history, which are hidden in the thresholds of consciousness" (Lévi-Strauss & Eribon, 1988/1990, p. 182).

From the myth to the logos, some branches of the scientific culture have fallen in the metaphysic belief in which the reality would be completely disenchanted through reasoning as a criticism of the mythical beliefs. Nevertheless, the rational criticism of the myth is only one possible path concerning an object of human reflection. The same object could be explored in the paths of arts, religion, or politics, for instance. Besides, regarding the object, reasoning is not able to regard itself in its real historical situation: the rational self-comprehension is always delayed in relation to its praxis, evincing a limit to its aims of achieving a full awareness of its position (Gadamer, 1954/2010, p. 63). These hermeneutic propositions assert that it is only by comprehending the role of the myth in the process of knowledge construction that we can achieve a self-comprehension that includes but also surpasses the limits of reasoning. It is, then, relevant to pay attention to the extra-scientific truths (i.e., arts and religion) which are reunited, although not fused, in the poetics of knowledge construction.

Figure 11.2 shows the recursive process in which the scientific knowledge constructions emerge and develop as an argumentative criticism of the experiential and mythological narratives (as we discussed previously from Gadamer, 1954/2010). Some of the emerged elaborations are reconverted into mythological narratives in the field of social representations (Marková, 2006; Valsiner, 2012) and are the support for the elaboration of other institutionalized or noninstitutionalized discourses in religion, arts, politics, or common sense.

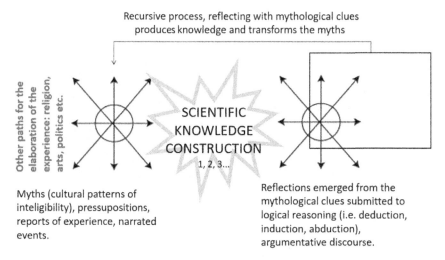

Figure 11.2.   Scientific knowledge construction between narrative and argumentative discourses.

Multiplying the Multiplicity of Psychologies

From the latest decades of the 19th to the first decades of the 20th century, a considerable number of projects for a scientific psychology emerged as an outcome of the intellectual production of researchers in Europe and the United States, from different academic backgrounds (philosophy, medicine, literature, biology, law, etc.). Publications of some precursors of contemporary psychologies are representative of the intellectual aims to achieve a general psychology, the basis for scientific ventures—for example, *Principles of Psychology* (James, 1890); "Project for a Scientific Psychology" (Freud, 1895/1996); *Introduction to Psychology* (Wundt, 1911); "Psychology as the Behaviorist Views It" (Watson, 1913); *Principles of Gestalt Psychology* (Koffka, 1935), among others. At this time, one of the most relevant reflections concerning the fragmentation of the psychological field and the efforts for its integration was documented in Vygotsky's work "The Historical Meaning of the Crisis in Psychology: A Methodological Investigation" (1997).

Vygotsky (1997) assumes the task of realizing the psychology as a science by the means of dialectically integrating the scientific knowledge already produced by the different schools. First, he identifies the fragmentation of psychology concerning the distinct subject matters focalized by the different schools, that is, the consciousness, the behavior or the unconscious, and the distinct starting points elected by the researchers, that is, the normal or the pathologic, the simple or the complex phenomena, the human or the animal behavior. Vygotsky observed that the answer each psychology had given to unify the phenomena of interest led to the emergence of dogmatic or eclectic positioning. That is, the former, by selecting an object of study—the observable behavior—and excluding the possibility of considering others such as the conscious or unconscious. The latter, eclectic positioning, tried to assimilate concepts emergent in different philosophical and scientific matrixes, fusing disparate theories.

One of the problems of the dogmatic attitude in psychology is that it ends up by fragmenting the field in distinct sciences, thus failing in the objective of creating a unified science. The eclectic attitude also fails because it does not take into consideration that

> the word that refers to a fact at the same time provides a philosophy of that fact, its theory, its system. When I say: "the consciousness of the color" I have scientific associations of a certain kind, the fact is included in a certain series of phenomena, I attach a certain meaning to the fact. When I say: "the reaction to white" everything is wholly different, (Vygotsky, 1997, p. 326)

Therefore, for Vygotsky (1997), it is relevant to understand the process of construction of scientific concepts, and he understands that the dialectic materialism provides the best methodology in order to integrate the two principles that he identified as the main source of fragmentation in the psychological field, the opposition between the objectivist materialism and the subjectivist idealism: "Dialectics covers nature, thinking, history—it is the most general, maximally universal science. The theory of the psychological materialism or dialectics of psychology is what I call general psychology" (p. 389).

> After all, our task is not at all to isolate our work from the general psychological work of the past, but to unite our work with all the scientific achievements of psychology into one whole, and on a new basis. We do not want to distinguish our school from science, but science from non-science, psychology from non-psychology. The psychology about which we are talking does not yet exist. It still has to be created—and by more than one school. (p. 405)

The teleological, or prophetic, aims for the creation of the new man and the new society through the scientific emancipation of the mankind are still unrealized. Psychology, almost a century after Vygotsky's claims for integration, remains a field of dispersion in which the stereotyped repetition of the old ideas and nourishment of strained oppositions between schools of thinking guides the sterilization of the creative process in the expected scientific development of new ideas (cf. Valsiner, 2012). By contrast, the study of what constrains human creativity, in order to enlarge it, is precisely the aim of cultural psychology (cf. Boesch, 1997). Psychology, as a scientific, therefore, cultural knowledge, faces the fact that each culture cultivates its members in a self-centered way, that is, each culture has a proper systematized knowledge, notions, and methods to empirically understand and produce what the Eurocentric sciences call psychological processes.

Facing the Diversity

> Why do people feed and take care of small babies? They do it because babies are *kwamonuru*, "handsome, sad, little wretched ones, poor little things." It gives rise to *getwamonuta*, "discerning the sadness, pity, abandonment, graciousness of someone," that is an aspect of *nshinikanchi* [mind, intelligence, memory, respect, love]. *Getwamonuta*, "to discern the affliction," moves the older parents to an effort in order to satisfy babies' desire, leading to the formation of *nshinikanchi*, in the process of upbringing. (Gow, 1997, p. 55)

Which psychology would emerge if we decided to reflect on the Piro's[3] notions of *kwamonuru*, *getwamonuta*, and *nshinikanchi*, in order to develop it as a scientific concept, for instance, submitting the Piro's narratives to an argumentative logical reasoning, deductive and inductive analysis, or hermeneutic interpretation? Or which psychology would emerge from the development of Amerindian philosophical concepts (cf. Viveiros de Castro, 2006) into novel methods for general knowledge construction, from the deep and sophisticated local wisdom? How do we include the voice of other cultures in the epistemological debate concerning the universal knowledge of mankind in a pluralistic world?

The issue of knowledge demarcation, in opposition to the false, fantastic worldviews, is a relevant dimension in the process of interethnic subjugation. The demarcation between knowledge and lack of knowledge is in the core of the assimilationist projects of Amerindian peoples in Brazil, starting from the Catholic religious conversion projects to the secular efforts of the State to integrate the population. In Brazil, for centuries, the Amerindians were considered as unable to access civil rights. The State historically addressed their full integration to the National Society, despite the resistance of the peoples themselves.

Between the 19th and the 20th centuries, with the secularization of the State institutions in coalition with scientific knowledge, the opposition to the Amerindian traditions was strengthened, including their knowledge associated with fairy tales or myth as a product of fantastic imagination, in opposition to the scientific as the truth. Amerindian peoples have been resisting and constructing counter-discourses and pervasive practices that act on public opinion, aiming to reverse misconceptions and, consequently, develop more consistent ideas and social practices in relation to them (e.g., the documentary *Tenonderã: Um Olhar para o futuro*).

In this context, the dialogues between psychologists and Amerindian peoples presuppose an indefinite dynamics of approximation and distancing which are primarily affective, motivated by the availability to recognize an uneasy feeling in relation to otherness (Simão, 2003). Uneasiness, as the motor of epistemological curiosity and ethical approaches of the Self to Other, emerges if we are available to face the diversity of psychological processes, languages, myths, rituals, and memories that are constitutive of strong and peculiar perspectives on the basis of reflected, consistent, and coherent realities and worldviews.

Besides, we need a method to approach the Amerindian psychology without falling into dichotomist attitudes, claiming for an impossible communication between distinct culturally made knowledge, or eclectic attitudes, making cursory approximations between millenary traditions developing proper and sophisticated systems of knowledge. If there is a bridge between the Amerindian and European cultures, this bridge was broken about 10,000 years ago, and the last 500 years have contributed to intensifying such cultural distance, instead of creating communicative conditions to epistemological exchange. It means that Amerindian and European cultures were not stable from the period these people became geographically distant, and each one guided its cultural traditions to different ontological routes (Descola, 2008). If each culture developed resources to deal with foreigners, it is also true that the reflections emerged in each cultural frame are not transparent to the other (Rasmussen, 2011), there is always a zone of misunderstanding (Simão, 2003) or equivocation (Viveiros de Castro, 2004) in such efforts of interethnic translation. It is, then, necessary work on the gaps between both worlds in order to control or minimize the unavoidable equivoques.

When recognizing the mythopoetic as an inclusive part in the process of knowledge construction in its scientific path, psychologists are able to reflect on its belongingness to the social life of a specific community among others, that is, a perspective that implies a natural attitude and constructs a social objective reality (cf. Berger & Luckmann, 2003). The scientific knowledge emerges as a criticism of such socially constructed reality or natural attitude in order to understand and/or manipulate it. Recognizing its belongingness to a socially constructed reality, instead of assuming it to be universal when the psychological knowledge is local and mainly Eurocentric, psychologists constructing knowledge concerning interethnic frames need to reflect upon the images and associated feelings that emerge in the experience of diverse cultural fields as distinct trajectories of knowledge construction. Any cultural knowledge, including the scientific, needs to be approached from a critical perspective; that is, including nonscientific, ontological, and ethical evaluations as a strategy of self-reflection in order to become systematic, intelligible, and functional to certain cultural aims.

Other Fantasies and Other Images Grounding Knowledge Construction

In this chapter we focused "the forgotten dimensions of the human being, whose roots connect psychology to anthropology rather than to epistemology" (Cornejo, this volume, p. x), proposing that psychological knowledge is immersed in the images and fantasies of the cultural field in which it belongs. This unavoidable participation in a cultural field guides further reflections, addressing epistemological disputes and theoretical construction. Nevertheless, distinct cosmologies guide the construction of concepts based on images, fantasies, and desires, addressing notions of persons who are not similar to those who developed in the ontological trajectory of Eurocentric cultures.

William James (1890) presented and discussed three of the main sources of error in psychology. First, the absence of proper terms for the investigation and comprehension of thinking and feelings that are part of the psychical life; second, the confusion of the psychologist between thinking and the object of thinking; and third, the possible mess between the perspective of the psychologist and the psychical fact he/she investigates.

More recently, Hermans, Kempen and van Loon (1992) cited Jaynes (1976) in his observation that the language people typically use to describe psychical phenomena is derived from the visual and active experience of the being in space, as a metaphor for the mental processes, that is, slow thinking, agitated mind, brilliant ideas, open mindedness, and so on. These terms are all metaphors that belong to a certain cultural field; they are not completely invented in the scientific framework.

Altogether, these considerations call the attention to a sort of promiscuity between the scientific and the cultural knowledge in psychology: psychology has no proper terms. The terms adopted in the construction of the psychological science depend on the articulation of words and meanings belonging to a cultural conception of human being. Additionally, each person culturally situated takes as object of his feeling/thinking specific elements derived from the experience in social life: that is, the object of concern and the solutions given by an Amerindian shaman finding the cure to an illness are radically different from those given by bio-medicine.

Therefore, the cultural situation of psychology, that is, its unavoidable indigenous genetic basis, imposes limits to its aims of generalization if psychologists are focused on the regularity of behavior and the contents of mental life. An exploration of indigenous psychologies around the world would bring myriad novel terms and meanings to the same terms that enormously amplify the dispersion of the already fragmented psychological schools. Besides, the meanings of the cultural production of objectivity, through semiotic and other material elaboration, emerge from a social situation in which an already elaborated meaning becomes open to the singularity of the other.

In its singularity, the otherness ruptures the identity or unity of the knowledge, establishing a field of unknown as an ethical condition that instructs the processes of cultural differentiation and dedifferentiation. The susceptibility to the unknown precedes knowledge, demanding an answer as an affective and cognitive semiotic elaboration and action in relation to which the person is responsible.

Psychologists are, then, ethically responsible for their elaborations (fantastic, imaginary or those assumed as real), while moving across distinct cultural fields, as the Amerindians' diversities, to the same extent that each culture is responsible for the implications of its indigenous psychology. It is also necessary to think carefully about the consequences of building approximations and distancing, especially in the interethnic situations that involve psychosocial vulnerabilities, which are consequences of historical interethnic threatening practices.

If the psychologies have no proper words to express the universal contents of human minds, they can observe, reflect, and intervene in the heterogenetic process of meaning construction, as it appears as a general aspect in the diversification of cultures. Instead of producing transcultural correlations between psychological contents, cultural psychology could develop the sensibility to apprehend and the capacity to host the process of semiotic multiplication that takes place in concrete situations of a world in which people have the right to manifest their singularities.

Cultural creativity transforms the social incompleteness with autonomy and responsibility to a greater or lesser extent under specific conditions. Therefore, psychologists should not feel insecure because they do not have all the script prefigured to their practices in the interethnic zones: learned ignorance, as the recognition of the limits of the cultural immersion of the psychological knowledge, is a good starting point in order to develop novel knowledge in partnership with other realities that are representative of human semiotic-cultural creative conditions.

NOTES

1.   This idea was explored in a preliminary paper (Guimarães, 2012, p. 349):

> "At the psychological level, science may become 'a system of explanation and justification for which no rational proof or deduction is or can be given. It somehow encapsulates firm and unquestioned ideas of reality, its reasons and consequences' (Boesch, 1991, p. 123). The cultural psychologist Ernst Boesch described a representative situation in which a young girl started to perceive the Freudian Oedipus 'myth' as a scientifically proved explanation for the course of human development. The presupposed valid scientific explanation became a reference of true, and could be confronted with other 'fairy tales.' In this confrontation, the vast number of arbitrary myth stories from Asia to Greece and the Americas probably would be considered as 'non-committal' (cf. Boesch, 1991, p. 276). In such Boeschian case, a scientific discourse was converted into myth, working as a crystallized and unquestionable formula in the psychology of his patient."

2. That is, if we think in the theories as real explanations, they become unquestionable, but if we understand them as fictions, then we are able to criticize and develop other fictions we consider more consistent to understand the phenomena, the experience of the untranslatable real.
3. The Piro are a people who live in the Amazonian forest between Brazil and Peru.

REFERENCES

Almeida, A. V., & Falcão, J. T. R. (2008). Piaget e Teorias da evolução orgânica. *Psicologia Reflexão e Crítica, 21*(3), 525–532.

Aristotle. (1992). *Poética*. São Paulo, Brazil: Ars Poética.

Bacon, F. (1980). *Novum organum ou as verdadeiras indicações acerca da interpretação da natureza*. São Paulo, Brazil: Abril Cultural. (Original work published 1620)

Bahrani, Z. (2008). *Rituals of war. The body and violence in Mesopotamia*. Brooklyn, NY: Zone Books.

Berger, P. B., & Luckmann, T. (2003). *A construção social da realidade: Tratado sobre a sociologia do conhecimento*. Petrópolis, Brazil: Vozes.

Boesch, E. E. (1991). *Symbolic action theory and cultural psychology*. Berlin-Heidelberg, Germany: Springer-Verlag.

Boesch, E. E. (1997). Reasons for a symbolic concept of action. *Culture & Psychology, 3*(3), 423–431.

Cassirer, E. (1994). *A filosofia do iluminismo*. Campinass, Brazil: Editora da UNICAMP. (Original work published in 1932)

Comte, A. (1978). *Curso de filosofia positiva*. São Paulos, Brazil: Abril Cultural.

Descola, P. (1998). Estrutura ou sentimento: A relação com o animal da Amazônia. *Mana 4*(1), 23–45.

Descola, P. (2008, January 21). Who owns nature. *books & ideas.net*. Retrieved from http://www.booksandideas.net/Who-owns-nature.html

Duran, A. P. (2004). Relação eu - outro: Um Paradigma sob a Perspectiva do Construtivismo Terapêutico. In L. M Simão & A. M. Martínez (Eds.), *O outro no desenvolvimento humano* (pp. 131–144). São Paulo, Brazil: Pioneira Thomson Learning.

Fausto, C. (2008). Donos demais: Maestria e domínio na Amazônia. *Mana, 14*(2), 329–366.

Figueiredo, L. C. M. (1992). *A invenção do psicológico: quatro séculos de subjetivação (1500–1900)*. São Paulo, Brazil: Educ/Escuta.

Freud, S. (1895/1996). Projeto para uma psicologia científica. *Edição standard Brasileira das obras psicológicas completas de Sigmund Freud* (pp. 335–454). Rio de Janeiro, Brazil: Imago. (Original work published 1895)

Gadamer, H.-G. (1954/2010). Mito e razão. *Hermenêutica da Obra de Arte*. São Paulo, Brazil: Martins Fontes.

Gadamer, H.-G. (1981/2010). Mito e logos. *Hermenêutica da obra de arte*. São Paulo, Brazil: Martins Fontes.

Gow, P. (1997). O parentesco como consciência humana: O caso dos Piro. *Mana, 3*(2), 39–65.

Hermans, H. J. M, Kempen, H. J. G., & van Loon, R. J. P. (1992). The dialogical self: Beyond individualism and rationalism. *American Psychologist, 47*(1), 23–33.

Ingold, T. (2000). *The perception of the environment: Essays on livelihood, dwelling and skill.* Oxon and New York, NY: Routledge

Jahoda, G. (1999). *The images of savages: Ancient roots of modern prejudice in Western culture.* New York, NY: Routledge

James, W. (1890). *The principles of psychology.* New York, NY: Holt.

Jaynes, J. (1976). *The origin of consciousness in the breakdown of the bicameral mind.* Boston, MA: Houghton Mifflin.

Koffka, K. (1935). *Principles of Gestalt psychology.* London, England: Lund Humphries

Lévi-Strauss, C., & Eribon, D. (1988/1990). *De perto e de longe: Reflexões do mais importante antropólogo do nosso tempo.* Rio de Janeiro, Brazil: Nova Fronteira.

Marková, I. (2006). *Dialogicidade e representações sociais: As dinâmicas da mente.* Petrópolis, Brazil: Vozes.

Melo Franco, A. A. (1937/2000). *O índio Brasileiro e a revolução francesa: As origens Brasileiras da teoria da bondade natural.* Rio de Janeiro,: Livraria José Olympio.

Neymeier, R. A. (1997). Psicoterapias construtivistas: Características, fundamentos e futuras direções, In R. A. Neymeier & M. J. Mahoney (Eds.), *Construtivismo em psicoterapia* (pp. 15–37). São Paulo, Brazil: Artes Médicas.

Rasmussen, S. (2011). Encountering being, identity, and otherness: Reconsidering Guimarães's "Amerindian anthropology and cultural psychology" and Amerindian perspectivism, with insights from anthropology of religion, African humanities and collaborative ethnography. *Culture and Psychology, 17*(2), 159–176.

Simão, L. M. (2003). Beside rupture - disquiet; Beyond the other - alterity. *Culture & Psychology, 9*(4), 449–459.

Stengers, I. (2002). *A invenção das ciências modernas.* São Paulo, Brazil: Editora 34.

Todorov, T. (2010). *A conquista da América: A questão do outro.* São Paulo, Brazil: Martins Fontes.

Valsiner, J. (1994). Culture and human development: A co-constructionist perspective. In P. van Geert, L. P. Mos, & W. J. Barker (Eds.), *Annals of theoretical Psychology* (Vol. 10, pp. 247–298). New York, NY: Plenum.

Valsiner, J. (2007). *Culture in minds and societies: Foundations of cultural psychology.* New Delhi, India: Sage.

Valsiner, J. (2012). *A guided science: History of psychology in the mirror of its making.* New Brunswick, NJ: Transaction.

Viveiros de Castro, E. B. (2004). Perspectival anthropology and the method of controlled equivocation. *Tipití: Journal of the Society for the Anthropology of Lowland South America, 2*(1),1–22.

Viveiros de Castro, E. B. (2006). *A inconstância da alma selvagem e outros ensaios de antropologia.* São Paulo, Brazil: Cosac Naify.

Vygotsky, L. S. (1997). El significado histórico de la crisis em psicología. In *Vygotsky obras escogidas I: Problemas teóricos y metodológicos de la psicología* (pp. 257–407). Madrid, Spain: A. Machado Libros.

Watson, J. (1913). Psychology as the behaviorist views it. *Psychological Review, 20,* 158–177.

Wundt, W. (1911). *Einführung in die psychologie* (R. Schulze, Ed.). Leipzig, Germany: Voigtländers Verlag.

CHAPTER 12

GAPS IN HUMAN KNOWLEDGE

Highlighting the Whole
Beyond Our Conceptual Reach

Lucas B. Mazur

Over the last several centuries, human inquiry into the nature of knowledge has perennially confronted the challenge of how to unite the knower
with the known, a problem inherited largely from the Cartesian mind-
body divide. As discussed by Cornejo (this volume), in response to this,
the natural sciences and psychology have increasingly turned to quantification and mechanization in the hope that these tools will produce the
kinds of objective answers that the toolmakers themselves appear unable
to provide. Cornejo convincingly argues that this has led in many ways to
the devaluation of the notion of *fantasy*. As a result, we have come to cut
the world up into knowable bits, but bits that fail to capture the greater
whole and that fall short of the objectivity and universality we hope will
accompany them. The Truth for which we seek remains eternally just out
of reach. Rather than seeing the space between Truth and our imperfect
knowledge as a source of anxiety, this chapter will argue that we can see it
as space into which we might grow. In order to do so, we must have faith
in light of this Sisyphean task and trust in our engagement with the
world. In this sense, science and psychology share with faith traditions the

The Psychology of Imagination: History, Theory, and New Research Horizons
pp. 239–251
Copyright © 2017 by Information Age Publishing

ability to see imperfection and incomplete knowledge as that which makes their practices meaningful. It will be argued that fantasy, in the classical sense explored by Cornejo, remains an inalienable component of our search for Truth, as scholars continue to find doubt accompanied by faith, and the gaps that inevitably accompany knowledge, rich with meaning and value.

In what follows, we will first briefly review the problem of imperfect knowledge and how science and psychology have attempted to address, and "overcome," this issue. We will then examine how within science, psychology and theology we nevertheless see an awareness of the futility of these attempts to cross the divide from imperfect knowledge to Truth. This recognition and the doubt it entails are not, however, inherently a source of despair, but rather they are the source of curiosity, trust, and hope. Doubt in our ability to ever actually reach Truth and wrap our hands around it is what makes science, psychology, and religious faith meaningful in the first place.

The Cartesian Anxiety Accompanying Our Search for Certainty

Unable to find a stable bridge across the mind-body divide first promulgated by Descartes, much of Western intellectual history since that time came to be colored by what has been called *Cartesian anxiety* (Bernstein, 1983); the inability to rest peacefully with the awareness that our knowledge about the world may be incomplete or inaccurate, or what is even more unsettling, that we may lack the very tools necessary to even make such a determination of its accuracy or inaccuracy in the first place. This unease is intimately tied with a *spectator view of knowledge*, that is, the belief that we somehow stand outside, and apart from, the objects of our inquiry. In this view we are neutral observers of reality. This is also generally entwined with a *referential view of knowledge* whereby we expect Truth to be found in something to which we can point in the world around us. This global understanding of knowledge has come to heavily influence how we see the world and our place therein. For example, the challenge of the mind-body divide, in giving rise to the notions of (scientific) objectivity and subjectivity, would come to (ostensibly) divide the scientist from the artist, our scientific tools from their creators, and the study of mental reproduction from the study of mental creation (e.g., Cornejo, this volume; Daston & Galison, 2010).

However, as Cornejo (this volume) reminds us, in the centuries following Descartes, not all scholars were equally beset by such worry. While Kant sought the solution to this challenge in *a priori* rules, Goethe rejected the validity of the division between knower and the known, placing greater value on the unity between the lived experience of the scientist and the actual doing of science. Similarly, Giambattista Vico believed the social, human sciences to be of greater scientific merit than the natural sciences, as they spoke to a reality that we can actually hope to know, namely, that which is created by humanity, thereby bridging subject and object (Tateo, this volume). There have been, and continue to be, various schools of thought that push back against the spectator view of knowledge (e.g., different currents and scholars that are often lumped under various versions of pragmatism, phenomenology, and critical thought), arguing that it is in our actual subjective experiences that we come to know the world and that it is precisely here that we ought to search for true knowledge.

The history of psychology has also been marked by this tug of war between those seeking Truth in objectivity and those seeking it in subjective experience, although many have seen the founding of Wundt's experimental laboratory in Leipzig in the late 19th century as subjectivism's Waterloo. While the history of psychology as a whole is not so simple, since Wundt's time, the field has certainly come to be increasingly colored by the shift toward the (attempted) quantification of psychological phenomena by the increasing value placed on experimentation and by the assumed objectivity of the field's various tools (Michell, 2004). During the same period, attempts were made to remove the once valued notion of "beauty" from science, seeing it as more befitting the arts (Daston & Galison, 2010). As Cornejo (this volume) laments, a similar fate would befall the notion of *fantasy*.

This trend is also seen in the various subdisciplines of psychology. For instance, it is interesting to note that while the early development of social psychology was heavily influenced by the Frankfurt School with its focus on historical contingency, this particular field would be heavily colored by the period in which it burst forth upon the scene; a period marked by the desire for clear answers, primarily to questions of man's inhumanity to man. In the era following the Second World War, we see such influential projects as Adorno's work on the F-scale (Fascist-scale), which would develop into an enormous body of research by various psychologists on the authoritarian personality, Sherif's work on intergroup animosity and cooperation, and Milgram's work on cruelty arising from our purported proclivity to conform to authority. As scholars have begun to look back into the details of those seminal studies, we are gaining a better understanding of how much more complex the results of these various studies really were, and how much more complex was the actual thinking of the researchers. As the Western world looked for ways to explain the cruelty of the Second World War, interpretations of data were favored that suggested categorical explanations of interpersonal and intergroup cruelty. Sherif emphasized the expected conflicts between the groups of boys, downplaying gestures of disobedience to the researchers along the way, and similarly, Milgram's notes indicate that he thought the dynamics he was observing to be more complex than he would come to report, and infinitely more complex that the more simplified version that we generally teach (Russell, 2011). However, once these deep tracks in our thinking had been dug, and the specs of our research carts standardized via the use of ever more uniform research methods, travel in this manner and in this direction became increasingly easy and increasingly preferred.

Such research methods in the service of increasing objectivity impose artificial gaps onto a more complex reality, thereby generating frozen images of our social world. While these simplifying processes are often very useful and are certainly very alluring, they ultimately fail to cure the *Cartesian anxiety* itself. They may provide us temporary relief from the worry caused by the "big questions," but they leave them unanswered. For instance, stage models of human development have in many ways helped to paint a useful and meaningful picture of the human lifespan, and they have, in some cases, arguably even furthered the cause of social justice (e.g., by helping to put children in schools rather than factories). At the same time, it is important to point out that in such stage theories of development, with their categorical, linear phases, it is the very notion of development itself that often remains elusive (Valsiner & Connolly, 2003). Just because we now have more phases between birth and death does not mean that we are closer to understanding the notion of human development itself. If it did, that would mean that the new developmental phase, "emerging adulthood" (Arnett, 2000), would imply either that people in the West, where this phase is found, are aware of something that the rest of the world is not and thus are closer to the Truth of development, or that they are simply more developmentally advanced. Both of these positions are obviously untenable and absurd. Goethe observed two centuries ago that we perceive the world through the lens of useful but limited and limiting operationalizations. Commenting on the relationship between our categories, the gaps between them and the whole they represent, Goethe writes, "At first I will tend to think in terms of steps, but nature leaves no gaps, and thus, in the end, I will have to see this progression of uninterrupted activity as a whole" (Cornejo, this volume).

Similarly, William James spoke to the frequent inability of social scientists, and of humans in general, to look beyond our own vision of the world so as to imagine other ways that people can live and find both meaning and value in that life. James' essay, "On a Certain Blindness in Human Beings" (1899/1958), is a particularly honest and moving confession of his own failure to do so. In speaking to his own blindness to the lived experiences of others, quoting from Robert Louis Stevenson, James writes that in such moments of blindness "justice is not done to the versatility and the unplumbed childishness of man's imagination." Our lived experience is fueled by imagination, something that should be, according to the likes of James and Goethe, also reflected in our study of that experience. As Cornejo (this volume) argues, imagination is not simply recreation before the mind's eye, but "imagination opens new ways to understand life and its multiple aspects." In this way, it can help to overcome those gaps separating us from others, both as social scientists and as fellow humans.

In the face of such gaps, we need not however, choose only between embracing them completely, rejecting them entirely, or overcoming them as suggested in the quote from Goethe above. Rather, we can see in the gaps not only the outline or limits of our various constructs, but we can also recognize in them the limits of our current knowledge more broadly, something that itself implies there to be something more to learn; something beyond. In our doubt regarding the reach of our current knowledge, we see the roots of our search for something greater. What is more, in recognizing that such doubt will *always* be there, not just in reference to the particular constructs at hand, we implicitly learn to have faith that something will *always* be greater. This is the hope found at the core of the ever-correcting scientific method, from whose critical eye no "fact" is safe. This is the hope found within interpersonal trust that forms the foundation of interpersonal relations. It is also the hope found at the core of theological doubt regarding our ability to reach that which is greater than ourselves. We will now briefly examine some of the ways in which science, psychology, and theology are aware of the limitations of knowledge and how this is seen as being a fundamental and core, not transitory, state of affairs.

AWARENESS OF THE LIMITATIONS IN THE NATURAL SCIENCES, PSYCHOLOGY, AND THEOLOGY

> I am tempted to say that we do not look for truth, but for knowledge. But I dislike this form of words for two reasons. First of all we do look for truth, however we define it; it is what we find that is knowledge. And second, what we fail to find is not truth but certainty; the nature of truth is exactly the knowledge that we do find.
>
> —Bronowski (1964, p. 37)

> This is the paradox of imagination in science, that it has for its
> aim the impoverishment of imagination. By that outrageous
> phrase, I mean that the highest flight of scientific imagination
> is to weed out the proliferation of new ideas. In science, the
> grand view is a miserly view, and a rich model of the universe is
> one which is as poor as possible in hypotheses.
>
> —Bronowski (1964 p. 46)

The power of the scientific method comes in part from the fact that no finding, however robust, and no theory, however strongly supported, is immune from its critical probing. In opening all we know to critical evaluation, and in assuming that everything we know can, and eventually will, be changed (or rejected), we see doubt not as a weakness, but as a fundamental strength. While seeking for Truth, we are temporarily satisfied with truth, and despite knowing that there will always be room for advancement and thus that we will never arrive at Truth itself, we nevertheless continue the pursuit. While science pushes for greater precision, simplicity, and above all, testability (for the *impoverishment of the imagination* as Bronowski writes) at the same time, this push is understood to be never ending. The scientific method is above all a method for searching, and only in the most fleeting of senses, for finding. In this sense it is perhaps counterintuitive, as Bronowski reminds us, that while we may search for Truth and certainty, the scientific method leads us to truth and knowledge. While it can lead us to new heights, it also pulls us back to Earth, hence the paradox.

This valuing of Truth as a goal toward which we strive, but not as an end state at which we can ever say we have arrived, has been frequently discussed within the tradition of pragmatism (Bacon, 2012). In this regard, pragmatism has been able to speak to the gaps in our knowledge as something positive, as room into which we can grow. Scholars working within this tradition, broadly defined, have also much discussed and much debated what justification for our scientific endeavors is left, once we have removed the possibility of actually arriving at Truth. This discussion echoes Wittgenstein's rejection of the very plausibility of the purported end goal of logical positivism. If we cannot claim that science will allow us to grasp the Truth, once and for all, on what grounds can we justify the use of science itself? The scientific method is not a justification for the use of the scientific method; science, by itself, is not a justification for science. This fundamental challenge is often given voice when people defend the value of pure science (versus applied science), by pointing to the utility to which it has eventually been put, as if to imply that the findings were rich with meaning and value, but that we simply did not appreciate that until we found a use for them. In other words, we find justification elsewhere, again, as the scientific method does not itself provide a justification of its use (as in Donald Davidson's assertion that we use some beliefs to justify others; Davidson, 1986).

Rather than awakening anxiety, this openness to growth is one of the scientific method's central strengths. It has been argued that this approach should be taken in all areas of human inquiry, not just science, reflecting what might be understood, in simplified language, as our unending capacity to learn (Bacon, 2012). Some areas of research in psychology arguably reflect a more global shift toward seeing value in understanding our constructs to be *underdetermined*. In some ways, the field is reinstating the *productive* elements of its constructs, in addition to the purely *reproductive* ones that came to be favored in the field's initial shift toward experimentalism and quantitative measurement (Cornejo, this volume). We have come to see memory, not as the ever elusive *black box*, or *engram*, in which data is stored in unadulterated form, but rather as a truly creative, productive, and ever flexible, changing, and context-dependent process (Wagoner, 2012). What is more, these characteristics of memory are not seen (solely) as a weakness by focusing on memory "errors," but they are seen as part of what makes us adaptive, social, inquisitive beings with unique individual pasts. The fact that various psychological processes are underdetermined can be seen as a strength, not a limitation.

The idea of doubt in human knowledge has been even more explicitly explored within faith traditions. The separation of humanity from the Divine is something that all faith traditions explore, even those that deny the ultimate reality of such division (e.g., by seeing it as an illusion). This tension between the ultimate, unlimited Truth and our desire to somehow capture, or represent, it in a way that we can wrap our minds around, has found expression over the ages in various forms, such as the differing theological opinions on the utility and even acceptability of artistic representations of the Divine. This finds powerful expression not only in art, but also in the Christian notion of the Trinity: "Since the Word became flesh in assuming a true humanity, Christ's body was finite. Therefore the human face of Jesus can be portrayed ... in the body of Jesus we see our God made visible, and so are caught up in love for the God we cannot see" (Catholic Church, 1995, pp. 476–477). In a wide range of ways and arguably by definition, faith traditions recognize, and wrestle with, the limits of our knowledge: "On the boundaries of the finite the infinite becomes visible" (Tillich, 1948, p. 9).

The Importance of Work *in the Face of Doubt*

As we have discussed above, any discussion of Truth, be it in science, psychology, or theology, need necessarily include the possibility of error, which is to say that it need necessarily include a degree of doubt regarding our current positions, otherwise there would be no discussion at all, but rather certainty. Most philosophical theories of truth need necessarily leave open the door, at least a crack, to the possibility of knowledge being incomplete or imperfect. Even those philosophical traditions that reject the ultimate division between knower and known generally see something less than the Truth as accompanying us on the path we are currently following (such as Mahayana Buddhism's notion of *upaya*, "expedient means," whereby flawed thinking and methods otherwise imperfect can be intentionally, temporarily used to guide one toward enlightenment and Truth—perhaps not entirely unlike consciously lying to children about the existence of Santa Claus in order to teach them the greater value of generosity and kindness in a way they can understand at that point).

Despite knowing that any discovery we make may, and ultimately will, be replaced by something else, scientists continue to work. Despite knowing that the nature of human life will remain out of our grasp, psychologists will continue to explore it, to classify it, to subclassify it, and to ultimately reclassify it. Despite the divide between humanity and the Divine, faith traditions encourage us to seek. In all of these traditions, it is the limited, fallible nature of our current understanding that serves as the empty field providing room in which new knowledge might grow. It is this space that also helps to define such positive and constructive notions as participatory democracy (à la John Dewey), transcendental reevaluation (à la Hilary Putnam), evaluative fallibilistic pluralism (à la Richard Burnstein, which requires openness and imagination), and Giambattista Vico's tacitly anthropological approach to understanding the Other (for a discussion of these issues, see Bacon, 2012). What all of these approaches have in common is that they recognize not only the particular limits of whatever knowledge is in question, but also the fact that all knowledge that we might possess is open to further scrutiny, change, and ultimately to being replaced. Even those operationalizations we might argue to be inherently "good," such as laws intended to guarantee human rights, should be open to reevaluation as their well-intended ossification can enshrine forms of injustice that we either did not see or did not foresee (see also Mazur, 2015). Similarly, one might even argue for a connection on these points with Augustine's assertion that all true learning is good (van der Meijden & Wilczyński, 2015). These approaches to knowledge do not advocate relativism, but rather they take pains to avoid it. This is arguably the main appeal of pragmatism; the central role it gives to both fallibility and anti-skepticism. What we know is not valueless, nor are our efforts to know more. Rather, they are both simply never complete.

The Importance of Work *Because of Doubt*

Were we to truly lack doubt, we would be certain. Cornejo (2014) has eloquently argued that social relations cannot be, by definition, marked by certainty. We can perhaps claim a certain degree of certainty in the social world, not as the result of careful scrutiny (leading to Truth), but rather as arising out of *pre-reflexivity*; the state of interpersonal anticipation that exists before the relationship is examined. For example, a child might be "certain" of her parents' aid, even if no logical or experiential reason for this conclusion exists. However, when we think more about this relationship, we see that no actual certainty exists, but rather *trust*. The more one examines this relationship, the more evident it is that we are necessarily dealing with individual actors who are free and independent from each other and whose interaction is based on trust, hope, and acting in good faith. The foundation of such hopeful action is the unjustified (and ultimately unjustifiable) state of *belief* that engenders the lived experience of *trust*. While we can not be *certain* of the actions of others, the resulting doubt need not lead to anxiety, but rather can form the basis for trust. What is more, we generally do not actually strive for certainty in our relationships, as certainty would require the use of propositionally based logic that would ultimately sow mistrust (as we would not act until we were certain). Cornejo beautifully illustrates this point with the metaphor of dancers, who can only move together in as far as they trust each other. The moment they try to thoughtfully and rationally calculate each other's moves, is the moment they fall out of sync.

One can extend this difference between certainty and trust to science itself. While we can feel certain of a great many findings when dealing with them within certain set parameters, especially once we have seen their application to a particular problem within a particular context, upon wider reflection we generally come to see their contingency (e.g., the justification being determined not by its ultimate and final truth, but by its utility in addressing a separate problem, à la Karl Popper, or by its fit within an internally coherent worldview, à la Thomas Kuhn). Confidence is not achieved by having identified an unchanging fact that has been established beyond all doubt, for all time, and in all conditions, but rather, by acting in trust while treading the waters of the gaps in our knowledge. Again, within science, all findings are open to future revision and even rejection. And yet no one would claim the findings of science to be pointless, or useless, or futile, or a waste of time. Rather, they are worthy of our trust until that time when we deem such trust to be unfounded; we do not actually challenge all knowledge because of its inherent limitations (although we could, and eventually may), but only those that we deem in need of "fixing." To reject all knowledge because of its flawed nature would be to act on what Charles Sanders Peirce (1934) called "paper-doubt." Trust to act in the face of paper-doubt, unlike certainty, necessarily requires both belief in the face of a lack of absolute certainty and a willingness to act on that belief. By engaging with both science or social relations, we enter into a dynamic marked not by certainty, but by a sense of uncertainty; an uncertainty that need engender a sense of faith and trust if we are to act at all.

Paul Tillich has similarly defined *faith* within Christian theology. Tillich calls the drive toward the (ultimate, complete) Truth our state of being *ultimately concerned* (Tillich, 1957). We are driven to grasp the Truth, which ultimately lies eternally just beyond our grasp. In this yearning for the Divine/Truth, we need necessarily recognize the divide separating us from the Truth. Were we to arrive at the truth, thus crossing this divide, we would have arrived at *certainty*. Instead, precisely because of the divide, we have *faith* instead. In other words, were there no doubt, no recognition of our incomplete knowledge and our inability to cross this divide into certainty, there would be no faith. According to Tillich, faith constitutes an *attitude of trust* (Peterson, 2013). Faith (like *trust* in social relations) arises not only out of our awareness of our inability to cross the divide, but also, crucially, out of our continued desire and attempts to do so, *in the very face of that division we know to be uncrossable*. In the 16th century, St. Teresa of Avila expressed this experience as follows:

> When the vehemence of love and the great impulses of this pain [of the loneliness of being separated from You] increase, there's no remedy, my God. For the intellect is disturbed and the reason is so kept from knowing the truth of your omnipresence that it can neither understand nor know. It only knows it is separated from you and it accepts no remedy.... O true Lover, with how much compassion, with how much gentleness, with how much delight, with how much favor and with what extraordinary signs of love you cure these wounds, which with the darts of this same love you have caused! O my God and my rest from all pains, how entranced I am! How could there be human means to cure what the divine fire has made sick? Who is there who knows how deep this wound goes, or how it came about, or how so painful and delightful a torment can be mitigated? It would be unreasonable were so precious a sickness able to be mitigated by something so lowly as are the means mortals can use. How right the bride of the Canticles is in saying: My Beloved is for me and I for my Beloved, for it is impossible that a love like this begin with something so lowly as is my love. (Cameron, 2015, pp. 277–278)

St. Teresa's call is that of a lover for the Beloved, for the Divine. The desired union between lovers, even a sensual or sexual union, is not an uncommon metaphorical expression of the desired union with the Divine/Truth in faith traditions, particularly within mystical writings. Similar metaphors have also found their place in more common language. For instance, nuns are described as the "brides" of Christ, they are "wedded" to the Church, and so on. In St. Teresa's call we see the core elements of Tillich's understanding of faith: an awareness of the division between lover and Beloved, an awareness of the futility at the lover's attempts to cross it, and nevertheless both the desire to cross that divide and continued attempts to do so. This is the "leap of faith" in the face of an uncrossable divide.

In St. Teresa's text, we also see the lover, in her *belief* in the Beloved, reaching for knowledge of the Beloved (as in Saint Augustine's notion of *Fides quaerens intellectum*—faith/trust seeking knowledge). The lack of certainty in no way impedes faith, but rather engenders it, and faith in that which is beyond our grasp engenders our search for greater understanding. Augustine understood faith to not only involve the intellect, but to be largely constituted by it (van der Meijden & Wilczyński, 2015). The idea of growth arising from our imperfect knowledge is beautifully captured in Nicholas of Cusa's notion of *docta ignoratia* (learned ignorance), whereby our ignorance is fundamentally and intimately entwined with our desire and hope to know the Truth (as discussed in Cornejo, this volume).

In all of the traditions discussed above (theological, social, and scientific), we see an explicit awareness of the uncertainty, or doubt, that is seen as necessarily accompanying, but also engendering, our search for the Truth. These positions see our inability to reach the desired goal, not as a weakness, but as a strength; as it is the gap between us and the Truth that provides the room in which we can grow. When we see how pervasive doubt and trust are in our lives, the notion of us "living by faith" takes on a powerful meaning, and one that does not divide our various attempts to reach the Truth, but rather unites them, be they secular or religious, scientific or artistic. Doubt in what we know accompanies our continued search in science. Doubt in our social relations illustrates both our independence as social actors and our interdependence based on trust. Doubt in our current relationship with Truth is what gives faith wings.

CONCLUSION

We are a "symbolic species" that sees in our symbols not only the signifier and the signified, or only the act of signifying, but the existence of something just beyond the reach of both. In acting otherwise, and perceiving truth within any one of the symbolic elements themselves, we are acting *idolatrously*, in the language of Tillich (1957); which is to say that we are erroneously attaching ultimate meaning, Truth, to that which is conditional and bound to change. Within science and psychology, we see something similar when we become too attached to the operationalizations and metaphorical language we create out of the gaps we impose on reality (Bancroft, 2014; e.g., the notion of the "storage" or computer metaphors when speaking of memory, Wagoner, 2012; mechanical and personalized metaphors in physics, Jeppson, Haglund, & Amin, 2015). Rather than seeing these gaps as either capturing Truth, or as an expression of futility and meaninglessness, we can see them as signposts pointing to something beyond. Over the centuries, artists have used the limits of our symbolic language (in the written and spoken word, but also in music and the visual arts), to give expression to that which extends beyond the limits of the symbols (Eco, 2009). Lists appearing in literature can speak to vastness or endlessness itself, not just to what is actually listed. Still lifes can speak to the very notions of bounty or wealth, not just to the items on the table. The number of people drawn within a frame can speak to countless numbers. Symbols of time can speak to eternity.

There is no doubt that we can become overly attached to the symbolic language that we speak and that we can come to think of the world as being limited to the patterns we give it when cutting it up as we do. As Cornejo (this volume) has argued, in many ways this has left us with many a challenge, and at times, even an impoverished view of both the world and human knowledge. At the same time, the gaps that we impose on the world can be tremendously useful, as the overwhelming power of the scientific method has made clear. The trick is to not lose sight of the fact that the gaps we impose on reality actually speak to a greater whole; a greater whole of which we cannot help to grasp but pieces at a time. It is precisely our awareness of this that compels us to keep moving. As the pragmatists have reminded us, while we can doubt the truth or value of any and all particular claims, we cannot doubt the truth or value of all claims at once. In the words of Tillich, "There is scarcely one thing about which we may not be cynical. But we *can not* be cynical about the shaking of the foundations of everything!" (1948, p. 10). Acknowledging the ever-present gap and its accompanying doubt need not lead to anxiety, for it is this doubt that also lies at the heart of science, of trust in human relations, and of the faith that elevates us in our state of being *ultimately concerned*.

REFERENCES

Arnett, J. J. (2000). Emerging adulthood: A theory of development from the late teens through the twenties. *American Psychologist, 55*, 469–480.

Bacon, M. (2012). *Pragmatism: An introduction*. Malden, MA: Polity Press.

Bancroft, J. (2014). *Tolerance of uncertainty*. Bloomington, IN: AuthorHouse.

Bernstein, R. (1983). *Beyond objectivism and relativism. Science, hermeneutics, and praxis.* Philadelphia, PA: University of Pennsylvania Press.

Bronowski, J. (1964) *The identity of man.* Garden City, NY: American Museum Science Books.

Cameron, P. J. (Ed.). (2015). St. Teresa of Avila. *Magnificat, 16*(11), 277–278.

Catholic Church. (1995). *Catechism of the Catholic Church.* New York, NY: Doubleday.

Cornejo, C. (2014). On trust and distrust in the lifeworld. In P. Linell & I. Marková (Eds.), *Dialogical approaches to trust in communication* (pp. 237–253). Charlotte, NC: Information Age.

Daston, L. J., & Galison, P. (2010). *Objectivity.* Brooklyn, NY: Zone Books.

Davidson, D. (1986). A coherence theory of truth and knowledge. In E. LePore (Ed.), *Truth and interpretation: Perspectives on the philosophy of Donald Davidson* (pp. 307–319). Oxford, England: Blackwell.

Eco, U. (2009). *Infinity of lists.* New York, NY: Rizzoli.

James, W. (1899/1958). On a certain blindness in human beings. In W. James (Ed.), *Talks to teachers on psychology and to students on some of life's ideals.* New York, NY: Norton.

Jeppsson, F., Haglund, J., & Amin T. G. (2015). Varying use of conceptual metaphors across levels of expertise in thermodynamics. *International Journal of Science Education, 37,* 780–805.

Mazur, L. B. (2015). Prejudice reduction and collective action: A conflict or confluence of interests? *Journal of Social and Political Psychology, 3*(2). Retrieved from http://jspp.psychopen.eu/article/view/324/html

Michell, J. (2004). *Measurement in psychology. Critical history of a methodological concept.* Cambridge, England: Cambridge University Press.

Peterson, D. J. (2013). *Tillich: A brief overview of the life and writings of Paul Tillich.* Minneapolis, MN: Lutheran University Press.

Peirce, C. S. (1934). *Collected papers of Charles Sanders Peirce. Volume V, Pragmatism and pragmatics* (C. Hartshorne & P. Weiss, Eds.). Cambridge, MA: The Belknap Press of Harvard University Press.

Russell, N. J. C. (2011). Milgram's obedience to authority experiments: Origins and early evolution. *British Journal of Social Psychology, 50,* 140–162.

Tillich, P. (1948). *The shaking of the foundations.* New York, NY: Scribner.

Tillich, P. (1957). *Dynamics of faith.* New York, NY: Harper & Row.

Valsiner, J., & Connolly, K. (Eds.). (2003). *Handbook of developmental psychology.* Thousand Oaks, CA: SAGE.

van der Meijden, J. G., & Wilczyński, K. (2015). Reason and will. Remarks on Augustine's idea of power. *Orbis Idearum.* Retrieved from http://www.orbisidearum.net/pdf/issue_3.pdf

Wagoner, B. (2012). Culture in constructive remembering. In J. Valsiner (Ed.), *Oxford handbook of culture and psychology* (pp. 1034–1055). Oxford, England: Oxford University Press.

CHAPTER 13

NATURE LEAVES NO GAPS

From Scientifically Dissected Phenomena Back to the Whole

Meike Watzlawik

We are a "symbolic species" and symbols speak a language of division, but they also speak to the conviction that we can understand that which lies beyond the symbol. This confidence is shown by our belief that our symbolic language can actually direct us to that which is beyond the symbol— "Lived experience." Indeed, Goethe already believed that "every rational construction should start from the personal experience of being in contact with the phenomenon of interest" (Cornejo, this volume)—the lived experience itself.

Starting with a personal experience that triggered a research project on sexual identity research, it will be shown that the attempt to capture a certain phenomenon scientifically often implies taking it apart, thus creating gaps that later need to be acknowledged and "worked with." This isolation procedure, with which facts are obtained, leaves the researcher with the question of how the phenomena itself can be reconstructed from these facts. Identity research will again serve as an example for how these dissection processes have led to alternative methodologies and attempts to capture phenomena, even if "neither things nor ourselves find full

The Psychology of Imagination: History, Theory, and New Research Horizons
pp. 253–263

expression in our words" [= symbolic language] (Goethe, 1805/1998, p. 26) that can nevertheless direct us to what lies beyond. But let us first look at what triggered the specific research project.

"I Am Gay!"—Being in Contact With the Phenomenon

My interest in sexual identity development was first triggered by the Coming Out of a close friend. He told his friends and, shortly after, his family that he was gay and that he had fallen in love with another man. The friends were accepting from the start and appreciated his openness. His parents, however, needed time to adjust to the new situation. The first reactions (needing a drink, feeling sick to the stomach) underlined the shock of the parents, who did not have much information about homosexuality besides the stereotypical representations they were (and still are) confronted with in the media. Not knowing much myself, I then decided to write a paper for my psychology studies on Coming Out. Where are the stereotypes coming from? Why is homosexuality often not mentioned in schools? How do adolescents manage to form a positive sense of self when the environment is intolerant (if they manage at all)? The paper then triggered the interest of a professor of mine who encouraged me to turn the ideas presented in the paper into my dissertation project, which I did.

Writing Songs About Hatred Without Hating?

Cornejo (this volume) discusses a conversation Goethe had with Frederic J. Soret, in which Goethe apparently stated the following: "I have never uttered anything which I have not experienced ... I have only composed love-songs when I have loved ... How could I write songs of hatred without hating!" (Eckermann, 1850b, as cited in Cornejo, this volume). Can I only do research on things I have experienced myself? In some cases, the answer may be more obvious than in others. For example, I do not have to have experienced sexual abuse to do research on the topic. In fact, nobody should have to experience such violence, but since it happens, it should be studied to improve therapy and to help prevent such traumatizing experiences. In the example given above, I was the one who a friend trusted enough to talk to. I was therefore personally in touch with the "phenomenon of interest," but still I did not experience the Coming Out myself. Would that mean that I am disqualified for doing "good research" on the topic? In discussions with colleagues, it was stressed that researchers often have not experienced themselves that which is the focus of their research, but that it helps to have experienced similar things. For example, I might have experienced a similar feeling of being "out of control," or I might have struggled to find out who I want to be, even if I never really questioned my sexual orientation. Based on these (abstracted) experiences, I can thus imagine what a situation, described by somebody else, might be/feel like for the other without having experienced "the same." The story told by the research participant will trigger emotions (emotional interpretant, see Johansen, 2010) followed by recognition. Recognition may then lead to empathy that can be verbalized to check whether the "fictional world" I am imagining fits with what the research participant experienced. This is important as Gilbert (2007) points out that our imagination works so quickly and effectively that we are often not skeptical enough. In addition, what is imagined is very much influences by the present and past (cf. Watzlawik, Schachter, & Cunha, 2015, on recursivity) taken as reference or even "standard." Our imagination may thus be too conservative and it takes effort (if it is possible at all) to transcend the boundaries established by the time, place, and circumstances we find ourselves in. While on the hand, imagination can thus help to relate to and understand others, which Schiller (1784/1967) even established as educational goal demanding the "education of the heart"; imagination can also hinder the understanding of others if we do not question our own hypotheses and associations. Since research is also about giving voice to those who have not been heard (enough), we need to make sure that the voices are understood correctly. In the introduced case as well as in possible other cases, not the researcher, but the research participants are the "experts" for the "lived experience."

Capturing the Lived Experience

For the research project introduced here, I talked to quite a few adolescents and adults before putting together the online questionnaire with mainly open-ended questions to capture the thoughts and feelings when "first becoming aware of one's sexual orientation" (internal part of the Coming Out process) until (if at all) "first telling somebody else about how they felt" (going "public," external). During an internship at Massachusetts' Boston Children's Services supporting GLBT projects, I had plenty of opportunities to listen to personal stories and to participate in discussions. Of course, literature research was done in parallel. I nevertheless decided by myself which questions were most relevant for my project. I also added questions after the test run of the online questionnaire because a few participants said that they would have liked to add something to the topic, but that it did not fit any of the questions asked. These additional questions included a general one in the end: "Is there anything that you would like to add that we did not ask for so far?" The space for the answers was unlimited.

Should this be the "state of the art"? Did my participants (not subjects)[2] participate enough in the research process? Bibace, Dillon, and Dowds (1999) would still say that I "dictaded the overall field of inquiry" (p. 10). They suggest beginning the research with participant-generated questions. In my case, I could have asked the adolescents at the Boston Children's Services: "What questions do you think are important to ask in order to understand the Coming Out process?" In this way, the participants would have had their say in how to structure the online study around the issues they considered most important. The next step, according to Bibace et al., could then be to present a list of questions that was put together after reviewing the professional literature on the topic. The participants should be asked if any of the questions that they had not mentioned so far "were especially relevant to the experience" (p. 10). This approach contrasts traditional approaches as shown in Table 13.1.

Table 13.1 also shows that the research participants in the Partnership Research Approach should not only have a say in what kind of questions are asked, but also in the interpretation of the data gathered. Bibace et al. (1999) thus recommend the implementation of a feedback mechanism.

Table 13.1.   Partnership Research Approach

Traditional Approach	*Partnership Research Approach*
	Research Participant Generates Own Questions to Domain
	Research Participant Provides Answers to Own Questions
Researcher Initiates Questions	Researcher Initiates Questions
Research Participant Answers	Research Participant Answers
Researcher's Question	Researcher's Question
Researcher Evaluates Research	Researcher Evaluates Research
Participant's Answer	Participant's Answer
	Research Participant Evaluates Researcher's Questions re: Relevance
	Research Participant Evaluates Researcher's Means and Procedures
	Research Participant Evaluates Researcher's Discussion & Conclusions

Source: Bibace et al. (1999).

While "good" research does include making the results available to the partcipants, Bibace et al. go a step further. Before publication, the research particpants should be given the opportunity to comment on the researcher's means, procedures, and, most importantly, interpretations. By incorporating the research participants in this way, the methodological decisions and interpretations can, on the one hand, be validated. On the other hand, by not doing research on "subjects," but doing research with research participants, the danger of creating or even repeating the feeling of "powerlessness" is minimized.

Diverging Interpretations

What if the researcher and research participants disagree in how the answers given should be interpreted? Bibace et al (1999) state that the "feedback loop does not preclude researchers from making interpretations that participants do not agree with. However, researchers would be compelled to include these disagreements in their work" (p. 11). Diasgreement and being in dialogue already is part of the research process itself (e.g., through commentaries in scientific journals), but should include not only other researchers, but the participants as well. Disagreement and dialogue should thus be extended and be made more explicit as well as transparent in many ways.

In my case, the diverging interpretations of the results and interpretations that followed publication (since I did not incorporate a feedback loop at the time) were incorporated in proceeding publications (e.g., Watzlawik, 2014) and shaped follow-up studies. Another online study that included all questions that the research participants of the first study were missing (e.g., concerning sexual experiences, how and where one had met "significant others") was conducted right after the initial Coming Out project. For the follow-up study, the results and interpretations were presented to and discussed with adolescents, teachers, parents, and scientists before publication so that different viewpoints could immediately be taken into account (see Watzlawik & Heine, 2009).

Taking Phenomena Apart to Then Put Them Back Together

Despite all methodological questions, the question whether the "phenomenon" can be captured at all remains unanswered. Sexual identity development is a complex process and is influenced by multiple factors. Even the term *sexual identity* itself can be defined in many ways and is often confused with gender identity. I was interested in the Coming Out process itself, but even that does not occur in isolation. Individuals inter-act with others in different settings, and identity facets (e.g., sexual, gen-der, ethnic, religious, occupational) influence each other, as the literature on intersectionality has pointed out quite vividly (e.g., Meyer, 2012). Budde (2013, p. 248) even comes to the conclusion that "one would need an infinite amount of categories ... to describe the complexity of life situ-ations and power relations in an accurate and differentiated manner. Out of numerous reasons—mainly methodological and research-pragmatic ones—this categorical expansion is limited."[3] Also Goldstein (1995, p. 27) stresses that "as soon as we attempt to grasp [living organisms] scientifi-cally, we must take them apart." I thus decided to concentrate on the Coming Out process as part of sexual identity development (leaving aside other aspects like, for example, sexual activity, sexual ethics) and asked homosexual-, bisexual-, and heterosexual-oriented[4] adolescents how they experienced the moment in which they became aware of their sexual ori-entations, how long it took them to talk to someone about it (if they had done it at all) and why (not), how the first confidants reacted, and so on. For each of the open-ended questions, I looked for common themes in the answers given and then, later on, used Marcia's model on identity development to frame these themes theoretically. Marcia's model is based upon the dual criteria of exploration of possibilities and commitment. The absence and/or presence of these two variables describe in which identity status an individual is at the time of assessment (see Table 13.2).

In the status Achieved Identity, the individual has undergone explora-tion ("I first thought and hoped that I was bisexual, but then realized that I just like men.") and is currently committed ("I am homosexual."). The Moratorium describes a state in which the individual is presently in an exploratory period and commitments are vague ("I am not sure what these feelings mean, but I might be bisexual."). In the state of Foreclosure, the individual has not explored, but rather adopted alternatives. Commit-ments are present ("I cannot say when I realized that I was heterosexual.

Table 13.2. Marcia's Identity Status Approach

	Diffusion	Moratorium	Achieved Identity	Foreclosure
Exploration of different options	no sense of having choices	Yes	Yes	No
Commitment to a certain role/value	not yet made (neither willing nor attempting)	ready to make choices, but not decided yet	Yes	Yes

Source: Marcia (1993).

That is just how it always was. I never doubted it."). Diffusion means that the individual has "undergone only cursory exploration at most, and is not committed" (Marcia, 2007, p. 7).

With this approach and model, I was able to show that while heterosexual adolescents do not question their sexual orientation (it is as expected, heteronormatively speaking), homo- and bisexual adolescents often struggle with understanding of what their feelings mean, which could be described as Diffusion at first (Marcia, 1993), then, when starting to explore, as Moratorium, to later reach the temporary "state" of an Achieved Identity.

With these results, I was able to stress that (still) more information on this topic (e.g., adolescents explicitly wished for more information in school) and support is needed (e.g., some said that they did not have anybody to talk to), which triggered quite a few often fruitful, but sometimes also tiring and less productive public discussions.

The research introduced here, even though important, remains nevertheless fragmented, as Goldstein (1995, p. 27) underlines:

> and this taking apart nets us a multitude of isolated facts which offer no direct clue to that which we experience directly in the living organism.... What do the phenomena, arising from the isolating procedure, teach us about the "essence" (the intrinsic nature) of an organism?

The Coming Out process is not linear, it does not happen in isolation, and it is part of a bigger concept, which the term identity facet already implies. A glimpse at the complexity of the process is provided by the description of a male research participant given in the "open" section of the online questionnaire. He states,

> The inner experience ... starts long before age 16. The feeling of being "different," being interested in the same sex at first, then the interest in girls, accompanied by a need for distance, noticing the heterosexual behavior of other boys, accompanied by the thought that oneself might never get there, longing for this behavior and, at the same time, rejecting it, causes a profound marginalization which, again, influences perception. Especially, insecurity arises about how one is perceived/judged by others.... Most profoundly is the insecurity concerning one's own existence, which leads, among others, to the following questions:
>
> *Will I ever act out my sexuality, whatever it is?*
>
> *And if so, is it legitimate?*
>
> Which—because of the existential meaning of sexuality—leads to the question:
>
> *May I be the way I am?*

And finally,

"May I be?"

Now imagine negative reactions from the outside ... I don't believe that these kinds of experiences can be explained to someone who experienced his sexual socialization as straight, *just because they are not normal.*

With the results I arrived at I had thus only looked at a facet of the facet, at one part of sexual identity, which again is only one part of identity as a whole. Goethe suggests the following:

With any given phenomenon in nature—and especially if it is significant or striking—we should not stop and dwell on it, cling to it, and view it as existing in isolation. Instead we should look about in the whole of nature to find where there is something similar, something related. For only when related elements are drawn together will a whole gradually emerge that speaks for itself and requires no further explanation (Goethe 1995, as cited in Holdrege, 2014, p. 13).

With the example given above, other identity facets might be considered to be "something similar." We could compare developmental processes in different life areas with each other (gender, sexual, occupational, etc.), as has been done by Marcia (1993). We could follow the idea of intersectionality, saying that this comparison does not lead to meaningful results, because the phenomenon itself changes through interactions (cf. Budde, 2013). We could then look at the interactions of different social categories and examine their influence on identity development (cf. Meyer, 2012), but it would still remain something "simplified," because we would, pragmatically, choose certain categories.

Another challenge could be that we do not capture identity at all, since identity is nothing that "exists," but that is constructed in everyday interactions and, thus, changes all the time (McAdams, 2001). Examining a "status" or "state" would then not be possible, because individuals constantly (re)define themselves through stories that may be based on episodic particulars of autobiographical memory (big stories = narrative identities; cf. Singer, 2004) or that emerge in mundane everyday life situations allowing the individual to position his/her sense of self to, for example, others in interactions (small stories; Bamberg, 2012). This argument would support Goethe's observation that "[if] we look at all these *Gestalten,* especially the organic ones, we will discover that nothing in them is permanent, nothing at rest or defined—everything is in a flux of continual motion" (Goethe, 1995, pp. 63f). With his *Hymn to Nature,* Georg Christoph Tobler, a friend of Goethe, underlines this observation by saying "[nature] is whole and yet always unfinished. As she does now she may do forever. To each she appears in a unique form. She hides amid a thousand names and terms" (Tobler, 1782, as cited in Holdrege, 2014, p. 11). Scientists thus face the challenges of dealing with ambiguous terms, such as *identity*, and, even if definitions are agreed upon, with capturing constantly changing phenomena. While some researchers solve these problems by strict definitions and treating their results as "fixed" (e.g., in the status approach), others rather include the "flux" in their definitions (e.g., in the narrative approach) and look at the narrative means that allows the individual to make sense/explain what occurs and changes all the time, taking into account that "neither things nor ourselves find full expression in our words" (Goethe, 1805/1998, p. 26), so that even narratives remain an approximation to the phenomenon. Which leads to the following question.

What Do We Actually Know?

We know that humans are hypercomplex and that we, as scientists, need to be aware of the gaps that we create by dissecting the phenomena of interest (see also Mazur, this volume). Pretending that there are no gaps might not be the best solution, and to really be able to "imagine again a psychology with soul," as Cornejo (this volume) envisions, training future scientists to deal with ambiguity might be the better approach. For biology, Holdrege (2014) states that to bring back the soul into science, we need to "shift its emphasis from a focus on learning facts and theories to developing capacities: (p. 22). Already early on, he demands that students have to experience how "messy and rewarding scientific inquiry can be" (p. 22), and that learning a million facts from PowerPoint presentations will never be able to substitute this experience. I agree. I also have to confirm his unsettling observation that, in the current system, whether biology or psychology students, "can get a B.Sc.... without having once observed a living creature in its natural environment" (p. 22).

If we really manage to teach science as a process that is about going out and meeting the world, engaging with those that we study (e.g., by applying the Partnership Research Approach), we would maybe become more aware of possible connections between phenomena. We might also more easily treat existing theories and models as "temporary means" to help further exploration that have to be questioned when they turn out to hinder it. That would help overcome the contradiction so well described by Holdrege (2014):

What our culture has emphasized and trains is the ability to analyze and focus on details of the sensory world and the extended sensory world mediated by instruments, on the one hand, and on the ability to form generalizations that create a web of meaning for the facts, on the other. This has led to the duality of matter and mind and to all the fruitless attempts to make the world whole again by denying one of the two poles. Because Goethe's approach stays at all times within experience—but experience that encompasses thought and sense—the division that plagues modernity does not arise (p. 19f).

If it is thus about humans engaging with humans in different contexts and learning through experiences, we have to provide grounds for these kind of encounters—encounters in which the existing, valuable knowledge base is the starting point, but can be challenged at the same time. With a world population of about 7,327,990,524 individuals (11 a.m., July 12, 2015), there should be plenty of opportunities.

NOTES

1. This goes beyond neural mirroring that may facilitate social behavior, and, according to Iacoboni (2009), solves the "problem of other minds" (how we can access and understand the minds of others)" allowing for intersubjectivity.
2. Even if research participants are "subjected to" different procedures/inquiries, they are not passive in the process. The dialogue with the researcher is an especially coconstructive endeavor.
3. Original: "Man [bräuchte] unendlich viele Kategorien ... um die Komplexität sowohl von Lebenslagen als auch von Machtverhältnissen angemessen und differenziert zu beschreiben. Aus zahlreichen—vor allem methodischen und forschungspragmatischen—Gründen ist diese Ausweitung aber nicht beliebig weit zu treiben."
4. Today, I would add categories and I would also leave the option of not using categories at all when asking for self-identifications. Research is, as many human experiences, an ongoing learning process.
5. Answers like these were rarely given since it takes a high level of reflection and the ability to express oneself elaborately.

REFERENCES

Bamberg, M. (2012). Narrative analysis. In H. Cooper (Ed.), *APA handbook of research methods in psychology: Vol. 2. Quantitative, qualitative, neuropsychological, and biological* (pp. 77–94). Washington, DC: APA.

Bibace, R., Dillon, J. J., & Dowds, B. N. (1999). *Partnerships in research, clinical and educational settings*. Stanford, CT: Ablex.

Budde, J. (2013). Intersektionalität als Herausforderung für eine erziehungswissenschaftliche soziale Ungleichheitsforschung [Intersectionality as challenge for educational and social inequality research]. In S. Siebholz, E. Schneider, A. Schippling, S. Busse, & S. Sandring (Eds.), *Prozesse sozialer Ungleichheit* [*Processes of social inequality*] (pp. 245–257). Wiesbaden, Germany: VS Verlag.

Gilbert, D. (2007). *Stumbling on happiness*. New York, NY: Random House.

Goethe, J. W. V. (1805/1998). Symbolism. In D. Miller (Ed.), *Goethe: The collected works* (Vol. 12, pp. 26–27). New York, NY: Suhrkamp.

Goethe, J. W. V. (1995). *The scientific studies* (D. Miller, Ed., Trans.). Princeton, NJ: Princeton University Press.

Goldstein, K. (1995). *The organism*. New York, NY: Zone Books.

Holdrege, C. (2014). Goethe and the evolution of science. *Context, 31*, 10–23.

Iacoboni, M. (2009). Imitation, empathy, and mirror neurons. *Annual Review of Psychology, 60*, 653–670.

Johansen, J. D. (2010). Feelings in literature. *Integrative Psychological & Behavioral Science, 44*, 185–196.

Marcia, J. E. (1993). The ego identity status approach to ego identity. In J. E. Marcia, A. S. Waterman, D. R. Matteson, S. L. Archer, & N. Orlofsky (Eds.), *Ego identity: Handbook of psychological research* (pp. 3–21). New York, NY: Springer.

Marcia, J. E. (2007). Theory and measure: The identity status interview. In M. Watzlawik & A. Born (Eds.), *Capturing identity—Quantitative and qualitative methods* (pp. 1–14). Lanham, MD: University Press of America.

McAdams, D. P. (2001). The psychology of life stories. *Review of General Psychology, 5*, 100–122.

Meyer, D. (2012). An intersectional analysis of lesbian, gay, bisexual, and transgender (LGBT) people's evaluations of anti-queer violence. *Gender & Society, 26*(6), 849–873.

Schiller, F. (1784/1967). Die Schaubühne als eine moralische Anstalt betrachtet [Theatre as a moral institution]. In H. G. Thalheim, P. Fix, J. Golz, W. Hagen, M. Oehme, R. Otto & B. Pelzer (Eds.), *Schillers Werke* (Bd. 1, pp. 237–247). Berlin, Germany: Aufbau.

Singer, J. A. (2004). Narrative identity and meaning-making across the adult lifespan: An introduction. *Journal of Personality, 72*, 437–459.

Watzlawik, M. (2014). Homo-, bi- oder heterosexuell? Identitätsfindung in, zwischen und außerhalb der Norm [Homo-, bi-, or heterosexual? Identity within, inbetween, and outside the norm]. *Sonderheft der Zeitschrift für Inklusion* [Online journal]. Retrieved September 2015, from http://www.inklusion-online.net/index.php/inklusion-online/article/view/227/225

Watzlawik, M. & Heine, N. (Eds.). (2009). *Sexuelle Orientierungen. Weg vom Denken in Schubladen* [Sexual orientations. Thinking outside the box]. Göttingen, Germany: Vandenhoeck & Ruprecht.

Watzlawik, M., Schachter, E., & Cunha, C. (2015). Exploring exploration as a recursive process. In Z. Beckstead (Ed.), *Cultural psychology of recursive processes* (pp. 161–192). Charlotte, NC: Information Age.

PART V

NEW RESEARCH HORIZONS

CHAPTER 14

"WE ARE NOT FREE, ADMIT IT ... BUT WE CLING ONTO TOMORROW"

Imagination as a Tool for Coping in Disempowering Situations

Sarah H. Awad

Building on Cornejo's chapter (this volume), I will attempt to connect the concepts of imagination and fantasy to empirical research data in cultural psychology. In the context of the social and political changes that occurred in the recent years in Egypt post-2011, I will look at the aesthetic expression of imagination in letters written by political prisoners who were detained by the new regime after 2013, among thousands of other protesters, students, and journalists as part of a wider movement against protest and freedom of expression. The letters are analyzed as an aesthetic form of resistance to the confinement of prison as well as to authority. The analysis will focus on how ruptures, such as that of revolution and imprisonment, trigger imaginative thinking and reflection and how this form of imagination serves as a coping mechanism in disempowering situations.

The Psychology of Imagination: History, Theory, and New Research Horizons
pp. 267–281

First, the concept of imagination will be defined in the context of social change, rupture, and coping. Second, I will look at the challenges of observing imagination in research and analyzing it in empirical data, especially in an aesthetic form. Third, I will illustrate this form of imagination through excerpts from the data. Several themes in relation to imagination will be discussed from the letters: agency and resilience, social constraints, imagination as a dialogue, memory's interplay with imagination, and future imagination. Finally, the conclusion will draw on the correlation between imagination, agency, and resilience, as well as the value of the letters as a dialogical and aesthetic form of resistance.

Imagination and Coping

Imagination is discussed here as a sociocultural psychological phenomenon (Zittoun & Gillespie, 2016), understood as the human capacity to distance oneself from their here-and-now situation in order to return to it with new possibilities (Vygotsky, 1987). It is seen as a higher mental function that also involves vital feelings and aesthetics and is therefore not opposed to reason as Goethe emphasizes; rather, it complements the human capacity to fully feel the world and understand its interrelations (Cornejo, this volume). In this process, the mind experiences a "loop," where it disengages temporarily from the perceptual field and engages in a dynamic semiotic process that is not bound to the same linear or causal temporality as that of the socially shared reality (Zittoun & Gillespie, 2016). Imagination can therefore be oriented toward the past, the future, or an alternative present, and an imagined action in those spheres does not imply a causal consequence in them (Zittoun & Gillespie, 2016).

Ruptures such as that of revolutions and imprisonment trigger imaginative thinking. Such events question the taken-for-granted nature of daily life and create a demand for creation that is based on the lack of adaptation (Vygotsky, 2004, p. 29). Such times call for more work of imagination as the rupture "becomes the basis of sense making and narrative building, in those times imagination becomes especially crucial in replacing the unknown with representations, transforming obscure fears into actionable ideas and thus making new actions in future possible" (Zittoun et al., 2013, pp. 53–71). Imagination therefore allows us to alter our relationship to the world instead of reproducing it as it is. This process is essential in coping with constrained situations, as it enables us to decompose threatening social representations and reinvent new ones that provide projects into the future (Zittoun et al., 2013, pp. 53–71). Those new representations are the manifestation of the mind's capacity to imagine and fantasize, creating new meanings using symbols in their environment (Bühler, 1982).

Observing Imagination in Aesthetic Expression

As Goethe proposed, fantasy and imagination complement scientific inquiry rather than oppose it (Cornejo, this volume). We therefore need to utilize our own imagination to fully understand a phenomenon, more so, when we try to empirically inquire about a nontangible phenomenon such as the human capacity for imagination. One challenge in this inquiry would be that our analysis of the imagination of others would be bound by our own capacity to imagine. Another challenge would be that the observable side of the imagination process is in its articulation verbally or visually, and even though all humans have a capacity for imagination, their ability to express it varies greatly. Also when looking at the expressed form, we are limited by what the individual consciously chooses to share and manifest.

Observing imagination in aesthetic forms of expression such as a poem or a painting offers an opportunity to capture humans' subjectivity as they deal with their social settings. Individuals use aesthetic tools in their environment for reflection, intuition, and everyday resistance to what they perceive as threatening (Teo, 2015). Aesthetics therefore opens the horizon of our imagination to deal with the possible, the impossible, the ideal, and the implausible, allowing us to challenge the status quo. It also allows us through accentuation, exaggeration, and idealized representation to make sense of a problem or a disempowering situation as we experience it (Teo, 2015). On the other hand, analyzing those aesthetic forms of expression have their challenges too, one of which is how do researchers look for the subjective voice of the writer/painter and what they are trying to convey rather than attribute the researcher's own meanings to the object observed.

One way to attempt to overcome these challenges is to use a critical theoretical psychology that looks at subjectivity as an opportunity rather than a shortcoming, by employing a theory of subjectivity that is cultural-historical, socioeconomic, and embodied (Teo, 2015); to also look at imagination as a dialogical process that reflects agency and reflexivity, and to look at its expression as an invitation for intersubjectivity and empathy. This theoretical approach would also need to be supplemented with what Goethe terms *intuitive perception*, where we build our understanding of the phenomenon on our own self-reflection and experience, and looking, as Vico states, "within the modifications of our own human mind" (Cornejo, this volume). Incorporating this kind of perception in cultural psychology research has a potential to decrease the gap between human nature and our understanding of it.

Research Case: Imagination in the Aftermath of the 2011 Egyptian Revolution

For the inquiry of this chapter, I look at the case of Egypt in the aftermath of the 2011 revolution. From an imagination angle, the uprising in 2011 could be looked at as fueled by a socially shared dream of a better future. The change was triggered by a process similar to what Reicher and Haslam (2012) describe as mobilizing masses through reimagining their social identity, creating a vision of "what (they) might become" and organizing practical action that can turn this vision into social reality. As the revolution succeeded in overthrowing the president, those imaginations were nourished and the hopes for the future were multiplied. This "revolution euphoria" was soon challenged by several political changes, which included military dominance in transition periods, Muslim Brotherhood presidency, and finally the current military backed regime.

There are several manifestations of the revolutionary imagination and its hopes and future expectations. There are the written narratives of those who were part of the revolution (Awad, 2016) and there are also the visual illustrations of revolutionary graffiti in the city space (Awad & Wagoner, 2015; Awad, Wagoner, & Glaveanu, in press). The graffiti was a direct visual manifestation of the activist's work of imagination as it filled major squares and streets of Egypt in 2011. In both of these examples, the stories and graffiti paintings were material outcomes of the community's imagination and are seen as aesthetic acts of resistance that are oriented toward an imagined future of the community (Awad et al., in press).

This chapter will examine one of these forms of aesthetic resistance by looking at publicly shared letters written by prisoners during 2014 and 2015. These prisoners are supporters of the 2011 revolution and were imprisoned during the current military-backed regime for acting against authority, such as in the case of photojournalists covering clashes between security forces and protesters, or activists expressing their views in protests, the press, or online. The letters illustrate those individuals' imagination as they share their thoughts in the tangible form of written narratives. The letters serve different purposes; individually they allow the writers to express their thoughts in the solitude of the prison and communicate with their friends and families as well as with the wider community. It also serves as a social documentation of the authority's violations; letters mention cases of torture in prison, arrest without warrant, and indefinite detention without trial. This documentation also serves as a way of putting local and international pressure on government to release those detainees, as in this incident when president El Sisi pardoned 100 political prisoners a day before he was scheduled to fly to New York for a United Nations General Assembly gathering (Malsin, 2015). Lastly, some activists, who were known for their leading roles in the 2011 uprising, used the letters to confirm the continuation of their resistance and to inspire the general public to hold on to the revolutionary dream and stay hopeful and resilient.

The letters used in the data were shared publicly through families and friends of detainees on different online blogs, independent news websites, and social media (see Appendix). All letters were written in Arabic and few were translated into English when shared online. For data analysis, all letters were coded in Arabic then quotes used in the chapter were translated into English. Data comprised 17 letters written by 11 prisoners. The uniqueness of those letters lies in different aspects: that they reflect the rupture that happened in the sociocultural and political context of Egypt, sharing the high hopes of the revolution followed by unexpected events; the letters include imaginative forms of expression such as storytelling, poems, and fictional stories that reflect the imaginative process of the writers; and the constrained conditions in which prisoners write these letters reflects the capacity to imagine alternative possibilities even in the most disempowering situations such as that of indefinite detention, as most of the prisoners do not know when or whether they will be released.

Analyzing the Letters

The analysis focuses on letter content that deals implicitly or explicitly with imagination of the future as well as processes of sense making and reflection relating to the writers' feelings, memories, hopes, and despair. Attention is also put on the social constraints surrounding the writing of those letters as they help in the understanding of the content and reflect the writers' motivation for expression in spite of the consequences they might face. In many instances, the writers' safety in prison is challenged by the act of writing and sharing those letters:

> whoever dares to write inside the prison to share what is happening to those outside they put him on a black list and is punished by solitary confinement and is prevented from food, cloth, detergents, chocolate, newspapers, and books, but those who choose silence receive no harm. (Ahmed, photojournalist, Abu Zabel prison, February 2015)

Using thematic network analysis with a focus on the points mentioned above, the data codes were grouped into five overarching themes: agency and resilience, social constraints, imagination as a dialogue, memory's interplay with imagination, and future imagination. Below I will discuss each of these themes using excerpts from the letters:

Agency and Resilience

Imprisonment is a major rupture that challenges many of the taken-for-granted meanings in the writers' life. It becomes a trigger for the prisoner to reflect, reconstruct his/her identity, and to make sense of the new situation:

> But in prison you have nothing to talk about except yourself; time stops and your will is restricted to the boundaries of your body. When you talk about yourself with a freedom born of necessity—that's when you find yourself ... In the absence of despair and hope, nothing remains but the self. (Alaa and Douma, bloggers, Torah Prison, January 2014)

The writers reflect often on the injustice that led them into prison and whether there is hope for their release and a better future. The challenge of staying hopeful is very common in the letters. Being hopeful in spite of the social constraints seems very naive to some, while despair is seen by some as giving up on the revolutionary goals. In spite of the different perspectives shared regarding hope, 8 out of the 11 writers expressed a strong will to resist the disempowering situation. This sense of agency can be seen in expressions of being free from the cell and the walls that surround them, feeling less fearful of imprisonment or its consequences on their life, confirming commitment to the principles that led them to prison, and being keen to adapt. This reflects how imagination offers an escape from the perceptual field, allowing the person to become detached from the power of the situation and opens up an expanded environment (Gillespie, 2006; Zittoun & Gillespie, 2016). This concept of mentally refusing any constraints and reconfiguring the barriers of the prison situation is clear in these two examples: "But I give you honest advice: Do not try to tame a poet, the poet tames the world but cannot be tamed" (Omar Hazek, poet and novelist, Al Gharbaneyat prison, May 2014); "Your palace is not big enough for my dream, and the cell is pure absurdity. Have you ever seen a cloud on the move ask for permission?" (Alaa and Douma, bloggers, Torah Prison, January 2014).

The imprisonment for many also made them feel less fearful: "I hate prisons. I used to think earlier that I feared nothing more than prisons. But I am not afraid of prisons anymore" (Esraa, amateur photojournalist, 23, El Kanater Prison, July 2015). The resilience they develop through their experience is motivated by a conscious decision not to fall into despair and cling to hope: "Our main enemy is despair, we will win, losing one round doesn't mean losing the whole battle ... since I came here I feel stronger and more solid ... All frustration and despair are now gone from me" (Mahienour, human rights lawyer, 27, Damanhour Prison, August 2014).

Another motivation for hope was that out of necessity to be able to adapt in the day-to-day life in prison. Imagination of something better that awaits serves as a function for coping: "and life offers us light at the end of the tunnel, to let us forget the pain we are living" (Esraa, amateur photojournalist, 23, El Kanater Prison, July 2015). Another writer adapts to his daily life in prison through imagining the day he will be released: "I go on with a daily routine that doesn't change, living on the hope that I get out" (Salah, Member of the Movement for Justice and Freedom, 54, May 2015).

The capacity to imagine alternative possibilities also included fictional fantasies: "We keep on waiting for aliens to come over and save us ... but they never come. Prison is a wicked thing," and imaginative play: "Mrs. Rasha pampers us here and takes us up to her garden—the 3rd level of the bunk bed where she sleeps—where we drink chocolate shake and eat potato chips and chocolates. Up there we sing" (Esraa, amateur photo-journalist, 23, El Kanater Prison, July 2015).

Social Constraints

The attachment to hope and ability to imagine a better alternative is not always the case. As the constrained situation of prison continues, some letters express the inability to see an exit option and see themselves in a situation of despair: "I am alive yet dead from the inside, despair has spread into every part of me, my mind refuses even sleep ... nevertheless I don't fear death, I wait to welcome it for it is easier for me than staying here" (Shawkan, freelance photojournalist, 27, Torah prison, August 2015). The hardship of the reality and the inability to know when it would end threatens one's identity and challenges their capacity to imagine a positive outcome in moments of despair. The struggle between keeping hope and losing it and the risks that comes with adventuring beyond what could be is expressed in this poem:

> I know that despair is treason
> but the revolutionary in my country
> —even if he's a sinless prophet—
> when he sees the tyrant empowered
> and the oppressed silent
> amid the rejoicing of the poor

will lose his faith....

Why are we afraid to admit weakness? To admit that we are human, that military tanks destroy us and prisons make us lonely and bullets scar our thoughts and our dreams. We are humans suffering defeats, let down by our bodies, made weak by our imperfections, burned by our dreams and paralyzed by our nightmares. We are humans looking for love to support us against despair....

If despair is treason, what about hope? At least despair speaks frankly. Hope is treacherous and tricky. Is there any treason uglier than the one committed in the name of a hope you held? ...

Hope, like despair, is treason. But also, like despair, it's a normal human weakness. Here in my cell I wrestle with my dreams and my nightmares, and I don't know which hurts most. Despair and hope pull at me—but I am never a traitor. (Alaa and Douma, bloggers, Torah Prison, January 2014)

Similar to how moments of hope were associated with agency and adaptation in day-to-day life in prison, statements of despair were associated in many instances with feeling dead inside and an inability to do daily mundane activities:

Days pass here as if they are a copy of each other, they are all similar. Sometimes I think why do I eat? Why should I still survive, for what cause? I am starting to feel that life is dying within me ... I feel I am inside a tomb and pray to God that He revives me once again like He resurrects the dead from their graves. (Esraa, amateur photojournalist, 23, El Kanater Prison, July 2015)

This highlights the struggle to imagine an alternative reality when a person feels disempowered by the social constraints: "Is there a way to turn prison into heaven? Whoever claims that he can is a complete liar. They have robbed us of our freedom. We are living inside a grave" (Safaa and Asmaa, El Kanater prison, July 2015).

Imagination as a Dialogue

The letters transform the writers' imagination into a dialogue between them and their audience. The letters then become a shared story, allowing their writers to be agents in reconstructing their experiences (Jackson, 2002) and providing them with an opportunity to share their suffering and feel recognized. As in this example, where the writer asks the reader to do an exercise of imagination to understand what life is like in prison:

Want to know what prison is like?
Go into your bedroom, throw away everything and lock the door ...

Forget everything that you threw away because you will never leave.
Your life is frozen …
How many days would you live like this?
I have been living like this for 180 days, half a year.
If you want to understand the suffering of the detainees, imagine this approximate situation and try it even for one day to feel them, to realize how some of your friends are suffering the injustice of the authority.
Also know that you are not in their shoes. (Sherief, Assistant lecturer, Hadra prison, June, 2014)

The expressed imagination in this dialogue could be seen as a social act that is interdependent on several actors shaping its outcome (Marková, 2003). The writer initiating an act that is influenced by another actor (in this instance the authority) directed to the audience actor. This reflects a process of coconstruction of the letters in the social field, so even when alone in prison they are still imagining through the gaze of the other, or what they think some specific or generalized others might do or say in the future (Zittoun & de Saint-Laurent, 2015). This is of relevance especially to the letters written by activist who had leading positions during the revolution and their letters serve as a motivation for others to hold on to the revolutionary goals.

Similar to how the revolutionary graffiti in Egypt gets its power from the reaction of different actors and the government erasing it regularly (Awad et al., in press), the writers imagination is also triggered by the authority's reaction, as in the following example, where the writers compare their letter to graffiti, referring to the "new coat of paint" that the authorities put on to cover revolutionary expressions:

And finally: "Congratulations for the new coat of paint"
To erase—for the revolution—a page
is to give us a chance to think again and to write …
And it would be remiss not to thank the authorities—were it not for the new "paint" we would not have found the space to think and draw. (Alaa and Douma, bloggers, Torah Prison, January 2014)

Memory's Interplay With Imagination

Remembering plays a key role in the process of self-reflection and sense making. On the one hand, there is the interplay between memory and the future, remembering becomes an "imaginative reconstruction" that builds on their past experiences (Bartlett, 1932) and its reconstruction orients future thinking: "memories—modified by forgetting—become fictions that pave the way to the future" (Zittoun et al., 2013, p.

87). This is seen in how there were mentions of their past experiences in the letters in which new meanings of past events were constructed:

> The minute Mubarak stepped down in 2011, we all went out to celebrate. Then I noticed a young man sitting on the seashore, alone and crying. We asked him what was wrong, and he answered that a friend of his was martyred in the revolution and that at that moment he felt that his dream has come true. I know that the only true value of our lives lies in moments like this one. (Omar, Al Gharbaneyat prison, May, 2014)

There were also mentions of what they stood up for, and how events led them inside the prison, connecting those with the imagined future discussed later: "We must not forget our main goal in the middle of this battle in which we are continuously losing friends and comrades" (Mahienour, Damanhur Prison, May, 2014). This is closely related to how they identify themselves and what groups they feel they belong to. The prison space also triggered a collective memory that related the prisoners to fellow prisoners who occupied the same cell before them. Their constructed memories as well as the cell space defined this imagined community (Anderson, 1983) that the person now relates to. They share with this community their experience with the injustices of previous regimes (which was one of the factors that fueled the revolution), so the current prisoners are paying the price of this injustice just like others before them creating a kind of legacy: "The prison walls are filled with traces of injustice, with memories of all prisoners who preceded us, while the ritual of wall tagging continues with every new prisoner" (Shawkan, freelance photojournalist, 27, Torah prison, August 2015).

Memories also offered a connection with one's identity before the rupture and a temporary relief from wondering in the possibilities of the future:

> We've passed the stage of discussing whether there's value to our resilience and whether there is a chance of our release. After a month of disclosures nothing is left except memories ... and even though the revolution was—then—an "impossible dream," I remember me and find me there—in the past. (Alaa and Douma, bloggers, Torah Prison, January 2014)

Future Imagination

The externalization of imagination in a narrative form orients forward thinking and opens prospects toward the future (Bruner, 1987). The struggle between hope and despair mentioned above and the vulnerability of the situation hindered any detailed imagination of a secure positive future. However, in instances where writers mentioned future dreams, they resorted to forces outside their immediate control, associating future happenings to meanings, such as God, revolutionary power, or the temporality of life and the inevitability of death: "Faith keeps us going … I don't know what will happen, but all the time, every day I pray to God … God is generous" (Esraa, amateur photojournalist, 23, El Kanater Prison, July 2015): "I will live in this life for a predetermined time … If I die, they shall not bury my dream, my freedom, or the justice I have stood for" (Omar, Al Gharbaneyat prison, May, 2014).

> We fought for a day, one day that would end without the suffocating certainty that tomorrow would replicate it as all days had been replicated before … the revolution has a monopoly on our dreams … the revolution released our energies, we took it as our reason to exist. We did not preach the revolution or foresee it, but we dreamed of it and waited for it and so the square became ours … Not the ballot boxes or the palaces or the ministries or the prisons or even the graves are big enough for our dreams. (Alaa and Douma, bloggers, Torah Prison, January 2014)

This kind of external attribution with regard to the future could reflect a realization of their helplessness in the immediate situation in spite of their agency in creating their narratives and imagining beyond reality. It could also be a way of finding larger meaning in their existence in order to stay resilient in their current situation:

> If you think like me, you will feel no depression or disappointment. Because in these dark times, we have the chance to live by our own light, to live with what we have of love for freedom. In the darkest hours toward which we seem to be heading, a small beam of light still glitters calmly in the darkness. (Omar Hazek, poet and novelist, Al Gharbaneyat prison May 2014).

This resilience is also reflected in how in their personal future imagination, they hope for internal healing and to preserve their core identity and dreams through what they are enduring:

> I shall comfort the loneliness of my cell with a love unfettered by a jailer … I'm still waiting to learn how I can spend my life in the square without it taking my soul prisoner and emptying my dream, how I can stay inside it and still face the nightmares inside me. I'm still waiting to learn how I can leave prison without leaving part of me in the cell, and how I can forgive those who were unjust to me and those who let me down. How I can transform from a thorn in the side of injustice to a support for all those unjustly treated. (Alaa and Douma, bloggers, Torah Prison, January 2014)

CONCLUDING THOUGHTS

Throughout this chapter I have attempted to look at the adaptive mental function of imagination and its capacity and limitations in constrained conditions. The data provided examples of imagination processes and their expressions in an aesthetic narrative form. I would like to follow with some concluding thoughts about imagination as a facilitator for coping, the prison letters as an aesthetic form of resistance, and finally how those letters can help us to imagine the situation in Egypt.

The letters showed an example of how even in the most constrained conditions of prison, we have the capacity to imagine alternative scenarios that can mediate our coping and resilience. The writers' externalization of their imagination into a narrative form emphasizes their agency in reconstructing the past, reflecting on present, and orienting their future. This supports the understanding of human agency as having a symbolizing capacity to override environmental influences and impact one's development, adaptation, and change (Bandura, 2006).

The imagination of a positive future was challenged by different social constraints such as their situation in prison and the overall political situation in Egypt postrevolution. This created an internal struggle between hope and despair; however, writers who expressed hope also expressed better adaptability in the day-to-day life of prison. This supports the correlations found in research between hope and agency where high hope persons are correlated with perceptions of control over their life and positive affectivity (Snyder, 1994; Snyder et al., 1996). Hope, like imagination, is "a directing act of a cognitive kind" (Bloch, 1996, p. 12) that can therefore open venues for adaptation and resilience. High hope persons also resorted to external meanings (such as revolution), powers (such as God), or inevitable facts (such as death) to make sense of their situation. This made their current situation appear of less influence in the larger constructed meaning of life and allowed them to be able to imagine a positive future. This may suggest that the restoration to a greater meaning does significantly affect people's adaptation in difficult conditions, when the only freedom left for one is to choose one's attitude toward the situation and find a meaning for the suffering they are enduring (Frankl, 1959).

From a resistance perspective, the act of imagining and sharing this imagination in the letters is seen as an aesthetic everyday form of resistance. From one perspective it is the writer's attempt to resist the daily life of prison and "escape" the suffocating routine (Cohen & Taylor, 1992). From another perspective, it is in these low-scale everyday acts of resistance that the powerless get their weapons to fight an unequal battle and generate change (Scott, 1990). These acts become especially effective when shared in an aesthetic form with the wider community, as their story or poem creates a "virtual image" for the reader to be able to imagine their condition (Langer, 1955) and produce empathy as well as inspiration for resistance (Teo, 2015). It also shows the contrast between the two actors—writers and authority; the writers' act as one of peaceful resistance from the powerless situation of imprisonment in contrast to the authority's acts of illegal detention, lack of fair trials, and forced disappearance.

In this sense the letters are coconstructed by the different actors of the prisoners, the authority, and the wider community in the form of a dialogue. I would like to draw parallels here between the analysis of the prison letters and other forms of aesthetic resistance, such as revolutionary graffiti in their dialogicality (Awad et al., in press). Even when imagination may seem an individual act, especially when bound within the walls of a prison cell, it is an experience that is beyond the boundaries of one's own experience to the shared historical and social experience (Vygotsky, 2004); more so, once expressed and shared, creating a dialogical interaction in the wider community, triggering tension and creating a "force of change" (Marková, 2003). So the letters do not only serve as a personal reflection on a struggle but are also meant to feed into a larger imagined community of revolutionaries and the public.

Looking at the current situation in Egypt, similar letters continue to be shared as more political prisoners are detained indefinitely. Our understanding of their personal trajectories and imagination is limited to those who express and share their narratives as well as to what they choose to share, while the majority of detainees remain silent with untold stories. From the limited analysis of those shared, there is a common narrative of resilience and continuation of their resistance, rather than fear of the punishment they are experiencing, which challenges the effectiveness of authorities' tight grip on opposition and the use of prison as a way of eliminating opinions against the government. Those prisoners are commonly referred to as "opinion prisoners" or "prisoners of conscience," though the imprisonment appears to be only making those "opinions" more resilient and louder through new media channels where these letters are shared. This questions the expected outcome of the continuation of the same state strategy in dealing with opposition, especially that this strategy was one of the reasons that led to the 2011 revolution.

In conclusion, the prison letters offered an aesthetic object that reflected the writers' imagination and agency in response to the rupture they are experiencing. The rupture of the revolution continues to have a strong impact on the sociocultural setting as well as on the lives of people who are part of it. It also continues to trigger imagination of "what if" and motivation for new ways of expression and action. Through those new ways, novelty and creativity emerge from the space between reality and imagination (Winnicott, 1971) and change on the personal and sociocultural level becomes possible.

We are not free
Admit it
but we cling onto tomorrow (Alaa and Douma's poem)

REFERENCES

Anderson, B. (1983). *Imagined communities*. London, England: Verso.

Awad, S. H. (2016). The identity process in times of ruptures: Narratives from the Egyptian revolution. *Journal of Social and Political Psychology, 4*(1). Retrieved from http://jspp.psychopen.eu/article/view/521/195

Awad, S. H., & Wagoner, B. (2015). Agency and creativity in the midst of social change. In Gruber, C. W., Clark, M. G., Klempe, S. H., & Valsiner, J. (Eds.) (2014). *Constraints of agency: Explorations of theory in everyday life* (Vol. 12). Springer.

Awad, S. H., Wagoner, B., & Glaveanu, V. (in press). The (street) art of resistance. In N. Chaudhary, P. Hviid, G. Marsico, & J. Villadsen (Ed.), *Resistance in everyday life: constructing cultural experiences*.

Bandura, A. (2006). Toward a psychology of human agency. *Perspectives on Psychological Science, 1*(2), 164–180.

Bartlett, F. C. (1932). *Remembering: A study in experimental and social psychology*. Cambridge, England: Cambridge University Press.

Bloch, E. (1996). *The principle of hope, Vol. 1* (N. Plaice, S. Plaice, & P. Knight, Trans.). Cambridge, MA: MIT Press.

Bühler, K. (1982). The axiomatization of the language sciences. In R. E. Innis (Ed.), *Karl Bühler, semiotic foundations of language theory* (pp. 75–164). New York, NY: Plenum Press.

Bruner, J. S. (1987). Life as narrative. *Social Research, 54*(1), 11–32.?

Cohen, S., & Taylor, L. (1992). *Escape attempts: The theory and practice of resistance to everyday life*. London, England: Routledge. (Original work published 1976)

Frankl, V. (1959). *Man's search for meaning*. Boston, MA: Beacon.

Gillespie, A. (2006). *Becoming other: From social interaction to self-reflection*. Greenwich, CT: Information Age.

Jackson, M. (2002). *The politics of storytelling: Violence, transgression, and intersubjectivity* (Vol. 3). Copenhagen, Denmark: Museum Tusculanum Press.

Langer, S. (1955). Expressive language and the expressive function of poetry. In H. Werner (Ed.), *On expressive language: Papers presented at the Clark University conference on expressive language behaviour*. Worcester, MA: Clark University Press. (pp. 3–9).

Malsin, J. (2015, September 23). Egyptian President Sisi pardons political prisoners. *Time*. Retrieved from http://www.time.com

Marková, I. (2003). *Dialogicality and social representations*. Cambridge, England: Cambridge University Press.

Reicher, S. D., & Haslam, S. A. (2012). The role of social identity; cognitive alternatives and leadership in group mobilization and social transformation. In B. Wagoner, E. Jensen, & J. A. Oldmeadow (Eds.), *Culture and social change: Transforming society through the power of ideas*. Charlotte, NC: Information Age.

Scott, J. C. (1990). *Domination and the arts of resistance: Hidden transcripts*. New Haven, CT/London, England: Yale University Press.

Snyder, C. R. (1994). *The psychology of hope: You can get there from here*. New York, NY: Free Press/Simon & Schuster.

Snyder, C. R., Sympson, S. C., Ybasco, F. C., Borders, T. F., Babyak, M. A., & Higgins, R. L. (1996). Development and validation of the State Hope scale. *Journal of Personality and Social Psychology, 70*(2), 321.

Teo, T. (2015). Essay on an aesthetics of resistance. In J. Cresswell, A. Haye, A. Larrain, M. Morgan, & G. Sullivan (Eds.), *Dialogue and debate in the making of theoretical psychology* (pp. 303–310). Concord, ON, Canada: Captus.

Vygotsky, L. (1987). *The collected works of L. S. Vygotsky. Vol. 4: The History of the Development of Higher Mental Functions*. New York, NY: Plenum Press.

Vygotsky, L. (2004). Imagination and creativity in childhood. *Journal of Russian and East European Psychology, 42*(1), 7–97

Winnicott, D. W. (1971). *Playing and Reality*. London, England: Routledge.

Zittoun, T., & de Saint-Laurent, C. (2015). Life-creativity: Imagining one's life. In V. P. Glaveanu, A. Gillespie, & J. Valsiner (Eds.), *Rethinking creativity: Contributions from cultural psychology* (pp. 58–75). Hove, England/New York: Routledge.

Zittoun, T., & Gillespie, A. (2016). *Imagination in human and cultural development*. London, England: Routledge.

Zittoun, T., Valsiner, J., Salgado, J., Gonçalves, M. M., Vedeler, D., & Ferring, D. (2013). *Human development in the life course: Melodies of living*. New York, NY: Cambridge University Press.

APPENDIX: SOURCES OF PRISON LETTERS

http://www.madamasr.com/sections/politics/graffiti-two-alaa-and-douma

http://egyptprotests2014.tumblr.com/detainees

http://arablit.org/2014/06/12/egyptian-author-omar-hazek-if-i-die-dont-bury-me/

http://www.almasryalyoum.com/news/details/774692

https://www.facebook.com/freealaa2013?pnref=story

https://www.facebook.com/freemahienour/notes

http://albedaiah.com/news/2015/07/11/93143

https://www.facebook.com/Al7oriallgd3an?fref=photo

https://www.facebook.com/FreedomforShawkan?fref=ts

https://www.facebook.com/shabab6april?fref=nf

CHAPTER 15

FEELING ONESELF INTO NATURE

Reflections on Picking Flowers
in Japan and Denmark

Rebekka Mai Eckerdal

Interacting with and relating to nature has been central throughout human history. Whether nature is used as an object of observation, an activity frame, or perceived as a source of oxygen, it is inescapably part of being human on this planet. Our contemporary ecological concerns—discussed in politics and philosophy—converge with the way in which ordinary people handle concrete objects in nature. The discipline of psychology is needed in order to bridge these two angles through a focus on imagination. This concrete context is illuminated through questions about breaking social rules, the meaning of the living, and such. Human beings, as a biological species, inevitably come from nature, but our cultural development leads to counter-positioning vis-à-vis nature. We do not perceive specific parts of nature, for example, trees, rivers, flowers, and the like, through the same lenses in every cultural frame. In other words, relating to nature is the primary arena for human imagination. At first appearance, nature seems perfectly natural: We are part of it, or conquer it. In reality we relate to our own imaginary construction in what we

The Psychology of Imagination: History, Theory, and New Research Horizons
pp. 283–293
Copyright © 2017 by Information Age Publishing
All rights of reproduction in any form reserved.

refer to as "nature." Picking a flower is an act of "killing nature," yet it is an activity that human beings idealize as "maintaining beauty."

In this chapter, I will look at the meaning of picking flowers in Japan and Denmark and how it plays out in different levels (viz. micro, meso, and macro). In Japan, the person belongs to nature (macrolevel), acts in ways that do not violate harmony with nature (by, for example, not picking a flower—mesolevel), and feels bad when picking a flower is simply suggested (microlevel). The act of picking a flower takes on different meanings as a function of how relating to nature is culturally organized. My aspiration is to introduce the reader to my experience of differences in feeling oneself in nature even in such a simple act as refraining from or picking a flower. I will touch upon the general topic of picking flowers in public places and connect this with a study in Japan. Finally, comments are offered regarding how we as researchers should approach nature as living. The chapter concludes that the difference between Japan and Denmark, when looking at being part of nature as an "organism," shows a similarity that generates opposite outcomes. I draw on perspectives of the Japanese anthropologist Kinji Imanishi concerning living things, plants as living creatures, and nonliving things, and link this to perspectives from de Waal, Valsiner, Bishnoi, Cornejo, and Goethe.

My Japanese Experience: Flowers Are Here, But Nobody Picks Them

In a recent study I asked a Japanese group about their feelings and thoughts with regard to flower picking. As I was born and raised in Denmark, I never reflected deeply on the behavior of picking flowers. However, when I picked a flower in Japan and afterwards realized that I was the only one doing so, I became aware that this was not a universal practice. It appeared to me that what was a clear matter to me was not the same in Japanese culture, even though they pay as much or more attention to aesthetics than Danes. I became curious as to how people can have such an exquisite art tradition with lacquerware, textiles, armor, dancing, and flower arrangement, and at the same time hesitate to pick beautiful flowers in nature.

During a 3-month research stay in Japan, I arranged a focus group with nine Japanese psychology students at Ritsumeikan University. I explained my experience with picking a flower in Japan and asked the participants to reflect upon the topic. One student began by stating that because flowers are maintained with public resources, it is considered wrong to pick the flowers in public. The other students followed him saying that they simply do not feel comfortable picking flowers—in their mind it is not right and that the flowers belong to the place where they grow. A student also explained how the situation (for instance, a bush, tree, flower field, and such) framing the flower cannot be picked (unlike a flower) and the beauty is in the collected picture which the flower is a part of—picking the flower would ruin both the "picture" in the nature and not turn out as a success in the home. They were all familiar with buying flowers for the home but no one picks flowers outside to bring into their home. Hence, it is accepted to have flowers in the home but only if the action of getting the flowers is not done by you; for example, picking the flowers in nature, but instead bought in a shop. Several students mentioned that they take pictures of particularly beautiful flowers, and when asked what they do with the picture afterwards, they explained that they show it to their friends, share it on social media, or look back at the pictures after a while.

Clearly the students were not used to picking flowers and were raised with the idea of flower picking as being something morally wrong. I therefore asked more about this and when they learned not to pick the flowers. Several students shared anecdotes from their childhood or youth at this point. A student who grew up outside Japan explained that he often picked flowers with his mother and when he was around 10 years old his parents explained to him that flowers are not to be picked and he stopped. Another student said he used to pick flowers until he was 10–15 years old and played with them along with other children. These two students agreed that social pressure from their peers also took part in stopping the picking of flowers—as the children got older, the peers would tell the flower picking child that they were weird or ask them "What is wrong with you?" This states the obvious, namely, that children are curious and therefore pick flowers but are afterwards socialized into refraining from doing so.

One of the students grew up in the countryside and explained that out there flower picking is common and not frowned upon. The other students backed her up by saying that they would not hesitate to pick flowers in the countryside even as adults because these flowers, whether a tulip or a flower on a bush, do not belong to a particular owner. However, no one would dare to pick flowers on private grounds, in the city or in the countryside, since these flowers belong to the owner of the grounds and should not be picked by anyone, not even small children. By this, a pattern of regional and spatial limits is seen which has become an internalized Japanese norm. The internal norms have been shaped within the group/category "Japanese people" through "a historical process of continuous attunement to consensually orchestrated community practices" (Baerveldt & Verheggen, 2014, p. 179), and people therefore expect each other to act according to these internal, standard ways or "lay themselves open to disapproval and the exercise of sanctions by other group members" (Fraser, 2001, p. 142). Before moving on, it is worth considering the lay notion that Japan is a society containing strong collectivist values and therefore "would be more ready to accept majority influence than people who live in a society with much stronger individualistic values, such as the USA or Britain," which is not a sign of weakness, but of willingness to conform because of consideration for others (Fraser, 2001, p. 145). As Goethe expresses it, our one-sided thinking makes us see the world only through our own perspective and accordingly arrogantly believes that the world is created by and for us (Goethe, 1824/1998, p. 45f in Cornejo, 2015, p. 11).

A Thought Experiment: Breaking Social Rules

With the notions of social rules in mind, I asked the group in the session to imagine participating in an experiment the day after in which they would be filmed by me from far away and then pick as many flowers as the surrounding people would "let them." Only one person said he could do it without a problem since it was just an experiment, while all others said they would refuse. According to Moscovici and Personnaz' (1980, cited in Fraser, 2001) approach, this incident illustrates an example of a situation where the minority (the single student) could change the opinion of the majority (the group of students), though this would require the student to stick to his view repeatedly and take more time than if it was the majority trying to convince the minority (Fraser, 2001, p. 146ff). In this study the single student was not able to change the majority's opinion, which led me to the next step in the thought experiment. With Milgram's (1963) classic experiment in mind, I asked the Japanese students if they would fulfill the task if I added full responsibility on my account. Surprisingly the result stayed the same; they simply would not pick the flowers because I told them to or for the purpose of an experiment. Considering Festinger's (1950, 1954, cited in Fraser, 2001) argument that we compare ourselves to relevant, similar others (i.e., the fellow students) in order to "be influenced by social consensus, which can appear to imply a 'correct' way of viewing things" which will incline the students to accept the majority view (i.e., "I will not pick the flowers"), might be an explanation of the students' responses (Fraser, 2001, p. 153). When imagining how many flowers they would be able to pick before someone would interfere, the answer was 7–8 flowers, yet they would not do this. When I asked them how many flowers they thought I, as an obvious foreigner, would be able to pick, they said that no Japanese person would interfere, since they assume that the foreigner's flower picking is a result of not knowing the Japanese custom. I asked how they would react to this behavior themselves and they said that they would not interfere either, only look and think, "Oh, she is a foreigner" and pass on. When speaking about interfering with someone picking flowers, they all agreed that when someone makes a flower-picking person aware that the flowers should not be picked he/she should return the flowers to the place where he/she picked them and not bring them home. When I followed up with the question "This would not be a waste?" they shook their head or said no.

At the end of the session, I asked the attending women what their reaction would be if a man gave them a flower he had picked outside as a present. The first woman would accept it and take it as a compliment that he broke a social custom to give her a present. The other woman would accept it like the first woman, but added that she would tell the man not to do this again. The men in the room added that they occasionally buy flowers for women (e.g., for their girlfriend or on Mother's Day) but would not pick flowers for a present as a romantic gesture. The recurring points were that no one felt an urge to pick flowers when they came across them—even if it was legal or justified, they would not do it; they felt distress and uncomfortable when thinking about picking flowers and they all learned as children or teenagers not to pick flowers.

Danish Affordances of Flowers: Conquering or Admiring

As I have now explained my findings from Japan, I would like to focus on the conditions in Denmark regarding flower picking. However, before doing so, I want to stress, that the interesting point to be made here is not about differences but about similarities (Imanishi, 1941, p. 2). The relation with nature is universal, but its cultural patterning by way of just two social representations combined, for example, "the flower belongs to nature" versus "the flower is mine," give us diametrically opposite outcomes. It is my experience that it is not frowned upon if you choose to pick a flower in nature in Denmark, even though, as the Japanese focus group pointed out, someone spent their time planting them and everyone has been paying taxes to provide salaries for these people and thereby the flowers are owned by the municipality. If I were to ask a Danish focus group the same questions as I asked the Japanese one, they would most likely, due to their cultural heritage, laugh at me for being so silly as to make a problem out of picking and/or keeping the flower I picked. In Denmark we are raised with the thought that the affordance of a flower is to be decorative and in general made for us to use whether that means to look at, eat, pick, or possess it in other ways. Following this it is simply natural to me, as a Dane, to consume nature by picking the flower with the intention of enjoying it in a vase in my home. This is why the flower exists to me, that is my culture. Putting the flower back where I picked it from, simply laying it on the ground, would in this regard be a complete waste since it would not be used for anything useful. This stream of thought shows one of the clearest differences between Japanese and Danish ways of perceiving nature, to which we all relate. In the next section, I will further elaborate on this point.

The Theoretical Issues of Violating and Not Violating Nature

My starting point for this theoretical elaboration is the main premise that people of both Denmark and Japan share the commonality of being consumers of and surrounded by nature, and the main difference lies in the way we consume nature—in Denmark nature is part of me (I pick the flower) whereas in Japan I am part of nature (I *mederu*).[1] In order to substantiate this distinction and explain the foreign worldview, I use Kinji Imanishi's natural philosophy, which has had much influence in Japanese society. Kinji Imanishi (1902–1992) worked in the fields of anthropology, entomology, evolution, and ecology, and is the founder of Kyoto University's Primate Research Institute because of his substantive impact in the research on primates. In his work "*A Japanese View of Nature: The World of Living Things,*" he distinguishes between living and nonliving things and believes that by looking at each living thing we can recognize them but only interpret and express this in human terms. He collects his view on the relation between person and the surroundings by saying,

> Each living thing in its own place leads to an accurate perception of our human place. The objective of biology is not only related to the resources of our life, but also to provide the materials by which we reflect on our own entity by making it clear that we are part of this living world, having a biological affinity with it, and that the roots of our behavior are in the world of living things in general. (Imanishi, 1941, p. 7)

As we can see from this, Imanishi possess a holistic harmonious perspective with a focus on humans as part of the world, which is in contrast to the traditional Western dualisms of animal><human and nature><culture, which is also expressed in Plato's "great chain of being," where humans are placed above animals and nature (de Waal, 2003, pp. 294, 298). Although the Western dualism is strong, Goethe advocates that wholeness is superior to parts and that we should strive to pay attention to a holistic view in order to obtain knowledge about the parts (Cornejo, 2015, p. 5). These two contradicting perspectives (i.e., holistic vs. dualistic) are experienced throughout the world. An example of this can be found in a 1984 German film about an Indian story of the massacre at

Khejarli (Federal Republic of Germany, March 1984; Bishnoi, 1992). In the story from 1730 AD, 363 Indians sacrificed themselves for the sake of the trees near their homes when Maharaja Abhay Singhji ordered their cutting down because he wanted to build a palace for himself and needed timber in this process. The Indians believed the plants and animals were not to be killed without defense from humans, so the Indians placed themselves in front of and around the trees when they were to be cut, and because they were in the way, a person died every time they cut down a tree. To this story, which is deeply rooted in the Bishnoi population of India, the Germans expressed "three hundred and sixty three human beings giving their lives for dumb green trees!!" (Bishnoi, 1992). Thus, it is clear that some people see vegetation as on a lower level than humans, whereas others see it the other way around.

Another example emphasizing how feeling into nature can become personally salient is the childhood story of the German philosopher, Günther "Anders" Stern, who shared his pantheistic beliefs with his father, the German philosopher and psychologist, William Stern. When Günther was about 10 years old he experienced his aunt cutting a flower and presenting it to him, for him to hand to his mother as an expression of love. He reacted by slapping her and because of this, Günther's father tried to strike him and had to control him himself not to do it again; after this the aunt took care of slapping the boy herself. Moreover, William asked Günther to apologize to his aunt, which he refused to do since he thought that it was the aunt who should apologize for decapitating the flower seeing it from their shared pantheistic standpoint. The relation between the son and William Stern never became undisturbed again and the specific garden situation was not mentioned for another 30 years when William Stern was approaching death (Anders, 1971, p. 115; Lamiell, 2003, p. 25f). As we can see from these two examples, the value of nature can become central in actions and behavior for the involved parties.

The Special Meaning of *The Living*

Before addressing the seemingly simple question of when something is alive, I want to focus on what Imanishi says is the purpose of living. As Imanishi was concerned with evolutionary theory, he made his point clear in this regard; nature (cells, individuals, etc.) reproduces itself and thereby simultaneously reconstructs the world as it is, which then becomes the crucial objective for a living thing (1941, p. 24). When to live itself is the main objective for a living thing, then picking a flower, in Imanishi's perspective, is removing the ultimate objective. Here it should be mentioned though, that Imanishi is convinced that other organisms do not necessarily have purposes like humans do (p. 75). In his view then, the affordance of a flower is to live, whereas one could argue that in a typical Danish mindset the flower is there for the subject to use as he/she wishes. Furthermore Imanishi holds a materialistic view where body and life are inseparable and where the living thing represents life or spirit (seishin, 精神) (pp. 28, 33). In sum, his opinion is that the meaning of being alive is simply to make a living/work and secure our subsistence (p. 26).

Building on Imanishi's evolutionary approach to his understanding of the world, he argues that everything existing stems from one cell and that gradually develops (1941, pp. 13, 16). It should be clear to anyone today that the world is constituted of living things, but what is more blurry is what constitutes being alive. Imanishi argues that a living thing is alive when it has organic integrated exertion, and when the living thing is a combination of itself and its surroundings (pp. 15, 27). To this he adds that the surroundings only make the living things live if the living thing acts (i.e., food does not become food after being ingested, like meat does not become prey after being eaten). As Imanishi continues, "If organisms do not react, the environment presumably kills them and transforms them into matter" (p. 74).

Flowers: Living Things, Until They Die

Humans, animals and plants experience their surroundings in different ways (Imanishi, 1941, p. 29). But how do we even know that a flower is a living thing? Goethe defines the concept of nature from his genetic thinking as a living, developing organism, or simply the field of everything the natural sciences study (Cornejo, 2015, p. 4f). According to Imanishi, something is alive when it gradually develops, when it has organic integrated exertion, when the living thing is a combination of itself and its surroundings and when the living thing lives (i.e., swims, flies, etc.). From this perspective it should be clear that the structure of a living thing should be one that allows the thing to perform different functions—the plant should be autonomous. Imanishi emphasizes that a living structure, be it human, animal, or plant, cannot exist without both structure and function (1941, pp. 14–31). This specificity marks another similarity between the Danish and Japanese experience of nature: both in Denmark and Japan flowers have structure and function, albeit the functions are different from each other. Besides structure and function, Imanishi stresses that living things have integrity and a plant expresses this integrity by its separate form. He explains that the plant has control since there is a boundary between itself and its surroundings, which makes it an independent system in itself. He writes, "Apart from cells, a living thing in general presents itself as an individual expressing one self-contained independent system; this has an extremely important meaning and it seems to me that this independence and integrity cannot be considered separately anymore" (p. 24f). When considering integrity, it should be mentioned that we normally speak of brain or mind when thinking of the agent behind integration or control, but this does obviously not include plants even though these are living things like us. If plants have minds or consciousness in them, it is different from ours, but we might be able to speak of something in parallel since plants have wholeness and autonomy which we could identify as similar to the mind of higher creatures. To this aspect of theorizing nature Imanishi writes, "Some may insist that a plant is a kind of automaton or self-reproducing machine. In such a discussion this choice is a matter of opinion and nothing is certain: we cannot say this must be the case" (pp. 22, 31f, 62).

It is inevitable to ponder when a plant can be considered dead when focusing on flower picking. According to Imanishi, a living thing dies when it's integrated organic exertion of forces collapses, which a living flower expresses when it grows larger and grows buds (1941, p. 15). When putting the flower in water at home as we normally do when buying flowers, we delay the flower's decaying process, which makes the flower able to continue to live in this world (p. 17). Even though flowers go through a change by being picked, they stay alive since there is still structure, function, and integrity. When these criteria are no longer met, the living thing can be said to be dead (p. 19). The feelings attached to picking flowers and presumably killing them before their time are according to Nishida (1979) contributive in shaping a person's inner spirit. This is in accordance to what each person feels when picking the flower as seen in the examples with the sacrificing Indians and Günther Stern above (p. 225). Whether flowers in this sense have more power than we are aware of is a whole other topic, which can advantageously be taken up later on.

CONCLUSION

The ways humans relate with nature are culturally organized, which is underpinned by my study with a Japanese focus group of students who I asked to imagine situations of flower picking within Japan. Besides this, I have looked closer at some Danish conditions for flower picking where affordances are different from those of Japan. Throughout the explanations of this particular phenomenon I have used Kinji Imanishi's descriptions of nature to touch on the subjects of living things, plants as living creatures, and nonliving things. Imanishi emphasizes that things in the world are different although similar in essence, and that "difference presupposes similarity; by recognizing similarities, we can also recognize differences" (Imanishi, 1941, pp. 3, 20). What we as researchers get back from our relation to nature and the knowledge we construct from this, depends on the perception and projection that we make and the assumed perspectives we create in these interferences (de Waal, 2003, p. 293; Valsiner, 1999, p. 26). Here we can draw on Goethe's third feature and theory of knowledge; namely, to come face to face with nature and make a personal commitment by seeing, feeling, and touching the phenomenon under scope in the research situation and by this, capture what he calls the archetypal phenomenon. According to Goethe, fantasy is a necessary means of obtaining ideal science and hidden relationships of nature. We must therefore learn to see nature's inner relationships as they are and depict them naturally—"fantasy and organismic sensibilities play also a crucial role in science, as they express the connectedness between human organisms with the wholeness of nature" (Cornejo, 2015, p. 31). Theory construction should begin with a personal experience of intuitive perception with the phenomenon instead of being separated, which is often the case according to Goethe—or expressed in another way by Faust, "If you don't feel it, you won't catch it" (pp. 5–13). By this it can be said that Goethe advocates the abductive method, that is, when I went to Japan I did not know I could not pick the flowers, but because I was seeing, feeling, and touching the phenomenon of flower picking by incident, it became an object of theory construction, not the other way around. The difference between Japan and Denmark is actually a similarity that generates opposite outcomes. These outcomes have been elaborated throughout this text and can be summarized in two ways of being part of nature; nature belongs to me (Denmark) versus I belong to nature (Japan).

NOTE

1. When speaking with the focus group, two Japanese expressions were explained to me. The first one was *mederu* (愛でる) which means to *admire* or *love* without touching the object (e.g., nature, object, or flower). They explained to me that when Japanese people see a flower they intuitively think/act mederu. The other expression was *Oshibana* (押し花), which is pressed flowers in a frame typically in a pattern of animals, flowers, or figures. These are used to decorate the home indoors and can make it up for picking fresh flowers. These two expressions frame much of the group's understandings of flower picking: as a Japanese person, you are supposed to admire/love the nature without touching it, and you can buy other art that will make up for fresh flowers for home decoration.

REFERENCES

Anders, G. (1971). *Die geköpfte Lilie. Erinnerung an den Vater* [The beheaded lily: A recollection of my father]. Süddeutsce Zeitung, p. 115.

Baerveldt, C., & Verheggen, T. (2014). Enactivism. In J. Valsiner (Ed.), *The Oxford handbook of culture and psychology*. New York, NY: Oxford University Press.

Bishnoi, R. S. (1992). The great sacrifice & other sacrifices for trees. In *A blueprint for environment: Conservation as creed*. Dehra Dun, India: Surya.

Cornejo, C. (2015). *From fantasy to imagination: A cultural history and a moral for cultural psychology*. Santiago, Chili: Pontificia Universidad Católica de Chile.

de Waal, F. B. M. (2003). Silent invasion: Imanishi's primatology and cultural bias in science. *Animal Cognition, 6*(4), 293–299.

Fraser, C. (2001). Interaction in groups. In C. Fraser & B. Burchell (Eds.), *Introducing social psychology*. Cambridge, England: Polity Press.

Goethe, J. W. (1824/1998). Ernst Stiedenroth: A psychology in clarification of phenomena from the soul (Part One, Berlin: 1824). In D. Miller (Ed.), *Goethe: The collected works. Scientific studies* (Vol. 12, pp. 45–46). New York, NY: Suhrkamp.

Imanishi, K. (1941). *A Japanese view of nature. The world of living things*. London, England: RoutledgeCurzon.

Lamiell, J. T. (2003). Beyond individual and group differences. Human individuality, scientific psychology, and William Stern's critical personalism. Washington, DC: Georgetown University Medical School, Georgetown University.

Milgram, S. (1963). Behavioral study of obedience. *Journal of Abnormal and Social Psychology, 67*(4), 371–378.

Nishida, K. (1979). Affective feeling. In Y. Nitta & H. Tatematsu (Eds.), *Japanese phenomenology: Phenomenology as the trans-cultural philosophical approach* (pp. 223–249). Dordrecht, The Netherlands: Reidel.

Valsiner, J. (1999). I create you to control me: A glimpse into basic processes of semiotic mediation. *Human Development, 42*, 26–30.

CHAPTER 16

RUSSIAN REVIVAL OF THE ST. GEORGE MYTH AND ITS IMAGERY

A Study Based on Reconstructive Picture Interpretation and Psychoanalysis

Stefan Hampl and Dominik Mihalits

On April 22, 2015, the Russian online newspaper Pravda.ru tweeted a sharp comment on the public discussions emerging from the advertisement of the fashion magazine *Elle* in Ukraine. What caused the controversy? The original Twitter message or tweet consists of a photograph and a brief text (Figure 16.1). The photograph shows the May issue of *Elle* Ukraine at a public billboard in the streets of the capital Kiev. On its cover the American actress Michelle Williams is wearing an orange-black eel-leather dress from Louis Vuitton's spring 2015 collection. The same cover picture was used for the UK, Dutch, and Japanese versions of the *Elle* magazine without any specific public reactions. Hence, from an outside perspective the picture itself is not particularly revealing about what could be considered problematic about it. In order to investigate this question, it is worthwhile to contextualize the picture within the frame of the text of

The Psychology of Imagination: History, Theory, and New Research Horizons
pp. 295–315
Copyright © 2017 by Information Age Publishing
All rights of reproduction in any form reserved.

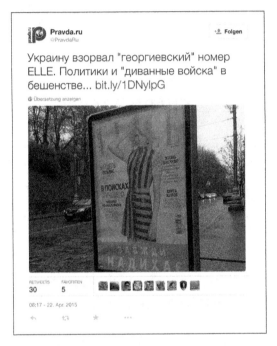

Figure 16.1.   Picture of *Elle* advertisement in the twitter message of Pravda.ru, April 22, 2015.

the tweet. The English translation reads as follows: "Ukraine was hit by a 'Georgish'[1] issue of ELLE. Politicians and 'couch soldiers' enraged."

Interpretation of the Tweet's Text and the Picture

What do we make of the tweet's text in reference to the picture? *The Interpretation of Pictures and the Documentary Method* (Bohnsack, 2010b) proposes a two-step process in order to systematically separate the literal from the referential interpretation. First of all we have to understand the literal meaning of the sentences (formulating interpretation). On the basis of that, we can then investigate what the literal meaning is referring to (reflective interpretation).

From a methodological viewpoint, one important aspect of Twitter messages is that they are limited to 140 characters. Therefore they force the writers to be concise. According to the ethnomethodologist Garfinkel (2004), the degree of how concise a message can be largely depends on its indexicality. A message is indexical if it refers to the cultural knowledge or common sense of a certain community. In effect it can be easily understood by someone from within the community, but is hard to decipher for someone outside of the community. Social researchers are typical outsiders to the field of investigation. Therefore their task is to reconstruct the referential meaning of the utterances of people from within the field. In the example of the presented Twitter message, we are confronted with a particularly indexical message. In the following we would like to demonstrate the methodological steps to reconstruct its meaning from within the Russian-Ukrainian sphere, where it originated.

Formulating Interpretation of the Tweet's Text

The first step of the interpretation is to paraphrase the text of the tweet in the common sense language of the researcher. The resulting text should be constructed along the principles of clear communication, that is, it should be concise but contain the key messages in an easily understandable way. In result, the original text can be paraphrased as follows: Politicians and Internet activists (i.e., "couch warriors") are angry after a "Georgish" issue of *Elle* was released in Ukraine.

The formulating interpretation vividly demonstrates that two levels of knowledge are necessary in order to understand the text: the level of generalized communicative (i.e., common sense) knowledge and the level of culture-specific conjunctive knowledge. While we are capable of decoding the first level of information with a little bit of imagination (i.e., couch warriors = Internet activists), we fail at decoding the second level (i.e., what does "Georgish" mean). In order to understand the word *Georgish*, we are simply lacking the necessary contextual information. According to Garfinkel (2004), however, there is a way of decoding Georgish by taking the formal principles of its use into consideration. This is where the reflective interpretation of the documentary method comes into play.

Reflective Interpretation

What we have understood so far is that *Georgish* seems to be a strongly indexical term. As already mentioned, according to Garfinkel (2004) an indexical term refers to a specific use within a specific community. Bohnsack (2010a) has developed a procedure of taking the indexical information into account and reconstructing the meaning of the term within the community of its users. We start by asking the question, what the word *Georgish* is opposed to in the twitter message. As soon as we have a lead on that, we will try to falsify and verify our findings within the frame of the text and later also within the frame of the picture of the twitter message.

"Georgish" in Opposition to "Ukrainian"

Following the logic of the twitter message, the "Georgishness" of the fashion ad is responsible for the anger of Ukrainian politicians and activists. A more focused inspection demonstrates that it is particularly the term *Georgish* that seems to be opposing the term *Ukrainian*. Hence, at the core of the text, two counterforces are presented to the readers: Georgish and Ukrainian.

Language of Force/Military Talk

If the Georgishness of the fashion advertisement is said to offend Ukrainians, the initial phrase "Ukraine was hit" and the expression "couch soldiers" strongly underline this impression. The first sentence sounds as if a bomb was dropped on Ukrainian territory and the "couch soldiers" are reacting to it now. Hence, the quite usual event of the "release of a magazine" is conveyed in an unusually strong assault language, more likely to be used in the context of an unexpected terrorist attack or a military operation.

Distancing and Ridiculing

With regard to the military talk, the author of the tweet takes an ambivalent position. On the one hand, he/she is distancing him/herself from any military connotations of the fashion advertisement. This becomes evident in the use of the third-person style of writing (e.g., Ukraine was hit … couch soldiers are enraged). This position enables the author to ridicule the "pathetic efforts" of "anti-Georgish" (Ukrainian) politicians and activists for falsely mistaking the cover of a magazine for a military offense. On the other hand, the author him/herself is actively fostering a conflictual understanding of the tweet by using military terminology. Why does this mode of communication not become immediately evident and turn against the author?

Credibility and Camouflaging: Making the Author Invisible

The principles of distancing and ridiculing are not only relevant with regard to the content of the tweet, they are also relevant with regard to the proposed literary genre of the text. The twitter message itself is drafted in the style of an officially authorized news bulletin (which it is not). In this shape, the text suggests a higher amount of credibility than, for instance, a personal message. However, the impression of "official authorization" is also supported by the fact that the tweet's author, @PravdaRu, is a collective body—the Russian Newspaper Pravda ("truth"). Simultaneously, whoever wrote the message, remains anonymous. Hence, the personal authorship of the tweet is camouflaged by using three oppositional modes of communication: (a) by proposing a seemingly official news bulletin style and simultaneously and ironically distancing oneself from it, (b) by proposing ironic distance from the actual content of the message while at the same time using connotations of serious military language, and by (c) issuing a personal message anonymously through the collective body of a newspaper.

Context

At the time of the tweet, war was actually taking place in Ukraine (inflicted by the Russian Federation's annexation of the Crimean Peninsula and its occupation of the regions surrounding Donetsk and Luhansk). Hence, dropping bombs, terrorist attacks, or military conflicts were happening every day and were in fact real threats to the people. Even from the side of anti-Ukrainian propaganda it would not have been popular to openly ridicule events that cost thousands of lives. However, particularly at times of war, it is possible to make fun of people who are seemingly unable to differentiate real threats from insignificant events. Hence, the Ukrainian politicians and Internet activists are portrayed as paranoid wimps, because they mistake the cover of a women's fashion magazine for hostile "Georgish" propaganda. For outsiders, the indexicality of the term *Georgish* is hard to decipher by looking at the text alone. In order to better understand what it is referring to, let us now focus more closely on the picture of the tweet.

Formulating Interpretation of the Picture of the Tweet

According to Bohnsack (2010b), the formulating interpretation of pictures consists of two parts: the preiconographic interpretation and the iconographic interpretation (Panofsky, 2006). The guiding methodological principle is to separate those aspects of the picture that can be understood independently of one's cultural background from the ones that require additional contextual knowledge (i.e., commonsense knowledge). The reasoning behind this procedure is to make empirically explicit to what extent the meaning of the picture is co-constructed by the culture-specific knowledge of the researcher (or any other common observer). The analytic differentiation between common sense and non–common sense enables us to create a distance to our seeing habits. We are forced to describe aspects of the picture that we might personally consider "negligible" or do not even consciously perceive as decisive. For instance, it could take us a long time trying to figure out what could be Georgish and problematic about Michelle Williams wearing a Louis Vuitton dress on an *Elle* cover. But simply excluding the names and the preknowledge that are common sense to us can provide us with new leads for a better understanding of the phenomenon. For example, it enables us to transform the initial question into What could be Georgish and problematic about a woman on public display, wearing an orange-black dress?

On the basis of these preliminary findings[2] of the picture interpretation, we can try to further narrow down our investigation of Georgishness. By attempting to understand the explosive potential of the picture within the context of its presentation in Ukraine, we are also following up on the military connotations that we found in the text of the tweet.

The Order of St. George and Its Ribbon as a Contemporary Derivative

Military symbolism in relation to the myth of St. George, combined with an orange-black color code, is paradigmatically represented in the Order of St. George, which has been one of the highest awards for officers in the Russian army. On the medal of the Order we find a representation of the Christian St. George on the back of a horse slaying a dragon. Historically, the Order unites tsarist, Soviet, and contemporary Russia as it has almost continuously existed up to the present since its introduction by Catherine the Great in 1769. With regard to our investigation of the Twitter picture, the most striking visual aspect of the Order is the orange-black ribbon attached to it that corresponds to the actress's dress on the Elle cover (see Figures 16.1 and 16.2). But is mere similarity between a dress and a military order enough to cause a public outrage? Actually, in spite of its long tradition, the Order has not even been a widespread symbol in post-Soviet countries. Our historical research, however, demonstrates that the orange-black ribbon itself has become more and more detached from the Order recently and was introduced into mainstream culture.

According to Fitzpatrick (2015), the first to pick up the solitary St. George ribbon was the Russian youth movement in support of president Putin, called Nashi (those who belong to us). They have used the orange-black St. George ribbon as a symbol to counter the orange ribbons of the followers of the Orange Revolution in Ukraine, which resulted in presidential reelections in 2004 (orange was the color of the opposition's presidential candidate Yushchenko). Following Fitzpatrick's argument, it was the Nashi's political aim to replace the narrative of "orange = revolution" with the narrative "orange-black = commemoration." In May 2005, the St. George ribbon became a central element of the Nashi's nationwide advertisement campaign for Russia's annual celebration of victory over

Figure 16.2.   Order Of Saint George, 1st class. Russian Federation.

Nazi Germany. In their pamphlet (Figure 16.3), the Nashi explained that everybody should wear a St. George ribbon in memory of those who lost their lives fighting for their fatherland.

The next time the St. George ribbon attracted public attention was in February 2014, during the annexation of Crimea. While the famous "green men" (soldiers without national identification) took control of the peninsula, the orange-black ribbons were handed out to the public to visually demonstrate their solidarity with Russia (Figure 16.4). After that the ribbons were also used by Russian soldiers and separatists in the Luhansk and Donetsk Regions of Eastern Ukraine (Figure 16.5).

The ribbon can therefore be understood as a "semiotic mediator" (Valsiner, 1999). Historically it was part of the military order awarded for

«Георгиевская ленточка»

идея акции - РИА Новости

«Я помню! Я горжусь!»

РИА Новости, Комитет общественных связей города Москвы и "Студенческая община" объявляют о проведении акции "Георгиевская ленточка" с 25 апреля по 9 мая.

Если война коснулась твоей семьи. Если ты знаешь, какой ценой досталась нам Победа. Если ты гордишься своей историей, своей страной, своей семьей. Если ты помнишь.

Сделай "Георгиевскую ленточку" символом твоей памяти - прикрепи ее на лацкан одежды, повяжи на руку, на сумку или на антенну автомобиля.

ФИНАЛ АКЦИИ – 9 МАЯ В 21:00 НА ПОКЛОННОЙ ГОРЕ И ПРОСПЕКТЕ САХАРОВА

➤ Как получить ленточку

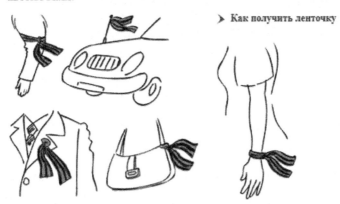

Source: https://web.archive.org/web/20050507120328/http://gl.9may.ru/

Figure 16.3.   St. George ribbon. Idea of the action—RIA Novosty (title translated from Russian).

Figure 16.4.   Russian nationalists outside Crimean parliament building in Simferopoldon[ating] distributing St. George ribbons on February 27, 2014 (Fitzpatrick, 2015). Arthur Shwartz/EPA.

Source: Getty Images.

Figure 16.5.   Camouflaged fighter in Eastern Ukraine wearing St. George ribbon.

the victory over the conquered enemies. As the ribbon has become detached from the Order, it was used to commemorate the martyrs fighting for Soviet victory. In very recent history, when Russia started seizing territories in Ukraine, the ribbon yet again altered its meaning while not giving up its military heritage. In the case of Crimea and Donbas, it was the first time that the ribbon of victory and commemoration was handed out to the conquered. In a psychological sense, this is clearly a (manipulative) invitation to unite with the conqueror and change sides. In this respect it can hardly surprise that Ukrainians will evaluate a cover of *Elle* magazine with a dress that resembles the ribbon of St. George by the same standards as the ribbon itself—as a demand for submission to the Russian conqueror. This is particularly the case as the *Elle* posters were put right into the streets of the Ukrainian capital Keiv (the street in Figure 16.1 can be identified as "Hrushevsky Boulevard," where the fiercest battles of the Euromaidan revolution took place in February 2014). Therefore it comes as no surprise that the seemingly neutral Louis Vuitton dress presented in the *Elle* May 2015 issue (the month of commemorating the Russian victory) can be interpreted as a hostile offense by many Ukrainians, even if the people who originally created the cover photo or the dress had no intentions to stir up such negative associations. As our example vividly explains, the fate of a product more strongly depends on the semiotic and sociocultural world of the users than on the motives of the producers.

DISCUSSION:
PSYCHOANALYTICAL INTERPRETATION OF THE RIBBON

On the basis of our reconstructive interpretation of the Twitter message as a cultural document (Figure 16.1), we now want to discuss the larger psychological and symbolic implications of our empirical findings. In our opinion, an effective and systematic way to achieve this goal can be to combine the epistemological potentials of the documentary method and historical research with psychoanalytic reasoning. Hence, along with the analysis of the content of the case material, this chapter can also be understood as an attempt to further develop qualitative research methodology.

From a psychoanalytical viewpoint, the documentary text and picture interpretation has highlighted the strong symbolic value of the St. George ribbon for contemporary post-Soviet societies in Ukraine and Russia. The historical research has provided us with the insight that the ribbon is originally of military origin. While it has only recently become introduced into mainstream culture, it has existed almost continuously across four centuries and various regimes. This unique characteristic of the ribbon provides us with an important lead for focusing on the psychological and political use of the St. George ribbon today.

The Ribbon: A Symbol of Coherence and Continuity

If we take a holistic perspective on the data gathered so far, it becomes evident that the ribbon symbolically transcends time and space. On the one hand, it has the capacity of synthesizing the past, the present, and the future of people who might have experienced severe forms of suffering or loss in their personal lives, families, and communities. On the other hand, it seems to be capable of reinstating the borders of the former Soviet Union and Warsaw Pact countries, regardless of the reality that many nation states have emerged within these delimitations since 1989. Hence, the ribbon has the power to create a strong sense of coherence for people in contemporary Russia, Ukraine, and neighboring countries. Evidently political leaders in Russia long ago understood its unifying potential and have exploited it to get people on their side. To achieve this end, they regularly made the compromise of supporting a symbol that in fact belonged to a previous regime, which was officially rejected (e.g., czarist Russia at the times of Soviet Union). The mere fact, however, that the ribbon has prevailed at all times even more strongly reinforces its symbolic power to provide real unity.[3] The colors of the St. George ribbon is of particular importance in this regard. Hardly another country would promote or tolerate the regular public use of colors competing with its national ones.[4] This is particularly striking as the orange-black stripes alone are already sufficient to trigger the association of the St. George ribbon. Before coming to the reactions against the ribbon, however, let us try to more profoundly understand the deeper psychology of this cultural artifact in its relation to a new concept of Russian politics: *Russkiy Mir.*

The Material Culture of Russkiy Mir

According to Kudors (2010), Russkiy Mir (Russian World) is a political program of Russian policymakers that bluntly comprises a "soft approach" to world domination. Following his explanations, it basically proposes the unity of everybody who speaks Russian, thinks Russian and acts Russian. By this concept, essentially Russia is, where Russians are, or people feel like Russians. Obviously, the St. George ribbon plays a crucial part in promoting the idea of Russkiy Mir in a material way. From a psychoanalytical viewpoint, the ribbon can be regarded as the totem and visible banner of belonging to a community that shares the narcissistic omnipotent wish of uniting the world under one Russian rule. Unchallenged by any other object, the ribbon synthesizes the material and psychological qualities of attachment. After all it is a physical symbol that people attach to their bodies or to their things of everyday use. Therefore, the ribbon is not only capable of connecting and embracing everybody who cognitively identifies with it but also those who are just using color-branded products. In Figures 16.6, 16.7, and 16.8 you can see some examples that demonstrate the proliferation of the St. George ribbon into everyday consumer culture. The mainstream use of political symbols in consumer products can be an effective way of exerting mass control on a certain community. However, as the selected examples vividly demonstrate, this process can also quickly get out of hand and become uncontrollable. According to McLuhan's (2003), successful media have the tendency to "overheat" if they are exploited too extensively. An exaggerated use of the ribbon could eventually ridicule its political symbolism. How can this process be moderated effectively? In McLuhan's terms "cooling down" the ribbon either requires a highly centralized system of product authorization or strong forms of systematic mass indoctrination. Russia has both. But the great efficiency of the ribbon's symbolism cannot be explained by the exertion of state control alone. At a closer look, the St. George ribbon itself provides us with leads on how to get people

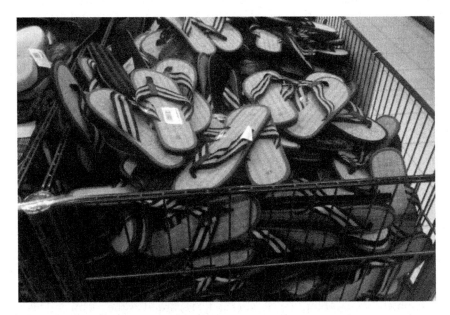

Figure 16.6. St. George ribbon of flip-flops.

Figure 16.7.   St. George ribbons as free gifts on sour cream packages.

Figure 16.8.   St. George ribbon on nail polish packaging. Special promotion from May 1 to10.

aboard voluntarily—by offering them a means of connecting to others and becoming part of something bigger.

From a psychoanalytical perspective, this is not a sufficient answer to our question yet. If people develop widespread enthusiasm for a cause, we need to understand the driving psychic forces behind it as well as the ways in which they are cultivated and regenerated collectively and systematically. This points our attention to the yearly ritual of celebrating Victory Day in Russia.

May 9th: The Ritual Celebration of Victory Over Death

On May 9, Russians literally "bring out the dead." It is Victory Day. In the big cities, the people march through the streets and hold up photographs of their relatives who died in the Great Patriotic War, as World War II is called in Russia. Like death itself, this event is the ultimate equalizer. No matter how old you are, if you are male or female, rich or poor, famous or infamous, and such, given that factually everybody has lost a family member during the war, almost anybody in Russia can participate on the same level of involvement. As the visual indicators of a community that shares a common destiny, the people personally attach St. George ribbons to their clothes. The orange-black stripes of the ribbon (that originally relate to fire and gun powder) remind us that this community has overcome death as a whole and is ready to even sacrifice itself. In Russkiy Mir, every victim is a hero. So do not mourn, but be proud of your personal loss and be ready to take your relatives' position at any time! On Victory Day, the "immortal regiment" (Figure 16.9) marches through the streets together with the living president. Be part of the moment, when the dead resurrect and you will always be remembered. Figures 16.9, 16.10, and 16.11 give a glimpse of May 9, 2016 marches in Moscow.

Russkiy Mir: Soviet Union Reloaded With Christianity

The apocalyptic frame of Victory Day vividly connects the contemporary construction of Russian history with Christian religious tradition. In this line of understanding, the St. George ribbon symbolizes resurrection from the dead, just like the Christian cross has promised to do for the last 2,000 years. President Putin's official speech on Victory Day 2016 demonstrates the symbiotic desire to create an immortal Russian nation, which knows no borders between people, state, and church:

Congratulations on Victory Day! An occasion where joy, memory, and grief have merged. May 9 is both a state and a very personal, family holiday. It has become a symbol of the sacred relation of Russia and its people. And

Source: rt.com

Figure *16.9.* "The immortal regiment," May 9, 2016.

Source: russkiymir.ru.

Figure *16.10.* Russian president Putin among other commemorators, May 9, 2016.

Source: russkiymir.ru

Figure 16.11.   Children in scout uniforms with St. George ribbon, May 9, 2016.

this unity devoted to Fatherland is a call to our strength, confidence, and dignity. (Chance, 2016, Kremlin, 2016)

While the rehabilitation of the Christian orthodox church in contemporary Russia is already a new quality for a nation under communist rule for more than a 45 years, the political doctrine of eliminating traditional borders does not seem to stop there. On May 6, 2016, a delegation of Russian parliamentarians participated in an audience with Pope Francis and attached a St. George ribbon to his robe (Figure 16.13). This act is of remarkable quality, as for the last 1,000 years the orthodox church (which is prevalent in Russia) has not accepted the pope as their religious leader (Figure 16.2). Is Russkiy Mir even capable of undoing the Great Schism?

CONCLUSION

Starting with the reconstructive document analysis of a disputed Twitter message, we have investigated the symbolic value of the St. George ribbon that has been recently promoted as a symbol of unity by Russian political

Source: BBC.

Figure 16.12. Orthodox Patriarch Kyrill I Blessing St. George ribbons.

Source: sputniknews.com

Figure 16.13. Pope Francis receiving a St. George ribbon from a communist member of the Russian parliament, May 6, 2016.

leaders. In studying how people use the ribbon in everyday life, we discovered its relation to the annual ritual of Victory Day on May 9 as well as to the even more elaborate concept of Russkiy Mir. According to our findings, Russkiy Mir cannot only be considered a political movement that simultaneously represents the romantic phantasy and (if necessary) the military commitment to extend the new Russian Empire beyond its conventional borders. In its extension, Russkiy Mir can be regarded as the most sophisticated utopian paradigm since the fall of communism. In the recent past, it has vividly demonstrated its factual power. Within a few years' time, postcommunist Russia has politically integrated capitalism and the orthodox church, both of which had been considered enemies of the state in Soviet

Figure 16.14.   Replacement cover for *Elle* Ukraine, May 2015.

times. Apart from this, Russia has also enlarged its territory by transgressing physical borders, as it has (fully or partly) annexed, occupied, or militarized other countries (Georgia, Moldova, Ukraine, Syria, etc.).

In the psychoanalytic understanding of Melanie Klein (1946), the denial of borders that exist in reality, combined with the narcissistic desire for a grandiose symbiosis of people, state, and religion, could be diagnosed as a paranoid-schizoid position: schizoid and narcissistic because those who promote the idea Russkiy Mir do not accept the objective realities and standards set by other people on the planet; paranoid, because this is the generalized response to anybody who questions (i.e., threatens) this Russian dogma.

Figure 16.15.   *Elle* Russia, May 2015.

The Twitter message (Figure 16.1) by the Russian newspaper *Pravda*, which marked the starting point of our reconstructive and psychoanalytical investigation, is a typical example of this paranoid defense mechanism. The first observation is that the author of the disputed tweet stays anonymous and hides behind the collective body of the newspaper. The second one is that he mocks himself about Ukrainian politicians and "couch soldiers" who would fiercely criticize a presumably harmless fashion advertisement. The condescending and ironic style in which the tweet was written further fits the pattern of the paranoid-schizoid position. Following the reasoning of its author, those who mistake the cover of a magazine for war propaganda cannot be taken seriously. They are either incompetent politicians or "couch soldiers." The mere fact that Ukrainians are sketched as helpless and defenseless (they do not even have "real soldiers") reinstates the author's grandiose belief in the superior power of Russkiy Mir. Kleinian psychoanalysis refers to this mechanism as projective identification, which has even a further consequence: the paranoid feelings that originated from the author of the tweet get eventually transferred to the Ukrainian community. This is exactly what also happened in reality. The perceived symbolic threat of the Georgish *Elle* cover reached such high levels in the end, that it had to be replaced by one with the same actress, but without the contested orange-black dress (Figure 16.14). In Russia, by contrast, *Elle* used a different *sujet* from the very beginning (Figure 16.15).

NOTES

1. We use the unconventional term *Georgish* in order to differentiate it from *Georgian*. This complies with the Russian language, which has separate words for георгиевсий (Georgish: in relation to the name George) and грузинский (Georgian: in relation to the European country Georgia).

2. We are skipping the reflective interpretation of the picture for reasons of conciseness. Please consult Bohnsack (2010b) for further reading on the concept.

3. The principle of creating territorial, societal, and political unity in an environment of frequent ruptures is also embodied in contemporary Israeli coins that contain the same depictions as to be found on ancient Jewish coins from centuries BCE (Lykke, 2015).

4. How naturally we usually associate countries with their national colors recently became evident when the global community demonstrated solidarity with France facing the terrorist attacks from November 2015. Facebook users added an overlay of the tricolor (stripes in blue, white, red) to their profile photos.

REFERENCES

Bohnsack, R. (2010a). Documentary method and group discussions. In R. Bohnsack, N. Pfaff, & W. Weller (Eds.), *Qualitative analysis and documentary method: In international educational research* (pp. 99–124). Opladen, Germany/Farmington Hills, MI: Barbara Budrich.

Bohnsack, R. (2010b). The interpretation of pictures and the documentary method. In R. Bohnsack, N. Pfaff, & W. Weller (Eds.), *Qualitative analysis and documentary method: In international educational research* (pp. 267–292). Opladen, Germany/Farmington Hills, MI: Barbara Budrich.

Chance, M. (2016, May 9). Russia marks victory day with Moscow parade [Video]. *CNN*. Retrieved May 20, 2016, from http://edition.cnn.com/videos/world/2016/05/09/russia-victory-day-parade-chance-pkg.cnn

Fitzpatrick, C. (2015, May 10). Russia this week: From medal of valor to ubiquitous propaganda symbol: The St. George ribbon. *The Interpreter.* Retrieved October 31, 2015, from http://www.interpretermag.com/russia-this-week-from-medal-of-valor-to-ubiquitous-propaganda-symbol-the-history-of-the-st-george-ribbon/

Garfinkel, H. (2004). *Studies in ethnomethodology.* Cambridge, England: Polity Press.

Klein, M. (1946). Notes on some schizoid mechanisms. *The International Journal of Psychoanalysis, 27*, 99–110.

Kremlin. (2016, May 9). Military parade on Red Square. *President of Russia.* Retrieved May 20, 2016, from http://en.kremlin.ru/events/president/news/51888

Kudors, A. (2010). "Russian world"—Russia's soft power approach to compatriots policy. *Russian Analytical Digest (Research Centre for East European Studies), 81*(10), 2–4.

Lykke, A. (2015, September 9). *Reign and religion in Palestine: The use of sacred iconography in Jewish coinage.* Wiesbaden, Germany: Harrassowitz.

McLuhan, M. (2003). *Understanding media: The extensions of man* (Critical ed.). Corte Madera, CA: Gingko Press.

Panofsky, E. (2006). *Ikonographie und Ikonologie.* Cologne, Germany: DuMont Literatur und Kunst Verlag.

Valsiner, J. (1999). I create you to control me: A glimpse into basic processes of semiotic mediation. *Human Development, 42*(1), 26–30.

PART VI

CONCLUDING RESPONSE

CHAPTER 17

CONCLUSIONS

The Reenchantment of Psychology

Carlos Cornejo

> It is in any case quite obvious to most people
> nowadays that mathematics has entered like a daemon
> into all aspects of our life.
>
> —Robert Musil, *The Man Without Qualities* (1930)

During the second decade of the 20th century, an unease about the scientific worldview crystallized in the form of a cultural movement reclaiming the lost sense of modern society. Technological development made us more productive but not necessarily happier; richer, but not wiser. This is the time of expressionist cinema; of the Bauhaus and the suprematist movement; of Arnold Schoenberg's dodecaphonic music. This is the context where Robert Musil—an engineer and doctor in psychology—published his famous novel *The Man Without Qualities* (1930). The scientific viewpoint had brought rational clarity in several domains of nature and society, but its progressive expansion to moral, spiritual, and experiential realms produced the ambivalent feeling of material progress and moral vacuity. The European cultural world sought for the lost sensibility by breaking traditional forms—tonal music, the ornaments of the bourgeois

The Psychology of Imagination: History, Theory, and New Research Horizons
pp. 319–333
319

society, the representation of objects—which felt as coercive armor. Artists and intellectuals reacted against this modern cosmology whose world was logically structured but devoid of spiritual and aesthetical features. Max Weber grasped this unease as the disenchantment of the world (1946) conceiving it as an unavoidable trait of modern Western civilization. In *The Crisis of European Sciences* of 1936, Edmund Husserl traced back this epochal unease to Galilean science, to the sociohistorical process of mathematization of the universe (Husserl, 1936/1970). At the dawn of the 20th century, not only nature, but also inner life became a matter of mathematical treatment. Of course it was not mathematics per se which caused the discomfort but rather the subtle, deep and pervasive metaphysical belief that every substance in the universe, including our selves, can and must be translated into temporospatial coordinates. Admittedly, science contributed to fulfill some primordial dreams of humankind. Paradoxically though, this was accomplished at the expense of the moral instance, where such dreams come from.

The analysis of fantasy proposed in the first chapter of this book reconstructs the slow transmutation of this concept into the modern imagination as used by present-day mainstream psychology. The fate of fantasy is, as I explained in Chapter 1 of this book, the fractal reproduction of what happened with those aspects of human experience that do not fit with the concept of mind developed during the 19th century. By doing epistemology with experimental means, 19th century psychology consolidated an anthropological model that reduces human experience to its knowledge functions. Fantasy progressively lost its ties to sensibility and feeling, mutating to an image-reproduction faculty that sets to work when no perceptual object is present. Under the guise of reproductive imagination, fantasy played an intellectual, yet secondary, role while its capacity to productively see the internal connections of a wholeness was dismissed.

It is not difficult to see that the metamorphosis of fantasy matches the disenchantment of the world. The new psychology pursued a place within the natural sciences, privileging method over subject matter. At the end of the 19th century, psychology defined itself as a nomothetic science, formally leaving the group of idiographic sciences (Windelband 1894/1980; see Cornejo, 2012; Lamiell, 1988). While strengthening its natural-scientific vocation, psychology limited its subject matter to the model of the intellectual mind, inherited from epistemology. As a consequence, psychology abandoned the inquiry of significant parts of the ancient soul, focusing on the catenation of sensation-perception-representation-memory. Along the 19th century, active soul functions, for example, synthesis, fantasy, will, were progressively eliminated or translated into mechanical terminology. As a consequence, psychology cut connections with disciplines such as aesthetics and history (see Klempe & Lehmann, this volume).

After reading the commentaries to the initial chapter, in what follows I would like to clarify certain thoughts developed in the text, as well as to foreground some consequences of the historiographical analysis offered.

Anthropology Instead of Epistemology

One of the bold tenets of Chapter 1 is that psychology's roots are to be found in anthropology rather than epistemology. The historical account shows indeed that what we contemporarily know as psychology is a late 19th century creation, so that the question of the origins of the discipline should actually be displaced centuries before what Sigmund Koch once named "Wundt's creature" (Koch, 1992). A very successful myth concerning the origin of the discipline establishes 1879 as its year of birth, when Wundt founded the first experimental psychology laboratory at Leipzig. The mythological character of this common belief is very well documented in Jaan Valsiner's book *A Guided Science* (2012). If we observe the big picture of the 19th century, Wundt's lab is rather at its end; Valsiner shows that what is usually presented as the irruption of a new discipline is rather the final consequence of a cosmological transformation that occurred along that century.

Fantasy embodies this metamorphosis through the passage from the productive fantasy to the reproductive imagination. While the first plays a central role in the anthropological model generated in the Romantic Era as a reaction against the rationalism of the growing natural sciences, the second fits better in the anthropological model constructed by epistemology. The first model of person was advanced by Hamann and Herder, but developed by J. W. Goethe; the second model of person was initially developed by English empiricism but metaphysically founded by Kant. Both models of the person recognize the same four traditional faculties of the soul: sensuousness or sensibility, fantasy, intellect or common sense, and reason. But while Goethe insisted on the integration of the faculties, particularly of those minimized in the rationalist worldview (i.e., fantasy and sensuousness), Kant raised reason as the highest human faculty, assigning other soul faculties to subsidiary roles.

It was argued in Chapter 1 that during the second part of the 19th century, scientific psychology absorbed the epistemological way of understanding human beings. It followed a Kantian model of mind; a model that supposes that the main human activity is to know the world. Psychology took the epistemic subject as a reliable equivalent of human being. Instead of describing the complexity of human experience, experimental psychology adopted the terminology developed by epistemology to explain human beings' thought. Kant created a metaphysical theory to answer the fundamental question for epistemologists: How is true knowledge possible? Taking for granted that good exemplars of true knowledge are Newton's gravitational theory and Descartes' analytic geometry, Kant designed a prescriptive model of what mind should be like to obtain those certainties. Against the statement made by Kant himself, psychology understood the epistemic subject as phenomenon and not as noumenon, becoming therefore the experimental wing of epistemology.

To be sure, both Kant and Goethe present an anthropology, in the sense that at the core of their respective theories of knowledge both do have a model of a human being. However, Kant's anthropological model is deeply rooted in the spirit of the *Aufklärung*, the German version of the French Illuminism, whose aim was to arrange a place for faith within an indisputably rational cosmic order (Taylor, 1979). Thus, after the *Critique of Pure Reason* (1998), Kant argued that moral behavior (in the *Critique of Practical Reason*, Kant, 2015) as well as aesthetical appreciation (in the *Critique of the Power of Judgement*, 2000) were ultimately governed by rational maxims. Thus, even though Kant pays great attention to freedom and aesthetics, as, for example, Klempe and Lehmann (this volume) and Christensen and Brock (this volume) remark, it should not be obviated that Kant's approach to these issues is guided throughout by the golden goal of epistemology: save the truth—truth being, of course, scientifically defined.

So, the claim anthropology instead of epistemology (or anthropology instead of metaphysics as Shotter [this volume] rightly points out; see also Tugendhat [2007]) does not mean that psychology should be conceived as part of or fused with the modern discipline called anthropology. The modern science known as anthropology, particularly at the end of the 19th century, made a radical turn toward symbolic structures at a supraindividual level, which led to a metaphysical gap between the individual and the collective, that is, between persons and societies. This gap defines the "micro-macro problem" or "mind-*Geist* problem" in psychology (Cornejo, 2007a). Therefore, anthropology instead of epistemology has nothing to do with the dilution of individual mind into the abstract collectivism described by (most of) modern anthropology, but with the recovery of an anthropological model of person which in fact existed during the first half of the19th century. It means that to recover the forgotten dimensions of human soul it is necessary to overcome the epistemological model of mind inherited by the discipline and to replace it with a model of human being (or a model of person: see Gaete & Cornejo, 2012). It means we must take seriously Wilhelm Dilthey's statement, "No real blood flows in the veins of the knowing subject constructed by Locke, Hume, and Kant, but rather the diluted extract of reason as a mere activity of thought" (Dilthey, as cited in Makkreel & Rodi, 1989, p. 50)

Kant and Goethe?

Christensen and Brock (this volume) maintain that the relation between Kant and Goethe would be a complementary one rather than a disjunction as I presented it. It would be "Kant and Goethe" rather than "Kant or Goethe." Christensen and Brock (this volume) miss especially the consideration of Kant's last major work, *The Critique of the Power of Judgment* (2000), where the philosopher approached aesthetic judgments and developed his conception of beauty and the sublime. In a similar vein, Klempe and Lehmann (this volume) argue that Kant's last *Critique* continued the program initiated by Alexander G. Baumgartner, so that Kant and Goethe would have more similarities than the mere reading of the first *Critique* allows one to discover.

Even though *The Critique of the Power of Judgment* (2000) was an influential work on Goethe and Schiller's thoughts on aesthetics, there are several reasons to put it aside in a historiography of fantasy. First, Kant's main impact upon scientific psychology was his theory of knowledge, which provided a prescriptive model of mind for the subsequent construction of a science of mental processes. In this respect, Kant doubtlessly exerted a massive influence on psychology; his doctrines on phenomenalism, the time-boundedness of human experience, and the discursive nature of thought are metaphysical conditions for an experimental science of mind. Yet Kant's theory of knowledge and his model of mind are to be found entirely in the *Critique of Pure Reason* (1998). Kant's second and third *Critiques*, besides their relevance in moral philosophy and aesthetics, scarcely made an impact on psychology.[1] Rather, the discipline absorbed Kantian epistemology and omitted his reflections on beauty and moral behavior.

In particular, the omission of *The Critique of the Power of Judgment* and the related cleavage between psychology and aesthetics can partially be ascribed to the fact that Kant's ideas on taste and beauty contradict any empirical description of those terms. It is in fact in this third *Critique* where Kant explains his peculiar usage of taste: "*Taste* is the faculty for judging an object or a kind of representation through a satisfaction or dissatisfaction *without any interest*. The object of such a satisfaction is called *beautiful*" (Kant, 2000, p. 5; emphasis in the original). Kant distinguishes the beautiful from the agreeable and the good; while the agreeable and good are interested feelings, the beautiful is "without any interest." The agreeable gratifies the person, which implies sensation; the good is something esteemed by the person, which implies the will of a certain value whose conceptualization implies reason. The beautiful merely pleases the person. Thus, although the three feelings produce satisfaction, the beautiful corresponds to a "disinterested satisfaction" (Kant, 2000, p. 2; emphasis in the original). The beautiful connects the subject to a universal satisfaction, object-unbounded and conceptless. It is a sort of objective feeling that serves as judgment without being either rational or moral.

The psychological unreality of these definitions is striking. How is it possible to imagine a satisfaction unrelated to an interest toward the world? Even though Kant does not offer a definition of satisfaction (*Wohlgefallen*) nor dissatisfaction (*Mißfallen*), one can fairly infer it is a positive subjective sensation that persons feel. But who can feel satisfaction independent of what is happening in the world? For Kant, this is the case of the actual feeling of beauty. Art, for example, is beautiful to the extent that the observer can transcend the artistic object accessing a satisfaction unrelated to the artistic object as well as to the concepts used to describe it: "One can say that among all these three kinds of satisfaction only that of the taste for the beautiful is a disinterested and *free* satisfaction; for no interest, neither that of the senses nor that of reason, extorts approval" (Kant, 2000, p. 5, emphasis in original). Kant's ideas about beauty rest on a model of person who is capable of separating the idea of beauty from the beautiful object that actualizes it. It is namely about a rational being who is capable of feeling satisfaction with no interest in the object that evokes such satisfaction. Again, as in the first *Critique*, Kant is not theorizing about real people: his subject is a rational being with the capacity to produce aesthetical judgments detached from the object of contemplation. This intuition becomes evident in the footnote attached to the adjective "disinterested" from the above quoted "disinterested satisfaction": "Only in society does it become *interesting* to have taste" (Kant, 2000, footnote p. 2; emphasis in the original). The agentive subject of Kant's aesthetical judgments does not pertain to society. Since it is counterfactual to think of real people apart from society, this footnote clarifies precisely that the rational being is not a socially formed being; it is not a person.

Contrary to what Kant himself declared and his adherents like to highlight, *The Critique of the Power of Judgment* does not overcome the rational-mechanistic model of mind he deployed in *The Critique of Pure Reason* (Hirschberger, 1991). It is undeniable that the third *Critique* is concerned with feeling (*Gefühl*) pleasure (lust) and displeasure (unlust), which implies a purposiveness and therefore freedom. But this concern remains throughout subordinated to the need of preserving the limits of science within the rationally constituted world of phenomena. In *The Critique of the Power of Judgment* causal determinism has paradoxical priority over the freedom to judge aesthetically. Thus, when Kant discusses the existence of an "end" in nature, that is, whether there is something like a formative force in the organic world—a teleology—he affirms "The concept of a thing as in itself a natural end is therefore not a *constitutive* concept of the understanding or of reason, but it can still be a *regulative* concept for the reflecting power of judgment" (Kant, 2000, p. 65; emphasis added). To have a sense of self-determination is not constitutive of human beings, but a regulative principle. We act as-if nature would be teleologically guided, but in reality there is just causal determinism (Hirschberger, 1991; Windelband, 2001). Through this position, Kant inaugurates a new form to refer to human will and freedom: the as-if-argument. Certainly this is not the last as-if-argument in human and life sciences.[2]

In sum, the third *Critique* is as rationalistic as the first one. Christensen and Brock (this volume) are plainly misled trying to raise a Goethean version of Kant. To this mistake they are probably led by the vocabulary that Kant used: intuition, thoughts, experience. But take notice that these concepts were entirely redefined by him in *The Critique of Pure Reason*! Christensen and Brock (this volume) quote recurrently this claim taken from the first *Critique*: "Thoughts without intuitions are empty, intuitions without thoughts are blind," and they assume this would express a form of Goethean holism. Nevertheless they overlook the crucial fact that in this quote thoughts mean strictly transcendental categories + sensorial impressions, while intuition means sensorial impressions or sensible data + a priori forms. The clothing of the language makes us believe that Kant and Goethe are alike; yet what Kant refers to with intuition is highly idiosyncratic, totally dissimilar to the traditional usage.

I do not want to minimize the huge influence that Kant exerted upon Goethe and many other younger intellectuals during the first decades of the 19th century. My point is simply that, at least in Goethe's case, this influence was *ex negativo*, that is, Goethe tried to argue against the rational-transcendental model of subject. The most eloquent demonstration of this is Goethe's discussion of the following paragraph written by Kant in *The Critique of the Power of Judgment*:

> And further, it is not at all necessary here to prove that such an *intellectus archetypus* is possible, but only that in the contrast of it with our discursive, image-dependent understanding (*intellectus ectypus*) and the contingency of such a constitution we are led to that idea (of an *intellectus archetypus*), and that this does not contain any contradiction. (Kant, 1790/2000, p. 277)

Goethe highlighted this paragraph in his own copy of the book. It is quite important, since this is exactly the point where Kant neglects the very possibility of *intuitive perception* (in the traditional sense). Against this statement, Goethe published in 1817 his significant essay *Judgment Through Intuitive Perception*, where he writes,

> Why should it not also hold true in the intellectual area that through an *intuitive perception* of eternally creative nature we may become worthy of participating spiritually in its creative processes? ... Impelled from the start by an inner need, I had striven unconsciously and incessantly toward primal image and prototype, and had even succeeded in building up a method of representing it which conformed to nature. (Goethe, 1998, p. 31f, emphasis added)

This quote reveals the deep differences between Goethe and Kant about *intuition*.[3] What Goethe calls intuition (or intuitive perception, after Douglas Miller's translation; see Footnote 2, Chapter 1 of this volume) is unachievable according to Kant due to the discursive, that is, categorically conformed, nature of human thought. On the contrary, Goethe, who was not caught by the metaphor of language as transcendental jail, states that intuitive perception is not only theoretically possible, but the appropriate method to capture the wholenesss of nature. It seems therefore equivocal to sustain that "common to both Goethe and Kant then was a view of absolute (divine) theoretical knowledge as being impossible for humans" (Christensen & Brock, this volume). To integrate sensuousness with conceptuality represents a Goethean ideal worth pursuing by contemporary psychology. But for the above-sketched reasons, such integration is not equivalent to integrating Kant and Goethe.

The Actual Soil of Earth

Goethe's claim to recover sensuousness (*Sinnlichkeit*) and fantasy corresponds to the insight that the wholeness of nature is only perceptible in the form of a felt experience, in which feelings and organismic sensibilities have a primordial importance. The perception of the *Ganzheit* is not purely a logic-rational exercise; it requires that human beings feel into their environments (Eckerdal, this volume; Valsiner, this volume). The right understanding of nature, not only in poetry, but also in science, does not correspond to the result of capturing abstract formalizations; we need fantasy to nourish them with "the actual soil of earth" (Eckermann, 1850, p. 220). Fantasy grants vividness and palpability to concepts, even abstract ones. It makes them intuitive.

Fantasy is centripetal, not centrifugal. Its work is not to transport us away from reality. Rather the reverse: It brings human beings back to earth, giving rational concepts the sentient vitality of sensuousness. Fantasy, in the Goethean sense, grants expressiveness to the world. This idea is tightly connected with the observations, made by pre-Wundtian psychologists, that mind modifies itself in order to reflect the features of the object, a phenomenon originally called imitation. The fantasy faculty allows persons to enter into the contemplated object to become it; that is, to feel into themselves the features and textures of life. Mind modifies itself in order to reflect the features of the object. Imitation, in Carl Gustav Carus and Ernst Stiedenroth, did not mean the purposive behavioral copying of a model but the spontaneous tendency of all persons to unreflectively feel into themselves the qualities of the perceived objects. We feel within ourselves the inner connections of nature. This anthropological fact was early described by Nicholas of Cusa as living mirror (*vivum speculum*). Vico also situates this crucial trait of human being: "man becomes all things by not understanding them (homo non intelligendo fit omnia) ... becomes them by transforming himself into them" (Vico, 1948, p. 405). A good example of this becoming-the-other phenomenon is Beckstead's (this volume) observation of the feelings we experience in front of ruins:

> The ruin is not primarily a text to be read, decoded, and analyzed. Nor can we understand our response to ruins simply through the laws of association; instead, the ruin is immediately and intuitively understood through our senses and because of the resonance between the ruin and our human nature, which involves the tension between the upward striving of the soul and the downward pull of nature.

The perception of the environment implies sensing its expressive features: the immensity of a mountain range (Valsiner, this volume) and the longing of ruins (Beckstead, this volume). These organismic sensibilities are neither subjective contributions projected on a neutral environment nor are they animistic traits of an anthropomorphic nature. What fantasy does "involves the tension between the upward striving of the soul and the downward pull of nature" as Beckstead acutely points out. This point is quite important for it shows a big difference between Kant and Goethe's theories of knowledge. Goethe's intuitive perception takes place before the Kantian subject-object division. During aesthetic contemplation there exists no separation between subject and object. As long as I feel into myself the expressive texture of nature, I am actually being the contemplated nature. There is no thing-in-itself beyond the mountain range while I am panoramically contemplating; I am immersed in it. No counterfactual thought comes up to my mind insinuating that this mountain range is not the real mountain range. Epistemological doubts come later. Such reflexive detachment corresponds to the ulterior egological moment when I realize that I am the subject and the mountain range the object. Then I start to think that what I see (not that what I organismically experience) is only a representation, and therefore that this is perspectival and uncertain; this is the core of the Cartesian anxiety described by R. Bernstein (see Mazur, this volume). Kant contributed to diminish this anxiety by asseverating that, even though we have indeed to give up the aspiration to get the world as it really is—the thing-in-itself—we can neverthe-less construct objective representations of it, because we all humans *a priori* share transcendental schemata by which we are bound to see the world as causally determined. Goethe is free from such Cartesian anxiety for he grounds certainty in the actual soil of earth, not in metaphysics. Human beings know the environment by its expressive value, graspable by the prerational faculties of soul: fantasy and sensuousness. Due to the fact that human beings are part of nature, they are holistically engaged in their environment by means of nonrational capacities long before they put reason in action.

Jaan Valsiner (this volume) complements the previous analysis with an additional element: my nonrational apprehension of nature produces in me not only a sensation, but at the same time it suggests in me certain ways to act in the environment. The perception of the environment is strongly united to the action in it. Thus, the perception of wholeness is not a merely contemplative sensation, but it induces concrete ways to actively engage in the environment. It is also an "affectivated *Ganzheit*" (Valsiner, this volume). Winther-Lindqvist (this volume) expresses similar concern by observing the experience of hoping in teenagers: "When imagining is involved in a phenomenon like hoping, it involves transfor-mation of the entire attitude or meaning horizon for the hoper" (Win-ther-Lindqvist, this volume). My entire engagement in a social situation promotes certain movements and actions, which change as long as my feelings also change. In certain social milieus it is natural for me to pick up flowers, as beautiful objects; in others my action is oriented to enjoy them where they are (Eckerdal, this volume). It is this powerful human capacity to be affectively activated by projected possible worlds that explains the interest of imagination as a liberating and potentially thera-peutic instrument (Awad, this volume; Zittoun, this volume).

Sensing Similarities

John Shotter (this volume) highlights the subtle intertwining of fantasy with sensing similarities. He writes, "In other words, in understanding 'things' poetically, or imaginatively, people sense them as being like other 'things' already familiar to them; and when they cannot make such 'out-side' comparisons, they must find a likeness 'from within themselves'" (Shotter, this volume). Shotter is rightly pointing to the tight connection of fantasy with the human capacity of sensing (not rationally inferring) similarities among objects of the world. To see connections where these are not superficial requires the skill to feel commonalities beyond the identity of the elements that compose the compared objects (Rojas, 2016).

In premodern times, fantasy was precisely the capacity that condensed such sensed commonalities: it condensed those features common to all sensorial forms. This is the reason why *phantasia* or *imaginatio* was considered as equivalent to the *sensus communis* in Augustine of Hippo, Avicenna, Averroes, Albertus Magnus, and Thomas Aquinas, among others (Sudhoff, 1913). This is also the reason for our pervasive use of metaphors and metonymies (Tateo, this volume) in ordinary life but also in technical uses of language. Metaphors do not work as the mapping of two abstract representations; rather, we identify poetically the sensed commonalities among juxtaposed experiences and microgenetically construct the wholeness (Cornejo, 2007b; Cornejo, Rojas, Olivares, 2013). We feel what is common between a mountain range panoramic view and our bodily proprioception when inspiring; that is why we understand expressions such as "a breath-taking landscape," even though we cannot give a clear-cut verbal explanation.

The capacity of fantasy to produce resonances between nature and person should not be envisaged as the discovering of a piece of knowledge behind certain features. Feeling the expressive texture of life does not correspond to a "deciphering process," as Guimarães rightly puts it (this volume). There is not a something that "lies beyond the symbol" (Watzlawik, this volume).

Nature does not hide contents waiting to be deciphered by our abstract reason. The impression of sensibilities occurs immediately, with no recourse to rational (e.g., inferential) processes. The immediacy of the inner/outer resonances coincides with the original description of aesthetical truth, introduced by Alexander G. Baumgarten:

> A poem can be experienced as evoking the truth, through perhaps irrational linguistic and musical configurations. Another example is the creation of new chords that have never been heard before. In such cases an *immediate concurrence* is experienced because there is a *complete compliance* between what is articulated physically by means of the words or chords selected and what is meant. This compliance gives immediately an impression of an expression as "true" or genuine. Hence, Baumgarten even talks about "aestheticological truth." (Klempe & Lehmann, this volume; emphasis added)

The connection of fantasy with Baumgarten's aestheticological truth expresses not only the inner/outer solidarity that describes the personal resonance with the environment (immediate concurrence, complete compliance) but also importantly the experience of vividness of the aesthetical impression. The inner resonance gives us immediately the impression of truth or authenticity. Mazur (this volume) describes the accompanying feeling of truth of the primordial expressive texture of life as a kind of faith or trust that contrasts with the rational certainty. Exactly the connection between the character of true of the aesthetical impression and the kind of certainty given by faith in premodern thought is encrypted in the meaning of intuition as used by Nicholas of Cusa, for example.

The environment in which my interiority immediately concurs can also be social. Fantasy is *sensus communis,* so it does not resonate individualistically. On the contrary, when we abandon the Robinson Crusoe model of mind, we do not start from the false premise that world understanding begins with thinking. Instead, in a Goethen spirit, we believe that life precedes reason and therefore that thinking is based on vitality. Such vitality is felt not from the solitude of my subjective position in front of a distant objective world. At this primordial felt experience, I am holistically feeling the world inside me. As long as I share the same anthropological condition with my fellows, I share with them a common experiencing, a common sense. In a different place, I called this primordial-sensed common experience co-phenomenology (Cornejo, 2008) as a way to understand intersubjectivity from a nonindividualistic approach. At the bottom of any human social relation, there is a shared common sense which is initially and mostly prerational. A theory of intersubjectivity cannot start from the Kantian subject as the core of the social relation, but it has to be based on human vital sensing. In real life, other people are not enigmatic objects endowed with mind. In fact, we share with other people a vast nonpropositional common sense, and it is upon this thick background that we interact socially (Cornejo, 2014). Thus, in ordinary life there is no such artificial problem called the "other mind's problem" that post-Kantian philosophy invented. For the same reason, the whole rational device known contemporarily as theory of mind is an unnecessary answer for a pseudo problem (Cornejo, 2008). Thus, as I see it, my exhortation for a psychology with soul does not deny a psychology with others (Glăveanu, this volume), unless the concept of "other" implies the modern "I," which is nothing other than the subject-object cleavage differently dressed.

Expressivity of Life

What I have said might perhaps be summarized as follows: our reality is and has always been expressive. We have never perceived such objects as stones, stars, faces, or noises. We perceive instead hard or cold stones, bright or distant stars, smiling or conceited faces, and sweet or annoying noises. What have human scientists done with this expressivity of life? Historiographical accounts show that psychology massively followed the rational-mechanical cosmology that simply ignores it. But history also teaches that making as if we interact with an inexpressive and neutral reality leads to a dishonest science (Merleau-Ponty, 2002): psychologists talk about behavior, but they intend action; they talk about beliefs, but they mean convictions; they talk about working memory, but they mean phenomenological experience. By neglecting expressivity, psychology behaves as if it were a natural science studying the same muted and silent universe that physics inquires. But not even physicists inhabit such an inexpressive world. Psychology, as human science, has the duty to confront the empirical fact that all our psychological life takes place in a world full of sense. Otherwise we will construct theories or models that, although they satisfy natural scientific criteria, we know in our innermost being to be naïve or plainly fake.

Incarnated in Goethe's tacit anthropology, I presented an approach to the human soul that recovers those faculties that disturb a rational model of man. In particular, I tried to show how fantasy is a centripetal force granting the "soil of earth" to concepts and abstractions. I also tried to emphasize that properly understanding Goethe's way of thinking demands suspending the epistemological attitude that cleaves subject and object. Calmness, longing, intensity, resolution, and hope are not properties of the reality "out there." Yet neither are they abstract ideas from the interiority projected onto an otherwise neutral reality. The most perfect form of knowledge is, for Goethe, the intuitive perception, a moment where I feel a wholeness conceptually and vividly. This kind of knowledge is fundamental for science to grow but, in its turn, can only exist when scientists work also by using fantasy. A poetic science should evidence the expressiveness of the world. This is the reenchantment of psychology.

NOTES

1. Incidentally it is expressive that the concept used by Christensen and Brock (this volume) to prove Kant's success in "bridging between sensuousness and reason," namely, *schema*, is introduced and developed in the *Critique of Pure Reason* (Kant, 1998), not in the *Critique of the Power of Judgment* (Kant, 2000).

2. In philosophy of mind, Daniel Dennett (1971) offers another example of as-if-argument of human consciousness by explaining the "intentional stance": we make as-if the clock would have mental properties (attibuting to the device, for example, the desire to wake me up), although we know this is only a fictional mode of thinking (Dennett, 1971). In theoretical biology, Maturana and Varela (1984) offer similarly another as-if-argument: we attribute meaning to the cat's behavior because we make as-if this has semantics; but in reality there are only behavioral coordinations of behavioral coordinations.

3. Goethe and Kant diverge also significantly in their concepts of *idea* and *experience* (see Hernández Maturana, 2014).

REFERENCES

Cornejo, C. (2007a). The locus of subjectivity in cultural studies. *Culture & Psychology, 13*(2), 243–256.

Cornejo, C. (2007b). Conceptualizing metaphors versus embodying the language. *Culture & Psychology, 13*(4), 474–487.

Cornejo, C. (2008). Intersubjectivity as co-phenomenology: From the holism of meaning to the being-in-the-world-with-others. *Integrative Psychological and Behavioral Science, 42*(2), 171–178.

Cornejo, C. (2012). What should idiographic science be like? In S. Salvatore & J. Valsiner (Eds.), *Making sense of infinite uniqueness* (pp. 21–33). Charlotte, NC: Information Age.

Cornejo, C. (2014). On trust and distrust in the lifeworld. In I. Marková & P. Linell (Eds.), *Dialogical perspectives on trust* (pp. 237–253). Charlotte, NC: Information Age.

Cornejo, C., Rojas, P., & Olivares, H. (2013). The physiognomic and the geometrical apprehensions of metaphor. *Culture & Psychology, 19*(4), 484–505.

Dennett, D. C. (1971). Intentional systems. *The Journal of Philosophy, 68*(4), 87–106.

Eckermann, J. P. (1850). *Conversations of Goethe with Eckermann and Soret, Vol. II.* London, England: Smith, Elder.

Gaete, A., & Cornejo, C. (2012). Psychology is about persons: On Brinkmann's expansion of Harré's hybrid psychology. *Integrative Psychological and Behavioral Science, 46*(1), 70–77.

Goethe, J. W. (1998). Judgment through intuitive perception. In D. Miller (Ed.), *Goethe: The collected works, Vol. 12, Scientific studies*, pp. 31–32. New York: Suhrkamp. (Original work published in German 1817)

Hernández Maturana, C. (2014). *Goethe und Hegel: Konturen eines epistemologischen Monismus.* MA thesis. Friedrich-Schiller-Universität Jena.

Hirschberger, J. (1991). *Geschichte der Philosophie, Vol. 2: Neuzeit und Gegenwart.* Freiburg, Germany: Herder Verlag.

Husserl, E. (1970). *The crisis of European sciences and transcendental phenomenology: An introduction to phenomenological philosophy.* Evanston, IL: Northwestern University Press. (Original work published in German 1936)

Kant, I. (1998). *Critique of pure reason.* Cambridge, MA: Cambridge University Press (Original work published 1781)

Kant, I. (2000). *Critique of the power of judgment.* Cambridge, MA: Cambridge University Press (Original work published 1790)

Kant, I. (2015). Critique of practical reason. Cambridge, MA: Cambridge University Press. (Original work published 1788)

Koch, S. (1992). Wundt's creature at age zero—and as centenarian: Some aspects of the institutionalization of the "new psychology." In S. Koch & D. E. Leary (Eds.), *A century of psychology as science* (pp. 7–35). Washington, DC: American Psychological Association.

Lamiell, J. T. (1998). "Nomothetic" and "idiographic": Contrasting Windelband's understanding with contemporary usage. *Theory and Psychology, 10*, 715–730.

Makkreel, R. A., & Rodi, F. (Eds.). (1989). *Wilhelm Dilthey: Selected Works, Vol. 1. Introduction to the human sciences.* Princeton, NJ: Princeton University Press. (Original work published in German 1883)

Maturana, H., & Varela, F. J. (1984). *El árbol del conocimiento.* Santiago, Chile: Editorial Universitaria.

Merleau-Ponty, M. (2002). *Phenomenology of perception.* London, England: Routledge.

Rojas, P. (2016). An expressive approach to affect and musical experience. In C. Cornejo, G. Marsico, & J. Valsiner (Eds.), *Annals of cultural psychology, Vol. 2.* Charlotte, NC: Information Age.

Sudhoff, W. (1913). Die Lehre von den Hirnventrikeln in textlicher und graphischer Tradition des Altertums und Mittelalters. *Archiv für Geschichte der Medizin, 7*(3), 149–205.

Taylor, C. (1979). *Hegel and modern society.* Cambridge, England: Cambridge University Press.

Tugendhat, E. (2007). *Anthropologie statt metaphysik.* München, Germany: Beck.

Valsiner, J. (2012). *A guided science: History of psychology in the mirror of its making.* New Brunswick, NJ: Transaction.

Vico, G. (1948). *The new science.* Ithaca, NY: Cornell University Press. (Original work published in Italian 1725)

Weber, M. (1946). *Science as Vocation.* New York, NY: Free Press.

Windelband, W. (1980). Rectorial address, Strasbourg, 1894 (G. Oakes, Trans.). *History and Theory, 19*(2), 169–185 (Original work published 1894)

Windelband, W. (2001). *A history of philosophy: With special reference to the formation and development of its problems and conceptions.* Boston, MA: Adamant Media.

CONTRIBUTORS

Sarah H. Awad: Aalborg University, Denmark, awads@hum.aau.dk

Zachary Beckstead: Grand Valley State University, USA, beckstez@gvsu.edu

Ignacio Brescó: Aalborg University, Denmark, ignacio@hum.aau.dk

Steen Brock: Aarhus University, Denmark, filsb@cas.au.dk

Bo A. Christensen: Aarhus University, Denmark, boac@edu.au.dk

Carlos Cornejo: Pontificia Universidad Católica de Chile, Chile, cca@puc.cl

Rebekka Mai Eckerdal: Aalborg University, Denmark, recker11@student.aau.dk

Vlad Petre Glăveanu: Aalborg University, Denmark, vlad@hum.aak.dk

Stefan Hampl: Sigmund Freud University, Austria, stefan.hampl@sfu.ac.at

Sven Hroar Klempe: The Norwegian University of Science and Technology, Norway, hroar.klempe@svt.ntnu.no

Olga V. Lehmann-O: The Norwegian University of Science and Technology, Norway, olga.lehmann@svt.ntnu.no

Lucas B. Mazur: Jagiellonian University, Poland, and Sigmund Freud University, Germany, lucasbmazur@gmail.com

Dominik Mihalits: Sigmund Freud University, Austria, dominik.mihalits@sfu.ac.at

John Shotter: University of New Hampshire, USA, jds@unh.edu

Danilo Silva Guimarães: University of São Paulo, Brazil, dansgui@usp.br

Luca Tateol: Aalborg University, Denmark, luca@hum.aau.dk

Jaan Valsiner: Aalborg University, Denmark, jvalsiner@hum.aau.dk

Brady Wagoner: Aalborg University, Denmark, wagoner@hum.aau.dk

Meike Watzlawik: Sigmund Freud University, Germany, m.watzlawik@tu-bs.de

Ditte Alexandra Winther-Lindqvist: Danish School of Education, Aarhus University, diwi@edu.au.dk

Tania Zittoun: University of Neuchâtel, Switzerland, tania.zittoun@unine.ch

CPSIA information can be obtained
at www.ICGtesting.com
Printed in the USA
BVOW06s1426080517
483371BV00004B/14/P